CALL ME MAURICE

Ruth and Maurice on their wedding day

Call Me Maurice:

the life and times of
Lord Fermoy (1885-1955)

Mary Burke Roche

ELSP

Published in 2008 by
ELSP
16A St John's Road
St Helier
Jersey   JE2 3LD

Origination by Ex Libris Press

Printed by CPOD
Trowbridge
Wiltshire

ISBN 978-1-906641-06-1

Dedication

For Sarah, Alex, Jane, Anya, Jo, Edward,
Charles, Frances, Maurice, Hugh –
and remembering Diana

Contents

Part 1

Life in America

Part II

Maurice and the Great War

Part III

Life in England

List of Illustrations

Introduction

M y intention in writing this biography of my father was to introduce his grandchildren to their unknown grandfather. Much of the information comes from his correspondence and his war diary.

I have set the man in the context of his times and have described some of the major events which were happening in the world around him. Throughout I have aimed for truth and accuracy. I have made it clear when I have quoted from family legend.

My researches soon led to the discovery of interesting facts about his parents and grandparents. I dug up the adventures of Jim Roche, his father, who effectively sold his sons to their rich grandfather when they were two years old.

Maurice's mother, Fanny Burke Roche, was a dominant force and influence in his life. Her diaries provide insight into her troubled years and the way they impinged on the lives of her sons. They also reveal the day-to-day life of a very rich woman in the Gilded Age in America.

Frank Work, his American grandfather, was another powerful influence in Maurice's early life. In the absence of their own father, Work took on that role, and endeavoured to instil in his grandchildren his own strict moral code. From being a poor boy in Chillicothe, Ohio – a daredevil who rode his horse naked down the main street – he became a very rich banker in New York and a despot who ruled his household with a rod of iron.

Maurice's twin brother, Frank, shared every aspect of his life until the First World War. They were identical twins and their relationship was exceptionally close. This book contains intimate and revealing letters, which Maurice wrote to his brother at times when they were apart.

I have included in its entirety, Maurice's war diary of his year in France in the First World War, when he was in the Motor Supply Train of the 78th Division of the US Army. This throws light on his internal and external experiences of the war in a very personal way.

In the context of Maurice's decision to get involved with British politics, I have given a lot of space to relating the life and speeches of his Irish grandfather, Edmund Roche, 1st Lord Fermoy. He was a prominent politician in the 19th century, who was inspired by his cousin Edmund Burke to fight energetically for justice for Ireland. He was unknown to Maurice, and many members of our family are unaware of this significant ancestor.

This book shows how Maurice, an American, integrated himself into life in

England at the age of 35. He took on the challenge of entering the political arena in Britain and succeeded in becoming a most popular Member of Parliament, both in his constituency and in the House of Commons. He was no parliamentarian or orator but did much to improve the lives of all his constituents, by his interest, his generosity, his warmth and his humour.

One of Maurice's grandchildren was the late Diana, Princess of Wales, which gives the book additional interest. However, I was inspired to write this book about my father in his own right. He was a great-hearted human being who led an extraordinarily interesting and colourful life.

I have included an Appendix on the life of John Wark, Maurice's great-grandfather. He was a Scottish civil engineer, who emigrated to America in the early nineteenth century. When I visited my American cousin, Nancy (Muffie) Swan, in Denver, Colorado, she showed me the Wark family bible, and lent me the journal of John Wark to transcribe. It describes his work in Baton Rouge, a town on the Mississippi river in Louisiana.

I have also added an Appendix on Edmund Burke, based on extracts from an address by the American Ambassador, spoken when he unveiled a plaque in Bath, in 1908, to the memory of Burke. The Ambassador's words capture the essence of Burke in an economical way. It is here for the benefit of those members of our family who know they are related to him, and even bear his name, but know little or nothing about this colossal personality who bestrode the eighteenth century!

I have many people to thank for the existence of this biography. My American cousins have greatly contributed. The late Guy Fairfax Cary gave me all the Roche memorabilia which was stored in the family home in Newport, Rhode Island. Abby Anne Van Pelt passed on her own files on the family history and a treasure trove of Frank Roche's correspondence. My first cousin Cynthia Russell has given me some firsthand memories of the family. Guy Van Pelt has also supplied me with some items of interest. John Maynard was a great companion on an expedition we made to Chillicothe, Ohio. Sheila and her husband Nick Platt were most hospitable and encouraging hosts to me in New York. My cousin Nancy Swan in Denver gave me valuable information.

I am grateful to my late mother, Ruth, Lady Fermoy, for keeping extensive photograph and newspaper-cutting albums; to my late brother Edmund, the fifth Lord Fermoy, who did much research into family history before his early death; and to his widow, Lavinia Corbally Stourton, who has carefully preserved these family records and has lent me the archive he assembled. My Irish cousin, Honor Smyth in Dublin, has shared her family history records.

I am indebted to the late Jose Ordonnez for chronicling the correspondence between Maurice and Dr Drury, the Rector of St Paul's School, Concord, New Hampshire; I acknowledge with thanks the help of Bob Rettew and David Levesque of the Ohrstrom Library at St Paul's; Lisa Long of the Redwood Library, Newport,

Rhode Island; Bert Lippincott of the Newport Historical Society; Paul Miller of the Newport Preservation Society; Stan Polny, historian of the 78th Division, US Army; and Patricia Medert of the Ross Historical Society, Chillicothe.

I am indebted to Her Majesty the Queen, Bernard Campbell, Franklin Conaway, Dorothy Davison, Guy and Alex Dawson, Simon Farnham, Desmond Fitzgerald, Hugo Merry and Joe Studholme for their help with my research.

I thank my family and friends for their interest, ideas and support.

I am grateful to Richard Brown for helping me all along the way and for proofreading the final version.

Finally, I am grateful to my publisher Roger Jones for his commitment, expertise, sound advice and help.

Simplified line of Maurice Burke Roche, 4th Baron Fermoy

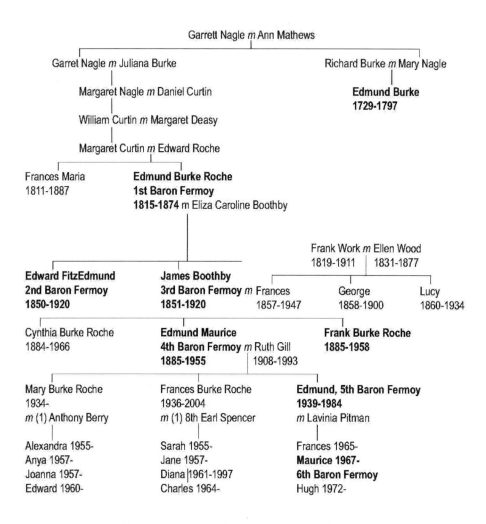

Garrett Nagle *m* Ann Mathews

Garret Nagle *m* Juliana Burke

Margaret Nagle *m* Daniel Curtin

William Curtin *m* Margaret Deasy

Margaret Curtin *m* Edward Roche

Richard Burke *m* Mary Nagle

**Edmund Burke
1729-1797**

Frances Maria
1811-1887

**Edmund Burke Roche
1st Baron Fermoy
1815-1874** m Eliza Caroline Boothby

Frank Work *m* Ellen Wood
1819-1911 | 1831-1877

**Edward FitzEdmund
2nd Baron Fermoy
1850-1920**

**James Boothby
3rd Baron Fermoy** *m* Frances
1851-1920 1857-1947

George
1858-1900

Lucy
1860-1934

Cynthia Burke Roche
1884-1966

**Edmund Maurice
4th Baron Fermoy** *m* Ruth Gill
1885-1955 1908-1993

**Frank Burke Roche
1885-1958**

Mary Burke Roche
1934-
m (1) Anthony Berry

Frances Burke Roche
1936-2004
m (1) 8th Earl Spencer

**Edmund, 5th Baron Fermoy
1939-1984**
m Lavinia Pitman

Alexandra 1955-
Anya 1957-
Joanna 1957-
Edward 1960-

Sarah 1955-
Jane 1957-
Diana 1961-1997
Charles 1964-

Frances 1965-
**Maurice 1967-
6th Baron Fermoy**
Hugh 1972-

Maurice was a first cousin five times removed of Edmund Burke

Prologue

Maurice Burke Roche came into the world on 15th May 1885. At the time of his birth, Queen Victoria was on the throne of England. William Gladstone was her Prime Minister. The Irish Members of Parliament held the balance of power in the House of Commons and Home Rule for Ireland was close to being achieved.[1] The 5th Earl Spencer was Lord Lieutenant of Ireland.

Grover Cleveland was President of the United States of America. The first skyscraper, ten stories high, was built in Chicago. The Canadian Pacific Railway was completed. The Statue of Liberty arrived in New York Harbour, a gift from the people of France. Ezra Pound was born.

In the same year, the first appendectomy was performed. Louis Pasteur discovered a vaccine for rabies; the first official cremation took place at Woking. The first automobile, the first motor bike and the first bicycle were patented. In July 1885, the Football Association announced that it was in the interests of Association Football, to legalise the employment of professional football players.

Maurice did not arrive alone. A few minutes after his birth, his identical twin brother Frank appeared. They were born at home in Pont Street, Knightsbridge, London, not many yards from Harrods (which had just been rebuilt following a fire in 1883). Their sister Cynthia, aged thirteen months screamed at the sight of them! Their mother was more than happy. The following day their father James Boothby Burke Roche wrote to Lucy, his wife's sister in the States, announcing the birth of his sons:

"61 Pont Street, London SW
May 16th 1885

My dear Lucy,
Fanny has done it this time and no mistake & 61 Pont Street is like the Foundling Hospital. The odd part of it is that she is so proud of it. The proceeds are large and apparently healthy and vigorous & both scream at the same time & what with Cynthia, take up all the available female help.

As usual, the event was unforeseen, at least by Fanny, & the Gamp[2] was not there, not being due until that afternoon, & it took place at 5am, but

---

[1] Gladstone's Home Rule for Ireland Bill was narrowly defeated in the House of Commons in 1886.
[2] Midwife.

Mrs Barlow & Sims appeared equal to it. So far, Fanny has gone on all right & the only difficulty is in getting "cows"[3] for the infants. I sent you a cable yesterday & received yours to-day, I don't think much of your names & you must fit 'em out with a better lot when you come over.

All my women kind are wildly excited about it all. The infants repose, head & tail, in your white cot, to prevent them being mixed, but I fancy they've been shuffled up once or twice already and failing any way of branding 'em that I know of, I suppose we must trust to luck to the right one getting his rights in the end. Cynthia goes into absolute fits when she sees 'em & can't be got to look at them at any price...

Affec, yours always
J B B Roche"

Maurice and Frank, aged 11 months

---

[3] Wet nurses. For centuries, the British aristocracy employed wet nurses to feed their babies because breast-feeding was seen as ruining a woman's figure, besides interfering with her social engagements.

Part 1

Life in America

1

Maurice's Irish father

James Boothby Burke Roche – known to the family as Jim – was a larger than life character.

"As 'Jimmy Roche' he was one of the best-looking men of his day. The story of his remarkable life from the time he left Cambridge would fill a volume. He dabbled in politics and racing but it was adventures in out-of-the-way parts of the world that appealed to him most." [4]

Physically a big man, over six feet tall and powerfully built, his enterprises and exploits were similarly on the grand scale, and the world was his theatre of operations. The second son of Edmund Burke Roche, 1st Lord Fermoy and one of eight children, he was born on July 28th,1851, at Twyford Abbey, Acton, Middlesex, the family home of his mother Eliza Boothby. The Roche family fortunes were in a bad way. Already in the 1850s his Irish landowning father was said to have required tenants to take out leases at increased rents in order to give a boost to his depleted finances.

Parliament was in session at the time of his birth and indeed that month his father, Edmund Burke Roche, MP for County Cork, spoke in the House of Commons, on the excess of pauperism in Ireland. The solution, he believed, laid in the encouragement of the manufactures in Ireland and in particular the cultivation of flax, which would provide employment for everyone.

The parliamentary session ended, the family returned to Cork where Jim spent his childhood at the two family homes – spending the summer at Trabolgan on the coast, and moving inland to Kilshannig in the winter. He led a carefree, outdoor existence. He learned to shoot and to ride at an early age, fearlessly jumping banks and ditches; he climbed trees, played Cowboys and Indians and invented all sorts of daring games.

Trabolgan,[5] which was approached by a long avenue, was a house of Georgian design, with a long façade, facing out to sea. It was vulnerable to Atlantic gales and stormy blasts, which were sometimes so fierce that it was impossible to open

---

[4] *Daily Graphic*, London November 2nd, 1920.
[5] From *A Guide to Irish Country Houses*.

the front door! There was also an entrance at the back, which could be used when the weather was wild. No wonder the family retreated to spend the winters at their more sheltered, inland home, Kilshannig!

Edward Roche, father of Edmund Roche, bought Kilshannig from the Devonshers for a sum of £7,500.[6] It is a fine house, standing in a commanding position, on a hill near Rathcormack. It was designed by Dukart, an Italian architect, in the mid-eighteenth century. It is built of brick, with arcades on either side of the main house, leading to pavilions.[7] It is said that the copper was stripped off the domes on the pavilions by the second Lord Fermoy, to pay off the family debts.

From an early age, horses were fundamental to Jim's life. He went out with the hunt and learned how to break in young horses. How disappointed he would have been as he looked at his twin sons in their cradle, if he could see into the future and learned that Maurice, his son and heir, only enjoyed riding once, and that was on the back of a donkey in Egypt!

Jim received a good education from tutors at his homes in Ireland, until he went to Trinity College, Cambridge, where horses continued to play a central role in his life. He belonged to a fast-living group including Moreton Frewen[8] and Hugh Lowther, later Earl of Lonsdale. Their principal interest was riding horses – at breakneck speed. Moreton wrote in his memoirs:

"We filled our niche not unworthily, and added no little to the colour and variety of the University life of our time. Without us there had been no polo, nor a pretty day's steeple chasing. For hounds we cared not a jot: they existed to give direction toward which we pointed our horses' heads." [9]

When he left Cambridge with his BA degree, Jim was certainly not well off but as one of the most striking and handsome young men of his day, a superb horseman and one of the best shots, the great country houses of England opened their doors to the debonair, young Irishman. Jim Roche found himself invited everywhere. A horse was provided for him, he was entertained and flattered. In turn, he was entertaining, being very ready to talk and an excellent raconteur.

We can get some idea of how he spent his time after Cambridge from this description by his friend Moreton:

"I chronicle my own times and seasons. From November to April (hunting at) Melton. Then a month's salmon fishing in Ireland and Punchestown

---

6   *Journal of the Cork Historical and Archaeological Society*, Vol 86, p. 64.
7   The present owner, Hugo Merry, and his parents before him, have carried out much restoration. See John Logan in *The Journal of the Irish Georgian Society*. Vol. X, 2007.
8   A sportsman, pioneer, inventor, champion of silver currency and politician, his numerous failed enterprises earned him the nicknamed "Mortal Ruin".
9   *Melton Mowbray and other Memoirs*, 1924.

James Boothby Burke Roche, 'Jim'

Trabolgan, 1948

23

Kilshannig

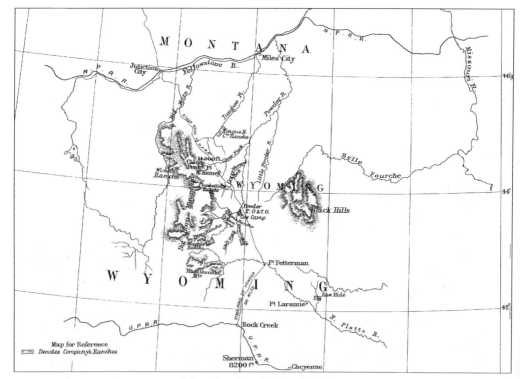

Map showing the Powder River

(races). In May, June the Derby and Ascot. Goodwood and Cowes. Some 'grouse' and Doncaster: next a broken week or two at Newmarket and a little schooling of young Irish horses after cubs. Such as this was the determination to pleasure of really the pick of our young fellows." [10]

The young fellows never thought of anything save their horses and their guns. When the ground was frozen too hard for hunting, Jim accompanied Moreton and Hugh to the casinos in Nice, where fortunes were made and lost. In 1877, Moreton invested all the capital he could muster into the great cattle rush in Wyoming. He had discovered the potential of driving calves from Texas to the untouched, lush grasslands of the eastern half of Wyoming. This vast area was unsuitable for agriculture since it could not be irrigated, but its plains and foothills provided sufficient pasture to maintain enormous herds of cattle. Winter feeding was unnecessary, as the grass in the dry climate of Wyoming naturally turns to hay, and was left uncut to provide winter fodder.

> "Young steers driven from Texas & wintered north of the 41st parallel attained a weight of at least a hundred pounds each in excess of those left to mature in the south... Texas is a better breeding country. Ours is a better fattening country." [11]

(In the severe winter of 1884, heavy snow covered the ground and vast hordes of cattle died from starvation.)

Pioneers of cattle ranching, Moreton and his brother set up their headquarters in the Powder River basin, which lies between the Big Horns and the Black Hills. [12] Moreton set in motion the construction of a large timber mansion, known to the cowboys as Frewen's Castle.

> "It was a two-storey pitch-roofed house. The main room was like a baronial hall, about forty feet square, with stone fireplaces either end, lined with rough-hewn pine logs. Rugs of beaver and buffalo skin tapestried the walls and draped the seats." [13]

It had a piano, a library and a massive staircase imported from Europe. There was stabling for seven hundred cowboys' horses. There he planned to live in a grand manner and entertain his friends.

Moreton returned to England and told his friends of the possibilities of making a fortune cattle ranching in Wyoming. His enterprises fired Jim's imagination.

---

[10] *Melton Mowbray and other Memoirs.*
[11] *'Free Grazing': A report to the shareholders of the Powder River Cattle Co. Ltd.*, p. 6.
[12] Not far from here, in 1876, several hundred soldiers of the US Army, led by Col. George Custer, were decimated at the hands of several thousand Lakota and Cheyenne warriors.
[13] *The Splendid Pauper*, p. 64.

Although his father Edmund Roche had large estates, Jim as a younger son needed to make his own way in life. His brother Ulick became a professional soldier but that would not have suited Jim's temperament, nor would the alternative occupation considered suitable for a gentleman, that of entering the church.

When Moreton invited him to stay, as one of his first guests, at Frewen's Castle, Powder River, he accepted with alacrity. Here was an opportunity to travel to America, to shoot big game, including grizzly bear, and to spend his days out of doors on horseback. Although he had very little money to invest, there was the possibility of making a fortune. It would be dangerous; it would require physical strength, courage, endurance and manliness. It would be an adventure which suited his wild, romantic, daredevil nature. "Only men of mettle could survive the rigors of all kinds of weather, battle the elements or fight off the raider or Indian."[14]

In 1878, Moreton set sail for New York on the good ship SS *Bothnia* with a party of six:

> "As the time of our sailing drew near, our party had been swollen to six: the other four, Sir Charles Wolseley, Jack Thornhill of Diddington, the (Hon) Gilbert Leigh of Stoneleigh[15] and J B Roche – the last three named, Cambridge friends of mine. Two nights before I sailed Chicken Hartopp[16] gave me a farewell dinner at a club in Park Place, St James's. We sat late and our mood was melting though fitfully hilarious." [17]

Seven years earlier, Moreton Frewen had married an heiress, Clara Jerome, the eldest of the three daughters of the American, Leonard Jerome, a successful entrepreneur and investor. His second daughter Jennie married Lord Randolph Churchill and was the mother of Winston. So the group had introductions to the most exclusive of New York society and an entrée to the Union and Knickerbocker Clubs. It was on this first visit to New York that Jim met the beautiful Fanny Work, herself an heiress, at one of the many social events to which the aristocratic, vigorous, young Englishmen were invited. In addition, Jerome lived in a fine mansion at 25, Madison Square, a few doors away from Frank Work.[18] She was then 21 years old and, like Jim, had a passion for horses.

The party remained in New York for several weeks, staying at the Brevoort House, a downtown hotel well known to distinguished travellers from abroad. On their way west, they called on General Sheridan in Chicago, who advised them

---

[14] *Sons of the West*, p. 138
[15] Eldest son of Lord Leigh of Stoneleigh. On a return visit in 1884 Gilbert Leigh died falling into a ravine which was concealed by tree tops.
[16] In 1869 Edward "Chicken" Hartopp, 10th Hussars organised the first game of polo at Aldershot where he was stationed. The game was known then as "hockey on horseback".
[17] *Melton Mowbray and other Memories.*
[18] Fanny's wealthy father.

that Indian trouble was brewing on the Upper Yellowstone, and that the party should go instead to West Wyoming. So they went to Rawlins where the six travellers were fitted out with horses, pack mules, guides and camping equipment. There was plenty to shoot – wapiti (elk), black-tailed deer and antelope, and ducks migrating southwards.

As well as big game shooting, Jim invested money in the cattle ranching company and secured an interest in a silver mine in Nevada. He returned to New York at the end of December, and sailed to England in February. Jim returned to America in May the following year, this time with his brother Alexis (and his greyhound Paddy) and his youngest brother Edmund Roche. The two younger brothers joined forces with Horace Plunkett,[19] who had formed his own cattle company and had a ranch close to the Powder River Cattle Company.

When later Moreton Frewen got into trouble, Horace Plunkett took over the management of the Powder River Cattle Company, with Maurice's uncle Alexis Roche as his partner. Plunkett left him in charge but Alexis was not a manager of men. Horace believed that he suffered from not having been to public school,[20] where he would have been humbled as a junior boy. As it was, he lorded it over the stable boys and caused problems.

"With all his ability he had made so much mischief, the country was too hot for us all. The position is most difficult as his people are on the verge of bankruptcy and are depending on him. At the same time, the conviction grows on me that he can never make a success of any work where he had control of others. We had to sack Alexis after a talk in which I tried to make him mend his ways but he only indulged in counter abuse."[21]

The two remained good friends and Horace attended Alexis' marriage to Maude, daughter of Viscount Goschen.

(Plunkett later wrote in his diary: "Found old Paddy the greyhound Alexis had brought out to the ranch had died. He had lived a hard life. Badly poisoned once, torn by wolves and badgers, scalded by prickly pears, his fighting days had been full of adversity.")

The following year, Jim returned to America and after two weeks in New York, Jim left for the West to join the Frewens, and to look after his own investments in Wyoming and Nevada. In July, he wrote to Mr Watson at Brevoort House, telling him that he was having great sport, hunting on the Yellowstone and that he shortly expected to welcome some friends from England.

---

[19] Sir Horace Plunkett (1854–1932). Anglo–Irish, son of Lord Dunsany, a politician and pioneer of agricultural cooperation. He aspired to make life better for small farmers in Ireland.
[20] *British Gentlemen in the Wild West.* p. 33
[21] *Horace Plunkett.*

Edward and Dick Swiveller

Fanny Work, Jim Roche, Lucy and George Work

On the 19th August, the proprietor of the Brevoort House received a despatch from Denver, Colorado, sent by a well-known guide in the West, announcing that the Hon. J B B Roche had been killed by Indians on the Yellowstone River. The newspapers reporting his death added that it was rumoured that he was engaged to a daughter of Frank Work, the well-known Wall Street capitalist.

None of his friends in New York had been told of his death and the following day the press were already regarding the report as unconfirmed. A friend was quoted as saying: "Roche was a thoroughly good fellow and well calculated to take care of himself anywhere. I can't believe that he has got away from his party and been killed."

Jim was in fact very much alive and he and his brother and the Frewens met up with Hugh Lowther and party[22] at Castle Frewen as planned. They had visited Niagara Falls, before travelling to Cheyenne and the Yellowstone Park. Hugh Lowther, the future Earl of Lonsdale, writing about this visit to Powder River, described Jim's extraordinary prowess at big game shooting.

> "Jim Roche was the most experienced hunter of the party. It was his second trip to the Middle West and he was a particularly keen buffalo shot. His method of killing them was unique, and founded on a strange lack of the instinct of self-preservation, which he had observed in the animals so far as white hunters were concerned.
>
> He had a technique of riding his horse right in amongst a herd, picking his animal and shooting it dead at point-blank range, between the shoulder blades – the surest way of hitting the beast's heart, which is placed very low down in its massive chest, between the forelegs. Being a sportsman in the best English tradition, however, he would always stampede the herd first and shoot the animal he had selected on the move, and the weapon he used was a .41 revolver!"[23]

The buffalo had to be killed to provide grazing for cattle. They also attracted marauding Indians and were destructive to posts and fencing. Moreton was unhappy at the wholesale slaughter of the great buffalo herds. He pleaded with his friends in power to extend the Yellowstone Park to include a low-lying area which was free from snow in winter, and which harboured 50,000 buffalo and 100,000 wapiti. Unfortunately, he failed in his mission and, within two years, the great game herds had disappeared.[24]

Jim and the Lowthers had returned to New York when winter set in.

---

[22] The party consisted of Lieut, Brocklehurst, the Hon. Hugh Lowther, (brother of Lord Lonsdale), Lady Grace Lowther, (sister of the Marquis of Huntly), the Hon. Charles Fitzwilliam and Capt. J F Hare. *New York Daily Tribune*. August 20th 1879 p. 3.

[23] *The Yellow Earl*, p.41

[24] *American Wonderland*, p. 25.

"The Lowthers stayed on in the Big Horn until well into November. Then they returned to New York with James Roche, to be met by a battery of pressmen. Even if the Wyoming cow-pokes thought little of the Frewen brothers and their aristocratic guests, socially-conscious New York was delighted with them."[25]

Jim fell into the welcoming arms of Fanny.

[25] *The Yellow Earl:* p. 43

2

Maurice's American grandfather

Fanny and Jim married in September 1880, with reservations on the part of Fanny's father, a very wealthy, self-made man. He was very much against the idea of his beloved daughter marrying a European. However, he was won over by Jim's kindness and his love of horses, a love which the two men shared.

From a very early age, Frank loved horses and riding. His father John Wark,[26] a civil engineer who had emigrated from England, died when Frank was four years-old, at their home in Chillicothe, Ohio. Sarah, Frank's mother, was left impoverished with five children to bring up. She was befriended by the wealthy Wood brothers, George and John, settlers from Virginia who made their fortunes in Chillicothe in property and pork packing.[27] George owned a stable and paddock for the exercise and riding of horses and young people were allowed to ride there. Frank became very skilful in managing horses. He was a daredevil child and his exploits became legendary.

One in particular was recorded in the *Scioto Gazette* in March 1936 under the heading "Quaint Tales of Old Chillicothe":

> "Frank Work as a young boy would often ride nude, astride a gaunt, gray horse, galloping down Paint Street. He would go to the river ford at Hickory Street with that horse, take off his clothes and bribe a companion to take them to his home in Mulberry Street; then he would make a grand entry into the city. He would come up the whole length of it.... Sometimes as he passed the market house, people would throw fruit and vegetables at him, trying to knock him off the horse. By this repeated practice he showed he loved swimming and horses!"

Frank earned his first money working as a clerk in the general, dry goods[28] store of John and George Wood, on the south-west corner of Paint and Main Street in Chillicothe. One day, when he was 15 years-old, the story goes that he

---

26 See Appendix A for his biography.
27 They reared hogs on their farms and packed the pork in salt, the method used to preserve meat before refrigeration.
28 Dry goods were woollen and cotton textiles, silks, velvets, laces, hosiery, buttons and thread. mainly imported. Spinning and weaving were mainly done at home until second half of nineteenth century.

ran away from home. According to one version of the story, a teacher in the local school chastised him by whipping the palms of his hands with a rattan switch. That was too much for Frank. He took his savings in the form of a five-dollar piece, and ran away from home, never to see his mother again.

Frank with his bold, daring, dynamic, personality, dreamed from an early age, of leaving Chillicothe and going out into the big world. He was very young when his father died, but he had heard the stories of his father's journey down the Mississippi to Baton Rouge, to survey some military buildings.[29]

Fifty years later, it was the ambition of the writer Mark Twain and his friends as boys, to become a pilot on a steamboat. He lived in a village on the banks of the River Mississippi. Mark Twain persuaded a pilot to show him the ropes and was taken on as a cub-pilot, an assistant who received no more than his passage but did "all the hard work while his master sat on a high bench and smoked." [30]

Steamboats provided a connecting link between isolated areas and the outside world. They brought newspapers and the mail, and news from far off cities. "But primarily the boats served the Herculean task moving bales of cotton and rafts of timber to distant markets returning with items needed for everyday life."[31]

And Frank, driven by the same ambition as Mark Twain, boarded a boat heading down the Scioto River to its confluence with the Ohio River, and onwards to Cairo where it met the Mississippi. With his independent, ambitious spirit, and love of the driving seat he, like Mark Twain later, found his way to becoming became a cub-pilot.

We can imagine what a steamboat looks like from this colourful description:

"The boat is rather a handsome sight. She is long and sharp and trim and pretty; she has tall fancy-topped chimneys, with a gilded device of some kind swung between them; a fanciful pilot-house, all glass and 'gingerbread'; the paddles boxes are gorgeous with a picture or with gilded rays above the boat's name; there is a flag gallantly flying from the jack-staff; the furnace doors are open and the fires glaring bravely; the upper decks are black with passengers; the captain stands by the big bell, calm, imposing, the envy of all; great volumes of the blackest smoke are rolling and tumbling out of the chimneys."[32]

To get an idea the scenery which met Frank's eyes, as he steamed down the river past Baton Rouge, we have Mark Twain's alluring description of Baton Rouge and the luxuriant south. Twain, making the same journey as Frank half a century later, tells us that the descriptions of foreign tourists fifty years earlier exactly

---

[29] See Appendix A.
[30] *Life on the Mississippi*, p. 177.
[31] *Steamboats and the Cotton Economy*, p. 4.
[32] *Life on the Mississippi*, p. 65.

Mississippi steamboat

portray the region as it appeared in his day, except as to the state of the houses. Negro cabins and big mansions alike had a decayed and neglected look – their shining white paint worn away by the blight of civil war.

"Baton Rouge was clothed in flowers, like a bride – no much more so; like a greenhouse. For we were in the absolute south now. The magnolia trees were lovely and fragrant with their dense, rich foliage and huge snow-ball blossoms...And there was a tropical sun overhead and a tropical swelter in the air...From Baton Rouge to New Orleans the great sugar plantations border both sides of the Mississippi. And now and then you see a pillared and porticoed great manor-house, embowered in trees."[33]

By contrast, Charles Dickens saw the Mississippi as "an enormous ditch, sometimes two or three miles wide, running liquid mud, its strong and frothy current choked and obstructed everywhere by huge logs and whole forest trees."[34]

We do not know how Frank viewed the great river nor how much time he spent on the steamboat. If he became a pilot, he would have earned good money. "The pilot, even in those days of trivial wages, had a princely salary – from a hundred to two hundred and fifty dollars month, and no board to pay. Two months of his wages would pay a preacher's salary for a year."[35]

[33] *Life on the Mississippi*, pp. 416–419.
[34] *American Notes*.
[35] *Life on the Mississippi*, p. 68.

By the time Frank arrived in New Orleans, he had some money in his pocket. New Orleans was the largest cotton port in the US, equalled only by New York as a commercial centre. As he was growing up, he had heard much talk in Chillicothe about the fortunes to be made in growing and marketing cotton. His elder brother John Clinton, ten years his senior, had a dry goods store in Columbus and was an important contact with the business world.

Cotton was a very rich resource in the US between 1815 and 1860 and was largely responsible for the rapid development of the US economy. The invention of the cotton gin, which separated the seed from the lint, had greatly increased production. With slave labour and rich land, landowners amassed great fortunes. And the growth in cotton production was in response to the enormous demand for raw cotton from the British textile industry. This, in turn, was the result of the invention of textile machines, powered by the steam engine.

Frank became a cotton broker, initially joining a firm of cotton merchants with a large-scale business. The cotton merchant bought the cotton outright from the planters in bales. These were further compressed in New Orleans, to reduce the bales before shipment to foreign ports, for buyers in the world markets. England was the main market. Over half of the cotton grown in America was exported directly to Liverpool from New Orleans. The merchants earned a commission of two and a half per cent of the gross proceeds. Frank left New Orleans in 1839, one year before a sharp decline in the price of cotton over the next few years.[36] Frank had made his first fortune just in time, and set sail for New York. He kept the five-dollar piece all his life, so the story goes.

He was twenty when he arrived in New York. He went to work in the dry good store of William Dailey, a former Chillicothe merchant, and soon became a partner. It was at this point that he changed the spelling of his name from 'Wark' to 'Work'. Horses were Frank's great passion and, in particular, he liked driving trotters (harness horses). He now had sufficient money to buy fast horses and to race them. Trotting races took place on the highways before the advent of cars. He drove his trotting horses until the end of his life, as this is article from a New York periodical reveals:

"When he began to drive in the road, that part of Broadway where the Herald Building now stands, was a popular speeding ground. Corporal Thompson's Tavern, on the present site of the Fifth Avenue Hotel, marked the end of the pavement, and from there, the old Bloomingdale road stretched away through miles of pretty, rural scenes in the vicinity of the Claremont, then as now a famous resort for the driving fraternity.

There was a good road across what is now Madison Square. Third Avenue was another speeding ground at that period and later came the

---

[36] *One Hundred Years of American Commerce.* Ch. XXXIV: American Cotton.

palmy days of Harlem Lane, Seventh Avenue, to be finally succeeded by the famous Harlem River Speedway. Mr Work is perhaps the only man now living who has driven trotters on them all when they were at their best.[37]

Of all the men who have driven fast horses over New York's million-dollar speedway, one of the most widely known is the stocky, hale and hearty old man who almost daily is seen bending over one or two beautiful harness favourites that take the dust of no man's horse."[38]

It was through their common love of horseracing that he got to know Cornelius Vanderbilt. The two met at Burnham's road house, at Bloomingdale and 76th Street, now upper Broadway. Cornelius was apt to be loud, rustic and coarse in his speech. He could not write the simplest words correctly and he only read newspapers. Unlike him, Frank was well educated, but in other respects, the two had much in common. They had both grown up in extreme poverty.

Cornelius was the son of a poor farmer. When a young boy, he saved up enough money to buy a rowing boat, in which he ferried passengers and farm produce from Staten Island to Manhattan. Next, he bought a sailing schooner and then like Frank worked on a steamboat. Before long, he was designing his own steam vessels and eventually owned a fleet of one hundred, including transatlantic liners. He was given the nickname of The Commodore.

At the age of 68, the Commodore turned his interest to railroads. "I am a friend of the iron road and like to see it stretching to every corner of the US." [39] He first acquired the New York and Harlem and the Hudson River Railroads in 1866. Two years later he attempted to take control of the Erie Railway but his purchase was prevented by the directors, Gould and Fisk, who placed fraudulent stock on the market.

Frank Work was Vanderbilt's representative on the board of the Erie Railroad,[40] and was a key figure in the Battle for the Erie, as it became known. In February 1868, he appeared before Judge Barnard of the Supreme Court of New York, to apply for an injunction, aimed at thwarting Gould and Fisk. He was unsuccessful, but his clever management helped to make his reputation. Vanderbilt's efforts to acquire the Erie Railway were abortive and he lost millions in the attempt and Frank too lost his own large investment in the venture. This was reimbursed to him by Cornelius.

Clearly, Cornelius, 25 years his senior, recognised qualities in Frank which inspired his trust, and to which he could personally relate. Frank was honest,

---

[37] There is a painting in the Museum of the City of New York entitled 'Frank Work Driving a Fast Team of Trotters' by John McAuliffe.

[38] *Men and women of the Outdoor World.*

[39] *The Vanderbilt Legend.*

[40] *A Chapter of Erie.*

bold, thrifty, practical, and hard working. His spirit was strong and indomitable. He possessed the very qualities which made the Scots such successful pioneers in America. Cornelius' young friend soon became his trusted ally and one of his stockbrokers.

Cornelius Vanderbilt was a remarkable man. He accumulated a vast fortune, making most of it when he was over 70 years-old. At his death in 1877, he left a fortune of $105,000,000, "For business opportunities and requirements of his period, Commodore Vanderbilt had unequalled genius," said an orator after his death.[41]

As his broker, Frank Work earned a commission on his investment transactions. Having amassed a large fortune, Work started a banking firm with William Y Strong, the son of another Chillicothe merchant and nephew of his future wife. His obituary lists a number of bonding and brokerage firms with which he was subsequently connected.[42] When he died in 1911, the poor boy from Chillicothe was worth $15,000,000.

Many fortunes were made in New York during that period of rapid expansion; E L Doctorow describes the scene:

"Nowhere else in the world was there such an acceleration of energies. A mansion would appear in a field. The next day it stood on a city street with horse and carriage riding by."[43] "There was a sense of the expanding, pulsating city pumping its energies outward furiously in every direction."[44]

Frank was 38 when, in 1857, he married a fellow Chillicothean, Ellen, daughter of his parents' friends, John and Eleanor Wood. Ellen's mother, who was born in Philadelphia, was the daughter of a famous physician and inventor, Dr Joseph Strong. His ancestor was Elder John Strong, who was born in Chard, Somerset, and left England for America in 1630, because of his strong Puritan sympathies. The mechanical inventions of Dr Strong anticipated the principle of the bicycle. More importantly, he invented the axle tourniquet for the control of bleeding during surgery.

When Ellen's father died in 1848, his widow Eleanor built a fine town house, in Greek revival style, in Chillicothe. In 2005, I visited my great-grandfather's birthplace with my cousin John Maynard. We were both strangers to the town. A man spoke to us in the street as we were taking a photograph. By an extraordinary coincidence, he turned out to be the present owner of the house that Eleanor built. His name was Franklin Conaway and he invited us to his home. A few minutes later, we were sitting by our great-great-grandmother's fireplace!

41 *Life and Later Speeches of Chauncey Depew.*
42 Work, Davis and Burton; Frank Work & Co.; Scott, Strong & Co.; Strong Sturgis & Co.
43 *The Waterworks*, p. 11
44 *The Waterworks*, p. 59

Frank Work,
Maurice's grandfather

Ellen Work,
Maurice's grandmother

Eight years later, Eleanor sold her home in Chillicothe and came to live in New York with her daughter Ellen, then aged 25. No doubt, she moved to be near her son George, who was working in New York. In addition, the metropolis would give her daughter, the lovely Ellen, greater opportunities for finding a suitable husband and perhaps she already had Frank in mind as a son-in-law. Eleanor and her daughter Ellen were the belles of Chillicothe. Frank had last seen Ellen when he left Chillicothe at the age of 15, and she was only two or three years old. The marriage may have been arranged but he fell in love with the beautiful, young woman. When he was wooing her, he sent her an extract from *The Lament of Tasso* by Byron. It is about a young man falling totally in love:

> "I found the thing I sought – and that was thee;
> And then I lost my being, all to be
> Absorb'd in thine; the world was past away;
> *Thou* didst annihilate the earth to me!"

Frank copied Byron's poem in his own hand and put it in a small envelope addressed to Miss Ellen Wood. It clearly spoke to her, as she kept it all her life and I have it to this day. And indeed, she married Frank, thirteen years her senior, now a rich man, handsome and generous. The poorest boy from the Dogsburg district in Chillicothe, married the daughter of one of the wealthiest men in Chillicothe. They lived in 13 East 26th street, overlooking Madison Square, which remained Frank's home until he died.

Frank and Ellen had three children, George, Frances and Lucy. Maurice's uncle George was born in 1858. His father sent him to St Paul's School, Concord, New Hampshire, a private preparatory school[45] with strong affiliations with the Episcopal Church. It was founded in 1856 by a Boston doctor who turned his country house into a school, so that his sons could be educated in a rural environment, where they would have contact with nature and be safely away from the outside world. Cornelius Vanderbilt III and his brother Alfred, the great-grandsons of the Commodore, also went to St Paul's.

George did not follow his father into the world of finance. Instead, he became a champion sportsman. When he was thirty, he put all his sporting energies into clay pigeon shooting, in which he excelled, holding the amateur record for the country, with 98 hits out of 100, in a match against a professional. He was known as the Beau Brummell of the traps, because he usually shot in his everyday clothes, which were elegantly tailor-made.

Photographs show that he was a very good-looking man with a fine physique almost six foot tall, well built and slim. He was a well-known figure in nearly all the elite Sporting Clubs in New York. He never married, although in 1899 he

---

[45] Preparatory here means preparatory for college.

intended to marry Mrs Constance Biddle, when her divorce came through.

To Frank's great sorrow, his adored wife died of double pneumonia and rheumatism in 1877 when she was only 46 years-old. After her death, his horses became even more important to him. This article in the *New York Tribune* [46] reveals his great affection for his champion team:

"In a plain stable in 55th Street are housed Frank Work's trotters including the celebrated team, Edward and Dick Swiveller, who held the world record for covering a mile in 2 minutes 19 seconds.[47] A *Tribune* reporter called at the stable the other afternoon and inquired if Mr Work were there. 'He is out riding,' said the head groom, but will be back very soon. The reporter took a chair and sat down to await Mr Work's return. A number of thoroughbred bull terriers gambolled about the floor.

The reporter had not been in the stable long when there was a sound of horses' hoofs outside and the groom threw open the sliding doors to admit Edward and Swiveller, driven by Mr Work. They were attached to a light wagon with bright red wheels and shining black body. They had been driven all the afternoon yet they came into the stable with not a hair turned.

The first thing one notices about Edward and Swiveller is their length of limb, which can take those large bodies over the road with the speed of the wind; nay, they can outstrip most winds and make those red wheels look like one long strip of carmine.[48]

The horses on being unharnessed went of their own accord to the box stalls which Mr Work has had made for them. Going to the stall in which Edward stood he said: "Come here Edward" and the horse approached and laid his nose in Mr Work's hand, gazing at the same time with his great eyes in an inquiring way at the reporter. 'Ah! Edward is very sweet on me,' said Mr Work, as the intelligent animal placed his head affectionately on his owner's shoulder. After patting Edward on the neck and smoothing out his mane, Mr Work took the reporter to the next stall, where Swiveller was anxiously awaiting his supper. 'I don't think I shall ever sell Edward and Swiveller.' said Mr Work. 'I have not a great while longer to stay in this world and I want all the enjoyment I can get out of life. Driving is an expensive folly that grows on one by habit and I have indulged in it for nearly fifty years and

---

46 October 22nd 1882. Frank Work was then at the height of his powers as a driver of fast trotters.

47 Two years later, racing at Narragansett Park, Rhode Island, they knocked three seconds off this record. It was broken by William Henry Vanderbilt in 1883, when 2 minutes 15 and a half seconds became the new world record.

48 In the painting in the Museum of the City of New York entitled 'Frank Work Driving a Fast Team of Trotters' by John McAuliffe, he is driving on a stretch of 8th Avenue, at the time a soft dirt road where there were daily speed parades.

49 Edward lived to be 36, spending his last years on a farm on Long Island. FW stipulated in his will that he should be taken care of and not driven.

am loath to give it up'."[49]

The reporter was then shown his new stable, under construction in Fifty-Sixth Street. He described it as being over a hundred feet deep with a frontage of thirty-five feet on the street, the front facade cut in Wyoming graystone, which resembles granite, and the rest of the structure in pressed brick. The interior was finished in polished oak. It would be used entirely as a stable for Mr Work's trotters.

The ground floor was taken up by a large hall nineteen feet high, with a walking ring, stalls for the horses at the back and space for the wagons at the front. The ceiling was supported by heavy iron girders and hung with decorative iron lanterns. There were no partitions or posts dividing the hall, which had a paddock of peat moss running the length of the building twenty feet wide. Great care was taken to thoroughly ventilate the building.

Stairs lead up to the upper storeys from the outside. Mr Work had a set of rooms on the second floor, and the third had accommodation for the men employed in the stable. When Dick Swiveller died, his owner spent the whole night in the dying animal's stable.

DELMONICO'S TWENTY YEARS AGO.
(Reproduced from THE SPIRIT of April 7, 1877.)

W. H. VANDERBILT.   JOE MORA.   SIR JOHN RAE REID.   HORACE PORTER.   WILLIAM TURNBULL.   FRANK WORK.   CIRO DELMONICO,
B. HOUSTON.   BEN WENBURG. CAPT. WM. CONNOR, ROSCOE CONKLING.   GEORGE DEWEY.   JAMES R. KEENE.
WRIGHT SANFORD.   CHARLES DELMONICO.   JOHN GARCIA,   F. GRAY GRISWOLD.   T. J. EDMONDSON.

Delmonico's cafe at Madison Square, 1877; some well-known habitués.

Sketch from *The Spirit of the Times.*
Courtesy of Mrs. Henry A. Campbell

Delmonico's, a favourite haunt of Frank Work

"His palatial private stable at 107 West Fifty-Sixth Street, adjoining Carnegie Hall is still the show place of New York as a home for light harness horses and is regarded as one of the most perfectly designed structures of its kind in the world," said the *New York Herald*,[50] in a tribute to his 85th birthday.

In 1876, the celebrated restaurant Delmonico's relocated from 14th Street to 26th Street, just across the road from Frank's home. It was the hub of New York fashionable society. Many masked balls were held in the restaurant's elegant rooms. Mothers introduced their daughters to society there. State dinners were held there. The entrance to the dining rooms and ballrooms was in 26th Street. At the other end of the building on Broadway was the men's café, where smoking was permitted. It was an important meeting place for Frank, especially after his wife's death. It was surely a blow for him when it moved in 1899 to 44th Street & Fifth Avenue.

He was still driving in his eighties, and in 1900 was arrested for reckless driving in Central Park by two mounted policemen.[51] He was highly indignant, considering the arrest entirely uncalled for and conducted in the most brutal manner. "I have handled horses all my life", said Mr Work, "and those who know me, know I have always respected the laws regarding driving. If it costs me 100,000 dollars, I'll see that the man who subjected me to this shameful and outrageous treatment is dismissed from the police force."

A reporter visited him at his home the following day and found him in a state of intense indignation. "I have been ill for nearly a year and yesterday afternoon I went out driving for the first time in a long while, with a couple of brown ponies." Mr Work explained. "The animals had not been worked recently and were very restive. They began to prance and feeling myself too weak to control them for any length of time, I drove to the Casino and sent for the manager of my stable. He brought me a single rig, but when I started driving the mare attached to it, I found she was also in a restive condition. Not at any time however did I violate any law of the road or indulge in reckless driving."

The magistrate agreed and he was dismissed without charge, much to the disapproval of the *New York Times* the following day. The paper found it extraordinary that the magistrate apparently had no difficulty in coming to the conclusion, that four or five park policemen had been perjuring themselves before them!

[50] *New York Herald*, July 17th, 1904.
[51] *New York Herald*, September 29th, 1900.

41

3

Maurice's American mother

Frank's daughter Fanny inherited his bold, pioneering spirit.

"It was at Sherry's one Sunday night that Mrs Stuyvesant Fish and Mrs Burke Roche launched a minor, social revolution. In London, they had seen aristocratic ladies dining in fashionable restaurants, on the Sabbath, hatless and wearing low-cut evening dresses. Resolving to flout New York tradition they caused a sensation at Sherry's by appearing with heads uncovered, in gowns that offered a shameless exposure of flesh. The innovation was widely disapproved: even the press deplored this scandalous example set by two members of the highest rank. But soon after Mrs Astor on a Sunday night swept regally into Sherry's wearing a coquettish raiment of white satin, with the tiniest headdress and her famous pearls."[52]

Fanny's décolleté was said to be the most beautiful in New York!

Sherry's was the most fashionable restaurant in New York in the Gilded Age. It was a time when great fortunes were amassed – from mining, iron and steel, railroads, banking, trading and industry. A wave of immigrants, attracted by the opportunities and the freedom which America offered, contributed to that wealth.

The Gilded Age had begun a few years before Fanny's birth, with the discovery of gold in California: "The terrible glitter of the mines has crept into every fashion of life: tables glitter with galvanised plate; hotels glitter with vanity-teaching mirrors; boats glitter with chandeliers and stained glass; churches glitter with gilt crosses & guilty clergy."[53]

The Gilded Age was so called because of the luxurious, ostentatious way of life of the newly rich. The millionaires competed to outdo each other in extravagance and excesses, in grander houses, more extravagant parties, more expensive clothes. Their full social life provided the opportunity to show off their wealth: "Evenings were given over to balls, to dinner parties; evenings at the Opera, where every woman wore full regalia, enormous sapphires and emeralds, such a profusion that the problem was to find a novel way of wearing them."[54]

---

[52] *Incredible New York.* p. 246.
[53] *Harpers New Monthly Magazine*, April 1853.
[54] *King Lehr and the Gilded Age.* p. 59.

In 1903 a gas company tycoon held a dinner on horseback for 36 guests at Sherry's, in the fourth floor ballroom, which was covered in turf. The horses were taken up in the luggage lift. The guests ate from trays balanced on their saddles. They sucked champagne through a tube from chilled bottles in their saddlebags. Another millionaire gave a dinner in honour of his dog, which arrived wearing a $15,000 diamond collar!

Some wealthy individuals in the Gilded Age had a private railway coach, which was attached to a regular train, or was even drawn by its own engine. This was a home on wheels, fitted with bedrooms, a sitting room, dining room, a kitchen, a bathroom, servants' quarters and even a library.

Maurice's mother was born Frances Eleanor Work on 28th October, 1857 in New York. She was the second child born to Frank and Ellen. Her parents wanted her to have the best of everything. The education of girls focussed more on accomplishments than academic study. She had a French governess and learned to speak excellent French. She did not go to school but was well educated by tutors particularly in English literature.

She was very well read and her diaries are punctuated with quotations from Shakespeare, Swinburne, Browning, and Arnold, for example. She also developed a keen interest in painting and furniture. She could draw very well. She was highly intelligent and had she been born without her father's great wealth, and in a different age, she could have excelled in a profession, as an actress, a teacher, artist, translator or a writer, for instance.

The values she inherited from both her parents, her serious interest in reading, in the arts and politics, and in intellectual matters, place her in 'old' New York. She had no need to be a social climber but her love of expensive clothes, of lavish entertaining, of being seen, of spending money, of displaying her wealth, place her equally, in the world of the *nouveaux riches*, of the new wealth.

Paul Bourget, a French writer who visited America in the 1890s, described the young women of high society as being physically strong with a love of fresh air and exercise. They took pride in their figures and in their complexions; they were supple in their movements and were full of vitality. Their teeth were well polished and had gold fillings.[55] Fanny was no exception. She rode every day and hunted in the season. She was tall and lithe and carried herself well.

She grew up to become a great beauty and was a belle of New York society. In common with rich women of her society, she spent money liberally. Her wealthy father gave her a large allowance. Her clothes were made by the best dressmakers, she had luxuriant fur coats, she wore large, elaborate hats, and she had expensive accessories – parasols, gloves and shoes.

One year after the death of her mother, she met the dashing, charming, James Boothby Burke Roche, when he stopped in New York on his way to the cattle

---

[55] *Outre-mer: (notes sur l'Amerique)*

Fanny Work, Maurice's mother

ranch in Wyoming. Marriages between American heiresses and impecunious aristocrats from Europe were in vogue at that time. The most famous example was the marriage of the ninth Duke of Marlborough to Consuelo Vanderbilt, the railroad heiress, in 1895. The Duke was bankrupt and Blenheim Palace was in a depleted state, badly in need of restoration. A price was negotiated with her father, who paid the Duke a dowry of £2,500,000[56] as well as giving $100,000 each to the couple annually.

[56] About $300 million in 2007.

Jim was the second son of the first Lord Fermoy but his brother had no male heir, so Fanny had the prospect of becoming Lady Fermoy. The couple then came to live in London. Soon after Jim took Fanny to Wyoming to stay with his friends Moreton and Clara[57] at Castle Frewen, Powder River. The newly married couple sailed from Liverpool to New York at a cost of thirty guineas return.[58] Fanny easily embraced her new life. Through her American women friends who had married into the British aristocracy, Fanny naturally fell in with a group of young people. Lady Blanche Hozier,[59] the Duchess of Manchester,[60] Lady Leslie,[61] Lord Dunraven, Lady Lonsdale, Lord Hood and the Earl of Wharncliffe are names that appear with Fanny's in Clara Frewen's[62] journal.

Their year followed a set pattern:

"The Summer Session, the Winter Session, the Hunting season, the London Season, Cowes Week, the house parties in beautiful old mansions…all this routine, which it was imperative to follow, left little time for the upper classes to pay even fleeting visits to the nursery."[63]

Fanny played her full part in the social seasons, hunting and riding whenever her pregnancies permitted. In October 1882 at 69 Onslow Gardens, London SW, she gave birth to Eileen who died aged seven weeks old, from meningitis and convulsions. Cynthia was born in April 1884 at 28 Park Lane, Mayfair, and 13 months later, the twin boys arrived in Pont Street. Given the demands of the social calendar, Cynthia, Maurice and Frank saw very little of their mother. Jim continued to try his hand at schemes which promised to make his fortune – and regularly failed.

Throughout this period the couple were supported financially by Fanny's father. He was quoted in the press as saying:

"When my daughter married I agreed to make her an allowance of $7,000 a year. This was increased from time to time and in no year did I send her less than twice that sum. When the twins were born, I increased her regular allowance to $12,000 a year and was continually called upon for more. I was not only pressed for money by Roche himself but his mother and

57 Clara was the eldest of the three daughters of Leonard Jerome, a wealthy investor and speculator.
58 *The Splendid Pauper.*
59 Born Lady Blanche Ogilvy, daughter of the Earl of Airlie, her daughter Clementine married Winston Churchill.
60 Consuelo Yznaga, 1858-1909, half Spanish, half American heiress married the impoverished Duke of Manchester in New York in 1886.
61 Leonie Jerome, married Sir John Leslie of Glasnough.
62 *The Fabulous Leonard Jerome.* p. 291.
63 *The Fabulous Leonard Jerome.* p. 195.

intermeddling friends of his besieged me."

Frank Work might have continued to support his daughter and her opportunist husband, if he had not been informed that Roche was using his wife's money in the wildest sort of dissipation and extravagance. According to his father-in-law, three-quarters of his wife's money went to pay gambling debts. After Roche had squandered $100,000 in a single year Mr Work "stopped pouring money down a rat hole." Fanny's extravagant life style made its own hole in their income!

4

Maurice crosses the Atlantic

B y the latter half of 1886, the couple were in dire financial straits. The furniture was in the hands of the bailiffs. There were outstanding loans. Fanny, with the agreement of her husband, went back to her father in New York in December 1886, taking with her their daughter Cynthia. She left Maurice and Frank in London in the care of their nanny. Did Jim insist on keeping the boys? Did Fanny intend to make a short visit to beg for money? We shall never know.

Her passage was paid for by her younger sister Lucy, who was engaged to Peter Cooper Hewitt, heir to the great wealth of his grandfather, Peter Cooper. The latter was an industrialist who built the first steam-powered locomotive in America, and was well known as a philanthropist. He endowed the Cooper Union for the Advancement of Science in New York City. His daughter Sarah married Abram Hewitt, a formidable mayor of New York. Their son Peter was himself a scientist and an inventor.[64]

Three months after the departure of Fanny and Cynthia to New York, Jim, deep in debt and unable to provide for his family, crossed the Atlantic in March, with the 21 months-old twins and their nanny, Lizzie Flood. It is possible she was their wet nurse. She was then 16 years-old. Frank Work told the story of how: "When Jim Roche was on his way up the Bay with them, he sent me a telegram to have the maid come to the steamer to take them off." The party then proceeded to 13 Madison Square where the babies were left on the doorstep of their grandfather's house.

An interview took place the following day. Jim apparently agreed not to attempt to see his sons again, on strict conditions. My guess is that Frank applied both a stick and a carrot. The penalty for their father attempting to see his sons was that Fanny would have a minimal allowance, and the boys would grow up in poverty. The carrot was in the form of a substantial sum of money to pay off his debts. The press reported that Frank Work paid Jim's return passage.

Jim kept to the bargain and the boys did not see their father until their grandfather died in 1911. There was one occasion when he did speak to my father, who told me this sad story. He was walking around Madison Square when a very

---

[64] He invented the Cooper Hewitt mercury-vapour lamp which produced a powerful ultraviolet light.

Frank and Maurice aged two and a half

Maurice and Frank in New York

nice stranger spoke to him and gave him a silver dollar. When he went home, he told Lizzie Flood what had happened. She went to the window and looked out. There was a man standing by a tree. "That's him," said Maurice. "That is your father," Lizzie told him. Jim sometimes watched his sons at a distance, as they came out of school.

Frank Work's initial trust in his son-in-law had been seriously violated and for the rest of his life he held him in utter contempt, forbidding his family to have any contact whatsoever with him. His grandchildren were prohibited from visiting Europe and from contracting international alliances. In an interview when he was over ninety years-old he gave vent to his intense feelings on the subject:

> "I cannot express my contempt for these helpless, hopeless, lifeless men that come over here to carry off the flower of our womanhood.. American men don't marry money, they make it. But they don't want to pay those noble paupers' debts.
>
> I can't see what our fine American women are about, when they want to contract an alliance with those impecunious adventurers who only consider the splendid women they marry in this country, as so much money for the patching up of their ramshackle estates. The only way to stop international marriage and ruinations to this country, is to levy an enormous tax on imported bridegrooms, and encourage native wedlock by reward. It's the women's fault. Our men are not to blame. The women are attracted by the social position they think their marriage to noblemen insures them. In nine cases out of ten, American girls haven't the rights of a humble peasant in their husband's country.
>
> My advice to the girls is to stay at home until they know better, and to realize that American men make the best husbands, even if they haven't a 'sir' or 'milord' or such tomfoolery attached to their name…if I had anything to say about it I would make it a hanging offence for international marriage!"

Fanny was soon restored to her father's good books, and able to resume her expensive way of life. Her friends were sympathetic to her plight and in spite of the prejudice against divorce in New York high society, Fanny survived her divorce from Jim Roche without social ostracism. Undoubtedly, the power of her personality, her grace, her intelligence, her good taste and beauty were responsible for this. Jim's irresponsibility as a husband was well known:

> "When she came back to America, bringing with her a burden of grief and babies, her friends sympathized deeply with her and during the years which have elapsed since, they have continued to sympathize."[65]

---

[65] *Providence Sunday Journal.* Sept 21st 1902 Article: 'A Society Woman beyond Reproach'.

Her friendship with Mrs Astor, the self-crowned queen of New York and Newport society (the two societies were interchangeable) was a great help to her social status. When the Mrs Astor gave a ball in 1892, to which the four hundred socially elite of New York were invited, Fanny's name was included in the published list.

A month after the twins arrived in New York, an important social event took place at their grandfather's home. His younger daughter Lucy married Peter Cooper Hewitt in April 1887 and the wedding luncheon was served in a marquee in the garden. Many of the most prominent New Yorkers were present. One of the most expensive presents was the diamond crescent which Fanny gave her sister. The Cooper Hewitts lived in Lexington Avenue, next door to Peter's sisters and brother. The houses shared a ballroom where they held grand parties.

In 1890, Fanny divorced her husband in the Wilmington, Delaware Court. Her father was a powerful man with friends in high places and he pulled out a big gun. He enlisted the help of no less a person than former Secretary of State[66] the Hon. Thomas F Bayard, a resident of Delaware. It was his first appearance in court, in a legal contest, since he became a Senator in 1869. The Secretary made a powerful argument in favour of granting Fanny an absolute divorce on the grounds of desertion and non-support.

Her husband, he said, had ordered her "home" to America. "Seeing that her father would no longer accede to his demands for money, he did not wish to support the two children he had kept in London," said Mr Bayard, "but sailed for New York. On his arrival, he took the children to the door of their grandfather, inside of which their deserted mother had taken shelter. He pushed them inside the door, rang the bell and drove off. The next day an interview was held. In that interview he showed no love for his wife or children. He simply showed a desire for money. No money was forthcoming and he left never to see his wife again."

The divorce was granted with custody of the three children given to the mother. Jim Roche was ordered to pay the costs. The case was the most notable divorce contest ever known in Delaware at that time.

[66] Thomas F Bayard was US Secretary of State from 1885-1889. The Secretary of State is the Head of the Department of State concerned with foreign affairs.

5

Summers in Newport, Rhode Island

C ynthia, Maurice and Frank grew up in the lap of luxury. Every summer, their grandfather rented a house by the seaside, initially on Long Island. But from the time the twins were seven years-old, they spent their summers in Newport, Rhode Island. A French governess called Josephine took care of them.

Newport has a long history. Its name was originally Aquidneck, which is Indian for the "Isle of Peace". Much of its colonial architecture has survived today. It had a large deep-water harbour which contained the British fleet from 1776-1779 when the British were in occupation of Rhode Island, during the war of the American Revolution. In 1779, the British withdrew, to concentrate their forces in New York. In 1780, the French landed in Newport and, for the rest of the war, Newport was the base of the French forces in the United States.

Newport, with its good climate and beautiful scenery, had been a fashionable "watering place" for more than one hundred years. There were many "cottages" – temporary wooden structures – to let for the summer season and, since the 1850s, southern planters had sought the relief of Atlantic breezes from the humid heat of the deep south. Several fine beaches made it an ideal summer resort.

Henry James lived in Newport before he went to Harvard. He studied art but soon discovered his talent lay in writing. He loved "the dainty island of Aquidneck with treasures all its own, a thousand delicate secret places, far away little lonely, sandy, coves, rock-set, lily-sheeted ponds, almost hidden, and shallow summer-haunted valleys with the sea just over some stony shoulder." He lamented the summer visitors, who over the years had piled on their gold, "put things into it, things of their own, and of all sorts, and of many, ugly and of more expensive sorts; to fill it substantially, that is, with gold, the gold they have ended by heaping up there to an amount so oddly out of proportion to the scale of nature and of space." [67]

Edith Wharton (née Jones), twenty years younger than Henry James, spent most of her summers in Newport from the time she was born. She too loved the island, which was a rustic paradise for children, a haven for artists and intellectuals. She had a home there after her marriage, but developed a distaste for the new wealth and, like Henry James, she detested the changes brought about by the

[67] *The Sense of Newport.*

millionaires with their ostentatious 'cottages', their vulgar displays, their libraries where no-one read books. "Wharton ached to escape the "flat frivolity" and "watering place trivialities" in Newport society of later years."[68] In 1903 she moved to Europe where she met Henry James for the first time. They became close friends.

In the early 1880s the wealthiest families of the Gilded Age began to frequent Newport. They built magnificent mansions, palaces and chateaux on Bellevue Avenue, which, on the ocean side, had lawns sloping down to the shore. They were still called 'cottages' after the simple structures which they superseded. Pleasure yachting began in Newport and was on a grand scale. The yachts of the Gilded Age were magnificent and expensive.[69]

Paul Bourget in his description of Newport, wrote:

"There are more millions of dollars represented on this little extremity of this little island than in the whole of London and Paris combined...the dwellings are only lived in for six to eight weeks a year. Each one has with it, as a matter of course, horses, a coach and four, one or two yachts to cruise along the coast by sail or steam, a private railway coach to be able to feel at home on all the railway lines...One has an English abbey in the style of Elizabeth I, so exact that it could have been transported stone from stone...Another, in love with France, has a chateau of the French renaissance reminiscent of the chateaux of the Loire." [70]

Maude Howe Elliott wrote: "Nowhere can one see so many fine summer villas as in Newport. The Ocean Drive winds its way through twelve miles of incomparable beauty. A marble palace glistens in the sunshine, an English manor house crowns a hilltop, a medieval castle looks seaward, a red-roofed Normandy farmhouse nestles by the road side.

The island is a leafy paradise. Here are magnificent trees; flowers are incredibly profuse. Spring spreads a carpet of crocuses and daffodils. Great piles of rhododendrons only make way for drifts of roses. Flawless emerald lawns stretch to the cliffs' edge; blue hydrangeas repeat the singing color of the sea." [71]

Many architectural styles were represented. The Astors purchased Beechwood in 1881. They commissioned the architect Richard Morris Hunt who worked in Gothic Revival style, to renovate it at a cost of two million dollars. Beechwood became the centre of Newport social life during the Astors' eight-week summer

[68] *A Summer Salon: literary and cultural circles in Newport, Rhode island, 1850-1890.*
[69] Later Newport hosted important yacht races each summer. The America's Cup races were sailed off Newport, from 1930-1983.
[70] *Outre-mer.* pp. 59-60 .
[71] *This was my Newport .*

Frank and Maurice aged six

Bellevue Avenue, Newport, 1886

season. Mrs Astor moved with all her followers, to spend the summer months in their cottages in Bellevue Avenue. She held an annual summer ball, as well as exclusive dinner parties, where her servants were dressed in blue livery.

According to one source, Newport was a favourite haunt of Commodore Vanderbilt. He and some friends started Crumbs House which was a famous gathering place for the evening.[72] In 1888 William Kissam Vanderbilt, his grandson commissioned Richard Morris Hunt to build a marble palace, with a marble hall and a gilded salon, on Newport's Bellevue Avenue. It was modelled on the Trianon at Versailles. His elder brother Cornelius Vanderbilt II built the Breakers, the grandest of all the mansions, a seventy-room house in Italian Renaissance style, with a great hall, 45 foot high. In 1892 Ogden Goelet, a banker and developer from New York, completed the building of Ochre Court, a 50-room mansion also by Morris, inspired by Chateaux of the Loire. It is now Salve Regina University.

The Newport Casino, which opened in 1881, greatly enhanced Newport life for the very wealthy during the Gilded Age, becoming the centre of activities. A six-acre complex designed as a social and sporting club, it contained a theatre, which doubled up as a ballroom; a real tennis court; facilities for billiards, bowling, croquet and archery. Amateur theatricals were very popular and dances held regularly in the ballroom were well attended. Costume balls were all the rage in Newport as they were in New York society. The members loved dressing up as kings and queens, princes and princesses and historical figures. Gowns were made specially for these occasions.

The Casino is the oldest tennis centre in the world. It is even older than Wimbledon, which opened earlier but was rebuilt in 1922. It had the finest grass courts and was expertly managed. The players and officials were feted by the enthusiastic and generous patrons who welcomed them to their palatial homes and expensive yachts.

New York society transferred to Newport for the summer season where the natural setting and space provided the passionate party givers with great scope for exotic settings:

"The balls in Newport are unparalleled for beauty and authentic magnificence. I go to a ball in Newport as I would go to a ballet in Russia. Sometimes I find myself in some fabulous vineyard, where from the branches of the great trees, hang thousands and thousands of huge, green and purple and crimson grapes... Or tonight's ball may be a visualisation of all the dreams we had while we listened to a Hungarian rhapsody, hundreds of gypsies wandering over a lawn, grouped around their camp fires, singing their melodramatic hearts out."[73]

[72] *Good Old Summer Days.* p.186
[73] Mrs Oliver Harriman. *Harpers Bazaar*

A spectacular dance, given at the end of August 1895 at Marble House, illustrates the immense wealth of the hostess, Alva Vanderbilt, and the heights of extravagance, magnificence and of exotic imagination she reached:

"There was a remarkable floral feature near the grand staircase, a large bronze drinking fountain, surmounted by an immense bevelled plate-glass mirror. The basin was filled with tall lotus, water hyacinths, and tiny fairy lamps, while all around swarmed a flock of live humming-birds. Hovering around the open flowers were also brilliant butterflies and bees, which Mr Hodgson, who had charge of the decorations, had imported for the occasion. The many house servants and Berger's army of waiters were dressed in Louis XIV style. There were nine French chefs in the kitchen; one course alone consisted of 400 mixed birds. Three orchestras played."[74]

Alva gave this party to introduce the Duke of Marlborough to Newport society and to show off her daughter Consuelo. The Duke was impressed by the splendour of the occasion. Two months later he and Consuelo were married in New York.[75]

In 1892, Frank Work rented Elm Court, Bellevue Avenue, Newport from the Duchess of Dino, for Fanny and her family's summer vacation. Elm Court, was built in 1853 for Andrew Robeson who had made a fortune in the whaling

Elm Court, Newport, Rhode Island

---

[74] *Good Old Summer Days.* p.115.
[75] *Alva* p. 208

industry.[76] It is a dignified, elegant mansion with simple classical lines, built in the days before the invasion of the super-rich. Its distinguishing feature is an octagonal tower on the south side:

> "The present fine villa is in the Italian style and is built of brick and brown stone. The broad terrace in front of the drawing room windows on the south side, the gardener's cottage and the large stables are of the same materials. In the garden there are extensive graperies, early and late, peach houses and conservatories.
>
> The billiard-room, dining rooms, halls and passages are finished with a heavy wainscot in hard woods; the floors are in Neapolitan tiles and parquetry; and the drawing room takes the form of the large octagon tower on the left. The well-graded lawn scattered with fine trees, sweeps up to the house on all sides: the beds are filled with a profusion of the choicest flowers; many of the external walls are covered with bignonias and honeysuckles."[77]

Four generations later, the grapes have gone, some trees have been cut down, others have grown up. An elm tree fell on the porch in 1944 and opened up a whole new vista, which led to the creation of the garden room. Elm Court is still substantially the same and still in our family.[78]

The other fashionable centre of Newport was Bailey's Beach where there was, and still is, an exclusive club called the Spouting Rock Beach Association. This consists of a large pavilion and 81 outside beach huts (cabanas), many owned by the same family for generations. The bathing at the Eastons public beach is superior but unthinkable for the rich and famous. Conditions at Bailey's are far from ideal. "At Bailey's one often had to wallow about in a thick ooze of seaweed through which tiny marine monsters scooted." [79] Jellyfish, even stinging Portuguese Men o'War, were also a hazard when I was there in 1948.

When women bathed in the sea at the beginning of the twentieth century, they wore full-skirted bathing suits and long black stockings which protected them from these hazards, although they wore them from modesty and the prevailing conventions. Men too wore one-piece bathing suits.

To Bailey's Beach, the young Roches went every day, driven by their French governess Josephine in a donkey cart, which they drove themselves when they were old enough. The sun is very burning in August, and children in my father's days, before sun protection lotion, were only allowed to stay in the sea for twenty

---

[76] In 1871 Elm Court was sold to Joseph Sampson. His daughter Adele inherited the house and his vast fortune. She married, secondly, in 1882 the Duc de Dino. Frank Work bought it in 1896 for $115,000, furniture included.

[77] *Newport and its cottages.* 1875. ch. Frederic W. Stevens, Esq.

[78] The property of Guy Van Pelt, Frank Work's great-great-grandson.

[79] *This was my Newport*, p. 127.

minutes. When they emerged, large hats were put on their heads and their skin was covered with towels to protect them from sunburn.

Tennis played an important part in my father's life. From an early age, the Roches had tuition from the best professional coaches. They were also inspired by the world champions who came to Newport every August. The first US Men's Single Tennis Tournament was held in Newport in 1881. This tournament became the US Open Championship, which continued to be held there until 1915, when it moved to Forest Hills, because there was not enough space for spectators. In adult life, both the brothers played against the top players in the world at real (court) tennis and both were very good lawn tennis players.

Growing up with a mother and grandfather who were mad about horses, it was inevitable that they would start riding at an early age, first on ponies. As they grew, so the animals grew in size. My father never enjoyed riding on horseback, but Uncle Frank became a fine horseman.

The first Horse Show in Newport was held in the grounds of the Casino in 1896 and became an annual event. During the week of the Horse Show, Fanny gave two special parties:

"Mrs Burke Roche, who has given several dinners and luncheons during the week, is completing her arrangements for the lawn dinner and dance for young people on Wednesday evening next at her father's cottage, Elm Court. 30 young people will be seated at tables on the lawn under a large tent illuminated with small electric lights. And in another tent close by a Hungarian band will be stationed to play during the dinner and also for dancing afterwards. A week later, Mrs Burke Roche will also give a dinner on the lawn for older people at which Sidney Woollett and probably Miss Evelyn Harris will recite." [80]

Fanny Burke Roche was famous for her entertainment, for her beauty and her grace. "Two perfect specimens of stately grace were Mrs Burke Roche and her sister Mrs Peter Cooper Hewitt who moved with a sort of somnolent, unhurried grandeur through the Newport gatherings." [81]

The first party was for Cynthia, Maurice and Frank, then aged 15 and 14 respectively and their young friends. Maurice loved girls and dancing so no doubt had a great time that evening. Susceptible as he was to the opposite sex, he probably fell in love that evening – again! He would not have enjoyed the party the following week, listening to Mr Woollett reciting long passages from Shakespeare and other poets, and Miss Harris reciting French poetry.

The day after the end of the Newport Horseshow, on September 7th 1899 in

[80]   *New York Times* August 13th 1899.
[81]   *Good Old Summer Days* p.110.

the afternoon, the first ever Automobile Parade took place in Newport:

"The event was the most original Newport has ever witnessed and fully 2,000 persons saw the start and thousands lined along the route over which the parade passed. The weather was perfect." [82] Automobiles were rarely seen on the streets at this early stage of their development. The models in the parade were steam-powered (steamers) or electric. Petrol-powered engines were being produced in Europe and America but were still rarities. Unfortunately, the description of the parade does not name the make of the models.

The vehicles themselves were of sufficient interest to draw the crowds but in addition, they were decorated in elaborate and exotic fashions. Mrs Hermann Oelrichs, who won first prize, placed twelve white doves among pink and white hydrangeas and more doves on the dashboard and shafts, holding satin streamers in their mouths. Seventeen vehicles took part. Prizes were given for the best-decorated automobile. Mr M M Shoemaker driving Mrs Burke Roche won a silver floral vase as second prize. His vehicle was "a favourite with the spectators consisting of wheat, poppies and corn flowers with an immense corn flower umbrella over the carriage." [83]

Horses played a very important role in fashionable Newport. They drew the carriages transporting their owners from one social activity to another during the day, and delivered and collected them from a ball in the evening. They were an intrinsic part of the general spectacular show. Every afternoon their owners emerged for the daily parade down Bellevue Avenue.

"The horse was as important as his mistress's Paris gowns and jewels in the lavish parade of fashion. No Rolls Royce of the twentieth century can convey such an impression of fabulous extravagance as did the Newport turn-outs of the eighteen-nineties.

The afternoon was the best time to have a look at them. Soon after the elaborate and formal luncheon was over, the rubber-tired wheels would start spinning noiselessly down the driveways of Newport. Between the huge grilled gates of the Breakers, Mrs Cornelius Vanderbilt's carriage would emerge, make a neat turn into Ochre Point and go whirling down Bellevue Avenue...the ensemble was just perfect, down to the last minute detail – the short manes braided just so, not a hair of a clubbed tail out of place. The white breeches of the men on the box were just as immaculate as the long kid gloves of the ladies sitting behind them." [84]

[82] *New York Times*, September 8th 1899
[83] *New York Times*, September 8th 1899
[84] *Good Old Summer Days*, p. 70

Mrs Burke Roche, from a photograph by Du Pont

Coaching and polo attracted the finest horses in the country. The first Newport coaching parade was held on September 1st 1884. Eleven four-in-hands were in the line, each filled with gaily dressed ladies and gentlemen, the guests of the owner, lined up. It was a prestigious occasion. The leading coach was driven by August Belmont, President of the Coaching Club. (It was rumoured that Belmont horses were bedded down on white linen sheets embroidered with the Belmont Crest in gold thread.) At his side was the 21st President of the United States, Chester Arthur. The parade drove to Mr Belmont's farm where they had luncheon on the lawn served by liveried waiters. After the lunch, the parade went to the polo grounds to watch the match." [85] In 1899 there were twelve coaches in line and Fanny was on the box seat of W Forbes Morgan who drove four pretty bays.

Fanny had many suitors whom she was free to marry after her divorce in 1890. There were rumours at various times that she was going to marry the widowed J van Alen, or William Waldorf Astor, or Lord Roseberry or Bourke Cochran. Her friends insisted that she was wedded to her home and her family.

[85] *New York Times:* August 27th 1899

6

St Paul's School, New Hampshire

The summer of 1899 in Newport had been a glorious one for Cynthia, Maurice and Frank. They had seen the greatest tennis players in the world competing in the Lawn Tennis championships, and played tennis there regularly themselves. They were invited on board the most magnificent yachts. They had taken part in the daily parade of carriages down Bellevue Avenue and watched the Coaching Club Parade and the polo. They rode their ponies and drove themselves to Bailey's Beach, where they swam most days. They had visited Alfred Vanderbilt at his home at Oakland Farm, where he kept a stud farm of seventy to eighty horses.

They had danced in the ballroom at the Casino and been entertained by the amateur performances in the theatre, where the boys were ushers or sold programmes. They had done all this in the company of their friends by day and in the evening, when they were invited to numerous parties for young people in the "cottages", as well as having their own dinner dance on the lawn at Elm Court. They had been on a moonlight sail on the Vanderbilt yacht, sitting down to dinner at a party for a hundred young people.

That summer a moonlight clam bake took place on the beach at the Clambake Club. A shallow pit is dug in the sand. This is then lined with rounded stones and a pile of wood is burned on top of them until the stones glow red. A barbecue grate is put in position and this is covered with a layer of seaweed. On top of that, – alternating with layers of seaweed – go potatoes, corn on the cob, smoked sausage, clams, mussels and lobsters. A wet tarpaulin or wet sacks cover the whole bake and the ingredients are steamed until tender. The corn is served with hot herb or garlic butter.

In September it was time for the boys to go to boarding school and for Fanny to be bereft of her darlings. They went to St Paul's School, Concord, New Hampshire where their uncle George had been nearly thirty years earlier.

In the autumn of 1899, George's health seriously deteriorated. He had been ill for some years, suffering from tuberculosis caused by alcohol abuse, and was living in St Moritz in Switzerland. When the news came that his health had worsened, his sister Lucy sailed to Europe and took him from St Moritz to Davos, then the last resort for consumptives. She returned to the States in December when his health had stabilised.

A few weeks later, in February 1900, Fanny and Lucy received the news that their brother was dying. They immediately set sail, and arrived at his bedside a week before he died. George Work's obituary described him as "being so prominent in many branches of sport, that his name had become a household word. With one possible exception, he was the best gentleman jockey in the country. His hands were perfect, soft and caressing to a horse's mouth as a woman's, yet hard as steel when necessary. He was a champion steeplechaser, very plucky and skilful over the jumps and equally successful in winning races on the flat."

The twin brothers were 14 years-old when they entered St Paul's School. That was the start of the profoundly important relationship with their school, which lasted all their lives. After Maurice had left, and until he married, he had a paternalistic attitude to his old school and took care of it as if of his own family.

The campus covers five square miles, which includes part of the Turkey River, large areas of dense woodland and many ponds. The beauty of the scenery struck me when I visited St Paul's, particularly a large natural lake with a background of trees, which is visible from the school. St Paul's claims that there the first ever ice hockey game in America was played. Known as Lower School Pond, the lake freezes hard every winter, and used to be boarded off to form nine, separate ice hockey rinks. Hobey Baker,[86] a legendary American amateur ice hockey and football player, learned to skate on this lake, when he came to St Paul's in 1903.

The earliest letters written by Maurice that I have come across were written to his brother Frank at St Paul's when the two were separated. Maurice was recovering from a life-threatening illness. He was 16 when he wrote this letter to his twin from Elm Court:

Sept 24th 1901

Dear Boy,
It was a little while before I could get to sleep last night. I kept thinking of you and new surroundings. Mr Bumstead came and while he was here, Dr Knapp came in. He asked Mr Bumstead if he had noticed anything concerning my studies, & Bumstead said he noticed that I had forgotten a lot. Boy, Dr Knapp said that he knew some cases where they could not remember anything for one year. So if I cannot pass my exams, I will go to Dr M Coit and tell him what I have had & why I flunked. Then Dr Knapp said that I could do what I wanted.

Cynthia came back to-day. She said she had a fine time, it was very rough & she saw Grandpa (Boy write to him) ... (Boy I will not paragraph so I will have more room). I had my usual Knap and at 3, Miss Beers & I went out in the victoria and the Ocean Drive. I looked around for ducks

---
86 1892-1918. He was killed in a plane crash in France, shortly after the armistice in November 1918.

but saw none. I hope you passed, tell me about the papers, journey and other things. Boy, I miss you very much. Miss Beers goes tomorrow I think. I wore my hat to-day. It is alright.

I just had five o'clock tea. Boy, remember that if there is anything that we want, just write. I hope you got my yesterday's letter alright. Good-bye Boy, hope you are well, think of me here in Newport.

Many kisses & love MR"

The letter reveals his close attachment to Frank and how hard it was for him to be parted. One year later, the brothers are separated, again by Maurice's illness. Fanny described him, in a letter to Frank, as lanky and hollow-eyed, but there are no clues as to what he was suffering from.

"Elm Court,
September 23rd 1902

Dear Boy
I am awfully sorry you are gone now, I miss you. I hope everything went alright, that is, your journey. Look out for your money when you get installed, because there are a lot of strange maids and they might take it.

Boy during the first half hour of my knap, I could not keep my mind off you, thinking about your new surroundings & how the summer has passed. I then slept for 1 hr and was very hot when I woke up and my mouth dry.

Boy, I hope you fulfilled all my directions about exams, room, and our things at the Lower. If there is anything you want first write as I am supply station No.2. If there is anything that neither of us have thought about, just write.

Play foot-ball if you want, but <u>do not get hurt</u>. Boy I will write every day Good-bye boy, Tell me everything when you write, as I love to know everything.

Many kisses & love
MR"

This time Maurice, again writing from Newport, reveals his plan to leave home earlier than his mother wishes, making a secret, early morning escape:

"Elm Court,
September 30th 1902

Dear Boy

I received your letter this afternoon and I was very glad to hear from you. I did not do much to-day. I packed my trunk, which took only a little while. I will tell you about it later in the letter. Mama, Cynthia and Anne went to the Brockton Fair. I was so glad Anne went because she would tell Catherine about my sneaking off.

Well, I will now tell you all about my sneaking away from home. First Mama said that I could not go before Monday. I could not stay here this long. I was going to the Brockton Fair, but I could not go to school from there, as I could only take a valise with me. So I thought of the plan of escaping. Lizzie & Celia are the only ones who know about it. I am going to escape as follows: I will have my trunk packed and I am going to order the Express Man here at 7.30am and Lizzie is going to be around to show him my trunk. Meanwhile I will be making a breakfast down stairs. At 8.00 I am going to leave the stable in the Old Reliable.[87] When I get to the station I will check my trunk & put an 'Armstrong tag' on it, and I will thus escape.

Boy, the trouble lies in getting money. I have over $5 and Catherine is going to give me five more. I guess that will be enough. I am going to buy my ticket the day before, so I won't get left. Boy, I am of course unable to buy all those provisions. But have all the cooking utensils coming when we go in town we can buy things.

Boy when you get this letter do not write any more. And when I telegraph, meet me at the Farm, if you can, as my money might give out and I will be unable to pay the cabman, which will be $2. I am going to borrow some, as I will have enough to cross Boston and other things. Boy, I will get on all right, meet me if you can. Boy, I must stop. I hope you get this letter. I leave here on Friday morning at 8.20. I will soon see you.

Love. Kisses MR"

In fact this plan did not work as his mother got wind of it, and managed to prevent him from leaving. He was forced to spend another week fretting at home.

---

[87] A motor car made by Ford.

"Elm Court,
Oct 5th

Dear Boy,
I am really leaving on Wednesday. I am studying hard and I am ahead of you in Virgil. I am now able to buy the eatables which I could not at first. I have:
4 cans of condensed milk.
1lb of cocoa
A jar of pure honey
1lb of hard chocolate & other things.
I am going to keep a little money for school. I have been very bad about writing but I have been having a good time. I play poker a lot at the Huhns. I am having my friend Louis Johnson & Louise for lunch tomorrow.
Cynthia just gave me some roasted chestnuts. They were fine. Are the chestnuts ripe at school yet?
Edith Colford is a peach. I think she is one of the best girls I have ever seen.

Love. Kisses."

Boy, please see right away about a place for me to sleep, as I <u>will come</u> <u>sure this week.</u>

At the start of 1903, Maurice now nearly 18 is again recovering from an illness, this time possibly diphtheria. He writes from 13 Madison Square North, his grandfather's house in New York, the day after Frank had returned to school alone. Maurice is clearly once again very lonely and bereft without his twin.

"13 Madison Square
Jan 7th 1903

Dear Boy
It is now 5 o'clock by the Library clock and I have been thinking of you all the time. I have not done very much to-day, only reading the papers. To-morrow I am going to study some Virgil, and a little Greek so that I can get in practice for it. We have a lot to do this term.
It is so funny I have really nothing to say, but when you read this letter, which most likely will be at table, hold it down. I thought that when I could go out, I would try a little motor and have some fun with it. Boy, it seems so funny to be alone again. It seems that I did not treat you right when you were here. I have thought of what station you must be at, but now you are there safe, I hope.

I am of course going to Brooke Bros. and get another suit. It will be dark so as to resist dirt in its days to come, as all our suits have hard work.

I hear Cynthia, and as this letter is near its end, I close. I hate to do it.

Good-bye MR"

"13 Madison Square,
Jan 8th 1903

Dear Boy,

Another day passes but this one was very nice. I woke up after a good night and then had a good breakfast. I read the papers, cleaned the bird and played with Flosey till 11. Then I got dressed and I went out the first time this year. The weather was cold, and I liked it and walked over to the garden, and I saw all the chickens, pigeons etc. Boy, I liked those ducks so much. I always wanted to have a small duck place at Newport, but circumstances would not permit. Those big geese, my! but they were fine! The pigeons I liked and I thought I would like to have some at Newport, but the temptation of shooting them would be terrible. We might have a loft on top of our house, but they might fly away, but let us think that over if we stay at Newport another summer.

The incubator I liked and I thought how nice it would be if we could only have a place and raize some pheasants. I asked a man about them. Boy, the eggs have to be turned over twice a day, until there are signs of hatching. Then they are left until they are dry. There were a number of eggs hatching, and one place I remember, you pressed a button and inside the incubator, you could see the little things, all wet, etc.

I stayed as long as I thought best, and then I went out for a little walk in the square. I came home and Cynthia and I had a good lunch and I fell asleep. I woke up with that terrible taste and other complications. I thought of you and each time I looked at the clock, I thought of what you must be doing.

Boy, the doctor comes tomorrow and I think he will let me go Saturday, as I feel so well. Boy, do not forget to pray, and to be thankful for what we have. This will probably be my last letter. Lots of love.

Boy, I am going to write this one more sheet. I am going to tell you, Boy, that we must be more together as when the doctor came the other day he said he thought I have had diphtheria or at least going to have it. So God has been kind enough to spare my life twice. And now I am going to lead a new life. This year has gone very well so far. You must write every Sunday to Grandpa as his life is now getting shorter.

I took a good shave today as I needed it very badly. I love doing it. I first took some soap and wet my moustache. and then shaved. I had quite a lot of down on my razor. Boy, I hope you are well and studying. Play hard in the afternoon. Do not think of staying in, but when you come in from playing, study just as hard as you can. Good-bye, Boy, I hope you have much luck. I feel very lonesome but I will soon be with you.

MR"

The following letter reveals the problems the brothers have with Latin and Greek and Maurice's dream of sharing a house in the woods with his brother:

"13 Madison Square,
Jan 9th 1903

Dear Boy
I passed another day in peace, that is, I had a pretty good time. I had to stay in the house till the doctor came then he told me that I had better stay here till Monday.

I got your letter and I was very much stricken with it, how rotten it is to be in such a state. I hope you and I get through this year alright, because I am sure we can make the Vth (form) by the end of the summer. We must study hard and do our best. It must be terrible to have special Latin & Greek, but that is of course better by far than going back. Boy, I do not see how we can be put back in Latin, as it was our first flunck. (sic) I suppose you did your best.

Well after I saw the doctor, I got on my clothes and I went again to the Poultry show. I looked harder at those ducks, I also bought a book (25 cents) and it is great. It tells all about their ways, breeding, their food, where they should be kept, what they need, the different kinds. It might be useful to use some day. Boy, I saw some Belgian hares, my! but I would like to have them. They would be better than the ducks, because we could have them in a small place and they live on everything. This is what I would like. Have a place like the Laniers had, in those woods where they had their huts, let a lot of rabbits loose and have a regular rabbit hunt at Christmas time. Buy a good "ferret" like Morley has at school, have each a gun, let the ferret down a hole and trim it as it comes out. ...But we have not time and it is useless now.

Boy, there has been very cold weather here to day and there is skating in the Bronx and Van Cortland Park. Mama got a letter from Doctor Coit[88] but he failed to mention anything about the studies, which I rejoiced greatly.

---

[88] Rector of St Paul's, who was appointed as a young clergyman at the age of 24 and who presided over the school for its first 39 years.

St Paul's School Halcyon First Crew, 1905

St Paul's School Hockey Team, 1904–5. From l to r.: Mr Gordon, Roche, Pitts, Boughman, Coit, Trudeau, Willette, Beste (Cpt.), Irving

Ice rinks at St Paul's School

Frank and Maurice, 1909

Tomorrow I have arranged to go to the oculist, which I know is better for me, as the eyes get worse if you neglect them. I am going to the place where I saw Dr Burke's glasses were made. It shurely (sic) must be a good place. It is 126 East 23.

As I am writing here, Cynthia is sitting in front of the fire reading the Mail & Express. I am at the desk writing, at this very moment it is five minutes to six and Grandpa has gone to Delmonicos. Sadie and Francis have just left a lot of gardineas (sic) and a number of different flowers for Cynthia.

Boy, I am going to take this whole page to say good-bye. Now remember you will get this letter Monday noon most likely and I will telephone you all about when I come. Boy, go in my alcove and see that things are a little strait. I am glad I am in New York now, but I will study hard when I get back to school. Boy, think of me a little. I will bring a little candy up and everything will be all right. Boy, lots of love from you brother.

MR

I hope this letter is interesting but there is nothing that can show more my desire than to do the things mentioned."

These intensely loving letters reveal the deep closeness and interdependency which existed between the brothers. Their relationship is a secret one which no one must know about. Maurice reminds Frank not to give their mother an opportunity to read the letters, which he is sure she will open if given the chance. Neither must their fellow students at school know that Maurice is writing to his brother, as the injunction "to hold the letter down" if Frank reads it at table, reveals. I have transcribed them without correcting the spelling.

The affinity permeated every aspect of their lives. Equally weak academically, they were both outstanding at sports. Rowing on the large lake at St Paul's was an important sports activity. There were two rowing clubs, Halycon and Shattuck, each having four crews.[89] Both brothers were keen oarsmen and in the first crew of the Halcyons in 1904 and 1905, Maurice sat at No. 2, Frank at No. 3 was Captain.

The annual races between the rival clubs, held each spring, were a time of great excitement. This was a very important event in the school year. The crews were transported to and from Long Pond in motor lorries or old-fashioned wagons drawn by four horses. Boisterous singing of rowing songs was a feature of every ride to the pond and back. In 1905, the Halcyons had a great triumph, all four of their crews crossing the line first in a close finish. The Roche twins were heroes of the hour among Halcyon supporters!

[89] At Henley in 2004. St. Paul's School, Concord, the New England champions, beat Abingdon School to win the Princess Elizabeth Challenge Cup, open to public schools.

Maurice was the captain of the first Ice Hockey team in the winter of 1903. and in the following year. Both brothers played Forwards in the field. They were less successful at football, both playing in the Third Eleven of the Old Hundred Football Club. Frank was Vice-President, Maurice Secretary of the Athletic Association.

Their almost identical achievements in the field of sports are remarkable. Maurice at six foot tall and weighing 155 pounds was one inch taller and one pound heavier than Frank. It appears from their photographs that they dressed in identical clothes, at least until they left University.

7

Fanny and her riding instructor

With the boys away at school, there was an emptiness in Fanny's life, which she filled with her riding and her driving. At this time the whips, the drivers of the coaches, were all men. Fanny the feminist, the bold, the pioneer, could see no reason why women should not drive four-in-hands. She attended the Central Park Riding School in New York where she was taught by Aurel Batonyi, whom she had met at horse shows where she exhibited. He was an expert horseman, a good-looking man, who had come to the US from Hungary. His real name was Kohn but he changed his name to the more romantic one of Batonyi. For a while, he called himself Count but later dropped his title saying that it cost him money.

He was employed at the Central Park Riding School as a riding master but gave this up to drive show horses. His expertise was in driving four-in-hands at which he was particularly skilful. He also drove a public coach known as Good Times in New York, from Holland House and the Waldorf. However the business failed and left him out of pocket.

Under his skilful tuition, Fanny became proficient and was the first woman to drive a four-in-hands in New York's Central Park. This was not an easy accomplishment and required poise and skill rather than muscle. Fanny employed him to exhibit her horse "Masterpiece" and others of her string. She bought a stock farm at Middleton, a few miles from Newport, called Two Mile Corner Farm and made Aurel her manager. He lived in a small house across the road from the farm, which she called 'the cabin.' He ran his coach service again, driving "Good Times" between Newport and Naragansett Pier but once again his enterprise failed.

At the Newport horse show September 1902, Fanny won prizes every day. On the first day she won the class for horses shown in harness and for the under saddle class. On the second day, she took first prize in the Runabout horse class with her bay gelding Carman driven by Mr Richard F Carman. On the final day in the Champion saddle horse class, she won the championship with her black mare Iris.

And on September 1st, 1902, Cynthia Roche had a brilliant introduction to Newport Society. The only debutante ball of the season was given at Elm Court by Mrs Burke Roche in honour of her daughter Miss Cynthia Roche aged 18.

Fanny and one of her beloved mounts, c. 1904

Cynthia had been one of the most popular belles of the summer, and had attended many social functions, but this was her formal introduction into society. The Grand Duke Boris Vladimir of Russia was present! He was quoted as saying that nothing in St Petersburg could begin to compare with the opulent extravaganzas of Newport Society.

"Many novel and beautiful floral pieces were sent to Elm Court. One was a large sedan chair filled with lilies-of-the-valley. The color scheme throughout was blue and white. The reception room where Miss Roche received with her mother was a perfect floral bower.

Mrs Roche had constructed on the lawn a temporary ballroom. Dinner was served at eight small tables for about eighty persons. After dinner, a large number of additional guests arrived for the dance. Later there was supper served on small tables, all of which bore centre pieces of white and blue flowers.

The cotillion was led by Elisha Dyer Jr. with Miss Roche. The favors were fancy card cases and ladies' purses in hogskin, Malacca canes, whips and other small articles suggested by the Horse show. Two bands furnished music during the dinner and for the dancing, a hundred and twenty five couples participating in the cotillion."[90]

Cotillion dances were in vogue. Chairs were placed all round the ballroom where partners sat side by side. Six or so couples were chosen to start dancing. At a signal from the leader, they separated and each chose a partner from those seated round the room. Each time you were chosen, you received a favour in the form of a corsage or a rosette, which was pinned on to your shoulder if you were a girl and your lapel if you were a man. The favours were exchanged for very expensive items.

Fanny continued to win prizes showing her prize horses. Aurel was very much part of her life as the manager of her farm in Newport. He also excelled as a driver of other owners' horses. In 1903 at the National Horse Show in Madison Square Gardens, Lord Brilliant won the single harness championship class. The horse belonged to Dr Wentz and was superbly handled by Aurel Batonyi, "the best driver in the world" according to the owner. After his sensational win, Dr Wentz announced that he would retire from the horseshow ring and sold his entire stable to J Campbell Thompson. Frances Burke Roche acquired his three champion horses Lord Golden, Lord Golden II and Lord Brilliant. She now owned the top show ring horses in the country.

In August 1904, Fanny scored a triumph at a horse show at the Durland Riding Academy: "A perfect storm of applause went up from the critical spectators of

---

[90] *New York Times*, September 2nd 1902.

fine horses when in the runabout class, Mrs Burke Roche's superb pair of bays, faultlessly driven by Aurel Batonyi, won the first award." [91] At the National Horse Show in Madison Square Gardens in November of that year she entered three pairs in the tandem class, styling herself as Frances Roche in the official entries. She drove Lord Golden in the harness class, with Aurel Batonyi at her side.

She also had a great interest in and knowledge of pedigree dogs. *Town and Country* carried an item in April 1904, headed "Atlantic City Dog Show":

> "Mrs Burke Roche was a prominent exhibitor of the Dalmatians, bulldogs and bull terriers and was herself present and personally interested in the judging."

Fanny Burke Roche, 1905

Her daughter Cynthia was unhappy about her liaison with Aurel. Fanny was very keen for her daughter to marry Arthur Burden. According to the family legend, Cynthia made a pact with her mother that she would marry Arthur if Fanny gave up Aurel.

And on June 11th 1906, Cynthia married Arthur Burden at Grace Church at one of the largest weddings of the year:

"The bride wore a princess robe with a train of white satin, with lace corsage and sleeves. Her lace veil was caught with orange blossom and she carried white flowers…As the bride and groom left the church, chimes rang out and a crowd of curious spectators on the pavements pushed the police about in an effort to see the wedding party. Her brother, Maurice Roche, accompanied her to the altar and gave her away…The reception and wedding breakfast was held at Sherry's. Two hundred guests attended. As a rule, the costumes worn at morning or noon weddings in town in the summer are marked by simplicity, walking skirts and coats suitable for the usual railway journey into town, but yesterday's wedding brought out some very handsome gowns…Mrs Burke Roche, mother of the bride, wore mauve chiffon cloth over mauve silk. It was trimmed with mauve and white lace. She wore a large round hat of mauve Neapolitan, trimmed with mauve ostrich plumes."[92]

But Fanny had not kept her side of the bargain. In August 1905, a few weeks before the boys went to Harvard, she secretly married Aurel. The news of the marriage became public when it was announced by Frank Work, one year after it took place, in response to reporters demanding to know if the rumours were true. The *New York Times* reported:

"Mr Work desires to say that Mrs Roche was married to Mr Batonyi and had sailed for Europe. Mr Work does not know of his daughter's plans. All information as to when the marriage took place was refused. Mrs Roche sailed for Europe several months ago to procure the trousseau of her daughter Cynthia who was married recently to Arthur Scott Burden. It was said that Mr Batonyi followed her on a boat which sailed ten days later."[93]

Judging by the timing of this bombshell, it would seem that Fanny kept the marriage secret until after Cynthia's wedding. Her relationship with Aurel caused a catastrophic rift between herself and her father. Cynthia too disapproved of her mother's second husband and would not associate with him.

[92] *New York Times*, June 12th 1906
[93] *New York Times*, July 15th 1906

8

Harvard and heartbreak

Fanny's life now changed dramatically. She left her father's home in New York and moved out of Elm Court. She went to live with Aurel in her stock farm, Two Mile Corner Farm. She was happy to have the love and companionship of her new husband, and to have escaped from her difficult father. But it soon became clear that her happiness came at a price. She spent Christmas 1906 alone at the farm with Aurel, in a state of great unhappiness. This was how she described it: "No relations: no wires: no presents: no communications of any kind. Deadly depression. Aurel very angry. Telling me to go back to my family."

In January 1907, Mr and Mrs Aurel Batonyi sailed to Europe on the *Konig Albert* for a four-month tour. Daphne, Fanny's toy bull terrier went too. The day before they sailed, Fanny had a luncheon party in New York for her women friends. Maurice and Frank came up from Harvard to dine with her that evening on the eve of her departure. They had a happy evening together in the hotel where she was staying, dining in the restaurant, and then going up to her sitting room to talk.

On the day of her departure, she called at her father's home and kissed him good-bye. She stopped at a flower shop and ordered his usual red carnations. Maurice and Frank came in Lucy's automobile to see the couple off. Lucy did not come to the pier herself. She sent them four dozen fresh eggs.

Fanny and her husband visited Italy, Egypt, Turkey, Greece, France and England. She wrote this letter to the boys from the Grand Hotel in Naples:

"Jan 26th 1907

My dear Boys,
I think of you constantly and wish that you were here. We landed yesterday and today is just two weeks since that pouring day that you two stood on the deck and saw me off. I hope you will enjoy yourselves but don't forget that the studies are for the present the serious thing, and bend all your energies upon them. They are the foundation to your future – in fact your whole life depends upon you using your opportunities.
    We met etc....

I hope to hear from you frequently.

Affectionately yours (sic)"

The year at Harvard had not started well for Maurice and Frank. They had both extended the Christmas recess in order to attend a party! In January, the Administrative Board put them on probation for this departure from the rules. In addition, Maurice was informed that his college record was one which would put him on probation.

Two months later the following correspondence further reveals the problems Maurice and his brother were having with their studies. Their mother was disappointed and displeased to receive this letter:

Letter to Mrs Frances Batonyi (Burke Roche)

"Harvard.
March 14th 1907

Dear Mrs Batonyi,
I am sorry to have to inform you that at the request of the instructor, I have had to exclude your sons from Anthropology 5, for their neglect of the work in this course. Both had unsatisfactory grades at the mid years. Maurice had a grade of D, and Frank a grade of D-. Since that time, their work has deteriorated, and for their neglect, Professor Dixon has asked me to exclude them.

In their other courses, their work shows on the whole, I think, a little improvement, although some of their grades at the mid year are lower than they were at November. Their records do not yet warrant their relief from probation, but I hope that they will so much improve them at April, that they may win restoration to good standing.

Sincerely yours. Castle"

Maurice and Frank expressed their unhappiness with this decision, and this led to their tutor writing to the Professor of Anthropology.

Letter from Mr Castle to Professor Dixon

"Harvard.
March 8th 1907

Dear Dixon,
The two Burke-Roches told me that they did not like to be excluded from anthropology. May I talk over their records with you some time? They are of the quieter sort.

Sincerely yours. Castle."

Professor Dixon responded favourably to this appeal allowing Maurice to resume his anthropological studies, although predicting that he would fail the exam.

"Harvard
April 3rd 1907

My dear Castle, I've readmitted E M B Roche to Anthropology 5 but told him there was little chance of his passing. He got a grade of D- for the April examinations.

Sincerely, Roland B. Dixon"

In other respects, Fanny was having a happy time with Aurel on their European tour. He was kind and attentive and bought lozenges for her persistent cough and sore throat; they enjoyed each other's company and their sightseeing. She mentions that they read up about the Parthenon over dinner; they walked in the sunshine in Monte Carlo; they enjoyed their lunches in Paris; she ate the same thing every day – eggs in some form or other, followed by cold salmon with *sauce verte*. She liked being able to socialise freely with him in Europe, which she could not do in New York and Newport.

In Paris, she spent part of every day buying clothes. Her dresses came from the *haute couture* house of Paquin. Aurel went to London to order boots and shoes to be delivered to their ship at Southampton, and to find a mate for Daphne. He returned with Johnnie, whom Fanny found adorable. Unfortunately, the new puppy became ill after a walk in the Bois de Boulogne without his coat, and in spite of all her efforts, including rubbing him with eau de cologne, he died of pneumonia. She was heartbroken.

She returned to New York, to the St Regis Hotel, to find that many of her friends were out or busy when she called. Her sister Lucy and Cynthia wanted nothing to do with her or Batonyi. She had weathered her divorce from Jim Roche through the power of her personality but her marriage to Aurel Batonyi was not accepted. Her closest friends would see her, but even they would have nothing to do with her husband. After a few weeks of suffering from this ostracism, she went to Newport and was relieved to leave New York.

She was delighted to see her horses and dogs again. She bought 27 Plymouth Rock hens and one cock. She revelled in nature – the wild flowers, the trees coming into leaf. She acquired an automobile, which was "a great convenience". She and Aurel went for long drives in a carriage every evening. She wrote of her happiness and freedom at having escaped from the prison of her father's house.

When the vacation arrived, Maurice and Frank, who were unshakably loyal to their mother, stayed with her and Aurel at Two Mile Corner Farm that summer. With the closure of Elm Court, they were barred from the summer home they loved. Fanny's reign as a social queen and brilliant hostess was over, depriving them of the wonderful parties she gave.

Their own social life was otherwise not affected and they spent most of their time with their friends. They played their full part in the social whirl of the Newport season. They had a great time, playing tennis, swimming, yachting, watching polo and having picnics by day. It was fashionable to hire a sailing boat to visit the Fort when it was garrisoned, to hear the band play on the parade on Tuesday and Friday. There were elaborate dinner parties and dances most evenings. There was the annual moonlit clam bake on the beach.

Maurice and Frank at the gates of The Breakers, Newport, Rhode Island

In the middle of July, Maurice was invited to Sagamore, the rustic retreat of Alfred Gwynne Vanderbilt, his close friend, grandson of the Commodore. Sagamore was situated in a densely forested estate, overlooking a lake, in the Adirondacks in northern New York State. The Lodge was built in the style of a Swiss chalet, faced in split birch with log porches. There was a large stone fireplace in the dining room. There was a bachelor hall called the Wigwam, for hunting parties and single male guests. Alfred also built a tennis court and a hydroelectric plant for electricity. There he and his wife entertained their friends who in spite of the natural location dressed formally for dinner and were served by British staff wearing livery.

Both sons were kind and attentive to their mother when they had a free moment.

Fanny worked at making the house comfortable for them, redecorating Maurice's rooms in the colours of the AD club at Harvard. She was well aware that it was because of her that they were not living in their beautiful home as usual.

Her day followed a regular pattern. She went into Newport every morning to the Casino where she was warmly received by her friends. These included the three social queens of Newport society, Mrs Oelrichs, Mrs Stuyvesant Fish and Mrs August Belmont. Mrs Astor was the supreme queen but kept herself apart from the daily scene. Fanny was invited to ladies' lunches but Aurel was not included in snobbish Newport society. Then she did her shopping, buying fish and fruit, and household items. She came home for lunch with Aurel and occasionally the boys.

After a rest, she rode her horse, and every evening she went for a drive down Bellevue Avenue and on to Ocean Drive. On Sunday, she went to Trinity Church, usually with Frank, always splendidly dressed. On July 14th she "wore mastic (pale yellow) skirt, Paquin blouse, black tie. Blue hat, sulphur feathers. Green boa and umbrella." Towards the end of July, she began to be unhappy:

> "*July 24th* Very unhappy. Called Morri, out. Everyone playing polo. All in a jar. Dissonance with lovely day. The riot of roses and "honeysuckle round the porch has woven its wavy bowers.' [94] Aurel very critical of many things. In some things quite right. I am not practical…I am a person of extreme moods. I feel so intensely.
>
> *July 26th* Maurice brings home Whiteman late for luncheon, unexpectedly. I desert. I feel that it was not right on my part. I was not dressed up. But this is no excuse.
>
> *July 30th* Terribly depressed. Just as unnerved and useless as I used to be. Out of conceit with myself. Lunch Aurel and I. Maurice late for lunch. Depressing talk after with Aurel. Fear the end will come…Passed Faxon[95] (in Bellevue Avenue). Did not bow. Slept badly. Heard automobile at 1.45.

Fanny was in the deepest depression that day, finding it hard to stand the strain. She had received an unsatisfactory letter from the family lawyer, apparently containing a cheque for a small sum and informing her that so long as she continued living with Aurel, her future prospects and those of her children were jeopardized. Maurice also had a very disagreeable letter from his grandfather. She went to a ladies' lunch party and told them her problems.

"I showed them the cheque etc. They were all very kind trying to help me.

---

[94] *The May Queen.* Tennyson.
[95] Her name for Frank Sturgis, who owned Faxon Farm. He was Frank Work's banking partner and lifelong friend.

My situation is very sad and terrible. This beautiful day is ruined for me. I have no place & never had in this rich happy community. I am not of it or in it. I feel like hiding somewhere out of sight."

"*Aug. 2nd* Aurel left for Boston to find coachman and wife. I am absolutely out of courage. There is so much fighting, intrigue. I cannot think it over any more. I thought I did right. It was all so awful at home. My life so impossible and my self-respect so impaired by all the conditions. Aurel is such a good man and fine character. True, upright, clever, executive. I cannot understand all the opposition and unpleasantness. It must come, I suppose, and I go back to prison… Divine light in evening. Maurice & I sat together in twilight."

Fanny was forced to accept that she could not bear to be on bad terms with her family and ostracised by some of her friends. Without a great deal of money, she could not live the life to which she was accustomed. Her very identity was affected by the reduction in her allowance. Besides her own deprivations, the situation was adversely affecting her beloved sons, who were being abused and derided by their grandfather. He was threatening to put Elm Court on the market. Fanny thought it was very important that the boys had a place at Newport. After some weeks of despair and misery, she reached her heart-breaking decision.

On August 8th she took the night boat to New York with Maurice. Frankie went in the brougham. She and the boys met with Harry Work, Frank's nephew and lawyer, at her sister's home. Harry spelled out her father's conditions. Aurel should be expatriated and she must give up the farm in Newport and her horses. Fanny indicated that these conditions were unacceptable.

She dined with the boys and the following day they returned together to Newport and had a long talk with Aurel. They all agreed that Fanny should go back to her father:

"Aurel and I simply broken-hearted. A long drive. Iris' mane so neatly pulled, coat like satin, harness blinking in the sunshine. All around familiar roads. Eglantine, wild bay, elderflowers: the grey crags of Paradise Rocks. My heart broken, my head dizzy with grief. Boys lunch. Not much to eat. I [was] sorry about small domestic shortcomings. Horrible day. Nervous headache. Cannot control myself."

On August 12th, she had lunch with Maurice, Frank and Aurel for the last time on the farm and left for New York with the boys, spending the night at the St Regis Hotel. On August 13th, she went to see her father to capitulate. Excerpts from her diary describe the next six unhappy weeks:

"*Aug. 13th*. Arrived at 26th Street with boys. He was in his sitting room. Boys went in first. He was very disagreeable. Then I went to the Gift Room & had a cup of tea. Such a breakfast! Such thoughts. Then upon William coming in the Square for me – who was sitting on bench, I was too noticeable with the dog when I walked around – I entered. I saw my father. I told him I wanted to do as he wished and leave Aurel. He said he never said anything of the kind and did not want me back – when he had said: "She can come back at any time & I will reinstate her." Most stormy & disagreeable talk. Called Aurel names. I worked over it for some time.

Two Mile Corner Farm. Aug. 16th: Once more on the farm. Lovely air. Screen of pine trees, blue sky, telegraph poles, hydrangeas just breaking in flower. Every tree and bush eloquent. My heart is breaking. This good, good man. So devoted, so kind, so clever, unselfish. Losing my right hand! …I cry bitterly. Alone for ever.

Aug. 23rd Such a lovely day! I look out at this farm, which meant everything to him. On every hand, evidence of his care. How we expected to live on it & develop it and be together. Last night I had a dreadful attack of heartbreak. It is so cruel and could so easily have been avoided. Different trustees, that's all. Tennis tournament. Wore embroidered muslin & hat with long cream feather. Frankie sat with me. Talked to everybody. Boys went in brougham to Boston for club dinner.

Aug. 24th Maurice returned from his Club dinner in Boston. What will become of me? Frank and Maurice home for luncheon. I write Harry Work. I rest all afternoon. Maurice lies on floor beside me. We talk many things of interest. They both dine Sandy Point.[96] I send them in brougham. I eat no dinner. Bed. No refuge but bed.

Aug. 25th Ruin, desolation. My new state of health is strange, uncomfortable & trying. I must try and adjust myself. If only my outlook were not so horrible and so humiliating. The going back, the appeal to a Father so hard-hearted. The giving up all I had carefully built up for 3 years. It is bitter, bitter.

Aug. 26th Home. The house so lonely. Boys away. Just what I married to avoid! Long walk Daphne in lane. Transfigured sky, all rose & green trees. Very, very, sad. No dinner – my choice…

---

[96] Home of Reginald C Vanderbilt.

Aug. 28th Letter from H Work. Lovely day. I go to Casino after writing to Papa. Very good tennis. I feel very much alone.

Maurice & I lunch. Talk. Agree that there is nothing for me in any direction. I caution him. Victoria at 4.

Aug. 29th Telephone Cynthia. Busy, will telephone tomorrow… Desperate sadness. When I reach home in afternoon, I cannot become reconciled. Maurice & I dined. He is as broken as I am.

Sept. 3rd Aurel goes for good at 9 o'clock. There are no words to describe my desolation, the wrench, the utter blackness, emptiness. My terrible situation with father, family, world, financially, all. The whole thing was madness on the existing financial basis. I will be really curious to see how I can possibly fare in future. For there is none!

Sept. 8th Articles in paper about separation. [The *New York Times* reported that Mrs Batonyi had given up her husband with whom she was happy, to protect her sons' inheritance.] Reporters call me. I decline to talk. All articles said I would go to town to see Father. So I cancelled going. Maurice & I talked all day. Ticket refunded.

Sept. 9th Wetherall man here. Packed my best harnesses. Also to Elm Court, go ladies driving phaeton pole shafts. 2 runabouts. Poles, shafts & screens & Brewster gig. French chaise. Governess cart. Left in stable – Mail phaeton. Old gig. 4-wheel pony trap.

At 4. victoria and bay cobs so neatly turned out, such clean shining brass. Drove in back country. Wire: 'Wait till you hear from Harry Work. I will not see you. F.W.'

Sept. 10th Maurice receives wire: 'It is a matter of indifference to me if you come or not. F.W.' This shows how he is in everything. Of course, he (Papa) wants to see him and so I have always begged him to go. Begged. But he is fond of pleasure & hates to leave.

11.30 Victoria. Went to Elm Court Stables to see carriages stored. Maurice & I lunched. One day more frightful than the last. Why did I do such a fearful thing? Maurice went to town by the night boat.

Sept. 12th Maurice back. I in fever of anxiety. Went in at 9. He had helped me very much. He saw Papa, Lucy, Cooper, H. Work. First moment of relief from anguish. They will all help me & look after me if I am sincere. And will do nothing if I do not keep faith with them.

Sept. 13th A perfect day. I slept wonderfully woke in much better shape. Unsatisfactory letter H Work. All refreshing effect of sleep undone. Maurice & I lunched...
Rode Iris. Frankie returned at 7 with golden beard. Maurice dined out, Charlie Lanier & Frank dined in. After dinner, F talked in my room; tried to keep up my courage. It is at vanishing point.

Sept. 24th I saw Frank in the morning. I nearly fainted when he told me he had good news. My father was sorry for me. Would send money to relieve my necessities.

Sept. 28th Maurice dined out. Frank with me. We had venison Maurice shot. He went to Oakland[97] for dinner."

The following day was the last day of the boys' vacation from Harvard. Frank left Two Mile Corner Farm. Fanny packed some things to be stored at Elm Court, then left the farm with Andrick, her personal maid and Daphne her toy bull terrier, to take up residence in an apartment at Robinson's Hotel in Newport.

"*Sept. 30th* Told telephone to disconnect. See my faults more glaringly every moment. Deserve almost the frightful punishment I have. Full of apprehension & doubts. No doubt expect worst."

It was with relief that Maurice and Frank returned to Harvard. The vacation had been a mixed time for them. They went to Washington to stay at the White House to see Teddy Roosevelt, their friend and fellow student at Harvard. They had played their full part in the social whirl of the Newport season and in the numerous sporting activities.

At the same time, they were deeply concerned for their mother, whose reversal of fortune affected them directly, both emotionally and financially. Fanny's intense distress put great pressure on her kind, compassionate sons. Then there was the embarrassment of having a stepfather who was not socially acceptable. After Aurel's departure, they had serious worries for the state of her mind, half-crazed as she was with grief and remorse. They had a new responsibility for helping her to keep her equilibrium.

One or other son was with her almost every day, from the moment she decided to leave Aurel until the end of the vacations, a period of six weeks. It was to Maurice that she turned for advice on her best course of action. She confided her anguish and despair in him, and found her long talks with him comforting and helpful. He was keenly affected by the situation and responded to her appeals for

---

97   Oakland Farm, home of Alfred Vanderbilt. Equestrian centre and polo ground.

Frank and Maurice, 1909

their help. He interceded on her behalf with his aunt Lucy, his grandfather and Harry Work, conveying her extreme plight and having some success.

Her sons' loyalty to their mother unjustly made them the victims of their grandfather's wrath and hostility. Their own future life became tainted with uncertainty. They were hapless pawns in the battle of wills between Fanny and her father. His threats to deprive them of income and their home in Newport put pressure on Fanny to give up Aurel. For her part, she used them to intercede with her father, knowing of his affectionate relationship with them.

Distance provided a buffer to their mother's despair although she kept them in close touch with developments by letter. Her father, while he was kindly disposed towards her, affectionate in his way, thought it best for them both if she did not move back into his home in 26th Street. She remained at Robinson's Hotel in Newport, where she suffered extremes of loneliness and despair. Her nights were spent in agonies of regret and remorse, haunted by fear and dread.

Worse was to come! On November 13th· the *New York Times* reported that Aurel Batonyi had come to Newport to see his wife and inspect his property. He had called to see her at her apartment at the Robinson. She refused to see him, telling him that she would like to see him but she was forbidden to speak to him or see him or communicate in any manner or form, and that only in compliance with these conditions could she get any money from her father.

On being denied an interview, he was outraged and went to the Lawrence Club where he announced that he was suing Frank Work, Mr and Mrs Peter Cooper and Frank Sturgis, for $500,000 each – a total of $1,500,000, on the grounds that, individually and collectively, they had alienated from him the affections of Mrs Batonyi.

"*Nov. 14th* At 3, letter Harry W. telling me of the two actions. I am paralysed with fear. That miserable liar. I am so unhappy. To have been duped by such a horrible villain. On reading this I can hardly believe I could be so blind, such a fool."

She asked Frank to come for the weekend in view of the new desperate situation. Aurel telephoned many times each day over the weekend asking her to return. She soon developed immunity to his demands. He had become a scoundrel in her eyes, and she had no difficulty in refusing him. At the same time her heart was breaking. On Sunday, she and Frank went to church and on to a lunch party.

On Monday, she met Mr Little at Elm Court Stables, to arrange the sale of her carriages, horses and dogs. Later she met Harry Work at the Farm. She presented him with a proposition that for the sake of her family and to save them, she should return to Aurel. He would not consider it, it would not save them. A letter from Maurice, who had been at Sagamore, comforts her. Her women friends do their best to support and distract her. She is restless, lonely and consumed with sadness.

Nov. 20th Wrote Lucy regret at newspaper notoriety…Overcome in evening with frightful sadness of situation…mortal sadness…It is as if an earthquake had swallowed up everything. I have nothing to do and all my occupations, plans - life, utterly upset & routed. I read, I exercise, I pray. But it is all so difficult, so blank. I am so hopeless, no light ahead, I read continually.

Having checked through Harry Work that she would be accepted there, she decided to go to stay with her sister Lucy. Lucy had disowned her elder sister throughout the Batonyi years. Now, given the new circumstances, she agreed to have her sister to stay. Fanny wrote to Maurice and Frank at Harvard telling them of her plans and set off early the next day for New York by train and on to Tuxedo. On arrival, she found that her sister expected her the following day and was in town. She had dinner alone in front of the fire and went to bed early.

In the following days, Lucy was kind and they went for drives together in the afternoon. She took long walks alone with Daphne when Lucy went to town for social engagements. The news that Aurel was pressing his legal actions against her family filled her with anguish and shame.

In December, the boys came to New York on vacation from Harvard, staying with their grandfather. She describes her delight at seeing her sons again, whom she described as the handsomest creatures possible. She was soon off to Newport, with Andrick and Daphne, staying at the Robinson's Hotel, to sort out things at Two Mile Corner Farm. She was very annoyed with herself, as she had no receipts and no proof of what she had bought. She was appalled at her foolish, trusting conduct which had allowed her to fall into the power of a very shrewd, clever rogue.

Back in New York she spent most of Christmas Eve with Maurice. They went shopping together and then had a long talk. He was unhappy, finding it very upsetting living with his grandfather, in what he described as a "morbid house". His friend Charlie Lanier was getting on his nerves. He (Maurice) had some debts. Frank Work, now 87, was in a negative state of mind and had reduced his grandsons' incomes. It was Fanny's turn to do her best to console and encourage him.

On Christmas Day, she sent roses to her Papa and went to have lunch with Lucy. The boys were there, and she received a card from Cynthia. Fanny wrote that the circumstances were in some ways happier than the previous Christmas, which she spent alone with Aurel at the farm, suffering from isolation from her family.

On Boxing Day, she puts some of her jewellery in a bag to go to Tuxedo. "Pearls, little pearls and drops, ruby bracelet, ruby earrings, ruby crown, bracelet three pearls, sapphire and pearl bracelet, big diamond ring, sapphire and diamond ring, sapphire two diamonds, small ruby single diamond ring, antique necklace, watch chain, sapphire barette & earrings." She left other jewellery in the safe of the Seville Hotel. The year ended with her and her boys at Lucy's home at Tuxedo. They went to the Tuxedo Club after dinner on New Year's Eve, where they danced and had supper with the Mortimers.

9

The highs and lows of 1909

Fanny's divorce suit, charging Batonyi with adultery, and his counter charge first reached the Supreme Court in March 1908, but was adjourned. Her father reinstated her allowance but relations with him remained frosty.

The highlight of the Newport season that summer was a large dance given by Alfred Vanderbilt at Oakland Farm on September 5th. Maurice and Frank dined with Reginald Vanderbilt who gave a large dinner party at Sandy Point Farm before the dance. Guests drove into the show ring. There was continuous dancing to three orchestras in the trophy room, where there was a specially laid floor. Favours for the cotillion included cigar lighters, silver picture frames, bridge scorers, leather calendars. Shortly after midnight, supper was served on the roof garden in the open, above the show ring.

Frank had completed his work at Harvard for his degree and was given leave of absence for a year. For Maurice another year of struggling with his studies lay ahead.

By the beginning of January 1909, Fanny's life had changed out of all recognition. She was living with the faithful Andrick and Daphne at Hotel Le Marquis, 12 East 31st Street. She was full of happiness and thankfulness. She had Daphne to sit on her lap. Her birds were hopping about though not yet singing after the move. Frank was living with her and working at a bank. When Maurice came to New York from Harvard, he stayed with his grandfather, paying frequent visits to his mother.

On the first of the year, she lunched with him and then they took a car to her father's stables at 56th street where they take Hump II out for an hour's drive in the park. "He expressed himself delighted with everything. I laughed incessantly." She then showed him the pride and joy of her life, a magnificent horse called Superb. He agreed with her that he had never see a horse with such beauty, finish and marvellous way of going.

Maurice came again in the evening. She had sent Andrick out, so Maurice hooked her dress. They went to dine in Pompano's, a very good restaurant. She told George, the Greek head waiter, that she needed a page boy to do errands and be useful. George told her that he had a brother aged seventeen, very small and quick. His name is Pericles Climax, Perry for short!

Perry is duly engaged and equipped with livery. Her great joy is to go out in the afternoon in her gleaming victoria carriage, a groom and a coachman who also wears livery. All eyes are upon her, as her high-stepping bay mare 'Glenna' trots down Fifth Avenue. She describes a particular occasion:

"Feb. 1909. Victoria at 4.15. Bitter cold. People all look at the bay mare, Monks (coachman) in fur robe. Me in chinchilla with yellow roses and fur turban with yellow. Daphne in yellow. Down Avenue at good clip, everyone looking. Lovely, lovely day. I enjoy my drive beyond words. I get on victoria and drive."

Her days are now perfectly happy. Most mornings she drives in the Park. Her beloved mare Iris has come to town from Newport, fat and woolly but in good condition. She rides her adored, high-mettled horse Superb every day at Durland's Academy every afternoon. She often mentions how well she got on, and quotes people who admire her handling of the horse.

Her wardrobe occupies a great deal of her time. Part of every day is taken up with visits to her dressmakers, either to order new ones or for fittings or to her milliner or to buy underclothes and accessories. She delighted in her valuable, tropical, caged birds and suffered much sadness when they were ill – or worse. A Japanese nightingale fell ill but "a few hours later it stopped shivering, ate and drank and began to mend. I am so glad. He is a pretty, dear little thing. I thought him dying at 2 o'clock." The following day: "The Japanese bird appeared to be dead even after having whisky administered. Wrapped him in cotton wool. Covered eyes so as not to see him dead. Lo! He resurrected himself." The bird hopped and moved normally but did not sing until a few days later!

In April she arose to find, to her great sorrow, that her beautiful Brazilian bird, Lincoln, was dying. She had fed him worms the previous evening and he seemed well. Again she administered whisky and wrapped him in cotton wool. She sent for the bird man who told her he was dying and that she should never force a bird to take a bath. Lincoln died half an hour later. He was immediately replaced by an orange troupiole and an Indian thrush.

In February she is still marvelling at how happy she is: "Some late lark singing in my heart. So happy. Happy beyond words. Impossible to be more serene and even excited over the future." Her horses, dogs and birds give her great pleasure. She has Daphne and Nellie with her, others are kennelled at Sherwoods. She loves her pretty things, arranging flowers. She entertains, goes to the theatre and the opera, attends lectures. As always she reads a great deal. She is knowledgeable about paintings and is overwhelmed by an exhibition of Sandby – portraits, landscapes, flowers, children bathing: "Not Latour, not Sargent even, can paint like he does. All are marvels. No doubt the greatest living artist. I am in pieces over it."

She asks to be introduced to him, inviting him to lunch but he declines, saying he will call.

In the middle of the month she fears that Maurice will not take his degree. This makes her sad and disappointed. She consoles herself by thinking of Frank. "That sweet Francis, lovely and kind...What a joy to have such a son." Frank is still living with her, working at a bank. He is having his portrait painted by Funk.

Fanny's relationship with her sister was complicated, a love-hate relationship. Fanny was fond of her and needed her support and help, but often suffered at her hands. One day having tea with her and Peter, her husband, Fanny told them about the plan she had to open a Greek restaurant, called Little Athens.

"I talk at tea with the Hewitts meaning to be amusing & told them of my plans. It was particularly dull of me as I had made the same mistake as before. It give them all an opportunity to lecture me about my fantasies, and to criticize."

In March, Fanny visited Lucy who accused her of being a designing woman, encouraging Frank to make a mercenary marriage with a girl whom Lucy described as having the appearance of a woman off the streets, whose family were Jewish and who had poppy eyes. With superhuman self-control Fanny managed to control her wrath. She calmly told her sister that nothing would give her greater grief than such a marriage. She asked her sister why she had not taken the trouble to find out how things were before letting go such a flood of unjust abuse?

With only occasional moments of loneliness when she wished she had someone to talk to who was not a servant or a dog, Fanny's rapturous happiness continued until April when her divorce case loomed. She fell into low spirits, much troubled over her debts and troubles. She wrote to Maurice regularly, telling him of her fears and misery.

Diary: *April 13th* My life is so fearful that I can never contemplate it from any point of view with anything but utter discouragement & despair. I cannot feel that it is my fault. For 20 years I did what everyone approved: and it was a martyrdom. No woman could have kept her equanimity under such a cruel, unjust, hopeless system. All my beauty, intelligence force beaten; ambitions have only made it more of a mockery and hardship. How I kept intact my inner consciousness & my standards I wonder at myself...Eyes to the front!

For the first time that I remember, my dogs and horses have given me no pleasure, no relief. Usually, turning from 'the inhuman dearth of noble natures,'[98] their faithful presence has been a happiness for me. For the past few days while I have not hated them, I have found their care irksome and wished several times that I had not bought the horse and Nellie."

Maurice's sister Cynthia

Her mood soon swung back up and a few days later, she was thanking God for her happiness. "But oh God why can't I have a little luck & peace." She drove Iris in the park that morning and rode Superb in the afternoon. Her mood changed after a meeting in the early evening with Harry Work, which led to intense discouragement. She walked in the park looking at the blossoming daffodils and a red sun setting behind them.

She found Maurice when she reached home. They dined together at home.

[98] From *Endymion* by Keats.

On this occasion, he gave her no comfort. "He was rather fussy, I thought, and out of his plate. So selfish. He went to see his sister." The following day when she visited her sister Lucy, she was told by her brother-in-law that the case was to be heard that day. This threw her into a fit of nervousness. She had visions of the poorhouse, the ruin of a fortune. That evening in a state of total despair, she talked over the case with Maurice. She had a sleepless night, tossing in an agony of mind.

In the morning, she telephoned Harry, who told her that she had lost her petition for divorce by default. Her counsel had asked for an adjournment, as a witness could not be found. The judge refused to grant a further delay to this much-delayed case. Batonyi's petition for separation was heard the same day. The jury decided that his wife had deserted him and he won his case.

Fanny was outraged and indignant. Maurice and Cynthia had lunch with her and sympathised and consoled her, as well as admiring her new dresses, which had arrived that day. We get an idea of the conversation from her diary entry earlier that day.

"Dresses from Granese to be completed or I do not take them – how trivial all these things seem. Dresses. Why dresses? Who cares? What part have such frivolities of life in face of my martyrdom or misfortune? He won the case by default. I cannot understand how my lawyers could accomplish so little. He has had his way in everything. I have always known his ability, his adroitness. The lawyers laughed at it. 9.30 Granese with dresses. Very nice."

Frank Work exercised iron control over his grandchildren as well as his daughter. In May, Fanny received a telephone call from Murphy, her father's secretary. Her father is very annoyed because he has read of Cynthia's appearance as the Bacchante in a Greek pageant, performed to raise money for the Manhattan Trade School for Girls. In it, Cynthia wore purple and a tiger skin, and performed a Greek dance, ending in a whirling flourish! Fanny must stop her appearing again or he will stop her allowance. She goes to see Cynthia who tells her that she does not intend to appear. Fanny speaks of her son Frank's "abhorrence of a control so cruel and soul-killing. He is willing to work and glad to do his duty but claims the right to see something of the world."

After a pleasant time at Le Marquis she is obliged to leave for financial reasons. Her father requested that she does not attend the Mineola Dog Show, where Nellie is entered, as there would be a large photo in the paper. "I acquiesced. I am absolutely the saddest person you ever saw. A poor ruined woman." Andrick went to the show. Cynthia rang to tell her that she had won four prizes with Nellie. She invited her mother to stay at her home, Jericho Long Island. Fanny stays a week then returns to town, staying at Le Marquis. She leaves Daphne who is due to have puppies imminently at Sherwoods Kennels.

"Poor little Daphne that I have loved so well & in whom I took such pride. I expect never to see her again. All my little life that was so full and contained so many interests is slipping, slipping from me. I grow to be the hunted, lonely woman with no home, no belongings, no resources – in hotels. All is dead & gone. Existence is reduced to the barest limits and no hope even, remains."

New York was intensely hot. Fanny was suicidal but she was about to have some good news. At the end of the month, Maurice wrote to the Dean of Harvard petitioning for his degree:

"A D Club, Harvard.
June 29th 1909

Dear Mr Hurlbut,
Miss Mullen with whom I board, informs me that I must get in my petition for a degree before the morning.
    I am writing in hopes that the board will excuse my condition in plane geometry. Mr Parker with whom I am tutoring says it is impossible for me to pass, altho' I am going to make the attempt Monday.
    My college work is completed. I have twenty courses passed, and my full number of C's. Only the geometry prevents me from getting a degree.
    I do hope, with my past college record in attendance & not having ever been on probation for lessons, will help to give me what I am striving for.
                                Very sincerely yours, Maurice B Roche"

He did not have long to wait for the reply.

"July 1st 1909

Dear Mr Roche
I send just a line to acknowledge your note of last Friday. The Administrative Board, as you know, forgave you two points of condition and recommended you for your degree.
                                        Sincerely yours E H Wells."

As soon as he received the reply, Maurice rang his mother to give her the wonderful news. On July 2nd she wrote:

"At 5 Maurice. Tells me the good, good news that he has his degree. My relief is unspeakable. This is the only piece of good luck that has happened to me – to us – in the longest time."

Maurice had struggled to obtain his AB[99] degree but had shone at sports, excelling in rowing and tennis. He was bow oarsman in the University Second Freshman Crew and also at bow in the Sophomore eight.[100] In his first year, playing with his brother in the University Tennis Championships, he reached the semi-finals. In 1908 he reached the quarter-finals in the singles in the same tournament, and was a finalist in the doubles playing with R H Eggleston Jr. He was also in the University Cricket team and Association Football teams. He belonged to the AD and Kalumet Clubs. The many friends he had made while he was at Harvard remained in his affections all his life.

[99] Artium Baccalaureates, Bachelor of Arts in the UK.
[100] This position in the boat is more responsible for the balance of the boat than any other position.

10

At his mother's side

With great difficulty, Daphne gave birth to one large puppy. Fanny saw her a few days later, lively and bright before going to Lucy's home at Tuxedo Park, where she spent the next two months, while her sister was on a cruise. Her adjourned divorce case weighed heavily on her and she was in a very depressed state. She wrote in her diary that she contemplated suicide. Her family were very concerned for her state of health. As soon as Maurice had graduated from Harvard, he started planning to take her on a trip to the National Parks and the west coast. A protracted journey with her beloved son would be therapeutic. Although his grandfather would not allow his grandsons to visit Europe because of the risk of them seeing their father, internal trips were permitted.

Maurice left the Newport season to come to Tuxedo to collect her. They left in early August. Meanwhile Frank took a vacation travelling by train and boat to Bar Harbour where he boarded a friend's yacht. They moored at Bar Harbour for a few days, one evening entertaining a hundred people on board. They then sailed to Newport where he attended many parties and watched the tennis at the Casino.

Maurice wrote to Frank from Seattle telling him about their planned trip to Alaska and describing the Seattle World Trade Fair:

"Hotel Washington, Seattle
August 1909

Dear Boy,
Everybody here has told us not to miss the trip to Alaska so we are going – the trip occupies nine days, and the furthest north we go is to a place called Skagway.[101] We leave Saturday night. I went and bought the tickets this am. $60 dollars round trip. Boy, just think Mamma and I going to Alaska. The steamer follows the shore almost the entire way between islands so that the open sea strikes us but for two hours.

At first I was not very keen for the trip, but the more I hear of it the more pleased I am. We get back here September 6th, so Boy, will you please

---

[101] Skagway was the starting point of a route to the Canadian gold fields of Yukon., which entailed a 500 mile trek over the mountains.

send any mail etc. in a big envelope to me, New Washington Hotel, Seattle. Write me also a line telling me how you've been and what happened in the East.

Monday morning we went out to the Exhibition. My! How I did enjoy it all. First, the grounds are perfectly wonderful – so wonderfully laid out. All the buildings represent different industries, for instance the mines building show things that are mined – the US Government building shows the fish department; coast survey; making coins etc, etc. One could spend days at such a place, looking over things carefully.

Let me tell you of the people I've met. Boy, the girls are all so attractive. In the hotel, the place is filled with them. We play bridge, fool around. The orchestra is very good. They play "Havana" and all the popular tunes.

Worse luck, a perfect "peach" left today – and I never had the chance of meeting her. Boy, she was too lovely.

There are about eight fellows I play around with – from Yale, Princeton etc. so on the whole you can see what a heavenly time I'm having. Mama and I are going to see "The Bewitching Hour" tonight. They say it is good. You probably will be quite surprised when you see my moustache. It is quite a success, according to Mamma.

Boy all I can say is that I'm having a very good time, the very best possible. Send a line how Grandpa is; also how you've been enjoying yourself etc.

We go after that to San Francisco then back here and home
Good-bye, hope you're well, love, Maurice"

The first Seattle World Trade Fair in 1909 celebrated the tenth anniversary of the Klondike Gold Rush in Yukon in 1897.[102] Known as the Alaska-Yukon-Pacific Exposition and publicising the north-west, it was set up on the campus of the University of Washington, where some of the buildings still survive. Sadly no letter from Maurice survives describing the Alaskan cruise. His mother's letter written after the trip to Alaska tells us something of the end of this great trip to the west coast.

Fanny to Frank:

"Sept 22nd 1909
Hotel Alexandra Los Angeles

"Another night journey and here in the morning. Without resting we breakfasted, took a trolley to Pasadena. There hired an automobile for an hour and saw most of the prettiest residences with their gardens. Geraniums grow high here and form hedges – red and pink. Bougainvilleas, that purple

---

[102] Postponed for two years because it clashed with a fair in Virginia in 1907.

flower that grows in greenhouses with us covers piazzas and clusters around terraces. Oleanders of a beautiful shade of red flower and palms grow everywhere. It is very pretty.

Home for lunch – an excellent lunch. In fact these fine hotels with every comfort are to be found throughout the big cities. In afternoon, 22 route by trolley to Long Beach. But it was only a cheap Coney Island. Did not pay for the trouble. Maurice hired a suit and took a dip in the Pacific. I sat and watched him. We were going at 9.40 this morning on a 'balloon trip' in trolley seeing about 20 small places. I was too exhausted. He went alone. Andrick and I are taking a car to do sight seeing in Los Angeles. We leave tonight or tomorrow for Grand Canyon then across continent. We will have travelled about ten thousand miles. And we like the East best, which is natural. The people are a little nicer looking here. Just one degree!

How are you my dearest Boy! I think of you so very much! I wonder how you are? Is 13 26th Street very dreadful? And is Papa is very difficult? Bear it all with patience, dearest: don't let restlessness & rebellion drive you into any action. 'Flying to ills we know not of' seldom helps a situation. I have done a terrible thing for any old man/or any parent to bear. Our own character is the better for exercising patience & trying to help on a situation, and believe me, everyone has something that he does not like. Forgive me if I preach: I think parents <u>should</u>. Some of it <u>sticks</u>. Would I had had a counsellor to make me pause and reflect.

How is your M? I do hope you will not be drawn in! Do you see the young Villiers, today's paper says, parting by agreement? Better for people to reflect before – he was married too young. Like Alfred (Vanderbilt). It is too bad. You two boys must <u>not</u> be pig-headed & 'know it all' on account of <u>me</u> & your own future.

With deep affection & interest. Yrs FR"

On September 30th, Fanny and Maurice returned to New York to be available for her divorce case. She moved into Le Marquis. Maurice went to see Frank at his bank the following day, sporting a fine moustache! A week later, she dined with Maurice and Frank. Frank had seats for Maurice and Fanny to see the Dollar Princess: "Frank has seen it five times. Very kind, but my pet aversion is musical comedy with its inanities…M had been to dentist who reported 'all's well'."

Fanny wrote in her diary that she felt well, rested in mind and full of courage. Her weariness and uncertainty returned when she learned that her case was down for October 18th, but once she had collected Daphne from her father's house and seen her birds, her spirits rose. The next day Maurice came round before having his breakfast, with an urgent message from his grandfather: "He asked me to tell you that he wants Daphne back. She likes ice cream and sponge cake & he gives it to her three times a day. The only dog that loves him & you take it." Fanny replied no.

On October 18th she was in court with her sons. Once again, the case was adjourned but this time only to the following day. She moved to her rooms at the Gotham Hotel, her feelings alternating between hope and despair.

In court, her counsel exposed Batonyi's assumed name. He began by asking him what his name was. He answered. "Aurel Batonyi".

Counsel: "Didn't you ever have another name."

"I was born Kohn. That was my family's original name. They changed it to Marburg."

He then admitted he had changed his name to Batonyi when he came to America. Evidence was then presented to the court on which the jury were asked to decide if Batonyi was guilty of adultery. No verdict was reached that day and Fanny had to wait until the following day to hear their decision.

At 10.30am next day, Harry Work telephoned her to tell her that the jury had returned a sealed verdict finding Batonyi guilty. She had won!! "I WON," she wrote in her diary, in large letters. She described herself as wild and light-headed with joy. In addition to having got her divorce, the actions Batonyi was bringing against her family, for their part in alienating her affections, would now be invalidated. She rang her father's home first to give him and Maurice the wonderful news. Then Cynthia and Lucy. Frank was at work so she did not ring him. The world was suddenly a beautiful place:

"Cynthia called for me in new auto. Very pretty & smart!! Blue doucet costume, complexion lovely. I showed her my purchases…to Grandpa's. He had cold. I didn't go in. To Lucy's. Very happy!! Lucy really lovely in beautiful French dress. Home."

In the afternoon, they went to the Stables to see a runabout which she gave to Lucy. Lucy was very pleased. They go to see Superb.

"They (the staff) whisper as I go out: "Were you victorious?" I say: 'Yes, thank you.' Home. Maurice on telephone. Said he had been celebrating. Frank on telephone, overjoyed & he had been celebrating. Dinner with Maurice. Had met friends and passed a gay afternoon rejoicing at my freedom. He sleeps in my room. Boys very kind and affectionate."

The next morning when she woke up, Maurice had gone. She went to the Stables and rode Superb. Maurice turned up too late to see her ride. They lunched together. She made him report for work at his office at the Delaware, Lackawanna and Western Railroad Company.

After her rest, she dressed in her new Paquin dress and went by taxi cab to Renard's, her dressmaker for a fitting of dresses which were copies of French fashion houses. She carried "a sable muff & stole with big, handsome tassels that are a novelty this season. Every one in Renard's came & looked. I tried on my green Barnard day dress, also lovely Drecoll turquoise blue-black, and gold and silver on body. Quite lovely. $300 at least in Paris. $100 to me. Home 6.50cents to chauffeur."

On Friday October 22nd she wrote: "Maurice goes to the Delaware & Lackawanna depot in Hoboken. Began yesterday – wages. Lovely son day!"

The Delaware, Lackawanna and Western Railroad was built to transport anthracite coal in Pennsylvania's Lackawanna Valley. Eventually it ran from the Valley, west to Buffalo and east to Hoboken. It prospered in the early twentieth century, but with the decline of coal heating and the rise of competing modes of transportation, its revenues fell. Frank Work had been on the board of the Erie railroad and pointed Maurice in the direction of this job.

The news of Maurice's employment was reported favourably in *Town Topics*, New York City in November 1909:

"I am very glad to learn that, like the sons of so many other great families in New York, Maurice Roche, one of the twin grandsons of Frank Work, is not too inflated with his youthful importance to begin a business career at the bottom of the ladder. How many of the vapid young bloods about town, who see Maurice at the Opera and the theatre at nights, dancing attendance on the season's belles, are aware that his alarm clock is set for 6 o'clock each morning, as his numerous duties compel him to be at his desk in the office of the chief train master of the Lackawanna Railroad at Hoboken at eight o'clock. A graduate of Harvard in the class of 1909, Maurice unlike a great many of his peers, has impressed me by the manner in which he has taken to his position, that of a car record clerk and the way he sticks to his duty until after six at night. If at any time he is late for the Opera, is not this sufficient excuse? Hoboken is very far away from New York."

Fanny was delirious with joy at her success in the divorce court. Now that Batonyi's actions against the family had been rendered futile by the divorce decision, she felt entitled to come back into the fold. She instructed her father's stable manager to engage a helper so that a coach can be at her disposition. She ordered a yellow rose to be sent to her every day, to be worn with her yellow waistcoat. She planned to give a Thanksgiving dinner for the servants.

On Monday, Fanny went on a spending spree. She bought a bracelet and a ruby pin and pendant to celebrate her victory. She also left a bid for a ruby and

101

diamond cross at Levy, and a list of other pieces to bid for. She ordered a golden yellow dress and cloak from Renard's. She saw Maher her masseuse. Maurice dined with her on Tuesday and described his work, which he finds interesting.

"*Oct. 28th*. My birthday. Up at 7. Lovely yellow chrysanthemums & bronze oak leaves from the 'Faithful geyser' (Andrick). Very <u>greatly</u> appreciated. At 9.30 pm. Without a tinge of bitterness, I say not another soul sent me even a wire or a rose."

Her next project is to smarten up her carriages. She gives orders that the top runabout is to be varnished and sent to Lucy. A Brewster runabout to be varnished and delivered to the Stables for her use. Her miniature victoria to be touched up and her drag to be varnished. The carriage clock to be replaced on the brougham. She designs a new, black fur rug for her carriage, lined in black moiré silk, trimmed with yellow silk. Her mink carriage rug is repaired. Daphne and Nellie, her toy bull terriers, have black and yellow sweaters and go out walking on a coupling chain. "Very smart, practically unique." Black and yellow was Fanny's favourite colour combination.

On November 3rd, she gave a dinner party for ten in the dining room of the Gotham. The *New York Times* commented:

"The dinner was a small one. It was the fact that it was given in the main restaurant, however, that it was looked upon by those who knew Mrs Batonyi as a sort of celebration of the verdict for divorce and of her social advent once more. While this suit was on, Mrs Batonyi had practically remained in seclusion."

The guests included Mrs Harry Lehr, Eleanor Whitridge, Charlie Greenough, J Chauncey Mckeever, the Nasts,[103] Laurence Gillespie and her sons Maurice and Frank. After dinner, she took her guests in a bus to the theatre and gave them supper afterwards.

Entertaining her friends fulfilled Fanny. She loved to make people happy. In a letter to Frank she explains her attitude to being a caring hostess:

"My one desire you know, was to give pleasure and make every one happy. I am quite gratified to find that many communicative women and men say – and it comes back – appreciative things about my hospitality, my excellent cooking, service etc. and they also are kind in declaring that I make every one happy and that it is a house where people enjoy themselves.

---

[103] Condé Nast, magazine publisher, acquired Vogue in 1909. He was married to Clarisse, a society woman of French origin.

It all takes money. I could spend it on pearls and sables. It takes time and I can fill mine easily with my many tastes and occupations. It takes thought and infinite pains, to please the people properly. And it takes, as well, patience, tact, and entire unselfishness to be a hostess. One seldom has a moment's talk with anyone one cares to speak, and it is because I know that I have the requirements, that if I work (for it is all work in this world) I may fill a niche badly wanted in this community, where the kind of woman that I represent in my breeding and traditions is rare.

It is no credit to me, if born of a most beautiful, thoroughbred mother and a father who had exceptional beauty, health, ability, magnetism and force, that there should have been at least some trace of my parents. But it would be a poor creature indeed who, with such a pedigree, did not at least attempt to be something and not let herself 'with the crowd to be spent'."

"*Monday Nov. 7th* Maurice came in after dinner and spent evening. We talked over his work. I am delighted. He spoke of riding in the Academy at Hoboken during the week."

On November 8th the annual National Horse Show was held in Madison Square Gardens. This year for the first time there was an international jumping event for officers in uniform. Alfred Vanderbilt, the President, invited British cavalry officers to compete. Mrs Burke Roche had a box. Fanny had resumed the name of her first husband. Maurice and Frank were there to watch their friends Alfred and Reginald Vanderbilt perform.

One winter evening she wrote: "In a dressing-gown with Daphne under my left arm and Nellie right, in <u>bliss</u>, enthroned I sit eating my dinner, happily, cheerfully, reverently in peace. So full & all gratitude & happiness." She makes frequent references to a late lark singing in her heart and regularly thanks God for her happiness. She is full of deep and lasting content.

In the middle of December, her finances are in a very bad state. She could not pay her bills and Andrick had to run to her bank for $500 as an emergency measure. Over the next few weeks, she has problems getting Murphy, her father's private secretary, to give her money to pay her bills. She has several meetings and telephone calls with Murphy, which she finds hateful and fatiguing. She makes strong appeals but he is not understanding. After telephoning Murphy on December 14th, she writes:

"Discouraged at humiliating, haggling for money. Gladly would be a dog just now, nicely washed, brushed, blanketed & taken out by Andrick. Situation is ridiculous. A very rich man fights and tries to avoid paying lawyers etc. I am seldom blue. Then it is physical I suppose. I am <u>tired,</u>

103

overdone. I feel as if I would wrench my paintings from the wall: pack up my desk & bookcases & sink out of sight in the country. Economize, rest, sleep, not pretend to live at all.

Everyone expects from us what we are supposed to have, & have not. 'What infinite heart's-ease must kings neglect that private men enjoy'[104] For 'kings' read 'middle class'. I am a sad lonely, debt-ridden woman only asking a little peace & freedom from anxiety. Denied that always…all my little, simple, unemotional life, so innocent & happy and satisfying for months, is ruthlessly disturbed and rendered insipid, by anxiety, suspense & indignation that we are treated as we are!! A dream to get away, to change this excellence for a new one, undictated to…

Thank God. I know that I am well off, and happy. Only irritated by this prolonged annoyance. Still today I want to hear music, to see pictures, to hear voices. I am too restless, & expected to ride & drive. The blood of the other individual who lives in me cries out today, for companionship, for intellectual comprehension. The book is in my blood.

Christmas Eve. I saw my "Angel Nipper". Ben drove him, for me to see him up and down!! The greatest piece of horse-flesh in the world, bar size! Never, never saw anything like the way he has improved. Lovely pink azalea tied with green ribbon from Frank."

She buys expensive Christmas presents for her servants – hats for the women, a fine angora waistcoat for Ben. She spent a happy Christmas day, feeling very blessed. She had lots of presents – flowers, red azalea and berries from Maurice. She lunched with her boys and their friends, Cecil St George and Reggie Lanier. In the afternoon, she visited Mrs E Hewitt (Lucy's sister-in-law) and watched a play written by her and acted by her children. "A lovely homelike Christmas spirit prevailed. I was very happy. Dinner Lucy. Home with Cynthia in horse cab."

"*Dec. 26th* Blizzard. Wind snow. A day of rest and thanksgiving. Ben called for his present. I read Guiccioli's[105] Byron. Re-lived my youth & all I had read of him. Up for luncheon in restaurant. Read, read. Tea at 5. Mrs West & I long talk on telephone. Little white dogs on my lap! Wind howls. Bed at 10."

The last days of 1909 end on a happy note. She is peaceful and content, enjoying some quiet time with her dogs. She read *The Memoirs of the Duchess of Dino*, former owner of Elm Court, which she found interesting. Every morning she goes

---

[104] *King Henry V.* Act IV. Scene 1.
[105] *Lord Byron's life in Italy* by Teresa, Countess Guiccioli, Byron's mistress.

to the Stables where she enjoys her ride on Superb, then lunges or schools Hump II and Nipper. She lunches at a German bakery which costs her 45 cents, "a great saving every day." She and Andrick walk the dogs in the afternoon. When they see carriages lining the Avenue waiting to take people to dinner, she is thankful she is not in one. She is glad not to have social engagements. Every day she shops for pretty things and presents.

"*Dec. 31st* Bought pretty ruby and diamond horse shoe for Papa. Went to theatre, 'School for Scandal.' The boys are living with their grandfather, and having a very social time Almost every night there is a dinner followed by the theatre or a dance."

11

1910

Fanny starts 1910 "perfectly and wonderfully happy". Her diary entries and her letters to the boys all speak of her happiness and serenity, her thankfulness in every fibre of her being. She is resting, enjoying her pictures, her birds, her peace. The weather without is disagreeable. Within her heart, some late lark is singing. She goes frequently to the theatre and the Opera, she attends lectures at the School of Applied Design where they praise her rough sketches. She also goes to an architecture class which arouses her father's suspicions!

On January 8th Maurice dines and tells her of a letter Lucy has written to her father, a critical letter apparently reporting that Fanny has attended political meetings. Also that she did not give Lucy a ruby bracelet for Christmas. Fanny weeps bitter tears that night from vexation and humiliation. Furious with her sister for being a mean sneak, the next day she writes this character sketch:

"Lucy is a very nice ladylike, good woman. A lady. Very right-minded, upright. In large things, important things, to be admired. Is it to be admired to be as careless as she is? After giving her a beautiful, new runabout costing $450, would one expect (or is it an unreasonable idea) a line saying, if not thank you, at least it has come! I could have kept it really. I gave it as I do frankly, gladly, only happy to give pleasure and share my things! Her letter to me so unprovoked so rude, so mean, I kept the rubies for myself.

She has a quick temper with no self-control. Her house is a weird place: and no one looks after things. There will be a very sad awakening sometimes. I would love to help. To spare her. To let her look into things. If she were being robbed, I would. But can I with her attitude of snapping, hissing at *everything*. 'Aunt Lucy is a cat alright', Frank said, and it is unfortunately so. Never a word of commendation, if a word, then a blow! And there is a nice woman with, what people say, is a lovely nature. So Mrs Rogers said only two nights ago. 'So beautiful & such a lovely nature.' I assented warmly as I always do & I was very glad to have her praised.

Lucy is very lazy in mind, very lazy in body. If the latter is feeble – and she is always well enough to do the things that amuse her – the mind might be, even be in bed, turned upon reading or writing, on directing work or interviewing, ordering servants..."

Two days later the storm is over. Fanny describes her own temperament as extraordinary and exaggerated. She attends a lecture on the political situation in England, which she found delightful. She has sympathy with the liberal views and the cause of the suffragettes. She gets various authorities to read. Very happy. She was told that a highly educated and superior woman had commented that she, Fanny, was the cleverest woman she knew. Fanny regards the compliment as unmerited but she is happy and encouraged that her desire to learn was noticed by this person. Exhausted she says a prayer of thanksgiving, deep thanksgiving for her escape from all her tormentors, before going to bed.

Lucy Hewitt at the Hewitt Ball, 1908

Soon after this, she wrote an important statement in her diary: "I will from this day take up any public cause in which I am interested. All hiding and shrinking to please my father are at an end."

Fanny was strongly influenced by the feminist reform movements. She read the literature of the New Woman movement, which believed it was time to examine the work of men, to see if they were qualified to arrange and manage the whole social system. A New Woman was independent, capable of using her own initiative and often earning her own living. She was a woman of culture who preserved her femininity. She wanted the right of suffrage.

Fanny saw a lot of Maurice who played an important supporting role in her life that winter. Their travels in the West had improved their relationship. He did odd jobs for her. He escorted her out to lunch and to the theatre, when he was not otherwise engaged. He frequently dined with her. His opinion was very comforting and often confirmed her own. On one occasion she wrote:

"Maurice for dinner. Very nice & I so fortunate in having him. Fancy him working away in Hoboken! It is wonderful. So very happy. We have a plain understanding. Talk over people. He gives his views. I feel that he is correct. Thinks a person (Lucy) scheming, jealous and a knocker. Lovely evening!!!!"

She continued to live way above her means. By the end of March, Fanny was broke. Once again, she had to borrow money from Andrick to pay her immediate bills. She wrote that she did not regret her expenditure on horses. "All days are bland if no riding or driving...the world is now so bitter, a ride can make it sweet." She showed Nipper and Chinchilla at the Atlantic City Show which she attended herself but ashamed of her poverty, she avoided people, wishing to remain incognito.

An unimaginable event took pace in the middle of April. Maurice, now aged 25, departed for Europe for a few weeks, with the consent of his grandfather! Amazingly, his grandson had found a way to relax the old man's adamant prohibition on travel overseas. On condition that he should not see his father, he gave Maurice permission to visit his cousins in Ireland and his French governess, Josephine, who lived in Asnières, a suburb of Paris. No doubt the fact that Frank had crossed the Atlantic the month before filled Maurice with envy and was one of his prime arguments. It was a relief to escape from the pressure of his mother's dire financial predicament and growing state of despair.

Maurice went to see Josephine at her home near Paris. He and Frank were devoted to her and for Maurice it was an emotional visit. She told him what charming children they had been and what big hearts they had. She loved them very much and was very proud of the direction their lives were taking.

As the days pass Fanny becomes more and more weighed down by her debts

108

and her loneliness. She went to see her father and he said he forgave her but she was killing him. She leaves him, saying she does not want to upset him and is herself unhappy to be on bad terms. Unexpectedly her father says she can open Elm Court so long as she does not entertain and if Cynthia goes with her. This throws her into a state of great confusion and uncertainty. She describes herself as suicidal with stress. She decides to refuse his offer, which throws him into a violent rage. He threatens to close his stable. She sends him a message saying that she is all in pieces, will sell everything and go.

In early May, Ben and Walter, a helper, took Fanny's horses, birds and carriages to Prospect Hill Farm, Essex, Massachusetts, which she had rented. They took the night boat to Fall River,[106] Massachusetts and travelled on to Gloucester where they spend a night. They suffered great discomfort and cold. A little nightingale died on the way. Fanny and Andrick took the night boat the following day and after a night on the way they proceeded to Prospect Hill Farm. She very soon realised that she had made a bad mistake in coming to live in isolation. Her horses are her only comfort, her one pleasure and recreation. She cut down on her expenditure and is able to pay off some of her debts which gives her some satisfaction. She dissuaded the boys from making the long journey to see her. "It is too far; two days journey for a few hours here. I must stick it out: sleeping a lot: driving a lot: putting memory and ambition to sleep; existing." She is very happy for a brief moment when she learns that Batonyi has withdrawn his actions against her family.

A letter to the boys expressed great regret that she has put herself out of reach. She asks Frank if Maurice is behaving himself and wonders if she should move to New York to keep an eye on him. She was concerned that he had drunk too much at the wedding in New York in June of Ted Roosevelt and Eleanor Alexander when he and Frank were ushers.

"Maurice is not as steady as you and I wonder very much how he is getting on in that low city with no one to look after him. Confidentially if you think I should, tell me and I will go to New York & stay there, if I can have any influence over him, if things are not as they should be. You know where my place is. You know I think families should look after their members, whatever the age, and stand by to see that no one gets off the sensible path of right, leading to hideous trouble, disaster, disgrace & loss. But we have been so hampered about money that I have not been able to live up to that."

She writes little in her diary of this period, avoiding writing about her gloomy disagreeable life. Besides Andrick, she employs two stablemen, a cook and two

---

[106] 16 miles south-east of Providence, RI.

maids. On July 5th, she learns that her father is going to sell his stables in order to cut expenditure. This news has the effect of making her suicidal:

"Hideous night of despair & conflict of emotions. 'To be or not to be' in fact. Would it make the situation worse were I to end it? Life for me is in outward form only – existence. Inwardly it is torture, daily, hourly. Would it be hideous egotism to leave? If I felt sure that there would be no conflict, that thought would settle it, forever."

More than anything she felt completely isolated from her familiar life, her friends and, above all, her boys. She is dying of homesickness and grief. She knows that she has only herself to blame for going to Essex. The intense despair like the heat recedes. Maurice writes to her that he has been promoted. She is very pleased and heartened. She decides to get rid of all her horses and to leave the farm on August 1st. She longs to be in Elm Court and to have the money to run it. She fears for her mind, wonders if it will give way. She has a continual nervous headache. "The situation for me is so hideous & so hopeless that I grow cold all over when I look at it. This summer the greatest sorrow & anguish I ever had."

Several months of apathy and deep depression followed. There are no diary entries from the last night at Prospect Hill Farm in early August until her birthday on October 28th. On that day, she wrote to her sons from Virginia, where she was staying at the Homestead, in Hot Springs – a historic, luxurious, fashionable spa hotel, which still exists today. She told them that her mental balance was getting adjusted, her nights were better. She has emerged from the terrible apathy of the last few months:

"I have to a large extent risen above my surroundings & I am facing life with courage and equanimity again, even if society, and much that I have had, be eliminated. Kipling's 'If', which I am memorizing, has helped."

From Hot Springs, she moves to the Gotham Hotel New York where she resumes her customary New York life. Still under doctor's orders, she rests each day but is now much calmer, less restless and impulsive. She buys some new clothes but not on the previous extravagant scale. She rides and drives her horses, making no mention of her father, other than to say that he regrets selling his stables and that he had done a stupid thing. She goes to the theatre often as before, particularly admiring the great actress Ellen Terry. She attends lectures on Architecture and Design.

She works on a translation from French into English and tries to find a publisher. She has an urge to justify herself after her hideous blunder – to remove her stigma of stupidity, by some accomplishment in an elevated activity. She believes she can make money out of writing, "making money out of one's sensibility, one's keenness of feeling, one's vibrating quality of sensation." She also considered giving recitations but decided that her prominence in society would be a stumbling block to that.

Her happiest days are when she sees her boys. On Sunday in late November, she spends a day with Maurice. They go to look at her horses, then have lunch together and then walk down 5th Avenue. They have great fun:

> "I am so happy. Maurice is so wonderful. So handsome, a high-bred and a 'dog'! A gay dog with the ladies. He has a very kind heart: tells of Thanksgiving party he gave for his 18 employees…a happy, peaceful day."

A month later Maurice darkened her life when, on Christmas Day, he came to lunch, bringing with him a Miss Mackay. He had told his mother that she was wonderful. Fanny had considered him to be a good judge of women, given his long experience of the best in society but was instantly aghast at his choice in this case:

> "What did I see? A tall, very awkward, stooped girl; pretty, nice complexion, good strong white teeth, the whole row advancing, to me a very ugly feature. Nice blue eyes, untidy hair. Big red hands, feet like fire shovels. A very affected English voice, very rapid speech with no gradations or stressing, very indistinct. No manners, no distinction. Not one comment on my pictures, furniture, pretty things that showed she knew what she was looking at…I was so extremely bowled over by Maurice's want of discernment & discrimination that I finally made no more effort to speak to her."

(I imagine this savage, critical scrutiny was brought to bear on each one of Maurice's girl friends who were one by one dispatched. This could explain his late marriage. I had experience myself of the importance his mother placed on physical appearance. She detested fat people. The only time I remember meeting her she looked at me, then aged three, and said: "Grandma Roche does not like fat little girls!")

12

Freedom from tyranny

In early February 1911, Maurice and Frank decide to go to Palm Beach. Their mother hears of their intention and writes in the strongest terms advising against this unwise move. Were it Canada or Mexico or the far west she would understand their course of action:

"My dear Frankie,
I hope you have not gone off to some foolish debilitating, piffling place like Florida. To play around aimlessly with those girls and lose your time, scrap your chances of any interesting holiday and get your Bank and your grandfather down on you?

Don't! It is most unwise. And what a silly profitless outing? Were it Canada, or Mexico or the far West, while I advise not going, yet at least I see why you want it. But Palm Beach! – the Long Island of Florida, with girls only as an attraction, is a perfect waste of time and energy – good material."

Fanny's experience has made her cynical about people and their motives and many of her letters contain advice and judgements on others. She continues:

"Don't be nice to people! Be nice to yourself. Regard your own safety, advancement, happiness. Really, not only it has been my undoing, but I look around. Who is worth much effort? They are for the most part a selfish, sordid lot. They have an axe to grind. They are out for something – big if possible! Failing that, then their advertisement of one's acquaintance. Keep your fine feelings for your work, your own ideals, your family & use the other people when you want them. Love the real true things."

In February 17th 1911, Maurice and Frank went to Palm Beach despite their mother's stern advice not to waste their time. She writes tempting them back to New York, requesting their presence at a dinner she is giving on March 17th, where there will be lots of young people. A week later, Lucy is planning a fancy dress ball and the brothers are expected to be in her French revolution group. Their costumes have been ordered at a cost of $5 a night. They are taken from pictures of the time. There will be vaudeville and a play. She adds that she is being invited to big receptions and dinner parties for 24 people.

On March 17th, the day of the intended dinner party, a dramatic event occurred in the life of the family. Frank Work died of pneumonia. His grip of steel, which he had clamped on the lives of his daughters and on his grandchildren, was suddenly able. No more chafing at the bit for his grandsons who were now freed to travel to Europe, to come and go, to see the world which had been forbidden during his lifetime.

Frank and Maurice in Palm Beach, Florida, 1911

Their grandfather, Frank Work, died at his home in 26th Street aged 92. *Town Topics* reported:

"Frank Work outlived his generation. Tragically for him his only, adored son George Paul Work, predeceased him. He had few, if any, close friends left, and he was never a man to be chummy with any one. His old partner Frank Sturgis, who is much younger remained faithful to the last, and carried the news and tattle of the horse world of Madison Square Garden along the block, to where he would find Mr Work's eagle eyes peering out from behind the iron trellised doorway, where the old financier delighted to sit in the noon day sun.

Mr Work has seen the tearing down of the fine old residential mansions in his street and the up-town march of business undoubtedly cost him more than a tear. The recent demolition of a large part of his block and the excavations now going on for another skyscraper were the final blow. In despair and disgust at the intrusion on his privacy his vigorous sprit and splendid physique yielded to the inevitable."[107]

Frank Work's will was 60 pages long. He left his home at 13 East 26th Street and the stables in 27th adjoining to his daughter Frances Ellen. Elm Court was left jointly to both daughters, who were to have an annual income of $70,000 dollars. He did his best to continue his tyrannical rule beyond the grave. All the provisions for the benefit of his daughter Frances and his grandchildren were subject to the certain conditions.

James Boothby Burke Roche should never set foot in his house. His daughter Frances should cease to exhibit horses or other animals in public shows or in exhibitions. He stipulated that Aurel Batonyi should not be in any way connected with Elm Court. "If my said daughter shall fail to comply with my wishes her entire interests shall be reduced to an income of $12,000 per annum."

His daughter and his granddaughter Cynthia were not at any time after his death, to visit or reside in the kingdom of Great Britain and Ireland or the continents of Europe, Asia or Africa. He claimed that these provisions were for the protection and benefit of his daughter and grandchild, and in the belief that they could find in the United States enough to interest, instruct and amuse them, and all the variety of climate for the purposes of their health.

Cynthia was to assume and retain the name of Work in place of that of Roche until her marriage. If she married a foreigner or anyone not a citizen of US, all her interest in his estate would cease. His grandsons should assume the name of Work and once they had obtained their majority, they should become American citizens and must reside in the US. They must not, during the lifetime of James Burke

Roche, reside in or visit the kingdom of Great Britain and Ireland.

He instructed his Trustees to set aside a sum of money so that Edward his beloved horse may have the best care and attention in his lifetime without being worked. He left a legacy to the Cooper Union for the Advancement of Science and Art, as a memorial to his son George Work.

A court decided that these terms were unreasonable. The lawyers drew up "a constructive trust", whereby the grandchildren could receive income and be free to travel the world and live where they wished.

As soon as they had access to their very large incomes, the brothers' first thoughts were for their old school. They gave the school a launch for use in the coaching of the Crews at Long Pond. It was a gift that all those who were interested in rowing warmly appreciated. The coach, Mr Dole, could now coach ten eight-oared crews from the launch instead of from his position as a cox for a junior crew. He would also be able to help if a shell (boat) was swamped, the launch thus contributing to the safety of the oarsmen.

Maurice soon made up for lost time. Now aged 27, he and his twin embarked on a grand tour of Europe, which included England, France, Italy and Turkey. Their first destination was to London to see their father, Jim Roche, whom they had not seen since they were two years-old, when he brought them across the Atlantic and deposited them in the care of their mother and grandfather. As his name was not allowed to be mentioned in their grandfather's home, and their mother had severed her connection with him, they went to meet a total stranger.

13

Maurice meets his father

Jim had been leading a full life since the day he handed over his sons to his father-in-law. Over the years, he had glimpsed them from a distance when he was in New York. On one occasion, he had spoken to them, incognito. There was a lot of catching up to do.

In 1896, Jim decided to follow the example of his father and go into politics. He joined the anti-Parnellite Nationalist party, who wanted Home Rule for Ireland by peaceful means. He was adopted as a candidate in a by-election in East Kerry, admitting in his adoption speech that although he was born in the neighbouring county of Cork, he was not known to most of them. The opposition claimed he had been foisted upon them. "In fact he knew as little of the constituency, whose suffrages he was wooing, as if they were at the North Pole."[108] His opponent Mr McGillicuddy, the Unionist candidate, had lived in the area all his life and had given many years of public service to the community.

Roche was initially supported by the Catholic priests. When he was adopted, it was announced in the *Daily Independent*, the Parnellite newspaper, that he was divorced from his wife. The Catholic priests were outraged and withdrew their support. Roche served a writ on the *Independent* claiming £5,000 for malicious libel. Records of divorce courts were searched. No petition containing the name of the Hon. James Roche was found and the statement that he was a divorced man was regarded as invention.

He retained the support of the Catholic priests, so much so that the local paper described the clerical influence as scandalous. "Not only did they tell every elector in the constituency of the dire consequences if they did not vote for Mr Roche, but they actually entered the polling booths and watched voters who were not illiterate marking their papers." [109]

The very day before the election, the *Daily Independent* reproduced a column from the *Freeman's Journal* of February 1891, reporting on the divorce suit by Mrs Burke Roche against her husband the Hon. James Boothby Burke Roche. "In view of this disclosure the action of the priests in East Kerry during to-day's

---

[107] *Town Topics*, March 1911.
[108] The *Kerry Evening Post*. March 1896.
[109] ibid.

contest is awaited with considerable interest."[110]

JBBR insisted that the divorce in America was not valid and the matter was put to arbitration. He promised to take an interest in local issues and to develop the tourist trade through his influence. He was elected on March 28th 1920 with a substantial majority,[111] on the understanding that he would resign if the truth of these charges was established. In moving a vote of thanks to the returning officer, Mr Roche said that a certain portion of the Press had cast on his good name what he could only consider as the greatest stigma that could be cast on the name of a man. He asked the electors to accept his assurance that he would be found in no way to be disqualified from holding the position to which he had been elected.[112] *The Times* reported the following day that although he had won the seat, the opposing Unionist candidate gained the highest vote ever recorded for a Unionist candidate in Kerry East!

Jim Roche's first questions in the House of Commons, as he had promised before he was elected, were related to local matters. They were concerned with injustice to Kerry residents and their neighbours – on evictions, tax demands and compensation for a bog slide. He reported the need for improvements in the delivery of mail to Killarney and Tralee and for a gunboat to be placed at the mouth of the River Shannon to prevent a French fishing fleet from shooting their mackerel nets within territorial limits. He asked if primroses could still be exported from Ireland by post following the Post Office's refusal to accept small boxes of flowers from abroad. The answers he received were mainly negative and unhelpful, at best non-committal.

It is known that he went prospecting for gold along the Klondike River in the Yukon. Gold was discovered in 1896. When he spoke in the House in February 1898, after a prolonged period when his name is not mentioned in Hansard, he raised the subject of Alaskan treaties with Russia at the time when the US purchased Alaska from Russia. It must be a possibility he had first hand knowledge of the Yukon, and that this had prompted his question.

Two months later, he returned to the subject, when he asked whether the time had arrived to finally define the disputed boundary between the Yukon district of Alaska & the North-west territory of Canada, in view of the importance of the Yukon district. The Secretary for the Colonies replied that there was good reason to believe that an agreement would soon be reached for a *modus vivendi*[113] at the passes on the routes to the mining districts.

Further evidence of his interest in that part of the world comes from a question he put in July 1898, when he raised a question about the Canadian Cattle Trade,

---

[110] *The Times*, March 27th 1896, p.7. °ol. F
[111] Result: Hon. James Roche (A.-P.) ...1961 Mr John McGillycuddy (C) ...680.
[112] *The Times*, March 30th, 1896.
[113] A working arrangement pending the settlement of disputed matters.

asking for a restriction to be lifted upon the importation of store cattle from Canada into Great Britain, as they were free from disease. The President of the Board of Agriculture told him that all animals from abroad were slaughtered at the port of landing.

In April 1898, he asked the Financial Secretary to the War Office asked a question about the hardship endured by soldiers in Egypt caused by their inadequate equipment. He stated that the majority of men serving in English regiments on the Nile, arrived in a practically bootless condition after three days marching. The Secretary replied that the boots supplied to the army in Egypt were not made of shoddy materials.

He complained about the lamentable loss of life from a gob fire[114] at the Whitwick Colliery. The Secretary of State for the Home Department told him that gob fires had existed in this mine for probably twenty years, always carefully watched with proper precautions to avoid danger.

Jim only served one term and did not stand in the general election in 1900. His regular trips to America combined seeing his children with business ventures. Different conditions applied to Jim seeing his daughter. When Fanny returned to New York from London with Cynthia, it was agreed that he could see his daughter when he was in America.

In May 1899, he wrote asking for his 15 year-old daughter to be delivered to the Albemarle Hotel where he was staying. Her mother told the person who delivered the letter that she was away at a boarding school, the location and name of which she refused to give. When Cynthia was not produced, he went to the Supreme Court and secured a writ of *habeas corpus* in order to have his daughter produced in court the following week.

The grounds on which Mr Burke Roche obtained the writ were that her mother prevented her from going to see him at the Hotel. He claimed that he had frequently seen his daughter since he separated from his wife and believed Cynthia was detained against her will at her mother's residence, 13 East 26th Street, and that she was anxious to see him. The cause of her imprisonment was, as far as he knew, the determination of his wife to prevent his daughter from visiting or seeing him during his stay in the United States. After repeated adjournments, an understanding was reached by which Mr Roche was to be allowed the privilege of seeing his daughter, but not as frequently as had been his custom in former years.

In 1899, the year he obtained the writ to see Cynthia, he was actively engaged in attempting to bring about a sale of the Lakes of Killarney to Tammany Hall[115] politicians. The Muckross estate, which contains the Lakes, was for sale. He failed in his mission and the estate was bought later that year by two Irish

[114] An underground fire caused by the spontaneous combustion of coal waste left on the mine floor.
[115] The Democratic party political machine which dominated politics in New York city. It had strong Irish connections.

peers for £60,000.

The following year he arrived in New York in April as was his custom, and booked in at Holland House (Hotel). He attended the Queen's Birthday anniversary banquet in the hotel on May 24th but then disappeared, without notice. The hotel kept his room until the end of June when they reluctantly put his effects in to storage. His mail piled up and no word was heard from him. "It was his custom to come to this country at frequent intervals; in fact he seldom remained in England a year at a time, and was an often-noted figure in Broadway because of his great stature, his long, sweeping moustache and his typically British bearing."[116]

His friends remembered that he had been reported killed by Indians in 1879 and this gave them hope that he was alive and well. The day after this item appeared in the press, a reporter located him in Washington, at the Arlington Hotel where he had been staying for three months, on strictly private business.

We next hear of him in Dallas Texas where he participated in an oil venture. The following letter was sent to my brother Edmund (5th Lord Fermoy) in 1972.

"Your grandfather arrived in Beaumont, Texas soon after the discovery of the great Spindletop gusher. Immediately he became an object of great fascination; I gather he was regarded as something of a man of mystery, inasmuch as he seems to have disclosed little about his past. Of course it was obvious that he was a man of breeding and education – facts that were often commented on. All agree he possessed great charm as well.

At any rate, in 1902 he took an option on a tract of land at Sour Lake, which lies north of Beaumont. As he had limited capital with him, he could not buy the land itself outright. He therefore enlisted the help of some prominent businessmen who comprised the Texas company, now known as Texaco Inc. They raised the money to exercise his option, and the tract proved immensely productive. It was in fact the start of Texaco's career as an oil company. How much profit your grandfather made from this I am uncertain but he seems to have done well. Shortly after he returned to England."

His oil venture was a success but I imagine his share of the profit was not great, bearing in mind that he put none of his own money into the purchase of the tract. In the same year, Jim became a founder member of the Pilgrims Society, a super-elite, mysterious, British-American society, founded to strengthen ties between the United States and Great Britain. Its membership comprised politicians, diplomats, bankers and businessmen. The name "The Pilgrims" was Jim's idea, expressing the notion of Englishmen and Americans promoting

---

[116] *New York Times*, August 8th 1900.

international friendship through their pilgrimages to and fro across the Atlantic. Joseph Choate, the American ambassador, opposed the idea initially. but was won over and attended the first dinner.[117]

Jim Roche's most astonishing adventure took place in 1904, when he carried out an act of great daring and boldness. He successfully delivered a torpedo boat destroyer, built at the Yarrow shipyard, to the Russian port of Libau, Latvia, one of the main ports of the Russian Empire at that time! The story as reported in newspapers was that he was in conversation with some Russian naval officers in a club in St Petersburg. The Russians were at war with the Japanese.[118] They complained that the Japanese were constantly obtaining ships and munitions from England yet Russia could obtain none, not because the British were unwilling to sell them, but because no Englishman could be found with courage enough to take a boat away and deliver it to Russia.

JBBR was put on his mettle and wagered £500 that he could deliver a boat to any port the Russians named. The offer was accepted and Jim's fertile imagination got to work. He sent a rich American friend to the Glasgow shipyard on the pretext of buying a yacht. Predictably, no yacht was available so he bought a torpedo boat destroyer. Some slight structural alterations were made to convert it to appear to be a yacht. The boat, the *Caroline* was delivered to London where JBBR organised a crew and supplies of food and clothing. The crew took the boat out into the Thames to test the compasses, leaving all their supplies on shore. Suddenly they received instructions to make an unauthorised dash for the open sea. They picked up supplies when they reached Cuxhaven in Germany.

At the eastern end of the Kiel Canal, a German officer refused to believe that the *Caroline* was a yacht and went ashore to make a report. Away went the *Caroline* full speed, ignoring the guns of the German guard ship signalling her to stop! She was well out of range by the time the Germans had got up their heavy ammunition. About sixty miles out from Libau, two cruisers met the *Caroline* and escorted her into port. The crew returned to England in a German steamer. Jim had won his bet!

We do not know how much of his adventures Jim recounted to his boys. He was probably more interested in hearing about their lives. According to family legend, the meeting between the father and his long lost sons was not a success. The boys offered him money and this offended the pride of their father, a proud man, and he brought the meeting to an end.

[117] *The Pilgrims of Great Britain,* p. 13.
[118] Russo-Japanese War February 1904–September 1905.

14

Hither and thither

Maurice and Frank then visited Ireland, staying with their Uncle Alexis and getting to know their cousins Moira, Sheila and Edmund. Their cousin Denis, the fourth sibling, was in Argentina working on a ranch, following the example of his father in Wyoming thirty years earlier.

They went on to tour Europe, visiting Rome, Naples, Pompeii, Florence, Genoa, Venice and Turkey. In April, Aunt Lucy wrote thanking her nephews for their letters from Rome and postcards. Then she invited them to stay with her in London from mid-May, where she has a small house – 25 Norfolk Street, backing on Park Lane. She fears it is tiny and they will have to rough it as there is only one bathroom.

She told them that their grandfather's two houses on 26th street had been sold for $500,000. The running expenses were mounting up dreadfully. Fanny had moved into 18 East 77th street. Shortly after her move, on April 14th, the *Titanic* struck an iceberg and went down with the loss of 1,500 lives. Three days later Fanny wrote an emotional letter to her boys:

"April 17th 1912

My dearest boys,
From Frank a card from Venice saying weather had been perfect etc. Here people frantic and appalled at the *Titanic* disaster: nothing else spoken of. I have been really sick over it. And the later accounts are so much less encouraging than the first. And after all the sympathy with the sufferers and the survivors, what prayers and thanksgiving that neither of you was on board.

I feel that if I had wired you to come, you, Frank, would surely have engaged passage in a new boat. Lucy was told last night that you were on board. I am nervous and fussy. I may wire for consolation. It is all too terrible: speed and useless luxury instead of precaution against accident are the reasons…"

It was only when they wired her from their hotel that she stopped shaking at the possibility that they might have been on board.

Laura Webb, a young friend of Frank, wrote that "the *Titanic* disaster put this country into mourning. Many of the people on the (Fifth) Avenue were dressed in black out of respect and all entertaining was given up for almost a whole week, very remarkable for New York. It is now three weeks since it occurred but it is still the general topic of conversation everywhere."

It was still on Fanny's mind when she wrote to Maurice in May 1912. She is missing them dreadfully and longing for them to come home. At the same time she is glad they are having a good time and will quite understand if they stay on in London with Aunt Lucy...

"Only I do hope Morrie that when you have thoroughly satisfied your curiosity about abroad, you will turn to serious work. It is a very poor occupation for a man to float around and amuse himself.

But oh! My feeling that you might have been on the *Titanic*. I do not think that I could have gone on with life if you boys had been on her; and so there is always so much to be thankful for. How wonderful the people were! It renews one's belief in human nature. But 'the pity of it'. Every word of the investigation proves more and more criminal carelessness.

Good-bye dearest Morrie. I love you both so much & send you both my love & my gladness that you have enjoyed so much.

Mamma"

The following month, Frank went alone to Deauville, while Maurice stayed on in London and played in a real tennis tournament. He wrote to his brother encouraging him to delay his return to Elm Court:

"*25 Norfolk Street, Park Lane, W.*
July 1912

Dear Boy
Lucy and I are delighted that you have found Deauville pleasant; also that there are some people to talk to. Do stay on and have a good time. Newport is always the same and I think you're not coming until later will greatly help in the general comfort of the house. As matters now stand, it looks pretty full if we have Shaw Mclean and any stray visitors.

My days have been pleasantly spent. I have seen Bridget daily and am growing more and more fond of her. I have just bought her a rectangular watch like Cynthia's. The presentation of prizes takes place this pm!!

I have but two days more. Tomorrow I expect to play Mr Foster. I had a good practice yesterday. It means everything for me to win. I hope I won't make such a poor beginning and lose the first three games as I did last time.

Drop me a line at the boat. Give me an outline of what you want done. *Take care of yourself. Maurice."*

Frank came home after three months abroad but Maurice stayed on.

"July 31st 1912
Palace Hotel St Moritz

Dear Mamma

Your letter was forwarded here to me from Paris and I read with interest everything you said about Newport.

Curtis Moffat's mother being taken suddenly ill forced him to give up our intended trip and to leave by the first boat for America. Paris being so very hot, I decided to come straight here – I came down with the Demarests. It is a very long trip as you know from Paris – but we were well repaid for our journey, for we arrived in this heavenly place, where comparatively cool hours are to be had and lovely nights.

Having heard Aunt Lucy discourse on St Moritz and (you) having been to Davos which is so close, I do not have to waste time telling you of the scenic beauties of the place. My room overlooks the lake which is opal in colour, while on the other side rises a high snow-capped mountain. It is a lovely view and I like looking at it very much.

I was glad to find many Newporters here to make the evenings more pleasant here. I sit with Mrs Widener, Mrs Willie Thompson; Mr Charlie Robinson and Fred Baldwin are among the lot. On the whole it is very pleasant here. We play tennis and golf and live a sensible Northeast Harbour life, if you remember what we did there. There is no bad influence here – the hours are early and we all exercise continuously.

I am very much surprised to see how primitive everything is here. Even this hotel looks poorly constructed and the rooms are meagre. However, you cannot always have everything, as we found in the Yellowstone Park – the hardships were plenty but the scenery marvellous.

Frank must be with you all now, telling you of our spring abroad and the interesting things we did. I hated to have him go back and feel selfish at staying. I hope you are finding Newport as pleasant as formerly. It is so easy for me to picture you all in the house together.

I am well, living a perfect life of exercise and rest. I will write again soon.

Much love Maurice"

123

Maurice to Frank, on board the Cunard *Lusitania*:

"Aug.1912

Dear Boy,

I found your wire when I came aboard. Unfortunately, the boat has engine trouble at present, and I hope we shall not have to put in at Liverpool again. It seems she has been ailing the last few voyages, going as badly as 18 knots.

My leaving London was easy as possible. Louis Bruguiere and his mother, Elaine Goelet, the George McFaddens and many familiar faces are aboard. My cabin on E deck is quite large and already I am well settled.

I gave Bridget a watch like Cynthia's which she received with much joy I can hardly make out that girl. She is so indifferent, I don't believe she gives a damn about a man. However, I had courage enough to put over a few this am before I sailed. She has a soft mug – believe me.

I cannot tell you how familiar everything is on this boat – the smell, that living room, the orchestra, everything the same. I have a frightful nightmare of going back. If there is much rain, a poor summer and a few family fights, I shall be up a tree. However the Cunard line will always be running. I hate the thought of going back to the Delaware, Lackawanna & Western. You know very well why I returned last year. I thought it would greatly help my cure.

Boy, as I sit here tonight the event of the last six months come before me. I see St Moritz, Italy and England. How glorious it has all been. Do you think we shall ever be able to do that again? At any rate, I am never going to do anything with the family again. Altho' it was all very nice, it would have been nicer with a motor car and more freedom.

I succeeded in beating a very good player my last day at Prince's – a player who is level with Mr Foster. I played really well beating him 6-1, 6-3 6-2.

Let me know if you have anything to be done for you. I shall be most conscientious and attend to everything. Let me hear about your life in Deauville and don't get into trouble.

Love MR"

The following summer finds him once again in a mountain resort, this time staying at the Homestead in Hot Springs, Virginia. Having spent the summer in Newport, he writes in September to Frank this somewhat reproachful and irritated letter.

"Mid-September 1912

Dear Boy

I suppose you have wondered much why you have not received any news from me all summer. The truth of it is that I never knew where you were to be next. You never told me you were going to St Moritz and when you did get there, you wired me if I advised your going or not. Then you went to Constantinople.

At any rate I am delighted you reached home safely. I had great fears for your catching some awful thing in that distant place. Typhoid is so easily caught and no doubt you have heard that Archie Alexander died of it only a short time ago.

What are your plans? For Heaven's sake, let us consult each other at length as to our future. What are you going to do, where are you to be? I have opened your mail and you may be much surprised the only thing worth saving was your steel dividend of April 1st.

I had a very unsatisfactory summer in Newport. Truthfully I hated it all. I almost knew I would. I began wrong, having met Miss Milholland at sea, she then came to Newport, and [I] being a weak individual, she tried to run my days and I did one thing after another till I was bored to death. I practically lived at the Marble House,[119] and spent most of my days doing the things I never wanted to do.

I am going to await your letter. I am done with Newport and that life, so if you wish me to join you in town, I shall do so, but not in Newport. I assure you I shall never spend a summer there again. Somehow it is not the same place it used to be.

I find Hot Springs a very dull place. There is nobody here I know and I don't know why I ever came. What boat did you return on? Do sit down and give me some idea of what you are going to do. Tell me what you have done etc.

I wish I had more to say. Newport was quite like other years, tho' I didn't care for any of the dances – for I wasn't drinking. I fell off the night of Mrs Cornelius Vanderbilt's, as Mamma will probably tell you.

How is your condition? Let me know if you have had any worries. I am not so sure about myself. I feel pretty well; have been playing a good deal of tennis, tho' badly.

I am anxious to hear, so do give me some details.

Much love, Maurice"

A few days later he was reassured when a letter arrived from Frank:

---

[119] Opulent house faced in pink marble, built by Alva Vanderbilt, wife of the Commodore's grandson.

"The Homestead, Hot Springs, VA
Sept 20th 1912

Dear Boy,

I was delighted to get your letter this morning as it gave me some idea of your plans and a look into the future. I want to first answer the points you brought up in your letter in order not to omit anything.

I have already sent £100 to the Bank in Cork that Moira[120] asked me to make the deposit to. It should have reached her about the first of the month, as I sent it about August 20th from Newport.

About the fancy dress, I arrived at the Colfords without a domino.[121] In the men's dressing room, somebody gave me a white striped one to wear, which I did, but as I did not know its owner, I left it on the bed in the room and came away in my regular dress clothes. Just say that the fancy costume was left at the Colfords.

Boy, Mrs Conover asked me one day during the tennis tournament to come out and see her. Well I never went. A short time ago, she wrote me a hard-luck letter, and wanted $3,000, which I think is a good big sum of coin. Well, you know that there are lots of things we must do in this world that one does not want to. Mrs Conover certainly is a lady and I am sure she must be up against it with her husband making no money. Well, I sent her a check for one thousand dollars.

I am glad you found *Wilhelm II* such a nice boat. I shall never go on the *Lusitania* again. We were a day late getting in, and besides, as you know it never pays to do the same thing twice.

I have been corresponding all summer with Bridget and she is anxious for me to return. I am considerably up a tree as to what I shall do. Do you think your travelling is over?

We are having quite good fun here. Oliver Harriman is here. They dance every night. As I said in my last letter I am leaving here Sept 27th arriving in town on Saturday am. I hope you can arrange to be there on that date. Tell me something about what you intend doing. I am anxious to go back abroad about Jan 1st. I want to take in Egypt next winter. Wouldn't you?

I am glad you bought yourself a watch. I don't see why you got stuck $42.00 duty when I got in with all the winter things, my new tennis bag, all for $13.50. There must be different systems.

Tell me all the latest.

Love Maurice"

---

[120] His first cousin Moira Roche, daughter of Alexis Burke Roche.
[121] A fancy dress costume with a mask, worn at a masquerade.

(Mrs Conover's letter from Concord asked Maurice and Frank to help a young farmer and his family who had fallen on bad times through ill health and the destruction of his house and stock by a bad storm. "The poor fellow & his wife have come pretty near to the end of their rope. They have five young children. Winter is facing them without coal [prices almost prohibitory – $10 a ton] & the house in unfit condition to live in & a mere shed only hastily thrown up out of old lumber for his horse to shelter in.")

The Homestead, Hot Springs.
Sept 24th 1912

Dear Boy,

I am delighted you are having such an excellent time, and that Newport has been so pleasant. I assure you I shall never spend a summer there again. Somehow it is not the same place it used to be. I really did not have a good time this summer. You were right in coming back just when you did and everything was fresh and new to you.

I gave quite a nice lunch party yesterday. There were 14 of us, up at Daniel Burn's cabin. I had some corn and on the whole it was rather good fun.

I spent several nights in town before I came here and I was most comfortable. The woman cooks well and is quite good enough for breakfast. There is no use in having additional expense. We can easily live in the town house and eat outside.

Am I to see you in town on Saturday? The Wiborgs, who were down for Russell Sard's wedding, asked me down to Easthampton for the weekend but the journey and my lack of interest in that family has not enough to force me to make the trip.

I am looking forward to my departure Friday. I don't see much attraction in this place. Certainly it is very much overrated – for I don't think it is pretty and there is not such a lot to do.

Send all mail to NY.

love Maurice"

Maurice spent the autumn in New York, working hard and playing hard, until he left on his travels a fortnight before Christmas. The following letter describes his ocean crossing on the Cunard line RMS *Mauretania*:

127

*Miss
Angelica
Brown and
Mr Maurice
Roche
doing a
Russian
dance at a
fancy dress
ball*

Dec. 1912

Dear Boy,

This trip has been like every other voyage. We were lucky to have the most glorious weather the first few days. It was as smooth as one would find it in July. I sat about on the top deck and wished you had been with me to enjoy the sunshine and warm air. The smell of the ocean gave me the sensation it was summer. Again I am on E deck and with Arthur's[122] services and a good bath steward, I am excellently taken care of. My day is much as we have had together. Called at 9.30, a cold bath. Breakfast. Walking – lunch – bridge – tea – dinner – listening to music. Bed.

---

[122] His valet who accompanied him on his travels, as was the custom for a gentleman of means. Ladies took their personal maid, families a nanny for the children.

I have a nice seat in the dining room with the Frank Blakes, Sam Chew and Charlie Winslow. We have an amusing time and pass our meal pleasantly. I am the only one who comes up for breakfast. The time has passed quickly, for already (it seems but like yesterday I sailed), we are but a little more than a day away. They tell us we shall expect to dock early Monday morning and be in London 3pm. Monday. I shall mail your letters as soon as I get in London.

Besides the people already mentioned there is Schofield Andrews & Pearl Bodine, from SPS [St Paul's Scool], Sir H Beerbohm Tree[123] and Tita Ruffo[124] whom I have met, and he has given me his photo and autograph. I have also played some cards with him.

But, Boy, everything else is the same – the elevators rush up and down, the steam shoots the coal out of the boat as usual, the dinner bugles and everything that pertains to daily routine is much the same. I always have the same opinion – that it's a big long haul across the ocean; and that there is very little fun attached. The women aboard are too awful.

I hope you may find time to write often. Send me clippings of engagements and any deaths that might interest me. I wish I knew who won the SPS game with Yale. I shall write continually.

Today the boat is rolling somewhat. We are having rainy weather, and it is cold and grey. Tomorrow, Sunday, I shall finish this.

Sunday
Another glorious day! I thought of you this morning in Massachusetts. I could picture everything at home and see things as I left them. Boy, never have I had such a crossing. The boat has not made a dozen lurches in the entire trip. Absolutely calm the entire time. Today they tell us we shall dock at 8am and are in London at about 3pm.

I propose going to Claridge's and if any of my friends whom I have written to are in London, I shall call. In the evening, I am going to take in a play. If there is a good waltz, I shall buy it and send over.

Boy, now don't be discontented with yourself. Travelling isn't what one dreams it to be. I have been rather wishing I had taken some job and settled this winter in town. I hope everything turns out right. I am wondering a good deal how [Aunt] Lucy's plans will come out, and if I shall really go to Egypt.

I have not much more to say. Take care of yourself. I intend being on the wagon & non-smoking. Don't let your nerves play havoc with you. I am sure you will have an excellent time and a good winter. My advice is – don't go ahead too fast. *Love, Maurice"*

---

[123] Sir Herbert Beerbohm Tree 1853-1917, English actor-manager.
[124] Italian baritone, famous operatic singer in first 30 years of the twentieth century.

On arrival in London Maurice wrote an enthusiastic letter to Frank, extolling the beauty of the countryside and London and Christmas time:

"Claridges Hotel, Brook Street. W

Dear Boy,
We arrived safely and I cannot tell you with what delight the beautiful English country met my eyes. It all looked more lovely than ever.

I spent the afternoon buying shirts, socks, pumps. I went with Tappe to see 'The Dancing Maid' – Gertie Millar's[125] new show, not over good. London certainly is great. Every smell and noise brought back last summer's memories. I fully intend being here another season if necessary. Christmas is a great event and the shops are gay with much decoration.

I posted your letters. I am off to Paris this pm. I hope to leave the following night for St Moritz. Hope you are well.

Much love, Maurice"

"Hotel de Crillon, Place de la Concorde, Paris
Christmas Day, 1912

Dear Boy,
My last letter told of my arrival and evening in London, that being Dec 23rd & 24th. Yesterday I spent the morning getting money, a high hat and hair cut.

I caught the 2.20 Charing Cross and had an uneventful trip to Paris, except that the Channel crossing was too rough for words. It was then that I appreciated your suggestion of bringing the fur coat. There was however no necessity of my having it on the ocean. Everybody very ill, but I not a bit.

My arrival at the Gard du Nord was as hitherto. Unable to get a taxi, I embarked with Arthur in a horse rig, and we soon were at the [Hotel] Crillon. Paris was all ablaze, the streets full of people, even the restaurants in the streets were crowded with people sitting having their drinks. The weather was mild. It had rained some of the day. At the Crillon, I find a note from Lucy telling me to come around; so with Arthur's aid I jumped into my evening clothes. I had made a point of having them ready.

I never imagined the Ritz could be so full. I soon found out why. It was the opening of the new part of the Hotel, and the management had invited the elite of Paris – and for their breakfast, in the new ball room, had a sort of vaudeville show. It was impossible to get a seat in the room. I found Lucy and Cooper. She looked well and after a talk and outline of the trip,

---
[125] Gertie Millar, popular star of musical comedies 1900-1915

she said goodnight, and went off to bed. I returned to the reception and fell in with Madame Mazinoff and Julia Thompson. Mazinoff said she had received a card from you and asked many questions. They invited me to have supper with them, which I did.

Boy, all Paris was present Casati,[126] Letaillier, Blumenthals, Graves etc, etc. We had supper in the hall as usual – and tables ran to the front door. How strange it was to be back again! Everything just the same. Numerous people asked after you. By the time supper was over it was 1am. Determined tho' to make a night of it, we returned to the ballroom where dancing was in order. Unfortunately Julie never let me go for several dances, so my dancing was confined to her and Mazinoff. The Casati had gone when I searched for her.

At 3am, Julie and I went to Ciro's but the mob was something awful. Christmas Eve is as great a night as New Year's with us. Everybody was tight, balls were being thrown around, confetti, streamers and general hell was raised. We decided not to stop, so walked to the Café de Paris where I saw the same thing. I then took her home and we talked and I found myself home here at 5am. I had had so much rest and not having had anything to drink I was not in the least bit tired.

Arthur called me 10.00; I shaved and stopped at a flower shop to order a plant for Lucy. What a queer Christmas it has been! I found Lucy & Cooper and we lunched Ritz, few people. I saw Scorville afterwards and we have decided to go from here Friday to St Moritz. Boy, Cooper was not nice at lunch. He refused to go to the play and Aunt Lucy looked hurt. That damn Bruguiere woman of course is at the bottom of it all. She came over with him as Scorville told me all about it; and she is here bothering the life out of him. You well know the kind.

At 3 pm, Lucy & I motored out towards Versailles. It was a beautiful day and as we motored along, I thought of you all. I really cannot make myself realize I am <u>here</u>. The Arc de Triomphe recalled so much! I thought of Robbin's party last night and also of this day at home. I feel so selfish having left everything for so little here.

The plans brief as they are, are as follows. The boat is not ready until Jan 15th. I find I can get a boat from Marseille Jan 8th in time. Lucy wants to motor down. I don't...[pages missing]"

The next letter was an ecstatically happy one from St Moritz:

---

[126] The Marchesa Luisa Casati was a scandalous *femme fatale*, famous in European society in the first part of twentieth century.

"Dear Boy

I hardly thought I could have such a good time as it has been here. It has been a week of heaven. In the first place absolutely every moment of the time I have been here, it has been sunshine, cloudless days and glorious skating. The ice on the bandy rink[127] has never been finer. During the past week, I have been working to make the team, and I am glad to say I am representing St Moritz, Sunday, in their game against Davos. The game is advertised everywhere. I have been doing well, making about 2, 3 or 4 goals a day.

Yesterday they had the annual gymkhana. I entered three events with Mrs Littlefield; and we won two of them. In all the events, there were several heats and we came in first every time, except in the final of the spade race. This race consisted of the lady skating the length of the rink with a snow shovel and when she crossed the line, she sat on the spade and the man pushed her back. In the final, Mrs Littlefield being over-anxious, failed completely to sit on the spade and in the mix-up we came in 4th.

In the balloon race I got down first with my balloon, and Mrs L won easily on the return. In the ski and skate, I won by hard work and with the advance of my Lunn's skates. I got two prizes, a stick pin and silver paper cutter. There must have been a thousand spectators easily.

The other night they had a fancy dress ball at the Kulm [Hotel]. As I expected, my costume was much admired. I am wearing the same here tomorrow night at their dance.

I must tell you of the Davos game that took place today. St Moritz won by 9-0. We never had any close shots like last year. The Davos team was too good to allow that. I must say our team was a corker, Cutter and I working together made six goals by perfect team work. Their goal stopped one of my shots in the air with his stick. There were quite a number of people present. I don't want to bore you any more with accounts of games.

I have certainly profited by my twelve days here. Each morning I have been up early to take photos and I shall send them back by Luis Trendwell to be put in the Album.

I have missed you very much. I have often thought of you these cloudless days at work in town. I often stop to think, and cannot realize that I am on this side of the ocean. I hope everything is peaceful at home. I am so anxious that you shall have just as happy a time as I.

Lucy said in Paris that she intended coming back through Algiers by motor. I hope not. I want to take in the Riviera and Paris and London. I am leaving here Wednesday, going down the Maloja Pass and on to Naples where I join the steamer for Egypt. I shall write you at length from the

---

[127] Bandy was field hockey on skates, played on a rink the size of a soccer field.

boat.

Take care of yourself. I am looking very well and haven't had a drink as yet – or a smoke.   *MR*"

15

Journey down the Nile

E arly in the New Year 1913, Maurice boarded a ship of the Norddeutscher
Lloyd Line, at Naples, bound for Alexandria in Egypt where he met Aunt
Lucy and Uncle Cooper:

"*Hotel Excelsior Naples*
Jan 9th 1913

Dear Boy,
I am here for the night waiting to board my ship tomorrow for Alexandria.
I wish so you were along. The journey from St Moritz here has been rather
lonely with Arthur. In brief I made the sleigh-coach drive down the Maloja
as last year, arriving at Milan 5.45pm. I then took the night train for Rome
where I arrived at 8.50am today.

Upon my arrival at the Grand Hotel, I found out that Mrs Oliver was
there. I sent up word asking that I might see her. When I was shown up, she
was rather short and sore because you had failed to send her any word for
two or more weeks. Whatever it was, to me she seemed commoner than
ever. Dressed in a riding habit, she was about to go hunting with Sangria.
Her voice also seemed worse to me than ever and I hated my visit. Boy
please don't send her a line and let her go as she pleases.

My train did not go until 1.35pm so I walked around the Borghese
Park, which was still as lovely as ever – I thought of you, Andrews, Curtis.

I am extremely well thanks to St M and my moderate habits. Don't go
and feel that you have to get married – how I love my freedom at this
moment. I am anxiously waiting the first glimpse of the Egyptian shore.

Love MR"

Aunt Lucy, Uncle Cooper and Maurice took a Thomas Cook cruise down the
Nile in the Steam Ship *Sudan*, one of the largest and most luxurious ships of the
fleet. This was the Belle Epoque of Nile cruises, pioneered by Thomas Cook in
from 1877. In 1881 he built the Hotel Cataract at Aswan, where it was necessary
to change ships in order to visit the temple of Abu Simbel.

A cruise on the SS *Sudan* lasted twenty days – a round-trip tour from Cairo to Aswan. Sixty to eighty passengers occupied three decks, with mini-suites on the top deck and small but comfortable cabins on the lower decks. Travellers brought staff with them, a valet for a gentleman, a personal maid for a lady, a nanny for children, and the vessel was organised with these needs in mind. In the front of the ship, there was a studio for artists who wanted to paint the banks of the Nile in watercolour. There were lounges for playing games and a smoking lounge for men.

Maurice wrote frequently to Frank and his mother during his cruise:

"SS Sudan'

Dear Mamma and Boy,

I want to thank you for your two letter of Jan 3th & 6th. I hope Frank has been showing my joint letters to you two, for I have written them with that purpose. I am delighted you had such a pleasant Christmas, and I read with interest every detail of what you did during that week. Your letter, I am glad to say, has the right tone and I am sure you are getting no end of pleasure out of your concerts, acquaintances and the many plans you are thinking over.

We are at present 'doing' Luxor & 'Karnak'. It has meant many long hours and hot rides across desert country to the tombs. But of course we have been repaid. I think it is all <u>too</u> wonderful. Personally, I prefer the tombs to the temples. The temples are in too great a stage of destruction to hardly give any idea – except in respect to the pillars and monolithic statues. To me the painted tombs, so much better preserved, and the coloration, is much more inspiring. But I have liked it all. We have entered with interest every cave, climbed over fallen pillars, crossed desert country to see it all. Cooper, with his scientific mind, and Mrs Cameron with her great knowledge, have helped a great deal towards it all.

I have gotten to know Mrs Cameron. She is a very kind and good woman. Her marriage has been a failure. But how else could it be! How can a woman find a peaceful home when she marries a man, widower, with a house full of grown children! She also has made herself very agreeable at meals and is most prompt for every excursion. She arrives always five minutes early for meals – which is <u>right</u>. We have had several talks together and she has very much the same ideas about life as you. Her ideas are normal and her experiences in life have given her a very sane mind. It is needless to say that she has spoken highly in every way about you. She is so tactful and clever; she never asks questions and is the least inquisitive woman I have ever met. She has given us the statement that she never gossips and so far she never has.

Today we have been busy looking over our photos, taken thus far. Mine are really too good. I have three dozen without a failure! Picturing every side of the native life – sailing vessels, camels, villages etc. I have placed them safely away and will have them mounted when I return. Cooper has had few good ones – he tries to take too many fancy ones; Lucy's are mediocre.

I am glad to report that Cooper's health and disposition has greatly improved. He is far less nervous. He seems to really enjoy things and the inscriptions have given him no end of amusement.

The other evening we went out on the desert to try and shoot some jackals, a specie of wolf. Cooper and his man saw one. I didn't but the delightful sunset and moon gave me a great sensation.

I trust you gather I am loving this trip. In the first place, by taking no coffee, drinks or cigarettes, my nerves no longer exist. In this frame of mind, I see everything in a normal way. I have each morning as I get up no regrets. I have made each day a golden one. Never have I enjoyed life so much. Of course I realize that one cloudless day after another does cheer me up, but still one must be normal to have the pleasures of life. Excitement followed by the reaction gives one unhappiness of one sort.

Tell Frank that I have paid my Knickerbockers [Club] dues; he wrote that he had just given them a check.

On my return to Paris, I shall have my portrait done by Boldini; I have the measures of Frank's. I find I am rambling. Write often if only a line. I hope the motor gives satisfaction. Don't let Frank make any foolish marriage – there is plenty of time

My best love
Maurice"

"*SS Sudan, Cook's Nile Service.*
Jan 25th

Dear Boy

We left Luxor after four days stay. I must say I found that place most interesting and the time passed too pleasantly. All our excursions to the Kings' tombs and temples were full of new sensation – for the first time in my life I found riding a joy. Of course I only rode a donkey, but still a donkey can gallop and that was such fun.

The tombs of the Kings are situated some four or five miles back from the river. Try and picture the palisades that distance from the Hudson, with the intervening distance, first farmland and the desert country. That is the condition here. Our dahabeeyah[128] was situated at the east bank of the Nile, and it was necessary when we made the visit to the tomb, to row across to the west bank. Upon our arrival there, we found donkeys waiting and soon we were galloping back towards the sandstone cliffs. Try and remember a glorious July day, and wonderful grass perfumes in the air, clear sky – that is what we had.

I think we visited six or eight of the shafts that led down into the ground. They were lighted by electricity. The walls were covered with pictures and all in color. These tombs have only been opened since 1904, by a Mr Theodore Davis, who lives in Newport, Ocean Drive. In most cases, the mummies have been taken to the Cairo Museum, but in one, Ramassis II, he still lies as he was buried 3,000 years ago. They have a glass case over the coffin. I can't describe how wonderful it is to be 300 feet below ground and to be in a room that has painted scenes of the dead man's life – his excursions to foreign lands, the return with prisoners, pictures of his life, his relations, birds, farm yard animals, cattle, and also men in active trades. I was greatly impressed by it all. We had lunch out near the tombs and came back at dusk.

Last night we dined with the Hamilton Carys at the Winter Hotel, Luxor. There was nothing unusual there – a very sad looking crowd of people. I forgot to say that I spent one pm playing tennis. I saw an asphalt court at the hotel and through a gentleman, had myself invited into a foursome. I played quite well. I could win from all the other men, they played about as well as Arthur Burden. My stomach muscles are all sore today from serving.

I wonder if you are coming over this spring? I have almost surely decided to stay over till the first of June. I want to get some tennis both in Paris and London. At any rate I want to have your advice on how things stand at home, what I must come back to and what for. I do feel happy to be on this side of the ocean.

My plan in London would be to go to either Claridges or Cavendish. I think the Cavendish would be better on account of its proximity to the Ritz.

I have read the St Paul's School report very carefully. I think the school is in excellent shape and hope Drury makes a big school out of it. If you and I are prudent with our money, we might devise a scheme whereby we set aside so much each year, in a SPS fund at some bank and by putting in from time to time a check, we might be able, every ten or fifteen years, to give them a building. By 1915, which will be our tenth anniversary, I shall have $60,000 saved up. We might combine some of this and give them

---

[128] Thomas Cook pioneered the use of Dahabeeyahs – shallow, flat-bottomed barges with two masts, fitted out as very luxurious houseboats for tourism on the Nile.

something nice. The more I see of these tombs, the more I wish to construct – think of the thousands of boys who would benefit by our gifts. And there is money well spent. Parties and balls don't count for much. There is nothing to show for it.

I feel as tho' it were the beginning of August. We have such clear and warm days – just as it was in Palm Beach 1911 – that it is difficult to believe that I shall be going back to spring weather after this trip is over.

Do give me full accounts of NY. Tell me something about how the motor is running and any engagements that may take place. I shall be glad when we get home for the Nile is a monotonous place. I thought I would get some shooting but the birds are as afraid as they would be in America.

Hope you are having a good time, take care of yourself.

My best love Maurice

"SS Sudan
Jan 30th 1913

Dear Boy and Mama
At 12.30pm today, we reached our southernmost point. It is here where our trip ends and from now on we force the SS *Sudan* home. I cannot say how really sorry I am. It certainly has been a wonderful experience – with each successive visit more interesting than the last. Today certainly was a climax, for we came to Abu-Simbel where there is, in my mind, the finest rock tomb of its kind. The entrance to the tomb has four sitting figures 65 feet in height. They are most impressive for they have been hewn out of the solid rock face. The proportions are perfect, so that you don't get the idea that there is too much of anything.

A rather queer thing happened when we were at the tomb. I saw a man carrying a cane and soon I came to where he was standing. Somehow the conversation started and in a few moments I discovered I was talking to Edward R Thomas.[129] I could hardly believe I had come face to face with the man I had so often wished to see. Later I found he was passing his honeymoon here. He gave me directions for dove shooting and immediately I set off that afternoon after tea to look for some. I saw them flying about the trees but they were very shy. However with stalking I managed to get 4, I killed one on the wing. They are pretty birds, having brown and gray trimmings.

I must tell you of our two days at Aswan. It is there where the English have placed the enormous dam. It is 130 feet high and one and a half miles long. When you think it is 98 feet wide at the base, some idea of the work

[129] President of the Seventh National Bank.

can be had. Most tourist steamers make Aswan their tour's end. But we decided to go up to the second cataract. There are four locks one goes thro' in order to mount the dam; they are very short but large lifts. It took us about a half hour to get up. The dam holds back the water in a lake about fifty miles in length and this is let out during the summer months for irrigation and by July 1st it is entirely empty. The Nile then begins to flood and remains so until Dec 1st. Towards the end of Dec. they close the sluices and catch the water by degrees until Feb 1st (now) when the dam has its full capacity. The amount of revenue it brings in to the people is 15 million dollars a year thus far. All most interesting in the development of the country. It cost Cooper $15 to go through the canal.

At the Savoy Hotel, Aswan, I met Mr Nurse and with his son and tutor, we had a very good four in tennis. I won 3 sets with the son against Nurse and tutor. It was an asphalt court and with new balls the game went well. I have missed you so for exercise on this trip. If you had only been along, we could have had lots of tennis, also what an excellent opportunity of learning telegraphy.[130] I practice continuously but that is never the same. What I need is to receive. As usual I wish I had brought a foot-ball, for there are excellent sand beaches when we tie up at dusk, but as nobody can kick, it isn't much use.

If I come again, I shall also bring a typewriter, for the motion is fierce, much worse than any liner (as you can see by my writing). Also tennis balls, a good rifle, better camera. If possible a single scull would be a great addition, for in the afternoons one could row an hour or two for exercise. As the boat has to keep in the Channel of the meandering river, cutting the corners and going across the shallow water would easily enable one to keep up.

This pm we reach Aswan again. Do write me what you intend doing this year. I think I shall come home by way of South America, so I can take in the Panama Canal. I would like to leave about July 10th for Buenos Ayres (sic) and go up by way of Chili (sic). Do you think you could join me to make that excursion? I wish you could see how well I look. I have a good tan and have not had a cigarette this year. Am still on the wagon.

Remember me to everybody. Don't forget details, clippings – marriages, engagements, etc.

Take care of yourself
Love Maurice"

---

[130] A telegraph machine transmits words using the Morse code, along a wire connecting two points a distance apart. When a key is pressed a pulse of electricity is sent along the wire— dots if the key is pressed quickly, dashes if it is pressed for three times longer.

"Feb 5th 1913

Dear Boy

I was delighted upon reaching Aswan the other day, to find your large envelope with the latest. I cannot thank you enough for all the trouble you have taken and how complete it all is. It was dated Jan 9th so I hope to get another today as we return to Luxor on our downward journey. I think we shall probably run into Elsie Vanderbilt[131] and her party. They ought to be somewhere about here. I must say I think it is cheap enough for her to be entertaining all those people at Alfred's expense. I certainly won't put myself out to see any of her crowd except Mrs Ames.

The other evening I engaged a man and went jackal shooting. Jackals are very much like coyotes and come in from the desert at night to prowl around villages. My guide had a place baited up so we left just about an hour before sunset. We rode donkeys out to the outskirts of the desert and dismounting we walked some ten minutes and came to a place where there was a half-eaten carcass. About forty yards away, we placed ourselves in a circular blind made of stones. We placed some fresh meat about and hid in the blind. It was very uncomfortable, so cramped up. Just about at sundown, we prepared for the jackals. I had a 12-gauge gun and No. 1 shot, also the .22 automatic. It was just getting dark when I noticed a dark object coming across the sand. I saw it first and touching my guide brought his attention to it. Well I shot but too soon and altho I wounded the beast it managed to get away.

Luxor

I was delighted to get your letters upon my arrival here this pm. I had my hair cut and a shave and went over to see Elsie Vanderbilt's boat. I saw them all. I am delighted not to be on that boat. They all seem to be "hooping" it up. At any rate, I have arranged for a tennis doubles tomorrow. We should have a good game, I will write results later.

This evening J P Morgan arrived. I called around and saw Helen Hamilton who was suffering with a bad ear: She spoke of having seen you before sailing. My conversation was interrupted by Mrs L and Miss P –two dreadful bores. I excused myself soon afterwards. As for bills I am paying them as fast as you send them to me. Don't bother about paying anything. I wish you had not taken so much pains in the Knickerbocker Club and hope you will get my check in exchange.

I also received a letter from Cynthia. Nothing in it, except that she said there was an article on St Moritz mentioning me as being a good bandy (ice hockey) player. I got a letter from George Scott, Tuxedo thanking me

---

[131]   Ex-wife of Alfred Vanderbilt.

for some photos I sent of the Cresta run. He said that he had had them mounted and placed in the hall for the benefit of the Toboggan Club.

I hope you undertake a trip of some sort to Panama. If you get off for the summer, we might go to Buenos Ayres or South Africa. I hate to think of you being in town for the summer and Newport is so unsatisfactory. It means late hours and fights. That has gone out of my life and I hope I shall not be there again for any length of time. Please continue to give me all the news. Grateful for any news from school. This is a scrappy letter. However have a good time and don't for heaven's sake get married yet. I rejoice each night that I am free. It means a lot of worry and no fun. At 40 yes. Grandpa is the best example we can follow. Certainly, he had an ideal life.

My best love, give me more clippings and details.

MR

Lucy enjoyed her letter immensely."

"Feb 11th 1913

Dear Boy,

We spent almost a week at Luxor. It was a week of tennis, hunting and sightseeing. The tennis I had with Philip Livermore, Lothrop Ames and Gordon Douglas. It was good fun as we all played our games. Philip Livermore asked me to play singles afterwards and I was much surprised when I beat him 6-3, 6-2. I always thought he could beat me. He has a very good Lawford stroke but I stopped that by playing to his backhand and giving him hard services. Gordon Douglas played the best, I think; he has a beautiful eye – and volleys without mistakes. There was a large gallery.

Uncle Cooper engaged some guides to try and get us an eagle. Well it was a damned expensive proposition. In the first place, we paid a guinea for a has-been donkey. This in turn was led out to the foot hills of the cliffs and dispatched. This mornings after we set out on donkeys at 8am to see what had turned up. The donkey had begun to decay and several vultures hovered about. Uncle Cooper sat in one blind and I in another. I had the fore-legs as decoy and he the rest. Our blind was made of mud and palm leaves. From above, it was impossible to see in. There was an opening facing the decayed meat to shoot from.

It wasn't long before I heard a loud thud on the ground, and looking out discovered a huge buzzard standing by the meat. The guide told me not to shoot, as it would decoy an eagle. It did not remain long and presently flew over to where Cooper was. I thought he would shoot it, but I found later his man had told him the same thing. However it was now getting near noon and when the buzzard came over to me, I raized my gun and gave him a bunch of No. 3 shot which did the business. He was about the size of a turkey and was brown.

I returned the next day alone but there were no birds to be seen. I did see some eagles hovering but they were at great heights. I managed to shoot about 8 wild pigeons. They are easy and one finds them in the trees, also a sparrow hawk. We also went jackal shooting again I lost an excellent chance by being asleep. I was watching two that were walking about the desert when suddenly one ran right by the blind from behind a rock. Of course I never even shot.

Boy, if I ever come again I shall bring a high-powered rifle, some steel traps and decoys. I could have a glorious time, for with the steel traps one could just sit and watch the jackals, wolves and hyenas walk into them. If you and I both came I would get a fake donkey outfit for the quantities of heron, cranes and ducks would be easy victims. They don't seem to mind animals and with you and I working such a rig, we could walk right near and get some fine shots- they line the banks but fly when either a boat or person approached. Also wooden bird decoys would be good.

If we could manage to come together, we could buy a pair-oared boat and by taking the Adriatic, land at Alexandria and put it on the Dahabeeyah there. Each afternoon we could row an hour or so – but we could cut corners and certainly do 6 miles. Also I would have a typewriter. It is damn near impossible to write as you can see by the class of this letter.

We also had the good fortune to visit two tombs that had been recently opened by Mr Davis. Nobody else had ever been there, and the whole experience was interesting for things looked so fresh and the colour of the paintings had been unchanged by the many thousand years of buried life. The sarcophagi were still there.

Boy, if you have any money I think it would be nice to give the Halcyon and Shattucks each a new shell. We could easily collect six hundred dollars a piece and give them a surprise. You could write to Davey in Cambridge and find out what the shells cost. They could be presented on May 15th the day of our birth. Please continue to send Horae[132] and such details of interest. I have paid the bills you have sent me.

I hate to think that out trip is about over. The days continue like the weather we had at Palm Beach; just such days as we experienced at the house boat that day we fished etc. I hope you are well. I am perfectly positive my trouble is over. I have not a regret, nearly six months on the wagon and no cigarettes this year. Much love. I miss you very much. Thank you for sending the mail as you do.

Maurice"

[132]   *Horae Scholasticae* – St Paul's School magazine.

142

The last letter from the Nile:

"Feb 16th 1913

Dear Boy,
This is our last Sunday on the Nile. Also but two days remain. We are now anchoring on the outskirts of Cairo, and from my window I can see the Pyramids in the distance. The Pyramids certainly are impressive looking things. I have always had a great desire to see them, since our course in Fine Arts 3 with Chase. I am determined to climb to the very top. Uncle Cooper says he will do it with me. I shall write you that trip.

If the Nile trip has not been sufficient in pointing out great historic monuments, it certainly gives me the idea where old age should be spent. This life is ideal for such a period. In the first place, the climate is ideal, perfect. Then there are no horrors, no worries and troubles. I never have had the sensation that this life has given me. The air which has always the smell of spring for it comes from the enormous fields of wheat, sugar cane and barley. I just delight in breathing in long breaths as I start off each morning on a donkey ride. Each day is like a fine June or July day with us.

Then it is very important to be comfortable. In my white panel room, I had everything laid out. I find great comfort in my flannel trousers, my sweater and panama hat. We always return in time for tea, which is so well given – the crew also are excellent men; dressed in white with red sashes. They dust you off, bring hot water and it is so pleasant to have tea, looking towards a setting sun. I have also used the telegraph machine to keep my hand in.

My one regret has been that you have not been with me. How many things we could have done together! My, right opposite is the most wonderful hard mud flat to kick a football you have ever seen! We could also throw balls, run behind the carriages, telegraph together and I suppose you could have just as well been along. I am sure business has been very bad and you probably have not sold much. Besides I think you needed a rest, you were so nervous and thinking about yourself. Sightseeing cures all that.

Anyway I hope to come again, next time by train, for the distances are too great by boat and the train service is marvellous. Boy, the Pullman coaches are all painted white and of course that makes them very cool. Next trip I shall go to Khartoum. A man told me it is a great place for lawn tennis. They have something like 40 courts there. But you must come next time.

Lucy and I go to Rome and then expect to do some motoring in Sicily. I don't see any use getting back to Paris before April 1st; we are going back by way of the Riviera stopping at Mrs Curtis. I hope I get to Spain to see a bull-fight. This June I should like very much to go to Buenos Ayres. Would like to go about July 10th.

You must write often and tell me what you think. I simply hate the thought of ever returning to America. Unless you kill yourself working, there is not a thing to do. For heaven's sake, don't think of getting married yet. I don't think there is any girl that I feel like giving up my freedom for yet. Each day I thank my stars that no woman can make me do what she wants me to. Hope everything is well.

MR"

"*March 1st*

Dear Boy,
Our three days trip to Naples is already over. It has been too smooth, and perfect in every respect. The Drexels very kindly asked me to their table and it has been nice talking over Newport and my life. Alice certainly takes a prize for being a bone-head. She is uglier every day, poor thing.

Boy, the day before I sailed, I saw about big game shooting. If I can manage to go, I would start from Kartoum on Jan 15th next year, and take a boat, hunting each day from the boat. Major Maddock said it was by far the most satisfactory thing to do. You go up the Blue Nile. There are plenty of elephants, hippos and small game. When you sight game, you tie up and chase them. By such a method, you can be most comfortable and there is practically no danger of being bitten by insects & catching fever.

I want to acknowledge another envelope the day previous to my leaving Cairo. Thanks very much for the Horae, and do please enclose it every time it comes to the house. I can hardly believe that tomorrow I shall be in Rome. I shall go to see Lowrie.

Give me some plans for the summer. Why can't you join me and we could go on a trip together to Australia, or somewhere where we won't have to dance or do the society act. I fully intend staying in London for at least a month. Hope you are enjoying your trip to Palm Beach.

Much love Maurice."

16

Maurice acts in haste

The visit to Rome did not go as planned! Despite his talk about no girl taking his freedom away from him, and all his advice to his brother Frank to delay entering the marriage game, seven weeks after his arrival in Rome, the *New York Times* of April 19th carried the announcement of the engagement of Maurice Burke Roche to Ysabel d'Alcedo, daughter of the Duke of Alcedo. Ysabel was bowled over by the handsome, tanned, fit young man who blew in to Rome, intending to stay a short while and then to go motoring in Sicily with his aunt! Maurice after weeks of looking at tombs and the monotonous Nile, leading a life of abstinence of all kinds, clearly fell head over heels in love with Ysabel.

The engagement was short-lived, as is revealed in the following letter from her angry father, written on June 2nd 1913:

"Villa Alcedo, Biarritz

Sir, This morning I received by post, anonymously, a cutting from the New York periodical 'Town Topics' of 22nd May. The article, written in terms which I find insulting, claims that you broke off your engagement to my daughter because I demanded that you pay my debts. Apart from the fact that I do not owe a sou to anyone, you know better than anyone else how libellous and untrue this accusation is.

I imagine that you would not wish to add this latest wrong to those you have already inflicted and I ask you, if you still have a shred of conscience or of honour to personally correct this infamous charge and to send me the newspapers which you instruct to print this correction."

The Marquis was a very angry man. Harry Lehr's wife, a friend of Fanny's, gives us this version of an amusing episode in her book *King Lehr and the Gilded Age*.

"One or other of the Burke-Roche twins always seemed to be passing through Paris. They would drop in upon us suddenly in the rue de Lille, with all the latest news from New York, London, the Riviera, wherever they happened to have been. Once Frank arrived full of indignation against his brother, who had just let him in for a most unpleasant encounter.

He told us that Maurice had got engaged to a beautiful Spanish girl, the daughter of the Duke d'Alcedo, with the entire approval of both families. But the engagement was of short duration, for almost immediately, the fiancés quarrelled, and Maurice left for Paris, from where he wrote to the Duke saying he considered himself unworthy of the hand of his daughter and that he was returning to America.

The Duke was furious. Spanish tradition had been outraged, no family of the nobility could swallow such an insult! He wrote to Maurice challenging him to a duel, and adding that if he failed to meet him and give him honourable satisfaction he would shoot him on sight…Maurice neglected to advise his twin brother of what had happened. Frank was amazed one morning when, on crossing the Place Vendome in Paris, he was pounced upon by an elderly Spaniard who was apparently thirsting for his life. As it was he had the utmost difficulty in convincing the Duke d'Alcedo that he was not the American who had slighted his daughter."[133]

The following letter confirms Maurice's silence on the matter:

"Princes's Club, Knightsbridge, SW1
May 18th 1913

Dear Boy,
I rather wish I could join you on your motor trip but I have been invited to go to Oxford on Tuesday and spend the night. I hate to have you always on the job as you have been these last five months.

I have received letters from Moira (in Ireland) begging us to come over. Do let us arrange a short visit. I think five or six days quite sufficient. I shall bring my gun and my rod and we shall enjoy the sport. I thought the second week in June might do; give me your views.

London is delightful. I have my new clothes – a cutaway and such a smart coat. My bill is £35. Not much. Tomorrow Lytton and Baerlein[134] play the tennis final. Lytton I think will lose, he is such a poor match player. Has no heart.

Boy how do you propose going home? Of course I think to arrive in America in June is fierce. It is so disappointing to start in tropical weather. How I wish you and I and Mamma would go to Berlin, St Petersburg and

---

[133] *King Lehr and the Gilded Age.* pp. 243-244
[134] E M Baerlein was the British amateur real tennis amateur champion 13 times between 1912 and 1930. He was also the British amateur rackets amateur champion nine times.

Japan. Newport offers nothing new. The same people, the same place. How delightful it would be. But with the possible danger of war, we might not be able to. I hate to think that in another month, something must come to an end. I cannot realize what NY could be after my lengthy holiday.

Paris, of course, must be at its best. I can picture each place – the wonderful open-air life. I shall always remember our first year of 1911 – nothing could ever touch that. Send me any letters that might interest me – anything from Pine or your boss. I like to read everything, just put the bunch in a large envelope and dispatch it here.

I am not smoking or drinking and really am looking well. London gives you colour. Hope everything is well.

Love Maurice"

Maurice sailed home on the RMS *Majestic*, a ship of the White Star line, a replacement for the *Titanic*, which had been sunk the previous year.

RMS Majestic
May 21st 1913

"Dear Boy,
I was delighted to get your letter, also to see Arthur again. I promise you I shall go slowly and try and live down this last rash step.

And you, too, I pray, will not get into any trouble. Olive, I consider so dangerous. Think what she might do, think that if she were able to produce you might be in an awful mess. Avoid her if possible. The place for us is home. I am going to St Paul's to try and recall the good old days there. Then to Cynthia's for the Polo.

Don't worry about me.

I am sitting with two agreeable men and the journey promises to be quiet and restful.

I hope trip is a great success – everything well – good luck to you.

My love
Maurice"

"Jericho, Long Island
June 1st 1913

Dear Boy,
Certainly, I never have regretted anything less than my return home. I arrived here Friday to find glorious summer weather. It did me good to be back here after so many springs abroad.

147

I have been playing tennis daily at Piping Rock, my game being not a bit good. Fortunately nobody asked me a thing about my experience abroad. It was a delight to see Mary Canfield, Leonie Burrill, H. Post etc. the other pm. Canfield asked me to spend next week end with them. I go to Concord tomorrow night.

Cynthia's house is a charm. I never smelt such a divine air that comes thro' my window at night. Nothing to compare with it abroad. After the polo, I shall look about for a job. Loafing is no life – and I refuse to spend the summer doing so; even if it is at some school.

I am delighted to be home. I hope your motor trip is a success and you will return June 14th as planned. Wire when you decide.

Am well.

affec MR."

17

Maurice the Benefactor

While Maurice had been abroad, he had been thinking about what he could do for his beloved St Paul's School. As soon as he returned home, he went into action. He first initiated four scholarships to St Paul's in memory of his uncle, to be called the George Paul Work scholarships. Each was for $1,000 a year. He told the headmaster Dr Drury that he had returned after his travels more filled with the loyal spirit he had for his great school than ever. The Head thanked him warmly for this gift.

"This money will be applied for Scholarships in the name of your uncle and I know it will do incalculable good. Making possible an education at St Paul's is indeed a far-reaching benefaction, and I hope that our choice of suitable boys will justify your generosity."

In the first place, Maurice wanted the donor of the Scholarships to be anonymous but was later persuaded that his example might inspire others, and for the good of the school, he agreed to go public. He gave the same amount annually for the next twenty years.

The next letter from Dr Drury asks Maurice if he would be interested in a Mastership at St Paul's for the next year or so, until he has decided what line he is going to pursue in his life. Maurice writes thanking him for this proposal adding:

"I never believe in fooling myself. I frankly think I could maintain a dormitory, keep study and attend to bounds, but I could not teach. True I have had the necessary work and have a Harvard degree. Could I be of any use then? I love St Paul's. I love the life. If you would accept me, I certainly would never ask for any salary. I have a fair knowledge at shorthand and can work a typewriter. Also I have a fair knowledge of book-keeping. Would that be of any help to you?"

Public knowledge of the Roche Twins' large inheritance made them vulnerable to begging letters. Maurice even received one from a master at St Paul's. In his reply he set out his situation in detail:

"18 East 77th Street
Nov 1913, Sunday

My dear Mr Gordon,
I have given your letter attention and please do not think that I was either rude or surprised to receive it, not to give it an answer before this date.

I wish this was March instead of November. I have so many things on my hands that I am cramped myself to give that sum. There is a general impression that my grandfather left us his money outright, also that it is of some millions of dollars. Someday I hope to be well off but at present during my mother's life time receive but a small income. Unfortunately my scholarships and the price of the new boats come now and December. I ask you then to try and get on until March 16th 1914. If necessary, at that date I have some money and if you still wish the loan, will gladly give it to you. I really wish you had given me a line earlier for I could have readily done it. My allowance comes in in monthly portions and as I have already sent promissory checks abroad and to parts of this country, I can not help you until the date mentioned.

I hope your school games were a success.

I am to be in Concord after the game this coming Sunday.

As ever, yours
Maurice Roche."

Most of his gifts were volunteered by Maurice when he heard of some real need. Having heard of a boy fainting in the Chapel because of bad air, Maurice wrote to Mr Forster, one of the masters at St Paul's and asked him if the Dr Drury's wish to install a fan and blower system for ventilating the chapel at a cost of $3,500 would be useful and necessary. "I have the necessary amount to cover the instalment of the apparatus which I would gladly give if you deem it necessary. Please don't mention my name in connection with this. I hate publicity so."

After spending the summer of 1913 in Newport, Maurice went back to work at the Lackawanna and to the social round of fancy dress balls, the theatre, the opera, concerts, girl friends and of course taking care of his mother and his aunt. Dr Drury wrote to him in December, telling him about a plan to build a new study building capable of housing a hundred boys where they would be housed, fed and taught. Drury recommended that Maurice gave this scheme priority. Maurice was enthusiastic and pledged $35,000[135] to the scheme. "Too deep commendation cannot be accorded to this alumnus who in self-effacing generosity proves himself one of the school's most intelligent supporters," wrote Dr Drury in his annual report.

---

[135] His total contribution to this project came to $50,700 dollars – over £1 million in today's money.

150

Maurice returned to London the following summer 1914. In July, he wrote to Dr Drury of his vision of a new squash court building to be erected the following year, with a swimming pool in the basement. Every boy would be taught to swim although he was anxious about the health risks from the water. "Very soon I must find out if the doctors have any objection to the pool. Personally I am in great favour of such a thing; we can have 'Pa' Dole teaching every boy to swim and during the spring months remove that great risk taken by some boys who visit quarries and other places without permission."

And the following year the squash court building was erected, without the swimming pool. The cost was $34,000. The Rector wrote:

"Mr Roche's gift, the Squash racquet court is now nearing completion. This is the best building of its sort in the country, both for size and equipment. Boys and masters will derive athletic benefit from this building throughout the year."

Maurice gave a squash racquet to each of the masters to encourage them to use the squash courts. Dr Drury wrote to thank him:

"It is indeed a happy way of enlisting the enthusiasm of our masters, thus to provide each with the implement of play! It is quite like you, in your quiet way, to make it possible for every master to enjoy your building."

18

Back to Europe

Maurice was back in London in the summer of 1914. He wrote to Frank from Claridges in early July, telling him that he had attended the Henley Regatta at the beginning of July when the Harvard junior varsity crew, competing at Henley Regatta for the first time, had won the major event – the Grand Challenge Cup.

"July 6th, 1914
Claridge's Hotel

Dear Boy,
I have received at different times long letters from Mama giving full details of your excursion. I am delighted you have had such good weather and that in all, everything has been a success.

I visited Henley every day except Saturday. There were many Harvard fellows present and as you know by now the Harvard crew, now the Union Boat Club crew, composed of six former crew captains were second. I saw all but the last day. The Harvard crew were racing crews. They hardly had anybody swing, and gained their victories at a terrific high rate of speed: as an Englishman said who was next to me "they certainly are stuffing them in". I was very impressed by the beautiful way the whole regatta was run. The first two days, most gorgeous weather. I saw a great deal of Dacre Bush[136] who was over here for his first visit. Several of the Union Boat Club men had their wives. The best race undoubtedly was Leander & Harvard – the latter won by three-quarters of a length – in 7 minutes flat. The course record is 6.51 minutes.

I saw the tennis one day – altho' I'm sorry I missed Sat. match when Wilding[137] was beaten by Brookes.[138] I'm delighted. The papers say it was a good match.

---

[136] S Dacre Bush 2nd, a Harvard graduate.
[137] Anthony Wilding of New Zealand. Capt. Wilding, an outstanding sportsman was killed in action at Flanders the following May.
[138] Sir Norman Brookes of Australia.

My clothes are all very nice, 3 new suits and white flannel trousers; new evening clothes – very cheap. I advise you to go to Burkinshaw & Knights, 7 Cork Street.

Tonight there is a Harvard dinner at this hotel to the victorious crews. Bobbie Grant expected fifty people.

Now as to plans. As you know, I am always pleased to be here in London. What I don't want to do is to return to Paris. Answer me here what day you expect to go to Le Touquet. The trip from London is short. Let me know the hotel and day. When I get there, you can run over here and do your shopping.

Had a wonderful week end in Dover. Went to Canterbury Cathedral and heard some beautiful singing Sunday. Had a nice letter from Tatine Turnbull thanking me for the new boat which I gave them for their pond.

I went to Lord's this pm to watch Oxford-Cambridge match. London agrees with me – am looking well. Certainly I do love this place. When do you think you will go home? What plans can you suggest?

Lots of Americans here. Have something to do each evening. Write here – am well.

Much love Maurice"

After a few weeks in Le Touquet with his brother and mother, Maurice is back in London. The Great War had begun. Two days after declaring war on Russia, Germany declared war on France on August 3rd, 1914. Hours later, France declared war on Germany. The following day, Britain entered the conflict, declaring war on Germany. Apart from arranging to bring over Fanny and Frank's luggage from Paris, Maurice's life in London continued as normal.

"Prince's Club, Knightsbridge, SW
Telephone No. Kensington 662
August 19th 1914

Dear Boy,

We are such a queer family. We never take the trouble to inform one another when we leave and where we are. I suppose you have sailed. Mama, when I left her was to wire me and write. I haven't heard a <u>word</u> from her. Fortunately I got all our luggage over here and am going to send Arthur home on the first available steamer with all your things.

When I wire, do take the trouble to go to New York and meet him so as to make the necessary declarations etc. He has behaved so badly lately that I have made up my mind to fire him when I get back. We want an older man and I propose not to pay him more than $50. Its always the way, he had been spoilt. He was very rude to Mama in Paris and she says she will not have him in the house. That gives us an excellent chance to get rid of him!

I have enjoyed every moment of my trip here. I found Claridges able to take me in. I am so comfortable. The theatres are open. I took Mrs Godwin and Miss Pruyn to the Cinema Star the other evening, and I did enjoy every moment of it. It is the American version of the Queen of the Movies. Tonight I am going with Eva Zetland to see the Belle of New York.

Sunday, I went to St Paul's Cathedral; beautiful service; sermon on the war, must have been 5,000 people present.

I have played court tennis three times improving steadily. I only play an hour and find that does not tire me at all. This is an excellent club, so nice to spend the morning and lunch here & write.

Mama was to come this week. I am anxious to go to Scotland to one of the Lochs to fish. My two trout have been mounted beautifully. I want to visit Edinburgh and some of the points of interest before returning.

I have just bought an excellent book on railroad management. It has 600 pages of facts which I am reading from time to time. I expect to really finish it before I get home.

I have ordered myself three new suits so I should be very smart this winter. If the war continues, I won't go to St Moritz this year but will go around the world on March 1st 1915 – providing the war ends, getting back in time for Anniversary at school June 4th.

London is cool and pleasant. I am ordering a fancy costume for a fancy ball I say we get Mama to give this year, in Christmas week. It is to be a beauty.

Send me a line. Tell me if Barbara Rutherford is there this year. I hope your party will be a great success. Let me know if you need any ties or such things before I return.

I went to see the Scott[139] pictures last night and they certainly are marvellous. The lecturer made everybody cry before he finished. The moving pictures of the seals, whales & penguins are too wonderful. They also show a game of association football on the ice. So long. Don't get in too deep.

Love Maurice

At the end of August, Fanny wrote to Frank from Paris, where she is anxiously waiting for a ship to take her back to the States. She is longing to escape from the horrors of the effect of the war:

---

[139] Photographs of the explorer Robert Falcon Scott's expedition to Antarctica (1910-1913).

"Hotel de Crillon, Paris
Aug. 28th 1914

My dear Frankie,
Again a change! The boat has been put back and *Chicago* takes its place!

I am very tired & heartsick over all these sad and dreadful happenings. I will be indeed glad to see the "Isle of Peace".

I am remembering that on this night was to have been your ball, and I am thankful to see that all gaieties have been suspended. Every day Lucy and her friends meet at Avenue Royale and discuss the news. I have done what I can to help in money and now I am eagerly looking forward to getting away from daily, hourly news so pitiful and so inevitable apparently. Think of our tour in that lovely country & of all those little gay towns, those happy industrious people, the cultivation, the magnificent homes, all that made it so charming and so peaceful!

And now! I do not know if the American papers have the horrible details but the inhumanity and savagery are indescribable...and no-one can stop it.

It is all a double nightmare. And when one thinks as we sit, protected and comfortable, of the hideous fate of thousands of human beings, one cannot see how it can be permitted.

Lucy has been very fine – generous. Her hospital will be used later certainly. But they will first use all those nearer the frontier.

The refugees pour in to Paris. Wild, frightened, houses burned, destitute. We have funds to help them before they are placed. The people of Paris responded very quickly..." [pages missing – end of letter not clear]

Aunt Lucy had to leave Paris in a hurry, by car, leaving behind most of her wardrobe and her maid. Maurice wrote to Frank about her plight, with which he had little sympathy:

"Claridge's Hotel, Brook Street.
Early Sept. 1914

Dear Boy
Aunt Lucy came yesterday giving me a good account of her escape from Paris *en auto*. I wrote her three weeks ago to come here, and if she had taken my advice, she would be here with all her clothes and O'Brien. As it is she hasn't a thing and left her devoted O'Brien behind. I think the whole thing served her right. Nobody has given her a clap for what she has done for the Red Cross. The world is too much taken up with bigger things; she says she has not yet received a single patient!

She is staying at the Piccadilly where she camps with Nellie & Sally Hewitt, telling of her hardships. She lunched with me today and I hate to see people give up the way she does. She says she needs lots of rest before she can do anything, but she is well enough to sit up and inhale cigarettes and drink coffee! I am delighted I have an excuse to get away Sunday night on my trip to Scotland. I can't stand any more gloomy meals.

Had I any sort of excuse, I would spend another month. They say the coast of Norway is too gorgeous in the fall of the year. I would have gone there, were there no war. My trip to Scotland takes in all the most important cities, lochs, etc. and I am glad to say I shall profit a little over my staying here. Sunday I go to lunch on the river with Elise Jamis in the pm, to play tennis with Laurette Taylor (Miss Manners). It ought to be fun.

I do hope it has paid to get back. I am sure just a few weeks in Newport have been sufficient. The tennis too must have been excellent.

Hope you are well.

Love Maurice"

Apparently untroubled by the war, Maurice was off to Scotland for a tour. He followed "the Royal Route" on a Macbrayne Steamer of the Glasgow & Highland Royal Mail Steamers. He was delighted by the scenic beauty and as always imagined the possibilities of shooting game and planned a return visit.

"Sept. 7th 1914

Dear Boy
Ned Toland and I left Edinburgh last evening and journeyed to Inverness. I never thought the moor country could be so interesting. Everywhere undulating country with the purple heather. It has been gorgeous weather. We are now boating thro' the Caledonian Canal. It is a large lake bounded on both sides by high hills – so like Bar Harbour. We reach Glasgow tomorrow and then on to Edinburgh and London.

What little I have seen inspires me to want to spend a summer here fishing. It is divine and cool – lovely scenery; and from the train one sees long winding roads. It would make an ideal vacation; either to spend in motoring or coasting along the shores – there is an excellent boat service.

We spend the first night at Fort Augustus. Last night was at Oban. Today we have motored forty miles and are now in a steamer coming down the west coast to Glasgow. If the weather is fine, we go to the Trossachs and then Edinburgh and back to London.

I don't like to think another vacation is over. Already I can see myself seated having breakfast in your room – another winter coming. But since

I've been here, I am glad I've taken this trip. Some day I hope to pass some pleasant times here. Had you only stayed, we could have had a most enjoyable month shooting stags. On account of the war, the places are letting for nothing. We could have had a splendid time. Why, on this steamer I have been looking at a stag's head of 11 points, on the way to a taxidermist. Some places one can shoot 100 stags in a season! However I hope to do that next year.

I expect to sail on Tuesday next (15th). I rather hate going back just at present. I wish I were going to South Africa first. There have been several people on this trip that come from there.

I shall spend three days in London getting a few more things and probably will go up to Liverpool on Monday pm so as to be sure of making the boat.

Fairfield Osborn was getting married in London yesterday. I thought the girl he was going to marry very cheap. He certainly is in for it! They won't like her in NY.

Aunt Lucy is in London. I took her motoring the other pm and she bored me to death over Uncle Cooper and what she is going to do.

Hope you are well.

Love Maurice"

Part II

Maurice and the Great War

19

The sinking of the *Lusitania*

On September 15th 1914, Maurice wrote to Dr Drury, the Rector of St Paul's:

"Claridge's, London

Dear Dr Drury,
As things now stand I have a cabin on the *Franconia*, September 15th for Boston. I expect to go to Newport after my arrival, and will make the school a visit shortly after its opening.

Fortunately my mother and brother have sailed for America and I am here with my aunt. We had all of us rather trying times while in Paris. The first two weeks of the mobilization were extremely interesting but I was much relieved when we reached English soil.

I am enclosing my check for the first instalment of the George Work scholarship.

Young Vanderbilt has been here in the hotel and I have given him a short talk on what is expected of him (at St Paul's School). He certainly is not a normal boy – either he is over-nervous or not strong. If such a thing could be possible, I would advise his being placed under the care of some master. He is unfit for dormitory life. He should be living at one of the masters' houses until he has more confidence and has grown older. His studies need constant watching too…"

He went back to New York to the usual round of social activities. America was not at war but the tone was sombre. There were no fancy dress balls. There was no trip to Europe for Maurice and Frank in the spring of 1915. Instead Maurice visited the Panama Pacific International Exposition in San Francisco, which was held to celebrate the opening of the Panama Canal, as well as providing an opportunity for the city to demonstrate its recovery from the 1906 earthquake.

The fair covered 635 acres. The most prominent feature was the Tower of Jewels, a building 43 stories high which was covered with over 100,000 cut glass coloured "jewels" which shimmered in the breeze and glistened by day in sunlight and were illuminated by searchlights after dark. The exhibits were presented in a number of Palaces, including the Palaces of Manufacturers, Mines and Metallurgy, Education and Social Economy. Maurice had been thrilled with the Seattle World Fair in 1907 and equally marvelled at this display.

As he set out on a journey by train to California, Maurice read in a newspaper, the sickening news of the disaster of the *Lusitania*. On May 7th, the ship was hit by a torpedo and sank in eighteen minutes, with the loss of 1,120 lives. Many were women and children. 128 were American.

The ship was eight miles off the coast of southern Ireland, due south of the Old Head of Kinsale, County Cork.[140] The captain tried to beach her, but the helm no longer responded.

Alfred Vanderbilt was one of the casualties. He was last seen on deck giving his life belt to a woman and child. There were no more life belts and he could not swim. His body was never recovered from the sea. He left a fortune of $26,000,000. Maurice was profoundly shocked and saddened by the loss of a lifelong friend. Alfred was eight years older than him but Maurice had known him since his early childhood through the friendship of their respective grandfathers.

Alfred Gwynne Vanderbilt, aged 38, the grandson of "Commodore" Cornelius Vanderbilt, had set sail on the British liner the *Lusitania* from New York on April 30th bound for Liverpool. He was on a business trip and travelled with only his valet. The Germans had placed advertisements in national newspapers warning travellers that waters adjacent to the British Isles were in the war zone, and that vessels flying the flag of Great Britain were liable to destruction in those waters. The *Lusitania* was the swiftest ship afloat and the optimists believed the luxury liner had the speed to out-manoeuvre German U-Boats. There was an added danger in that, unknown to the passengers, the ship was carrying munitions destined for the British war effort.

The sinking of the *Lusitania* outraged Americans and many wanted America to go to war. In 1914, President Wilson had proclaimed America's neutrality in the conflict in Europe. For economic reasons, his government wanted to continue to trade with both the Allies (France, Russia and Britain) and the Central Powers (Germany and Austria-Hungary). Furthermore, the President saw intervention as a threat to domestic peaceful coexistence, as many Americans were first generation Europeans, the German-Americans forming an important ethnic block.

Wilson, anxious to maintain America's neutrality, succeeded in pacifying the people in a great speech in which he said: "There are times when a nation is too proud to fight."[141] At the same time he persuaded the German government to stop their policy of unrestricted submarine warfare. America remained out of the conflict and life continued as normal for the people of America.

Maurice continued to have a good time, in between working in his office in

[140] 25 miles from Roche's Point.
[141] *Too Proud to Fight.*

Hoboken. At the end of January 1916, Maurice wrote to his uncle Fitzy informing him that he and his brother were citizens of the United States, and that all claims to the peerage had long been severed, and that their grandfather's Will prohibited them from living in Europe. His uncle was very disturbed by Maurice's renunciation of his right to succeed to the title. He wrote to Frank Work's executors, telling them if this was a final decision, he would be obliged to ask the King to alter the patent so that his third nephew[142] could succeed.

---

[142] Denis Burke Roche, who had emigrated to Argentina in 1912 but returned to fight for his country in the Great War

20

On the threshold of war

Two days after the sinking of the *Lusitania*, Theodore (Ted) Roosevelt, Jr. (1875-1944) son of the 26th President of the US, asked President Wilson for appropriate military measures to be taken. Since his early childhood, Ted had heard his father preaching the obligations of self-defence and willingness to fight for a just cause. These qualities were essential characteristic of manliness. The belligerent ex-President was at loggerheads with the pacifist President Wilson. President Wilson was not interested in military preparedness, so Ted approached General Wood and asked him if he would hold a summer camp for business & professional men who wanted military training. Thirteen hundred men enrolled for the summer camp in 1915 at Plattsburg.

Ex-president Roosevelt visited the Plattsburg camp and addressed a mass meeting. He disliked the President Wilson with all the scorn of a man of action for an intellectual. He "denounced the professional pacifist, the poltroon and the college sissy."[143] Later, General Wood was reprimanded for giving Roosevelt this opportunity to express his views. It was forbidden for officers to speak of the war in Europe without war office approval.

Ted, the ex-President's son, was a contemporary of the brothers at Harvard. They both visited him at the White House and in June 1910, were ushers[144] at his wedding when he married Eleanor Butler Alexander. Undoubtedly, Ted inspired both brothers to prepare to fight the enemies of Britain and France. Other powerful emotional factors pushed them in that direction. They were half-British and had a great love of and sympathy for France.

The following year, in August 1916, Maurice and Frank readily enrolled in the second military training camp at Plattsburg, which was on the shores of Lake Champlain, New York State. Besides many of his Harvard friends, a hundred St Paul's old boys joined him. Recruits travelled to the Plattsburg camp by special train.

---

[143] *When Gentlemen Prepare for War.*
[144] Letter from Ted Roosevelt to Frank Roche: 42 West 47th Street. Dear Frank, Eleanor and I have decided to be married on the 20th of June and I would like you to be one of my ushers. I have been intending to write and ask you for a long while but have put it off except for one ineffectual attempt to get you by telephone. I hope that your trip abroad went well and that you had all sorts of experiences. Yours T R Jr.

Maurice Roche, right, and an unknown, Plattsburg, 1916

"It was at 5.45 in the morning when the Business Men's special pulled into a siding beyond the permanent brick buildings of the camp. The men piled off the train sleepy but eager. Beyond a field, a tent city waited for them – long rows of brown pyramids, extending as far as the mist-shrouded Lake Champlain. At the quartermaster's tent, they received a rifle and a bayonet well smeared with cosmoline, a mess kit, water bottle and cup, web belt and pack. The supply sergeant in the tent beyond, issued them with three blankets, a sweater, a poncho, half a pup tent, and five aluminium tent pegs. Those without uniform were now given two pairs of olive-drab breeches, two olive-drab shirts, a pair of leggings, a cotton blouse and a felt campaign hat with a bright braided cord.

There were eight men to a dirt-floored tent, which was furnished with collapsible canvas cots, a lantern, a water bucket, and several tin wash basins. The newcomers set up their cots, sorted out their equipment as best they could, and tentatively essayed their uniforms. Later, in the clearing evening, they were free to explore the camp and the post beyond. Although men of affairs in their ordinary lives, now, in their temporarily adopted military life, they felt something of the uncertainty of all recruits. Regulars in their close-fitting uniforms and campaign hats with faded cords looked so very regular. The businessmen soldiers-to-be, wandering in groups past the post parade ground, were uncertain whether to salute the officers they passed or not, indeed were uncertain as to just who were officers…"[145]

The recruits were introduced to the basic arts of rifle cleaning, the manual of arms. They went on route marches and soon began to look like soldiers. After the first week, they were drilling as companies and, learning quickly, they appeared on the parade ground as a regiment after the second week. Each man spent two days firing on the range before the climax of the course – nine days of mock battles in the field, matched against regular soldiers, covering large tracts of the Adirondack country.

Maurice thrived on the routine, the outdoor life, the challenge of the discomfort. All difficulties were mitigated by the presence of so many of his friends, and inspired by the cause for which they were preparing.

In stark contrast, a few weeks in Newport followed for the brothers. Regardless of the war, the season was in full swing. There were two large debutante balls in August. The brothers were the guests of Governor and Mrs Beeckman at their cottage Land's End, before a dance for Miss Ethel Harriman at the Clambake Club. They also attended a dinner dance for Lucile P Carter at Ochre Point, attended by three hundred residents.

Newport was soon to be made aware that the war was at their very doorstep.

---

[145] *When gentlemen prepared for war*, p. 3.

The season was over, when a most disturbing event rocked the peace of the entire Newport community. On October 7th, the German submarine U-53 entered the harbour of Newport,[146] and its Commander Hans Rose paid official visits to Admiral Knight and Admiral Gleaves, the commander of torpedo boats. The German commander had been instructed to call in at Newport but on no account to take any supplies, apart from fresh victuals, to avoid giving cause for detention.

Rose wrote in his diary that once he had reassured the Admirals that he would leave after two and a half hours, Admiral Greaves showed great interest in the U-Boat and personally inspected it. Several young officers, their ladies, some civilians and reporters were also shown over. Commander Rose duly left, taking no supplies, although he needed extra fuel for the return journey.

He reached the Nantucket Lightship early the next day. There he decided to examine the merchant traffic outside territorial waters and to wage warfare, according to the Rules of Prize Warfare. These demanded that crews were warned before an attack, given time to disembark and to reach a place of safety before their vessel was torpedoed and sunk. Seven ships were stopped and then sunk, including a British passenger ship, the *Stefano*. Two hundred and sixteen persons were rescued. No-one was injured and there were no casualties. There was great anger and indignation in Newport naval and other circles, but all agreed that Germany had not violated international law.

Maurice and Frank spent Christmas 1916 with their mother in their new home, 23 West 53rd Street. For the next six months, with the prospect of going on active service in Europe and perhaps not returning, Maurice's gifts to St Paul's multiplied. In November he gave a finely-bound encyclopaedia, which the boys were told to treat with care. In Jan 1917, he asked for estimates for reconstructing two dormitories, installing wash rooms and lavatories. He was prepared to pay $10,000 himself towards the work.

In February, Maurice was excited to find a fine portrait of George Washington by Rembrandt Peel (1778-1860). He rejoiced at this discovery and bought it without hesitation, to donate to the school. It was initially hung in the Upper School dining hall. It is now outside the Rector's office on the second floor of the schoolhouse. Maurice was invited to unveil the portrait but a longstanding social engagement in South Carolina prevented him doing this.

Early in 1916, Maurice came up with a scheme for a new building for the School Camp. This was run by the Missionary Society for less fortunate boys. He had visited the existing Camp and found the conditions deplorable, the rain pouring in on all sides. He hoped that the new camp could be used by boys who lived at some distance from the school, during the Easter vacation, who under the guidance of a master, could spend their days tramping over the delightful countryside.

His interest in the School included the health of the boys. He was very

---

[146] From *Germany's High Sea Fleet in the World War.*

concerned to hear of several cases of mastoiditis. He related a story to Dr Drury of a young boy having the infection in the Vanderbilt Hotel. When he left the hotel, a middle-aged man took the same apartment and became critically ill from mastoiditis. Maurice offered to pay for a thorough fumigation of all the dormitories at the school during the coming vacation, to return the school to a "germless" place. Dr Drury in his reply reassured him that fumigation was already in hand.

When in the summer of 1916 there was a world-wide poliomyletis (also called infantile paralysis) epidemic, which was particularly intense in New York,[147] Maurice offered to pay for three or four men to daily swamp the floors with disinfectant, for the first month of the new term in September. This was a course of action recommended by hospital doctors at a meeting he had attended.

Later that year Dr Drury told him that one boy was seriously ill with pneumonia. When Maurice heard of the boy's improvement, he wrote: "I have worried so over it. Everything connected with the school seems so close to me." He felt for the school emotionally as for his own family.

He was thoughtful in small ways. In March 1916, he sent grapefruit to Dr Drury from Florida. In 1924 Dr Drury wrote: "Mysteriously and constantly year after year, nine magazines come to the Infirmary. I do want you to know what a real pleasure this gift of yours is, and how the boys, and the nurses too, do appreciate reading matter coming to them all the time. With constant gratitude etc. Sam"

American neutrality persisted and early in 1917, Maurice went hunting on Jekyl Island, situated off the coast of Georgia. His passion for shooting game was shared by many of his rich contemporaries. The island club was a very exclusive playground for the wealthy. The following letter describes his experiences:

"Jekyl Island Club, Brunswick Georgia
Feb. 1917

Dear Boy,
Before you get this, probably you will read about young Gould's tragic death. He had a racoon in a trap and having nothing to dispatch the beast with, he seized the barrel of the gun and hit the 'coon with the butt end and it went off and entering his groin, killed him. You surely must have remembered him – Edwin Gould – a tall lanky boy, not a bit good looking.

Yesterday pm I went off with my .22 & hearing a grunt I dismounted & knew it was a wild hog. I could see the palms move, but could not get a good look at the beast. Finally I looked up the road and saw one coming out of the palmettos. I was beyond myself for fear of missing it, but taking careful aim caught him a fatal shot in the side. I fired again and struck him in the head, which threw him on his back. Another finished him. I went up

---

[147] The nationwide toll for the States was 27,000 cases, 6,000 dead.

168

last night in a Ford & gave him to the gamekeeper.

I went for a long ride this am with Gardenia & fixed up everything. It was a divine day. I cannot make up my mind if I will join you in Palm Beach or not. Hope you enjoyed Washington. Am having a good time here.

Love MR"

21

Training to be a soldier

M aurice's life was about to undergo another profound change. On April 6th 1917 the United States Congress formally declared that a state of war existed between the United States and the Imperial German Government.

At the start of 1917, the war in Europe had reached stalemate. Millions of lives had been lost on both sides. The Allies desperately needed fresh supplies of men, ships and arms to break the deadlock but still President Wilson adamantly refused to enter the war. Two coded telegrams emanating from Germany and signed "Zimmermann" were intercepted by British Intelligence in Jan 1917.

The first informed Washington that Germany intended to resume unrestricted submarine warfare on February 1st. This meant that U-Boats would sink without warning, all shipping, whether enemy or neutral, found in the war zones. The German navy believed that their submarines would starve the British into defeat in a few months. Furthermore they judged that the Americans did not have enough trained troops to change the course of the war.

To ensure the Americans did not cross the Atlantic, a second telegram was sent by Zimmermann stating that if America declared war on Germany, in retaliation to unrestricted submarine warfare, Germany would form an alliance with Mexico and Japan and financially assist the former to recapture her lost territories of Texas, Arizona and New Mexico. At that time, General Pershing, with 12,000 men, was engaged in battle with Mexico, and Japan had long been hostile to the US.

It had taken years to break the code used in the Zimmerman telegram and Britain could not reveal that it had been cracked. They waited until February 24th when a stratagem was devised to pass it to Washington via Mexico. President Wilson released the document to the public on March 1st.

The newspapers called the Zimmerman telegram the Prussian Invasion Plot. Germany's intention to attack US territory meant there could no longer be any question of American neutrality. In fact the president of Mexico decided to stay neutral, and Zimmerman's hope of keeping America out of Europe failed.

Another significant factor, which brought America into the war, was the abdication of the Tsar in Russia in March and the outbreak of the Russian Revolution. Without the Tsar at the head of military operations, the Russians lost appetite for the war and began to withdraw. This allowed the Germans to re-deploy troops to the western front and made victory more likely.

There were even more powerful reasons for entering the war. In the first three months of 1917, the total British, allied and neutral shipping losses amounted to 1,500,000 tonnage, almost entirely caused by torpedoing without warning. The British lost more than 800,000 tonnage and 283 vessels in that period. On March 28th, three American ships were sunk by U-boats without warning. On April 2nd Woodrow Wilson informed Congress of the effects of Germany's policy of sinking every vessel that was bound for the ports of Great Britain, Ireland and the western coasts of Europe:

"Vessels of every kind, whatever their flag, their character, their cargo, their destination, their errand, have been ruthlessly sent to the bottom without warning and without thought of help or mercy for those on board…even hospital ships and ships carrying relief to the sorely bereaved and stricken people of Belgium have been sunk with the same reckless lack of compassion or principle…The present submarine warfare is a warfare against mankind. It is a war against all nations. American ships have been sunk, American lives taken, in ways which it has stirred us very deeply to learn of…That the German government means to stir up enemies against us at our very doors, the intercepted note to the German Minister in Mexico is eloquent evidence. It is a fearful thing to lead this great peaceful people into the most terrible and disastrous of all wars. But the right is more precious than peace and we shall fight for the things which we have always carried nearest our hearts – for democracy."[148]

Four days later Congress declared a state of war between the United States and the Imperial German Government. The President was authorised to employ the entire naval and military resources of the US to carry on the war. He appointed Major General John J Pershing as commander of the American Expeditionary Force in Europe, with the responsibility of training and supplying an army for Europe.

No words could describe the profound relief of the weary, depleted, exhausted Allies on hearing this news:

"Stalemated in the trenches, torpedoed on the seas, emptied of funds, they heard the sound of a huge fresh, new ally, coming to join them with ships and money and goods and men."[149]

---

[148] Woodrow Wilson, war messages, 65th Congress, 1st Sess. Senate Doc. No 5, Washington DC.
[149] *The Zimmermann Telegram*, p. 197.

The announcement of American support provided a huge psychological boost, but had little practical effect in the short term. Despite the serious possibility of war that had confronted the nation since the sinking of the *Lusitania*, a lack of foresight meant the country was unprepared.

General Pershing described the situation that faced him:

"Extreme haste in our preparation was urgent. We were called upon to make up in a few months for the neglect of years. The possibility of our being able to send a completely trained and equipped army within a reasonable time was remote, because of our woeful state of unprepared-ness. We had no such army and could not have one for several months to come."[150]

A trained army of two million men was mobilised, initially combining a small number of professional soldiers with a military draft. The only trained reserve army was the Officers' Training Camps of the Plattsburg Movement. The Government initiated extensive propaganda through posters, films, newspapers, instilling a spirit of patriotism and anti-Germany hostility. When the drafts came, there were no riots and nine million men were drafted, the required number then being chosen by lottery to serve. "Doughboy" became the universally popular nickname of all the American troops sent to Europe. It was June 1918 before more than one million men landed in France to engage combat. Their arrival persuaded the Germans of the hopelessness of their cause.

As soon as war was declared, Maurice informed Dr Drury that he had left St Paul's a considerable sum in his will in view of the coming conflict. In September 1918, he donated a further $15,000 towards the improvements to the Lower School Study Building. The Rector describes him as the most self-effacing of givers.

Maurice volunteered for the Army. He wrote to Dr Drury that he was having some difficulty getting into the Plattsburg camp over his naturalization papers. If he was refused, he had a letter to General Wilson in Canada and would go there if necessary. He advised the Rector to make contracts for the purchase of flour and sugar, as the prices the following winter would be "terrific". In early May 1917, he wired Frank that he had an excellent opportunity of joining the 7th Brigade Canadian Field Artillery, and was anxious to join. However, at the end of August he enrolled in the Harvard Reserve Officers' Training Corps, and was admitted to Plattsburg.

Frank was involved with the war in Europe from its outset. In January 1914, he gave an ambulance to the American Ambulance Hospital in Paris in the name of St Paul's School. He then occupied himself with recruiting 188 volunteer drivers,

---

[150] *My Experiences in the World War.*

and the same number of ambulances. In the middle of 1914, the Lafayette[151] fund was established "to be devoted to the immediate relief of the unavoidable suffering of the men in the trenches." Money was raised to provide comfort kits for French soldiers, containing a waterproof poncho, socks and mittens, cigarettes. A postcard addressed to the donor was included in each kit. Frank was the dedicated secretary and Treasurer. In a letter to the Editor of the *New York Times*, he appealed for funds for the Lafayette Fund, on the grounds that the French had fought shoulder to shoulder with Americans against the British, in the dark days of the Revolution. They had helped America win her freedom. It was right that America should help France in her hour of need.[152]

With his activities for the French occupying much of his time, Frank did not rush to volunteer in 1917. Friends chided him for not offering his services before the conscription bill came in. He would never live it down, they said, if he did not volunteer before he was forced to. Everyone knew that Maurice had volunteered. In fact the twins, aged 32, were outside the age range of the draft in May 1917, which was for men aged 21-30. A later one, in September 1918, targeted all men aged 18-45.

In May 1917, Frank enrolled in the United States Naval Reserve Force with the rank of Ensign. For the next two months, he was assigned to SS *Carolina*, a training ship operating in American waters. In July 1917, he was instructed to report for duty to the Naval base at Newport, Rhode Island. Newport had long been a naval base, with a Naval War College and a Torpedo Station. In August 1916, the battleship USS *Wyoming* operated out of Newport for some weeks. Frank may well have met some of the officers, even her commander at the time, Captain Henry A Wiley. He wrote to Dr Drury that he preferred this work to army life. He went out in a boat most days, for a practice spin, which was delightful – except when it was rough. He was trying for a Quartermaster's position.

After six months training at Plattsburg, Maurice was sent to Camp Dix. This was a training camp in Burlington County, New Jersey, chosen because the terrain was suitable for digging trenches. It was constructed in June 1917, for the 311th Infantry Regiment, 78th Division, which was composed of men from New Jersey, Delaware and northern New York. In four months, an area of woodland and farm was transformed into a town of 1,600 buildings, housing more than 50,000 thousand soldiers. A hospital with 2,000 beds went up in a week. The work had to be completed in three months.

July 16th 1917; Maurice wrote to Dr Drury:

"Tomorrow night we are to spend in the trenches. The work there consists

---

[151] The Marquis de Lafayette (1757-1834) was a French soldier and statesman who secretly sent military supplies to America before eventually commanding George Washington's armies himself, in the American War of Independence.

[152] *New York Times*, December 3rd or 4th, 1915.

Frank Roche modelling the poncho from the Lafayette kit for French soldiers

Capt. Roche with British and French experts who were training student officers at Camp Dix

174

in making reliefs or arranging the troops preparatory to an attack. The trench system we have laid out is quite complete. We have dug-outs, communicating trenches and barb wire entanglements. I regret to say the government has failed to recognize this battalion. It is a pity to disappoint some 1,300 men at urgent times like this."

Maurice complained that some four hundred officers in the camp were being held with nothing to do. During his first week there, he grasped the opportunity to join the foreign officers and was with the Foreign Mission. Veterans from the British and French armies were there in an advisory capacity, to pass on their first-hand knowledge of war. Maurice was with the French Mission, which was composed of two French officers and a sergeant. He lived with them, and ran their mess and helped them with translations from French into English, so he at least was kept busy.

On August 6th 1917 he wrote to his brother complaining that going to Newport on leave was a trial rather than a pleasure:

"…Boy, the truth is that Mama gets on my nerves, so that it is not a rest to go home. I have to be worried with one thing or other, or some luncheon that causes me to have indigestion, thru' sheer boredom to say nothing of hearing her 'crab' Aunt Lucy and the plans for that place up the Hudson!

I might have a chance to go on Gen. Scott's staff. I put my name down; we only live once! My French has improved a 100% & I am most fortunate in being here with three French men, and I know it. I am trying to do too much. I have taken a course in trench mortars, and in Lewis guns, am taking a course in grenades & have but little more to wrap the whole thing up…

love Maurice."

Maurice was flying high! General Scott was the Chief of Staff of the US Army, until September 1917, when he reached retirement age. In December he became Commander of the 78th Division when it was formed in August at Camp Dix.

The camp closed at the end of November. Maurice was ranked among the first 25 in his company (Company 11, 18th Provisional Training Regiment, New York Division) and was offered a captaincy in the inactive list, with the choice of taking first lieutenancy in the active army. A large percentage of the men were to be retired until the second draft army. This was not good news as all wanted active service.

The sugar famine Maurice had prophesied happened. He sent two flags to St Paul's, one US and a Union Jack, suggesting they were placed in the Chapel.

Frank, in naval uniform, visiting Maurice at Camp Dix, 1917

Dr Drury wrote back telling Maurice that the flags were carried in a procession at a Chapel service by two sixth formers ahead of the choir.

In February 1918, Frank visited Maurice at Camp Dix. The two played their identical twin trick and swapped uniforms. Frank, wearing Maurice's uniform, introduced his brother Frank who was paying him a visit! This was a trick they liked playing on their girlfriends, the brothers informing each other of the interests of the poor girl, and 'how far' they had got!

Back in their own uniforms, they had a photograph taken together. After the visit Frank wrote to Dr Drury: "I thought my brother seemed very well and happy as I hope the picture we had taken together will show."

In March, Kendall, a master at St Paul's died. It was his untiring efforts, Maurice claimed, that permitted him to go to Harvard. Maurice was immediately concerned for the finances of his widow and sons. As the school had no arrangement for pensioning a master, he offered to give her a pension from his own pocket. He donated $1,500 to a memorial.

Finally, in April, the long-awaited moment arrived. Maurice was appointed to the Motor Supply Train 303rd Company D, 78th Division. Maurice wrote to Frank that they were on standby for departure to Europe, although the actual date was not in sight. He planned to take a substantial letter of credit with him in case of necessity.

Most of the supplies to the American Expeditionary Force in Europe came from the USA entering France through Atlantic ports. They travelled by purpose built railways to base depots. The largest interior depot was in Gièvres, a small town 125 miles south of Paris. It was managed by twenty thousand men and covered 12 square miles.

"It had storage for 2,000,000 gallons of gasoline, refrigerator capacity for 6,500 tons of fresh meat, and warehouse space for clothing and food for 30 days supply of 2,000,000 men not to mention the thousands of tons of medical, signal, engineering, and ordinance supplies, excepting ammunition."[153]

There was a constant flow of shipments in trainloads, from these base depots to the storage depots in the Intermediate Section, which maintained a large fixed reserve of all supplies needed by the troops. Supplies were passed on as required to railheads in the Advance Section where 15 days supply was held.

General Pershing gives an example of the speed of the system:

"At 8.15 one morning in August, a telegram was received ordering exactly 4,596 tons of supplies, including 1,250,000 cans of tomatoes, 1,000,000

---

[153] *My experiences in the World War*, p. 346.

pounds of sugar, 600,0000 cans of corned beef, 750,000 pounds of tinned hash and 150,000 pound of dry beans. Ten hours later this colossal requisition, which required 457 cars for transport, was loaded and on its way to the advance depot."[154]

Maurice spent his time in France in the Advance Section of the Services of Supply, at the stage where delivery was by motor. Supplies had to be delivered promptly and regularly to points within short truck-haul of the location of the troops.

A Motor Supply Train[155] consisted of 16 officers and 485 enlisted men. They were organised as a Headquarters, 6 truck companies and 1 medical department. There were 7 motor cars, 6 rolling kitchens, 9 motorcycles with sidecars, 163 two-ton cargo trucks, 7 rations of baggage trucks, 6 repair trucks and 12 tank trucks. For weapons there were 45 pistols and 445 rifles.

The 78th was known as the Lightning Division. It had as its shoulder insignia, a streak of white or silver on a red patch. In France, during the summer and fall of 1918, it was the "point of the wedge" of the final offensive which knocked out Germany. The 78th was in three major campaigns during World War I – Meuse-Argonne, St Mihiel, and Lorraine.

---

[154] *My Experiences in the World War*, p. 346.
[155] Details supplied by Stan Polny, 78th Division Historian.

22

Maurice's war diary, 1918-1919

The long-awaited day arrived for the 78th division to leave Camp Dix and cross the Atlantic to join the battle in Europe. Two convoys set sail at the end of May 1918. There was in Maurice's mind, the very real possibility that he would not return. He viewed his death with a certain equanimity. He contented himself with the fact that he had led a full life and had done many of the things that he wanted to do. He had travelled extensively. He had taken care of St Paul's School in his Will.

From the moment he left Camp Dix at the end of May 1918 until his return thirteen months later, Maurice kept a diary on a daily basis.

"On Active Service with the American Expeditionary Force in Europe.

Monday May 27th, 1918
"At 2am we left Camp Dix to march to the station. The movement was made without noise and rapidly. We were put in day coaches and soon (3am) the train was under way. It was daylight at 5am when we reached Philadelphia and disembarked on a wharf and marched the company to the pier. We had a Red Cross breakfast sent by the ladies of Philadelphia. At 10am we marched on board. The boat, the Steamer *Mesaba*[156] is a 6,800-ton boat. It is evident that there is to be considerable crowding, the ship having been until recently in the cattle service. The officers are quartered in staterooms, the men in hammocks and bunks. Fortunately my company has bunks – two tiers, frightfully congested. The Roman days had nothing on this! The day was spent in disorder – terrific heat and the mess for the men was without system and the ranges not in order. We were moved from the pier. The night was welcome. To add to the discomfort there was a heavy shower which caused the water to run from the hatchways and make things disagreeable."

The opening lines of Maurice's diary paint a grim picture of the first day on

---

[156] Two hours before the *Titanic* sank, RMS *Mesaba* had sent her a message reporting that a huge ice field and a great number of icebergs, lay in the her path. The message was ignored.

board SS *Mesaba* – the heat, the overcrowding, the discomfort, the chaos. In addition the ship was dirty and there were rats in the kitchen. The crossing was a great strain particularly for someone of his nervous disposition. Two days later, as they waited outside the harbour at Halifax, where another eight ships joined the convoy, he expresses his homesickness and his love for St Paul's, the fears of all on board and his own distress.

"May 29th
"From early morning I realized that this was Anniversary. I could easily picture the events that make up this day at St Paul's. I saw the many pretty girls, the proud parents, the boys with their red ribbons. I hope for a nice day. I thought of the chapel service, the luncheon, the afternoon sports, the concert. How many times I had witnessed all these events! How different was this day for me! Here on the *Mesaba* we had an uneventful day. It was bitterly cold – the sea like glass. There were several drills. The hours passed by. In the evening, we had slowed down for it was passed around that we couldn't make Halifax before they closed the harbour. I saw a glorious sunset, and times after dark we had glimpses of the lighthouses on the coast.

I cannot close this day without saying that the experiences of all aboard are anxious. Officers walk about in groups. From time to time we have chats with the ship's crew, nearly every one of which had been torpedoed more than once. It is a ghastly experience and one I pray may never happen to us. I think constantly of the days before this horrible war, the days at Newport, the summers abroad, what I wish I had done... I can picture Cynthia's place, Aunt Lucy's and even the pleasant streets of New York are missed. Well, it has to be. They say we shall see France about June 12th. At any rate, I pray that this drear voyage may soon pass for I confess I don't like anything about it.

May 30th
This morning when I awoke I saw land and realized that we were entering the harbour of Halifax. The harbour had every appearance of a naval base, and with the many transports, other vessels, a solitary cruiser and several torpedo boats we could see an active port. We steamed up past where the disaster took place last fall – the hill sides were desolate & in some sections not a house stood. At the water's edge there was considerable wreckage."

The shore lines for nearly a mile, from the water edge to the top of the hills behind the city, were blackened ruins due to a serious explosion a few weeks earlier, when a hospital ship rammed a steamer laden with munitions of war.[157]

---

[157] *The History of New York State* Book XI, Ch 11, Part 1. p. 1363. Editor Dr James Sullivan.

"We anchored in the west harbour where there was about 8 vessels which had congregated there to go in our convoy. We had visitors from other ships, got some newspapers, took on stores, water, and also sent two men from here to the hospital, one had mumps, another broke his arm during boat drill.

The pm was taken up with a drill and an inspection to check up the property of the men. In the great disorder, we fortunately only lost a canteen cup. The evening I played bridge with Kurtzman, Howard & Marcus.

After dinner it rained hard. We had a visit from Col Markham of the *Dignitas*. It seems that his boat has been here some days. It is remarkable thing to see these camouflaged ships. They present queer aspects and give a peculiar appearance as they lie at anchor.

At an early hour tomorrow, we are to begin our trip to France. This convoy represents some 20,000 souls. What sacrifice they are gladly taking. What they have given up can never be put on paper.

June 1st Foggy
Much fog at the early morning drill 5am. After breakfast it was evident that we were preparing to go. Within a few minutes of 10, the first ship in our convoy weighed anchor, followed in quick succession, until the fifth ship found us in place. Passed out of the harbour, saw the fortifications & nets, the lighthouses, etc. In the distance we could perceive a bank of fog, and very soon we were in a thick fog. This we had until after supper, when it lifted, and it was then that we could see all the ships of this convoy – eleven, at the head of which steamed the English cruiser. As it was my turn on duty, I prepared for the night & at 9pm I reported, and with the most unfavourable conditions, I put on my pistol and prepared to stay up and watch the men in hatchways E & F.

June 2nd
Very foggy. It was an uneventful night, the hours passed slowly. From time to time, I went my rounds. All the men were sleeping soundly – those in hammocks less well than the others. It was a marvellous sight to see so many men ready to face untold hardships and death, at any moment ready to leap to their positions on deck.

It was as quiet as possible, only the vibration of the boat reminding us that we were under way and the pumping of the ice machine overhead. I walked around the tiers of beds the men silently resting. I wondered what their dreams were. Were they of the perils of the trip, or of home and the things left behind?... Had a few hours sleep in am, luncheon and again my bunk. Developed a fierce headache and felt depressed. Better at supper.

Talked after dinner with an enlisted man. Certainly I admire these men for what they are doing. They have given up everything. Bed at 9. Tired and depressed.

June 3nd

Foggy. Very much better. Had reveille at 4.30am; inspection at 9.00. At 9.30, meeting with Major. Instructions as to launching rafts/disembarking. Still no sign of clearing. Spent the pm reading Nicholas Nickleby and from time to time, looked out of the porthole only to see the most dense fog imaginable. ...the men look pale, most unshaven and not having had space to clean up, they look like so many ruffians. They have not had their clothes off for days. their shoes are wet and dirty. I marvel how they keep cheerful, for I admit I am more distressed than they."

Maurice was so terrified by the dense fog on the seventh night that he could not sleep a wink.

"June 4th

I was awake throughout the night. Glancing out of the porthole, I could see that we were barely gliding. The fog could not have been denser. I admit I was filled with terror, for with the fog horn over my head, it was like a stab each time they pulled the whistle. Our code was two long, two short, a long and three short. After you have counted that each time, you lie back waiting the next. Breakfast, inspection. I read NN until 11, when Col Battle told us at a meeting, to avoid rumours. Last night a doctor in the train was told by a number of the crew, that 3 sub[marine]s and two icebergs were reported. It got around like wildfire to the whole boat, causing anxiety."

After lunch, the sun came out and his spirits improved.

"I spent the pm on the top deck sitting in the sun. It reminded of the good old days when I crossed in peace time. By 4pm the convoy had arranged itself in formation. It looks like an Armada heading for its real purpose - to fight. It is evident that the whole ship is in better spirits. Supper proved gay. I forgot to say we had a boat drill. I spoke a word to the men about staying in the sunlight and the care of the rifle. The evening is a lovely one, the sea like glass. Thank heavens, the ship ploughs silently on. The air is warm. I am a different person. It was light until 9pm. I stayed on deck looking over the bow, thinking, as I so often do, of home. Bed.

June 5th

Glorious day. Reveille at 4.30am. It seems it is a good thing to have the men up before daylight. I make several appointments – 2 new sergeants and 2 corporals – before presenting the warrants, in each case saying a word to the men. Now have two new sergeants who have made good, and I think will be of great assistance. Another drill at 2pm. The wind is freshening and the waves getting larger each moment. The convoy tried to execute some zig-zagging. I forgot to say that we now have our life-preservers with us constantly, going nowhere without them. Had a talk with some of the English crew about the subs., England, USA, and the merits of the different governments. Bridge until supper, then read until they asked me to continue the bridge. Bed at 9pm.

June 6th

Another clear day, somewhat colder. Inspection at 9am, read for a while and then played bridge until 12 noon. Didn't enjoy it much. We are rapidly nearing the danger zone, and the anxieties will increase. Heard just before dinner that 13 vessels had been sunk off the American coast by subs! Our convoy practised some zig-zagging and other manoeuvres. Supper, than bridge and bed. Am in excellent spirits and hope that we have good luck throughout our voyage.

June 7th

Rather aimless day. Read many chapters of Nicholas Nickleby. Hope we shall arrive soon.

June 8th

Heavy seas and much wind and rain. Boat rocking considerably tho' few men ill. We are in the danger zone. Much laughter at supper. Plans for future discussed. Go on guard at 1am.

June 9th

Beautiful Sunday morning. Had an uneventful four hours on duty. Cook gave me a cup of coffee and a most delicious pork chop. It never quite got dark towards the north. Sat on the upper deck in the sun. On duty from 1pm to 5. Heard a short sermon from the chaplain to the men, read a little, saw a gorgeous sunset, the best one we have had since at sea. Light until 10pm."

The following morning the ship awoke to discover that seven destroyers had arrived to escort the convoy. This caused much interest and excitement. No-one was more relieved than Maurice to see them.

"June 10th
It has been a comfort to see our new protectors. They work feverishly back and forth, scouring in every direction. We have more feeling of security than ever. Much speculation as to when we get there. Beautiful sunset. Bed."

His agony was about to come to an end. He had every reason to be anxious. The risk of being torpedoed was high and, rightly or wrongly, the belief that they might meet an iceberg was alarming.[158]

"June 11th
A summer day. Shortly after two (o' clock) great interest over the firing of several depth bombs. The men deeply concerned as to the real cause. Luncheon. After that, we soon sighted Wales. Expect to land tomorrow. The pm brought two dirigibles, which caused much comment. They circled about the entire pm. I became officer of the day at 3pm. Tomorrow will see us safely home I pray, for I want to send home a telegram telling the news. It has been a fearful strain and I hope never to repeat it.

June 12th
At an early hour we were in the Mersey. Saw the lighthouses of Liverpool. It was the most welcome sight I have had for years. It was wonderful to see the English soldiers, the passing ferries that gave us a cheer. The first to be taken off were a couple of sick men, to the American Red Cross. When we disembarked, we fell into columns of fours. We then marched thro' the city which was lined with people. They cheered us and I was much impressed with it all. As we arrived at the station, a band was playing, the officers were assembled and on behalf of the King, some English officers welcomed us and gave us each a letter. Through some misunderstanding, the officers were not given anything to eat, so we travelled until 5pm before receiving a thing.

It is difficult to describe the many sensations that came to me as we travelled through England. It was perfectly beautiful, bringing pleasant memories before the war. We passed every kind of English country and at midnight arrived at Southampton. The march was made at dead of night to a rest camp. Before we finally got to bed, it was 3am.

---

[158] Three months later on September 1st while making a convoy voyage from Liverpool to Philadelphia in ballast, the SS *Mesaba* was torpedoed and sunk. There were 20 fatalities, including the ship's commander.

June 13th

...I took myself off to Southampton and bought a Sam Brown belt and also sent two telegrams home. I wish I had written more letters, so that I could have sent them.

June 14th

At 12.30pm we started for the boat to cross the Channel. Arriving at the station, we hung around. I had some eggs with an Australian and we spoke of the war etc. At 8pm a rainstorm came upon us. We embarked for Havre. The boat was crowded with Tommies, Australians and troopers. The most beautiful sunset. The trip to Havre was in a fierce sea. Much sickness in the night, it being very rough. I tried to get some sleep but we were so crowded that it was impossible. After some time at anchor, we drew into the harbour.

June 15th

At 6am we marched to a rest camp, arriving at eleven. The men were in poor quarters and as usual crowded. The officers were well taken care of. We found plenty of English officers and the mess was exceedingly good. I spent the pm taking my company some five miles up a mountain, to a gas school where we were distributed gas masks. It was a tiring day. I had supper and soon went to bed."

Between May 27th and June 6th all the artillery units, divisional troops and trains of the 78th division crossed the Atlantic. After a brief stay in rest camps they crossed the Channel to Calais with the artillery going to Le Havre. The infantry had sailed a week earlier and also proceeded to Le Havre. There were five trains: the Military Police, the Ammunition, the Supply, the Engineer and the Sanitary (Ambulance companies and Field Hospitals.) Maurice was in 303d. Supply Train, which was assigned to the 2nd American Army Corps, then operating with the British in Flanders.

The division moved to its training area in the village of Nielles-les-Blequin, a few miles west of St Omer where they were attached to the Second British army. Training cadres of the Northumberland Fusiliers, the 15th Highland Infantry, and the 15th Royal Scots took over the job of giving the division intensive training. During this period of training, the Division acted as reserve unit for the British.

"June 16th

At 10 am we got news that we were to pull out at 12.30. I wanted to get a few days rest and see something of the English officers. Marched thro' Havre to the train. After a little food, I got on the train and received rations. Was in the same compartment with Smyth, Quinn, Kurtzman and Dr

185

MacKitraugh. Slept on the floor. It was cold but I fared well. Had everything I needed.

June 17th
Awake at 5am. Spent the am making the circuit of Paris, could see the Eiffel Tower in the distance. Went thro' the prettiest part of France. Had much fun arranging the meals, which consisted of bully beef, beans, blackberry jam. The day passed in some sort of fashion – sleep, getting in and out of the train, talking to the French officials. Arrived at our destination at 9, but it being so late, we did not detrain. Had to prepare to pass another night on board.

June 18th
Early am breakfast. Have been picked Zone Major and had the pleasant job of having to billet the whole train. Had a good luncheon at a small café. The Company finally got settled in their respective places towards the pm. Much to be done. Very little food to be had and no rations. I am in a house with an old lady of 90. I have an excellent room and a fine bed. Could not be happier. After a good dinner I retired for I was all in, after the days on the train.

June 19th
Awoke much refreshed. The men had the am to themselves – cleaning up and arranging their quarters. Attended a meeting at 10am. Major Lanza appointed Sanitary, Policing and guarding units and certain subjects were discussed until luncheon. I had to interpret before the entire crowd. In the pm I also spent the time going around marking out places to put Loos. Wrote several letters. I could not go into details as to the number of people I spoke to – had a most interesting talk with a lady who owns a shop. Learned the conditions of the town etc. Bed at 10.

June 20th
Had breakfast at 9. Saw to the company drill also to procuring a doctor for the old lady opposite, who has organic heart trouble. He gave me some pills and certain directions as to diet etc. Luncheon. Had many small things to do. Also wrote some letters and talked to the lady down the street. Spoke to refugees from Verdun, a man who had some oxen, had a glass of wine with another. Supper with the company at 5.30, a glass of claret with Cris, – a long talk with more French, and to my room to write. Bed."

Letter from Maurice to Frank:

"France
June 20th '18

Dear Boy,
I wish I could go into the details of our trip over. We were so crowded and the days were unending. I tell you it was depressing. I was so glad to see the country of our birth, but unfortunately we did not stay there long. Boy, I cannot realize that I am here. I look at the sky and think of the happy years I had at home. I'm glad I loafed these last years – for I didn't miss a thing.

Perhaps your letters may not reach me. At any rate I shall write frequently. Boy, do take care of yourself. I am glad at least that you are on that side of the ocean and I hope you will never have to cross it.

At the rest camp in France, I met so many Australians and English. Boy, you soon realize the seriousness of it all out here. From where I am now, one can hear the big guns. I wish you could see the house where I am billeted – with an old lady with a cane – 90 years old. Boy, poor France, poor France. The old are just killing themselves in the fields and at home. I have details[159] of my men cutting wood about the village, helping – we are brushing the streets. There are no Frenchmen left; just the very old and young.

I sat on in the Square with the company. The food is much like what we had on the hike in Plattsburg in '16. I assure you I never looked better in my life, and I have everything I need. I have an excellent barber in my co. also Jeffrey, who was with the Goulds, & is quite as good as Herbert. All my stuff also came from home and I am nicely settled in my room.

Boy, just keep an eye on St Paul's. I made arrangements with Salkin to send all the funds that I have started to the Rector, my scholarships, George Work, and to the Orphan's Home, the SPS Camp; also for the payment of my life insurance policies. You and I have always been lucky, so don't give me a thought. I don't know if I shall hear from you but what is more important is that you should get news from me. I shall write as often as possible.

Let us all look forward to the time when we shall met again. I cannot tell you how glad I am to be over here. And I have no regrets at all. In the last few years at home I did everything I wanted to.

Much love, affec. Maurice."

---

[159] Small parties for special duties.

June 21st

Had mess with the company. Raining all am. Visited the new mess halls. Luncheon. Heard that one of my men had meningitis, made me frightfully worried. Wrote several letters and had talked with the people about here on things. Supper at 5.30. Read the NY Herald and visited around town.

June 22nd

Rain stopped. Sunshine from time to time. Nothing of interest to note. Beautiful day. Took a lady at 1.30 to have her tooth pulled. She was fearfully afraid and was nervous about the novocaine. Finally it came out quite easily She recovered and was a little hysterical. Not much shame. Visited some of the townspeople at 8. Lt. Quinn introduced me to two others, sat and talked and they played an old Victor.[160]

June 23rd

A beautiful Sunday. Went to the church at 10am. Very crowded with our men. Read the NY Herald afterwards. At 2pm met Capt McRae and we walked to another village house two miles from here. The walk was gorgeous, passing through typical French farming country – on either side were cherry trees. Met some medical officers and they took us to their quarters where they gave us an excellent supper, afterwards going to the old chateau and the church, which was founded in 1473. It was a beautiful old place, and I did enjoy every moment of it all. The walk back was equally as nice and I enjoyed Capt. MacRae's company. I stopped to see several friends, spoke to Monsieur Limard, the village harness repair man and my friend with the young child. Bed – 9.30.

June 24th

Breakfast in the village at 8.30. Went around to see Major Drewers. Met two YMCA representatives who had to be shown about the town in view of placing a branch here. Luncheon with the Co. Heard that Richard Mortimer had been killed – what a nice fellow he was – he will be missed around the North Shore. He was an aviator. Went to the Station to arrange the placing of certain men. Had a talk with the Station Keepers. After messing, there was general singing at the market place, and then a conversation with some people of the village and the lady with the baby. Have been pretty troubled with a flea that is attacking me fiercely. Bed at 0.30 pm.

June 25th

Had breakfast with Major Lanza. Then I watched a lady trim a large rabbit.

---

[160] A 78 rpm gramophone record player.

Received order to report back with company, but to still continue office of Town Major. Had several things to do – and at 4pm had a pleasant talk with Madame R. After supper there was general singing, and Cris and I took a walk over to a neighbouring village, where we met a young lady and her family, whom Cris had spoken to the day previous. It was the typical French house. The father and mother very affable, and the daughters. They produced cherries and we sat in a pretty garden, with a beautiful view. I heard their story, one son dead, another prisoner, and a third somewhere. It was a nice evening and I enjoyed it very much – a lovely walk home with the twilight. Had a very pleasant evening. Returning soon again. Bed at 8.30.

June 26th
Gas instruction at 11am. Busied myself about town: company policed its area. Inspected quarters for the installation of the dental unit: also infirmary. At 2pm took the company on a hike. Passed thru' some beautiful country, much like New Jersey. Arrived at a farmhouse where the men fell out and Cris and I talked over our life and what the prospects were for the future. Spoke to some of the people in the fields. Lovely sunshiny day. Came back and had a nice talk with Madame Riche, such a nice lady who owns a store in the public square. She is a very pleasant, smiling lady with nice children. I am constantly improving my French. She gave me cherries and the like. I have bought also several useful things from her. Talked for two hours with another lady of Vitrey, a pathetic story of pure loneliness. Bed at 10pm.

June 27th
Went around and looked for a place to put the stores; meat also other provisions. Took a look around town. At 7.30 went with Kurtzman to Betancourt to see the friends. Had a pleasant evening talking with the family. They seem to be very pleasant people; spoke of the US and its charms.

June 28th
Looked around with Hilbrandt for suspicious places, took Madame R to dentist. Nothing much in pm. Had an excellent bath with hot water. Walked with the people I met last night. Had some claret. Went to Hallikens room. Bed at 12.

June 29th
Company on guard. Not much in the am. A quiet Saturday. Took a look around the town as my Co. was on patrol. Sat about the pm with Madame R. Went after supper to Betancourt to get some eggs and have a glass of wine.

June 30th

A glorious hot day. Held Muster and talked to the men on various subjects. Spent an hour with the Riches. Luncheon. Slept after luncheon and then had a nice talk with several people. The NY Herald came to give us a little news. Sat around after supper until 10. Thus ends the month of June, which has been very pleasant in every respect.

Captain Roche in France, 1918

190

July 1st
Had the company doing drilling. Kurtz did not turn up. He has been put in confinement. Took the company out at 2pm to visit the Chauvirey Chateau. Then for walk in a roundabout way home. Such a glorious day. Cooley returned to company and heard that Greenleaf is well again.

July 2nd
Took the company down to the field and had drill. After luncheon had the men for a hike, which took us to a beautiful place on the hillside where we ate cherries and had a general nice time. After supper I dressed up and went to the Grandes where I enjoyed myself – had an excellent wine and cake. It was pleasant to be with nice people again. Back at 10.

July 3rd
Field work again. Practised for the 4th. Close order. Went for a hike and returned for an officers' meeting. Discussed plans and inspected council book. Played poker and did not enjoy it much.

July 4th
National holiday. Walked over to Pisseloup to investigate about a piano. Had luncheon over there with Kurtzmann. Returned for field sports. Had the usual games – tent pitching etc. In the evening the YMCA had a show. Some indifferent boxing, singing. Talked to Madame Riche."

On July 4th 1918, Ensign Frank Burke Roche sailed for Liverpool on HMS *Devonshire* bound for Rosyth, Scotland to report to the commanding officer of USS *Wyoming* for duty on that vessel. His exemplary conduct won him the honour of serving on this vessel. Since November 1917, the *Wyoming* had been in British waters, based at Scapa Flow,[161] patrolling off the British Isles. Together with three other dreadnoughts of the US Atlantic Fleet, they were invited by the Admiralty in London to form the 6th Battle Squadron of the British Grand Fleet.[162]

"July 5th 1918
Some company drill with exercises. Message transmitting. Pm took them for a walk, where they enjoyed some cherry picking – returned by way of Vitrey. Stopped in and had a glass of claret – supper. The Major, K & I sat in a cafe until 1.30pm. Bed."

---

[161] A natural harbour within the Orkney islands, off the north-east coast of Scotland.
[162] USS *Delaware, Florida* and *New York* accompanied the *Wyoming*.

Letter to Frank:

"July 5th 1918
Vitrey

Dear Boy,
You don't know what you are missing. I have been having the most interesting time. Whenever we are not busy, I have been talking to the people about here, whether in their kitchens or in the cafes.

I am about the only officer who can speak French at all fluently. I have the title of Town Major – and in connection with that, I have to sign all such papers that pass between this town and our Government.

Each day on these glorious trips, I find time to stop and pick the best black cherries you have ever seen. Boy, you should see the fields here, filled with poppies – the finest smell you ever had. Such glorious skies!

Often I sit and think of America, so far away. I can picture the people at the beach club... I must say I would infinitely rather be here. You would love it all. I get breakfast in a small cafe – 2 eggs, bread, butter, fine coffee, 1 franc. So you feel fine, for the air is always cool and no humidity.

The other day when I was walking to another village, I came across an old man cracking rocks. He pointed to a railroad cutting in the distance and said that 61 years ago he had his leg broken there, when they were constructing the railroad. He has been an invalid ever since, and has made his living so. He was nearly 80 years of age. It was pathetic to think of him having to work thus for a living.

We had a pleasant 4th July. There were some games which amused the inhabitants. It seems strange to see the men drinking claret at night. There is <u>no</u> more beer.

The men have a good time and the people are certainly glad to have them. Each day I detail men to help in the fields, and have men cutting wood about the town.

Still I shall be glad to get back to the States...Remember me to everybody. Take good care of yourself. Don't ever worry about me. I am so well and in the best of spirits –

love Maurice."

"July 6th
Held an inspection at 9.15 then a drill until 11.30. Wrote letters until 3.00pm then went over to the Bousquets. They got me a bicycle, sat around in the evening until 10.30pm.

July 7th

At 10 am I went with Cris to Jussey. It was frightfully hot but the trip was very nice. It was the first bicycle trip I had ever taken in France. We stopped from time to time. Arrived there and had a bottle of champagne. Good luncheon. Walked about the city and had a glass of wine with a lady who had lost her son. She showed me the book he had in his left pocket when he was killed. The bullet went right through the book. Went to a band concert where I spoke to the Mayor and was taken afterwards by St Blum to his house for tea. Had supper then afterwards reaching here at 9.30.

July 8th

Took 20 men to the parade ground. Too hot for work. Sat around. At 2pm went for a fishing excursion. No luck – had an excellent swim – the water was divine. Glorious evening – returned, had a poor supper. Went to have a glass of wine. Poor night's sleep.

July 9th

Company on guard. Went over to see some friends in the pm. Tried to write some letters but nothing of interest to write about. The inactivity is hard for officers and men – we hear constant rumours, with but little to do. Never any mail.

July 10th

At 9 took the company to Jussey. It is a fifteen-mile round trip. It had rained in the morning which made the walking good, no dust. The walk is up and down hill thru' nice country. We sang going thru' the various towns, arriving at 11.20. The men stacked arms in the courtyard. Luncheon in two sittings. K. and I had good lunch. Returned at 3.45pm, arriving tired at 6pm. All had a good time.

July 11th

Company attended the memorial service of the man in Company H. that died a week ago. Took company down to the field and gave them "gas alert" practice and close order. Went to a YMCA concert.

July 12th

Company on fatigue, wrote letters and looked after the Gaillard child who is really ill. At 1pm went down to the baseball field and at 3pm to the Bousquets, where I had tea and she prepared a speech for me to deliver on the 14th. Sat around in the pm and at 11pm went to Smythes room where we had some wine.

July 13th

Had company down to help with the baseball. Luncheon again at field. Went back to the town and sat around in the evening.

July 14th

National holiday. Everything went wrong. Had luncheon with Cris, no music appeared so the entertainment went flat. Went to Madame R's for tea. Sat around in the evening with her, then had some claret before going to bed.

July 15th

Drill in am. Very hot. Took the company to the river where we had a nice swim. In the pm sat around.

July 16th

Went on a hike thru' beautiful country. Men picked cherries while we rested. Have now covered all the walks in the vicinity. Certainly it is peaceful country. Weather has been rather too warm, but it has been a godsend to have this sunshine. As yet no mail, but that is to be expected.

July 17th

Took the men for a hike thru' Ouge over towards La Ferté. Very hot. Got back at 12 noon. Gave the men the pm off to get their wash ready for the trip.

July18th

News of our leaving tonight. Men prepared to go. Packed equipment. Rush order to be ready at 2. Said goodbye to Vitrey. Sat around in the pm until we left at 8pm. Pretty ride to Langres. Very dusty – rained from time to time. Reached Vaux at 2pm rained hard – men slept where they could. K & I pitched our tents and had a poor sleep.

July 19th

Woke up at 5am to inspect the guard – back for an hour's sleep. Had walk in the pm. Detailed to fit the trucks ready for the move at 6pm. Went to get some supplies for the night – eggs etc. went around town – struck tent."

The 78th division moved south to Roellecourt, near St Pol, west of Arras and became a unit of the British First Army.[163]

"July 20th

Prepared to leave in the pm. It was quite hot, bought some eggs and sardines

---

[163]   National Archives and Records Administration, Maryland, USA (NARA).

for the company. Broke camp at 5.30. Six sharp out of Vaux. Had 31 trucks in train. Everything went fairly well until we reached Langres. Here the ammunition went wrong. I went on to Fayl-Billot and arrived there – waited two hours without any reason. Then on to Vesoul. Arrived at Lure at 9. Had some breakfast. Saw Capt Maroni. Reached Belfort at 11.30, had luncheon. Camp at Chevremont at 2pm. Arranged for Co. to mess at cafe. Much worried and hot, found a bed for 2 francs.

July 21st
Awoke at 7.30 Had mess at Co. A and arranged for luncheon. Rest of train appeared. Marched up to Fort. Saw to arrangement of men in quarters cleaning and mess at 5pm. Officers meeting until 12 midnight.

July 22nd
At 6 am took breakfast and went to La Chapelle. Viewed the aviation field, loaded trucks, had a pleasant talk with Capt. Etienne. Saw a French SPAD return, with machine gun holes in it. Good luncheon with men. Started for Grandvillars. Reached there at 5, unloaded and came to Belfort where I had a shampoo and a good supper. Felt fine for the first time in days. Bed at 10.30pm.

July 23rd
Up at 6 am. Rearrangement of camp. I took the pm off and went to Belfort where I placed my laundry, bought things for the company. Also identification rings. Had a shampoo, and supper with the officers. Enjoyed it all enormously. Rained hard in the evening. Bed.

July 24th
Stayed around in the am. At 6pm took four trucks to La Chapelle where we loaded meat and ammunition. Lost 2 of our trucks in the dark. Returned to Fontaine, had a half hour rest and back to Valdoie and return to Fontaine. Up the entire night, cold and not much fun."

Letter to Frank:

"July 24th 1918

Dear Boy,
We have finally moved up to our job. We see daily aeroplane attacks; you ought to see the shrapnel burst around the Boche planes as they come over the lines! They are almost out of sight, and the puffs of white smoke that

appear all around the plane gives you the greatest thrill.

The journey here was very hard. I started with some thirty trucks all loaded with food & ammunition. I travelled at night, without lights and in a clear moonlight – the dust was fierce. I rode on the leading truck so got very little. We finally reached our destination – having only left two of them on the road for repairs. One had a broken steering knuckle, the other ran into the truck ahead & had smashed its radiator.

Boy, this is beautiful country. We are with another division, not ours. The work is at all times of the night & day. I was taking some ammunition out the other day when I passed an aviation field. While I was there I met such a nice French officer. He showed me the latest SPAD.[164] It costs a little over $12,000 and can do 170 miles per hour. It lasts only 60 hours; after that the engine is scrapped. They are "avions de chasse"[165] and only stay up two hours. They cannot volplane,[166] as they are so cut down that they can only travel at full speed. If your motor stops you are lost. A machine came in that had an engagement with a Boche & the wings were full of machine gun bullets. They fight at 15,000 feet elevation. It is very hard to see them with the naked eye.

Am feeling well. I hope that everything is well with you. Hear Quentin Roosevelt[167] has been killed flying. Am comfortable here; near a big city. Our postal number is 765. It is nothing for me to go the entire night without sleep. I thought I could never do it.

Love Maurice"

"*July 25th*
Reached camp at 10am. Went to bed for a few hours. Luncheon. Had the pm to myself. At 5pm mounted guard. After supper went into Belfort where I had a little champagne with Tom S., beautiful night, walked all the way home. Bed at midnight.

July 26th
Breakfast & shave 8am. At 10 went to Fontaine where I made purchases for the company. Most beautiful day. Luncheon. Spent the pm writing letters. Supper. Thought I was going out. Had a little trouble about not having men stationed on trucks.

---

[164] SPAD XIII. One of the most successful dog fighting planes of WW1., French designed and built.
[165] Fighter planes.
[166] Glide.
[167] President Theodore Roosevelt's youngest son. His father never recovered from this loss.

July 27th
Up at 7.30. Had a Sat. clean up. Rained in the am. Went down too Chevremont to buy some jam for the men. Good lunch. Shave, wrote letters went around to Howard's room where we had some "hearts". More rain – stayed in my room most of the pm waiting for orders. Never seems to be any possibility of getting any mail.

July 28th
At eleven I went into town & had luncheon with Quinn. It was very pleasant and the food good. I then went to a hotel where we met a Miss Colet & Miss Rochester. Very pleasant afternoon returning to camp at 6pm in time to take 8 cars to the front. First time I had to use password. "Verdun". Got them all there; home at 11.30. Very interesting evening – rode in a side car.

July 29th
At 8 set out for Chalonvillars where I met the convoy. "All present" & at 11.30 started for Lure. Luncheon outside of village with two nice officers in Signal Corps. Arrived at Luxeuil at 3.30. Return at 4pm. Met two very attractive ladies outside of Lure. Hope to see them again. Little car trouble – saw a huge dog run over by fast French auto. Poor thing, it was desperately hurt and a soldier sent him "home" with a blow on the head. Transferred soldiers and, while rest of train went to the front, I went to Bribotte & back. Back very tired at midnight.

July 30th
Had an easy time in the am. Investigation re what happened last night. Some sergeant hit one of my men. At 11.30 Miss Colet and Miss Rochester came out for luncheon. Spent the afternoon with Miss C. Very pleasant time, enjoyed it so much, lovely pm. Sat near the fort and discussed life. Walked back to Belfort, returned with Miss C and gave her a gas mask. Sat around and read Town Topics which amused me much. While in Belfort got laundry.

July 31st
Anti-aircraft guns in am. Saw the Major about things in general. At 2pm started for town, made a few purchases – sat in a music store and at 6pm took Madame Comby and her friends to dinner. Returned afterwards to dance, very amusing party with great success – home at 4am.

August 1st
Went to Belfort to get things I ordered yesterday. Bought Madame C a

bicycle, much pleased. Spent the pm sitting around waiting orders. Thought a good deal of home. Went to Belfort in the evening.

August 2nd - 9th
During these five days nothing of note. Nice dinner one night at M.C. great fun, danced. Have been unemployed. Weather has been raining and cold. Have nothing to report. Much time in town at Madame C."

On August 8th Maurice wrote to Frank:

"Dear Boy,
You cannot imagine what it is to be so long without mail. I haven't had a line since leaving the States. I hope everything has gone well and that you have been having a nice time.

We expect to move again soon. It has been particularly nice here. I have met some very nice people in a large town nearby, an awfully nice lady where I have had "tail" regularly. This city is large and it has been a relief to get a good meal, a barber shop and see some light.

We are billeted at present in a fort like Adams in Newport. Kurtzman and I have a room, our field rangers are set up outside. I have a particularly good pull with the chef and from time to time I have a juicy steak. I also buy things for the men to eat. Curiously though I have only spent four hundred dollars since May. I have still $1,600.00 plus my pay for June, July & August.

Boy, there have been some glorious days. Most of our work has been at night. You cannot imagine what is going on here. At night you see the Very lights in the front lines. We bring up all kinds of stuff,[168] even men. Our machines are running splendidly and the men making good in every way. Have seen only air-plane fights, none brought down.

Somehow I have not been able to write any letters of late. I simply cannot bring myself to the task. This is such a dull letter. I cannot bear to send it.

I am extremely well and let us hope that we shall all meet soon again. This must stop some day.

I trust you are well and keep an eye on St Paul's. You might notify me of any events in connection with the school.

With love
Maurice"

---

[168] Food supplies, clothes and ammunition.

"August 9th -15th inclusive
During these ten days the work was uneventful at Chevremont. The afternoons were spent in Belfort. Several nights were pleasantly spent at Madame Comby's. After having turned over our trucks to 104th, we have had little or no work. Each morning I have made it a point to have some physical exercise and then followed by a game of soccer. This has given the men much pleasure. I have given them passes for the afternoon. I spent one very pleasant Sunday, the 11th, a big luncheon at Charlis, then to Chaud to see the aviation. We were six at luncheon. Bought a very useful rest coat in town.

Had a nice afternoon with Miss Petrie at the Canteen. Such a nice girl gave her $100 for her work. Took her to dinner and thoroughly enjoyed it all. Belfort afforded much diversion after what we have had. Have had enough of it.

August 16th
Word came this pm that we are to leave tomorrow at 6am. Have no time to say "goodbye". Gave instructions to men to be prepared. Bed early.

August 17th
Up at 4. Not much time to get ready – fall the companies in at 5.30. At 6 am started for Fontaine. Men march too much overloaded; the hike proved to be a very great hardship. Many men fell out or were otherwise distressed. It was hot. Officers too were forced to carry packs. We arrived at Fontaine in good time and at 11 started (marching again). The curious thing of it all was the fact that we passed right through Chevremont again. Belfort was reached at 2pm. The journey was uneventful. Chris, Murray and Quinn were with me. We had plenty to eat. The night was spent at Epinal. I slept on the floor, not well.

August 18th
The am we passed thru' several towns, stopping one hour at a staff centre. Arrived at Neufchateau at 2pm. Detrained. and were carried 12 kil. to Sartes where we are billeted. I have a nice room and on the whole things are going very well. The men are in Adriance Barracks. Had some eggs at 6pm, met a gentlemen from St Die who had been placed against the wall by the Germans prepared to be shot. The fact that his wife spoke German saved his life. Bed at 10pm.

August 19th
Felt splendid after a restful night. Good breakfast. Saw that the company

had been settled. Spoke to various people. Luncheon. At 5pm held a "retreat" which caused the men to be in perfect condition. They were able to take baths. After supper Chris and I went over to an adjoining village where we had a glass of claret. Fine moonlight night. Bed at 10.

August 20th

Was late for reveille – in the morning company did close orders. I wrote some letters. After luncheon took a hot bath. Had a talk with the Major on certain forms wanted. Spoke at length with a French family. Retreat at 5. After supper walked over to the next village to hear a band concert. Also heard some stories of the life in the trenches. Beautiful moonlight night. Bed!!"

On August 20th, 303rd Supply Train left the British sector and moved to the area around Bourbonne-les-Bains, (Haute Marne).

"August 21st

At 8.15 went for a hike. Extremely hot. One man collapsed on the way home. Officers mess started. Sat around & censored letters until 3.30pm. In the evening went over to a large base hospital and had a very amusing time, dancing and talking with the nurses. Very nice Canadians.

August 22nd

Took the company over to the stream where we had a good morning's drill – exercise, close order and gas drill. Pm took bath, men also. Officers' mess started, very good. Sat around. Went over to next village.

August 23rd

Company on guard. Took reveille and made inspections. Very warm in pm. Not much to report. Heavy storm at 8pm.

August 24th

Held inspection. At 12.30 call round to get out. At 2pm trucks arrived. At 3pm left Sartes for Langres. Pleasant drive of 60 miles. Beautiful country. Passed many Yankee troops. Arrived at 8pm. Saw Ham Fish. He has been wounded slightly. Company placed in barracks.

August 25th

Year ago to-day I entered Plattsburg Camp. Breakfast at 6.30. At 11am started for Dijon to get transportation. Pleasant drive arriving at 4.30pm. Company pitched tents. Beautiful evening. Bed at 9pm.

August 26th
Good night's sleep. At 9am went into Dijon and looked around. When I returned, I found that I was pulling out at 2pm. Men pleased. Packed up and went to Motor Park where they gave me 40 AECs[169] & 4 motor cars. It was five pm before we started. Could hardly believe my eyes when I was told that I had to go to Vitrey. Travelled up to 1pm. Camped just near Gray. Beautiful night. Pulled my blanket roll off the truck and slept on the side of the road.

August 27th
Up at 6am Arrived Vitrey at 9.30. Everybody very glad to see us. Madame Riche most enthusiastic. Had lunch with her at 3.30pm. Took the sanitary train to Bourbonne-les-Bains, arrived at 6pm. Found quarters at the Town Mayor. 44 rue –. Bed at 10"

On August 22nd, the 78th Division left the British sector and headed for the American sector, looking forward to returning to their own rations!

"*August 28th*
Up early and spent busy day at the Park. Company C arrived, dispatched cars all day, also saw the 78th Div. on the march. Back and forth between Div. headquarters. At 7pm went over to see Madame Riche at Vitrey – had a very nice evening. Home at midnight.

August 29th
Busy in the am at the Park. Walked about and arranged the transportation system. Luncheon at park. At 4pm I went and took one of the baths. Nice talk with Dave Milburn. Water very hot. At 4.30 went to a band concert. Supper at 6.30 At seven pm went to Vitrey to pass the evening. Not a very pleasant visit.

August 30th
Had breakfast at the hotel. Came to Park. Things going smoothly. Bought things around town. In the pm worked on the ration slip and walked in the Park. Had supper at the hotel and then went around there later to hear some singing. Bed.

August 31st
Up at seven. Everything going nicely at the Park. There was much rejoicing for at 10am the first mail since our arrival in Europe came. I had a letter

---

[169] Armoured trucks.

from Maman, Lucy, Cynthia, Grace, Kimball, Mr White, Mrs Somerville, Zenabru. It certainly was nice to hear from them. I have read them over and over. Frank is near Liverpool. At 6pm went to Vitrey to look up gas question. On to see Madame Riche. Major Lanza and I had supper together. After that went to Madame Riche's for an hour.

Sept 1st
Sunday am at the Park until 12 noon. Then had luncheon and played around with Madame Ferney. Not pleased. Supper with John Butter. Heard the latest gossip from the States. Went to the "Thermes". Bed.

Sept 2nd
Dispatched two companies. Censored letters, lunched at the hotel. Went for a walk with Madame F. In the evening went to the Hospital to see some Red Cross people. Most gorgeous day I have seen since being over here. Preparing to leave tomorrow.

Sept 3rd
At 8.30 I started with 18 trucks. Uneventful trip to Bouzy. Some more mail awaiting our train; many reports to send out, much annoyed that my first sergeant not here. Bed early.

Sept 4th
At 7 went back to Bourbonne where I saw the remainder of my trucks getting under way. Back at 11. At luncheon, Major Lanza asked me to take Col Lembourg to Langres. Started at 3pm with an interpreter. Col. very talkative. At 5pm fell into Fair Osbourne and Ham Fish. Also Paul Mills. He told me of Phil's death by a rifle grenade. Got a burn, worse luck and came home late. Many regrets.

Sept 5th
Very ill am – resolved not to drink again. Poor day of it. Nothing accomplished at all. Kurtzmann gone most of day. All companies free but ours and A's. From now on it will not be much fun I feel. Bed at 8.30

Sept 6th
Company on guard. Bad day of rain. Much refreshed. Had the job of dispatches. Things went well. Gorgeous day. At 4 pm went up to the Lembourgs for tea, very amusing at tea and after that arranged for trip taking place at 3am.

Sept 7th

Up at 3. Hot breakfast. Went to Damblain, spent am loading, back at 12. Found letter from Frank & Edith Travis. Glad to hear Frank on North Sea. Had an excellent lunch with the Lembourgs. After luncheon, Jeffrey came to tell me that we were leaving. Went back and packed up. Left at 3.30, beautiful trip to Mannonville. Found to my great joy many letters from Grace, Cynthia, Frank, etc. Had a most beautiful time reading them over. Have had all my mail by now.

Sept 8th

Good night's sleep. Out at Park – duties all am. Lunched there & at 3pm – write letters etc; at 5pm talked to people about here. Bed at 10.

Sept 9th

Heavy rain all morning; up at Park, nothing much to report. Have been just looking around & attending to things. Not much to say. Have a good room. Bed early. Much rested.

Sept 10th

Up at 7. Took a trip to see about the road tomorrow. Rained hard all day, lunched at the Heurys. Saw 600 trucks pull by – assisted in rescuing a truck from the mud. Ate at the H. Bed.

Sept 11th

Orders to leave. Said goodbye to my friends and left at 10.30. Trip thro' pouring rain. Kept right thru' to Toul. Beautiful city. Barracks on the outskirts. Company much like at Chevremont. Had supper in town, bed early.

Sept 12th

Offensive on. It rained most of the am. Busied myself around the company. In the pm mail arrived. More from Grace, Maman, Cynthia. Very glad to get it. Went to Toul to visit 11th century church – home. Heard that there was a train out, jumped on – most interesting ride out to the front. Flashes of guns. Many German prisoners passed. Saw a huge gun in action. Home at 4.30am."

The St Mihiel salient[170] had been held by the Germans since September 1914. Two years earlier, General Pershing began to plan an attack on this position as the US Army's first offensive operating as an independent American army.

---

[170] "A salient is a bulge in a line between two opposing armed forces. Soldiers occupying a salient face the disadvantage of having to defend three sides." *Spartacus Educational.*

"The reduction of the St Mihiel salient was important, as it would prevent the enemy from interrupting traffic on the Paris-Nancy Railroad by artillery fire, and would free the railroad leading north through St Mihiel to Verdun in this sector on 11 September."[171]

Pershing assembled 500,000 troops, of which about 70,000 were French. Nearly 1,500 French, British and American aircraft were assembled, the largest air force ever engaged in a single operation. On August 22nd, the 78th Division parted company with the British and started for the American sector, travelling south over two days to Bourbonne-les-Bains where their headquarters were located. The Division was now a part of the First Army and received the order to send the Lightning into action: "The First Army (US) will reduce the St Mihiel salient."

The 78th acted as 1st Corps reserve in the American attack on September 12th. The troops moved into their reserve positions during the night of Sepember 11th, prepared to jump into the attack at any point where it might be necessary. The salient was quickly reduced by the assaulting American troops, before nightfall and ahead of schedule. General Pershing described the success of the operation:

"The rapidity with which our divisions advanced overwhelmed the enemy, and all objectives were reached by the afternoon of September 13. The American army fighting under its own flag, made a quick passage through wire entanglements. French officers were ordered to visit the terrain to learn now Americans overcame these obstacles. They used wire-cutters or walked over, forming a bridge out of chicken wire."[172]

The front which the Americans had taken over came to be known as the Limey sector. It was seven kilometres long. The mission of the 78th was now to hold and organise this ground for defence, while maintaining an aggressive attitude. Two days after the offensive, the Division relieved the 2nd and 5th Divisions and came under fire for the first time. The Germans, aware of the difficulties of organizing a front after an offensive, brought their artillery into play, pouring numerous shells into the town of Thiaucourt, reducing dwellings to ruins and causing numerous casualties among the troops.

The 78th's casualties in the Limey sector totalled 2,170 in seventeen days, of whom 329 were killed or died of wounds.[173] The First Army took 16,000 prisoners and 257 guns at a cost of about 7,000 casualties. This was an important boost to the morale of the Americans and the Allies.

---

[171] Primary records: John J Pershing on the Battle of St Mihiel, November 1919
[172] *My Experiences in the World War*, p. 587
[173] *War Story of the 78th Division* by Major Philip D. Hoyt, assistant chief of staff.

"Sept 13th
Little sleep, no breakfast – dull day. Heard that Major Lanza had been given a higher command. He is leaving. Thank heaven. A most inefficient man, utter disregard for his command. At 8pm I left with 10 trucks for Rosieres. Arrived, saw Major Lumley, came back and spent night in Toul. Will be with this ammunition train henceforth.

Sept 14th
Up at 6am. Started for Rosieres, where I got the remainder of the trucks there on an ammunition dump. Then on to Limey. Here is where the offensive began. Nothing remains of village. Saw just things relative to the war. Great confusion. Had no orders so stayed outside of town. At five I went to see where the attack had taken place. Soon came on a burying party. My first view of our dead. A Lt Wickersham & 7 men all buried together, much impressed with it all. After supper we started on thru' Limey. Many dead horses and several of our men were lying to the right and left of the road, & a German or two. After we got by the German front line trucks, we stopped to spend the night. Major Lumley, Captain Mitchell and myself. Heavy firing going on.

Sept 15th
I shall always remember this day for I saw more things than any other in connection with the war. When I woke up, I was cold. Not far away lay two of our Yankees dead – one had his right arm blown off, the other had received some shrapnel thru' his face. What a sight. After arriving at the dump we prepared breakfast. In the cemetery lay two Germans and a Yank. Saw a great air battle in which a Boche plane came down in flames, a fierce fight. Saw them bury the Germans. Came down, met Dr Milburn, talked over the situation and had lunch.

On the way back I saw a Boche bring down two Captive balloons. He had come over in an American plane and when within striking distance had opened fire. The observers jumped out and fortunately had parachutes and they came down gracefully to the ground. The balloons soon caught fire and it was a great sight. Returned to the Park, then I went walking with Jeffrey over the battlefield. Came back, reaching Toul at 8pm. Had a cup of coffee then to bed tired. We are leaving for another rail-head at 7am. By far the most impressive day of my life.

Sept 16th
Up at 6 and got away at 9am. Camped near Francheville. Luncheon. Sat about in pm. Wrote letters. Beautiful moonlight. Bed at 8pm under gorgeous sky.

Sept 17th
Rained in am. Went up to Limey. Battlefield cleaned up. Saw where a French truck carrying munitions had blown up, killing driver. Lunch at Limey. Nice drive home. Beautiful day. Watched some aviators perform. Gorgeous moonlight. Mail arrived one from Lucy, Cynthia. Very nice all of them.

Sept 18th
Rained hard all am, went to Neufchateau, had luncheon, saw Hennie Young who used to go to Allen's school years ago. Took side car and went to Manoncourt where the Heurys received me in great style. They were wonderful to me. Had a pleasant trip home arriving at 8pm. Bed.

Sept 19th
Rained early. Sat around and wrote letters in the am. A fearful rainstorm in the pm. I went in search of new billets. Nothing in Francheville. Finally at Bouvron returned – more rain – bed at 9.30pm Hear we are going on a trip tomorrow.

Sept 20th
Up by 7. Breaking camp. Started at 9.30 with rations – uneventful trip. First sect. arrived at 2pm. Went with Jeffrey towards Thiaucourt – saw pm shelling and town in distance – most interesting. Thiaucourt also shelled. Viewed one of our boys who had been killed at noon by a shell. Returned at 7pm, most wonderful moonlight night. Back to Bouvron where I have a very good billet. Talked for a few hours – Bed at 11pm. This was the first day that I have seen a bursting shell and its effect.

Sept 21st
Good night's sleep. Looked around and attended to company things. Went to the YMCA. Wrote several letters. Luncheon. Took a hot bath which was fine. In the evening I motored over to Base Hospital. I saw where Lufberry was buried. Also met Major Tilton who promised me to take me around. Bed.

Sept 22nd
Beautiful day. Church. After luncheon went to Manoncourt arriving at 5pm. The Heurys glad to see me, sat around and talked and had an excellent dinner. Spent the night after taking the aunt for her first motor drive.

Sept 23rd
Up at 5.30. Good breakfast and started back at 6am. Got here at 8am

found that nothing had taken place. Rained most of am. Quiet day. At 7.30 went over to see Miss Webster and Miss Townsend. Very pleasant evening. Nice girls. Saw many casualties coming in in ambulances. Bed at midnight.

Sept 24th
Officer of the day. Made the usual inspections, also wrote letters. At 3pm motored to Nancy. A beautiful city – wonderfully laid out. Walked about the city and had an excellent dinner. At 8pm returned. Much pleased with everything I saw in Nancy. Wish I had gone there in peacetime.

Sept 25th
Good night's sleep. Meeting at 8am to discuss train topics. A glorious am. Sat around. Luncheon went to the Pattis. In the evening went over to the Base Hospital where I had a very pleasant evening with Miss W & Miss Townsend. Long walk home, heavy firing. Leaving tomorrow.

Sept 26th
Left at 9am for Norian. A poor place, poor quarters. Village has been heavily shelled and has every evidence of the war's destruction. Good lunch at the Company's mess – getting settled afterwards. At five pm started for the Red Cross, got Miss Webster and Miss Townsend, went to Toul for dinner – fairly nice time. Returned at 8.30pm and after a talk with Miss Webster came back to bed.

Sept 27th
Up at 7. Have ration trucks today. Went down to railhead then to hospital to see Miss W. Returning witnessed burial of five men. Service by the chaplain. On to the dump. After luncheon witnessed shelling. Ration cart hit, two men wounded. Shrapnel fell around. Very interesting work. Back at 6.30. Had some mail from Elizabeth and Helen. Bed at 9.

Sept 28th
Nothing much all the am. Signed papers and busied myself around. At 3.30 pm I motored over to Nancy with Joe Hallihan. Went to a restaurant where we had some drinks and then picked up two women and took them to dinner. I got tired of mine and came back at 1am. Didn't have a particularly good time.

Sept 29th
At 9am went to ration dump – saw Miss W at the dump. Then back here for

luncheon and on to the front. Much trouble with the trucks which were horribly stuck. Saw some 9.2s fired, also anti-aircraft guns fired and much interest by all onlookers. Returned at 7, home 8.30. Wrote letters. Bed.

Sept 30th
Cool day. Spent the am. writing letters and censoring company mail. Read the newspapers after luncheon and had a nap. After supper, Miss Rochester and Sister arrived. Gave them something to eat and then motored back to Toul. Had a slight collision with side car. Nobody hurt, arrived at 11.30 and stayed at hotel until after midnight, when we returned home, puncture en route. Home at 2am.

Oct 1st
A dull cold day. Sat around in the am. Read the papers and censored mail. The months are passing rapidly and today Salkin pays the first instalment of the George Work scholarships. After luncheon, I received several very nice letters from home. At 5.30 went to Red Cross and played cards.

Oct 2nd
Cold day. Nothing much in am. War news excellent. Censored letters and made my rounds. Officers' meeting at 6.30. Discussed train topics. After meeting, I went to a prayer meeting at the YMCA and read some magazines. Bed at 9pm."

On October 2nd, the order came that the 78th were to be relieved in the Limey sector. At the same time, the 303d Ammunition Train was relieved. The relief began on the following night of October 3rd - 4th.

"Oct 3rd
Up at 7.30. Taking ration trucks up. Went up at 10am, spent the day near the front. Saw some shelling, also heard a man explain some of the movements of a big gun and the composition for drill. Back in time for supper. Sat around, wrote until tired. Bed.

Oct 4th
Nothing much in the am. Censored letters. After luncheon, there was nothing to do – our division being relieved. At 7 went down to see Miss Webster who was in tears having received some mail from the US that touched her. She lost her fiancé here in this war. Back at 10pm for bed. Two letters from Helen today.

Oct 5th

Nothing much to do this day. Saw to my pay (May-Sept) vouchers etc. Five months being sent home amounting to over a thousand. Took a bath and sat in the sun and wrote letters. Bed."

Letter to Frank:

"Oct 5th 1918

Dear Boy,

Ever since my last letter things have been very quiet here. I have only seen some artillery work with some huge naval guns. The shelling has been less, altho' one day I stood and watched it for about 3 hours. Several pieces fell very near to where I stood.

Not far away are some extremely nice Red Cross girls – one from Worcester and one from Washington. Cris and I go down several nights a week to chat and play cards. It kills the evenings.

Cynthia has been fine about writing. Mama has had one of her usual depressions in August. You and I know just what that means – just nerves from having nothing to do & worrying. I wrote her a stiff letter about getting interested in the Red Cross or even the Blue Cross.

Boy, if you could see the deal the horses get in this war. After the advance, you can see them standing like so many skeletons by the wayside. They have the most lonely death in France – not even a man to care for them or give them a drink of water. From where I am sitting, back of my billet in a shell-torn town, I can see several "wrecks" grazing & one has a left leg the size of an elephant's. He has been struck by a piece of shell. But this one is receiving attention and will eventually recover.

I have no news here. France is too lovely now. Lovely October days. It is hard at times to believe that I am over here. Boy, I never would have missed it for anything. It has your job beaten a mile. I have been in at least forty towns in France; have motored the whole distance, seen beautiful country, its been like a huge vacation. My nerves have been just right, I haven't had a moment's bad health all summer. I get a little tired of eating out of a mess kit at times, but the food is very good & the minute steaks I get some days would make your mouth water.

Much love Maurice"

"Oct. 6th

Took many trucks to Sorcey. Beautiful ride over there – place men in casual. Trucks loaded. News of Germany's trying to sue for peace eagerly received.

209

It does not seem possible that this war may be over soon! Supper and slept in a truck. Nice talk before retiring.

Oct 7th

Up at 6 and arrive at Pierrefitte at 8.30. Long day of waiting around & finally we drew away at 4pm. Found that I made a mistake by coming back here. Should have gone to Sorcey. Will be off in am again.

Oct 8th

Over at 8am to Sorcey. Took a section of forays to Les Islettes. A whole day's run, thru' a good deal of rain. Very pretty country over magnificent roads. Arrived at Pierrefitte, then on to Jubecourt, lost the train. Fierce fog going thru' Clermont, arrived to find much confusion – finally found a room with the 26 engineers – had a cup of coffee and opened my blanket-roll. Bed at 9.30, lot of strange men in the room.

Oct 9th

Fine night's sleep. Breakfast on the am. (*ammunition dump*). Managed to have the trucks dispatched. Good lunch with engineers, read papers. Fortunately we have had a nice day with sunshine. Met Jaime Fargo and we are eating together this evening. Had a fine dinner and talked over conditions, afterwards went to a moving picture place. Bed at 9.

Oct 10th

Up at 9. Cris arrived with the field kitchen. Went around to see when we could get installed. Everything going nicely. Passed the pm by going over towards Verdun. Supper in the evening sat around & played with the five Kitchs that are making their homes with us. Saw Thomas Robinson."

On October 10th, the 78th Division relieved the American 77th division in the front line in the Meuse-Argonne Offensive, where it participated without respite until November 5th. The targets were the two chief enemy strongholds of Bois de Loges and Grand Pre. The Division suffered heavy losses. Twenty companies were reduced to the fighting strength of a full battalion. 890 enlisted men and 17 officers were killed; more than 4,000 enlisted men and 135 officers were wounded. Among the 15 National Army Divisions at the Front, the 78th stood second in the number of men killed in action. "By engaging, wearing out and finally driving in headlong retreat, elements of nine enemy divisions during its operation on the Argonne front, this Division contributed its share to the final collapse of the German army."[174]

---

[174] Major Philip D Hoyt, assistant Chief of Staff. *War Story of the 78th Division.* Operations report on the Argonne movements of the 78th Division.

"Oct 11th

At 10am went towards the line. Saw much destruction and horror due to this drive. Had luncheon. Great confusion, many men about, saw huge German graveyards and their great constructions in this part of the world. Came back and sat around. After supper, came back and soon to bed.

Oct 12th

At 9 started for Chatel. Saw the results of the battlefield; many Germans lying here and there in fearful condition. Very much blown up. Burying parties here and there. Spoke to a French captain on the conditions just now. He thinks France will soon be cleared of the Boches. I sincerely hope so. Met Cris up there and we again visited the Battlefield where the men were strewn about; back in time for supper; had some mail from home – 2 from Maman, Lucy & Helen, Sue, Frank. Came back and read letters until bed hour.

Oct 13th

Glorious news that the Great War is about to close. May it only be true! Went to the railhead and saw to the day's programme and then at 12.30 I started for Varennes to arrange for the train. Never saw so many trucks in my life. Came back at 4pm. Marvellous work being done by the engineers. News of Germany having accepted Wilson's terms caused great excitement. Came back to room and talked over the future.

Oct 14th

Up at 7. Cris and Murray slept the night in Bar le Duc. Had most of the train officers for breakfast. Busied myself around company and censored letters. Cup of coffee for luncheon. At 2pm motored over to Verdun – the city is practically all in ruins. Several shells fell in the city when we were there. Visited the Cathedral 12th cent. Also viewed the city's fortifications. A twenty mile ride home. Found a letter from Frank. Supper. Returned to write letters."

Letter to Frank:

"Oct 14th 1918:
AmericanYMCA

Dear Boy,

I am glad to hear that you like your job, which sounds interesting. Also that you have done some visiting and seen dear old England. I must add a word about what our men & officers are doing here. The officers here behaved disgracefully in all the large cities. I have seen them in Belfort, Nancy, Dijon just raising "hell".

None of our men have any regard for anyone else, they are daily robbing gardens, they throw everything from the cars, search every place they go into, and have stolen hay from the barns to sleep on, burnt every piece of wood they lay their hands on. They have acted just like a wild mob, fiendish driving over the roads, insulting all the French women.

I have very little to do with the officers in this train because they are <u>not</u> gentlemen. A <u>lady</u> had to ask me to tell my lieutenant that she wished he would stop trying to kiss her for it annoyed her – just things like that. Their conversation is always with the usual vulgar remarks, and all other disagreeable things that you and I both dislike. They have never been trained.

I have recently seen another fierce battlefield & have never seen such injuries as those the men died from – heads cut open, arms off, even bodies in two – everything beyond medical repair. I saw a Boche who had a bandage on one arm & beside him lay the Red Cross man. A 75mm shell had killed them both. Another man had been run over by a tank. When I see you again I will tell you some spicy things.

Well I think this show is nearly all over. Let us meet [back] home as soon as possible. I have a trip which we must take – don't think of coming over here. I have seen every place including Verdun and I can assure you it isn't worth seeing – such devastation you have never seen. I have seen thousands of trees cut down, ruthlessly; beautiful houses blown up; churches smashed to pieces. Do keep away from it."

Love Maurice

"Oct 15th
Dull gray day. At 11am went up with the trucks to the dumps. Witnessed all kinds of interesting things on the road. Went to the wrong dump. Fearful congestion. At 4pm witnessed a French 140 in action – most interesting to watch – very pleasant officers. Back in Lt. Smith's car and had supper at 8pm. Raining hard. The idea of an early peace seems gone. Fell asleep all dressed.

Oct 16th
Raining hard at 1pm. I took 12 trucks to Lançon. Very tough trip, much waiting before getting to L. Arrived but nobody as usual to show dumps. Left at 10pm on French truck, had good luck and got a ride almost all the whole way back, by quick thinking and some running. Back at 1am. Heard from an ambulance man that I had been reported killed. They were glad to see me. Read the papers when I got back. Glad oh so glad to be home.

Oct 17th

At 7am Cris went up. Sat around and censored letters all morning. It has been such a dismal day. Continual rain. Sat around and talked. It was a day of rest. Wrote letters. Bed. Must say that an extremely nice chaplain passed the night with us. A Princeton man. Had an interesting talk with him.

Oct 18th

Beautiful smashing day. Everybody felt different. It was glorious. Had a hair cut & at 1pm jumped on a truck to go to Lancon. Beautiful fall afternoon which I enjoyed very much. Cup of coffee. & bed at 11pm.

Oct 19th

Cris gave me five letters from home. Drury on Roche scholarship matters, Helen, Salkin. Arranging system for ration trucks. Took the motor cycle and went to St Menehould where I bought some stationery. A pleasant pm. Nice rides home. Supper. Came back and talked to the chaplain who is a nice man. Bed.

Oct 20th

Pass the am in the orderly room and in arranging things. This is another Sunday. Rode last section up at 2.30pm. A fierce day of rain. Nothing could be gloomier. Back here by 8. Found a friend of Cris here named Backus. Read the papers etc. bed.

Oct 21st

Passed the am about here. At four went over to the Evacuation hospital with Cris. Band concert. Then on to St M, bought a few things and took my laundry. Supper – two letters. Then went back to Red Cross – looked at an operation on a man's hand, thru the door. Nice talk with Miss Young. Bed at 11.

Oct 22nd

Up at 8. Fixed up Co. book. At 10 went to railhead, then to St M. saw Monroe Robinson who gave me some good war news. Then on to Lancon. Went to "triage" where I saw some men from Vitrey. Viewed a dead Yankee Then back to St M and to the hospital. Saw some badly wounded, three men who were not expected to live thru' the night. Back to tea. Couldn't help but think of the horrors of this war. Bed at 10pm.

Oct 23rd

Beautiful day. Censored mail all morning. Real summer here. Luncheon and at 1pm started for Varennes. Like a June day. You never would believe there was a war. Arrived and could see the fighting in the distance. At about 4pm I saw the most amazing stunt pulled off by a Boche since I have been here. Three anti-aircraft guns announced his approach; and amid a blizzard of machine gun fire, he executed a nose dive and when directly over it, opened up with his machine gun and put the balloon in flames & escaped. It seems to me to be strange that nobody got him even after finishing his act. Shrapnel burst everywhere around him and he flew home in safety. Back by 7 and had supper. Sat around and read in the evening. Saw Snowden Fahnstock.

Oct 24th
Had a letter from Drury and Salkin. At 11am I started up to the dump with turner. It was a lovely day – had a puncture – tried to make myself understood with some German prisoners – none spoke English. After a jam sandwich, I went to the hospital where I saw some wounded – bullet wounds in the knee, leg, arm & back. Very interesting work. First I had seen in my life. Back at 4pm. Found a nice package of food from Madame Riche – nice woman. I shall always remember her. Wrote letters. Bed.

Oct 25th
Wrote letters in the am. Had a captain from the chemical warfare for luncheon. We talked of several topics and future plans. At 3pm I jumped on a truck and went to St. Menehould to look for my laundry. Had a bottle of champagne. Stopped at the Red X and met a Miss Lebrenk. Back at 6.

Oct 26th
At 9.30 started with Kreoh and Schrenk to go to Menil le Freme. Kreoh made a mistake and we went to the wrong place, driving aimlessly about the place. Back at 1pm and I found about eleven letters from Helen, Cynthia, Salkin and Grace. Sat around and wrote most of the pm. At five, Cris brought in a piano & stayed for supper, giving me a brief of what he has been doing since coming over here last March. Bed at 11.30: Nice letter from Madame Riche.

Oct 27th
It was just five months ago today that we came over. How much longer it does seem! Another month will soon give us our first stripe. Went up to division headquarters and got some cigars and candy for the men. Luncheon. At 1pm Marcus and Turner and I went to Lançon. It was a gorgeous day. We stopped to hear some music and saw lots of air activity.

At the triage, I saw some wounded and also had some nice talks. Long trip back, supper – a nice letter from Maman, Grace and the faithful Helen. Bed."

Letter to Frank:

"Oct 27th '18

Dear Boy,
Yours of the 7th just reached me. You say that this is about the seventh you have sent me. I can only say that I have had but two. I cannot understand why the mail is so bad between these two points.

Regarding the opening of mail in the US I have the same thing happen to mine – however I feel sure that Salkin opens mine – Mama has a rotten habit of doing that – and think it is damn cheek to do it. She hasn't been very good about writing these last two months. Lucy wrote that she has had the blues all summer – not to be too critical – but anybody who leads such a selfish life is bound to. I don't believe she is interested in a single thing at home.

It is out of the question my ever getting to England. I advise you not coming here. If you get any time off go to London or play about where you are. Nothing is more boring than to be where the fighting is going on. There is nothing to do. You can't see anything unless your unit is on the front. If you think that Paris would amuse you – go there.

Boy I saw a remarkable thing pulled off by a Boche plane the other day. I was just a little back from the front at a divisional dump. Overhead was a huge sausage balloon. In the west the bursting of shrapnel told us of the presence of a Boche plane. Well, if he didn't zigzag his way thru' the air and when directly over the balloon, open up with his machine gun and set it afire – while the observers came down in parachutes. It seemed a miracle that he escaped the rattle of machine gun bullets & shot; however I had the satisfaction of seeing one of our men bring down a Boche balloon at a later hour. It is extraordinary how you get used to seeing shells land & know by the sound whether they are coming your way or are flying over.

I stopped at a dressing station the other day & getting up my nerve I marched myself in. I saw very nearly every kind of a wound being dressed as the men came in. I thought it would make me feel faint – but not at all – the only thing that is unpleasant is to see abdominal wounds, for the intestines generally are pushed out. The men are so brave, but as they generally have morphine, they don't really suffer until later on. I saw three men that day breathing their last. One had a piece in his head, another gas

215

gangrene, another shot thru' the stomach.

Before one died he said everything was getting very black in front of him. The doctor explained to me that it was his failing that caused that. Boy, I had tears in my eyes as he said: "Good-bye Captain", for he never knew me, only he was a good soldier and felt that I was perhaps helping to save his life. I often go around to them when they are lying on the stretchers and ask them how they are and the story how they got hit. I always like to shake hands with them. They have had a fierce time of it. So it goes.

I am extremely well as usual. Let us hope that this war will soon end. I think it will…

love Maurice"

"*Oct 28th*
Beautiful day. At 10am C & I went to Ste. Menehould where we picked up two Red Cross ladies and went up to Lançon. Saw some wounded & then walked over to see a sausage balloon – picked up by an MP. Back on Bearers truck – lovely pm. Had supper at 5.30pm. Sat around and wrote letters.

Oct 29th
In the am attended to company matters. At 3pm went to hear Band concert. Saw an English aviator who had been shot in the legs. From outside the operating room, I saw them give him the ether and start the operation – one bullet was located at once – the other took some time. Went over to St M and had a few purchases to make. After supper, Cris and I went to St M to have a game of bridge. Pleasant talk with Miss L and Miss S. Talked war and other topics – back at midnight. Vienna states she is ready for separate peace. Bed at 12.30

Oct 30th
Beautiful day. Had some poor people of the village to take care of. Think peace is not far away. Took Capt. Ray and Wilson to the front. En route bought some things for the officers at the triage. Went over to chapel, witnessed a Boche trying to down a sausage. He was unsuccessful. Two men jumped out and I saw the whole thing. Listened to a band concert and then talked to a Vet. who was attending to a sick horse. Back with the officers to Rosecourt. Supper – back to write letters.

Oct 31st
After some company work, I went to St M where I had my picture taken. Then on to Lançon. Had a nice talk with the medics. Came back and after supper went over to St M and had a very pleasant evening, met some new

216

people and read the papers. Some paperwork here, the drive towards offensive on!

Nov 1st
Received word that I must move to Lançon. Arranged for transfer, comes up at 1pm. Looked around for a place to billet – have a place for the night – good supper – had a talk with the mayor regarding the English system. Very pleasant supper. Bed at 8.30pm.

Nov 2nd
Turkey abdicates. Watched some big field pieces – started to rain – my company arrived at 2pm. Busied myself around until evening.

Nov 3rd
At 8 started for Grandpré. Saw where all the fighting took place. Lots of our men lying about in shell holes – on to Briquenay – the advance is going so fast that our men can not find the Germans. Back at 8pm. Very tiring day. Letters from home, Cynthia, Maman.

Nov 4th
Good night's sleep. Company moving forward this noon. Beyond Briquenay. Arranged for departure. C. Co went at 9am. Started at 1pm. Arrived at 4 at Grandpré. Was a beautiful city. Major Howard arrived at 5pm. After supper I had just returned to my room when Lt Kurtzmann announced German planes. "Lights out". Plane dumped nine bombs – killing three men & seriously wounding several, one had his arm blown off. Great excitement. Fifteen or more treated. Bed at 8pm.

Nov 5th
Good night's sleep. Went around the town to see damage. Everything improving. In the pm I sent a letter to Salkin telling him to make the deposit with the Rector of the ten thousand dollars in memory of Richard Elliot. I had left it up to the Trustees as to what disposition they might make of it. . I hope it pleases them and it should come as a surprise – a Xmas present. At 5pm had a little supper then came back and had a nice talk with Cris. Then to bed at 7pm. My mind full of plans as to the future. How I pray this day a month the show will end."

On November 5th the 78th moved back to the region of Grandpré becoming Army reserve troops of the American 1st Army. There it was engaged in rest, training and refitting until the Armistice.

217

"Nov 6th
At 9am, Lee, Marcus and I went for walk – saw the destruction of Grandpré, the results of the shellfire etc. Also several graves of our boys. Our division coming out of the line. After luncheon I saw two US bodies that had been found under a building – just the skeleton remained. Several refugees arrived and I took them to Vouziers where I passed some 200 French ready for interment. Back at 8. Caught in a French convoy. Bed at once."

From November 6th to 11th the Division marched in stages to the Argonne, Les Islettes and Ste Menehould camps. On the 16th they entrained for Semur-en-Auxois, where they camped in the area until their return to the States via Bordeaux and Marseilles the following April and May.

"Nov 7th
This am busied myself around and had an early lunch and went to the railhead, where I heard that we were to move back to Les Islettes. Back by five pm. Sat around and talked to Marcus – supper – back at 9pm. The rumours of the end of this war are running wild. I pray so.

Nov 8th
Up at 7. Prepared to leave Grandpré. Left at 9am. Uneventful journey back. Thought of the future; at Ste. Menehould saw in the papers that Germany had sent ten men to talk peace. May God grant that this be true. Stopped at les Islettes but came on here. Le Four. Some letters from Frank, Lucy – distressed to hear of Bab's death of her chauffeur. General belief that the war is over! Supper – several letters from Frank.

Nov 9th
After a trip to the railhead, I decided to go to Manoncourt. It was a rotten day, raining most of the time, such fierce roads. Reached Toul at 3 pm, recalling so many memories. It was just 6 when I pulled up to the Heurys door – they had been supping. They made Jeffrey and I some eggs – and we drank white wine. Sarah had the grippe and almost died; fortunately she had recovered and looked so well. I gave them 500 francs. Bed at 10pm.

Nov 10th
Called at 6am. Both girls came into my room to say good morning. Off at 7am. Shortly after we had one thing after another – all caused by a dirty strainer – which Jeffrey never found. Stopped at Colombey-les-Belles for gas. Then more trouble, finally cleared up. At 2pm had another puncture and got home at 5pm. News of the Kaiser's abdication received with much

joy. Back to room to write letters."

Letter to Frank:

"Nov 10th 1918

Dear Boy,
At this moment the Kaiser has abdicated and the prospects for peace are excellent. Heaven only hope that it may take place at once.

Yesterday I received two old letters from you, and the one of the 27th Oct. The oldest was August 18th. You have cleared up several points in my mind and I hope that you have received my latest which tells you that I cannot get away at the present. If Peace really comes, I may. I have just come back from a night's trip where I returned to see a very nice family. There are two such fine girls. They have been so nice to me. When I arrived, they had a regular meal ready – eggs – wine etc. It was the first good dinner I had since going to the front. I gave them five hundred francs to help this winter.

I had a letter from (Aunt) Lucy which I am enclosing. If she comes over, I do hope we can get together. She can learn in Paris where the 78th is and you two might come down together – for the war being over it should be easy.

Boy, when we go home we must get together about either taking a trip or getting to work. After what I have seen over here, I pray that I shall not be seen at every deb(utante) dance. This must be a turning point in our lives and we must "make good".

I was glad to hear you say that you were still interested in the Orphans' Home. Yes, I have helped in France but I'm not so crazy about the French as I was before the war. All the 'poilus' do is to rob our men right and left. The families of France have done nothing but cheat us right and left, overcharging & passing "bum" money. They take things off our poor dead, and pick our garbage piles for anything they need. Uncle Sam has to pay for everything & when I think that we came over here to fight for them & then we have to pay for the use of their roads & the trenches we occupy – well that's the limit.

Then again, France is alive with slackers. Boy, don't you fool yourself that all the rich men have faced shell fire. Never. I have never seen so many useless individuals touring France as I have this time. Attached to our train is a perfect example of an "ambusque" – just a cheap sport who is playing the role of "interpreter"; and there are thousands of these in France. They are perfect stinkers and kick at everything we do. If I have any money to give, it will be to England. They have my admiration.

I bet there are lots of our friends at home that wish just now that they had "come over". I hope people are cold to them after we return. At any rate there will be two classes of men after this war – those that came over and those that remained at home.

The other night we had a fierce air raid. I was standing outside my billet when we heard the Boche come. The alarm was given and then the first bomb fell – then another – each time closer. Just outside our place was a shelter & Kurtzmann & I went into it. If you have never been in an air raid, you have no idea how terrifying it is. They do such a fierce amount of damage. Of course I knew there would be some killed, and after it was over I went down the street and helped carry a Major who had his right arm practically blown off. I saw an ambulance driver dead – and still another man who had evidently been killed looking out of a window at the machine. A piece of the bomb "got him" back of the ear. Fifteen other men were at a dressing station being treated. In the very instance, it is their own fault for they refuse to obey orders. The ambulance driver in this case was performing his duty.

Boy, the other day I saw two of our men who were found under a building that had fallen on them during a bombardment. They were so far decayed that their heads were skeletons. The burying party said that the rats were responsible, for they ate the dead. Another gruesome thing. I passed a place near Vouzier where I saw over three hundred French all collected for burial. They lay in every conceivable manner "Mort pour la France".

There are so many details in my life over here that only when I get with you shall I be able to describe them. It has all been too wonderful & I shall never forget it.

I am waiting to hear from you. Did I ever tell you that I have my own personal Dodge car! & chauffeur, to go about in ?

Take good care of yourself & let us look forward to a marvellous life after the war.

With love Maurice"

"Nov 11th 1918. Armistice Day
Paid the men at 8am and fixed up things; luncheon in the orderly room. Armistice supposed to have been signed this morning. Wrote letters all pm, had a hot bath and haircut. Sat around in the evening. Bed at 10pm. The war is over!

*Maurice on the day
before peace was
declared, November
10th, 1918*

Nov 12th

Was detailed to go with the ration trucks. At railhead by 8.30. First section off at 10.30. Pretty ride going there. St Menehould, the town beflagged and much enthusiasm on all sides. Reached Isle dump at 1.30 – good luncheon. Back at 4.30pm. Found a letter from Cynthia. NY Herald says "War is Over". Talked with the other officers – Bed at 10. Fine moonlight night.

Nov 13th

A cloudless day. Frost on the ground. Wrote letters and at 1pm motored to Fleury to the base hospital to have a man x-rayed. Visited the cemetery where over 500 of our men are resting – having been murdered by those unspeakable Germans. Had a puncture, then back at 5 – had supper. Then sat around and wrote letters. On rations tomorrow.

Nov 14th

Up at 7am. Gorgeous day. At the railhead at 8.30am, took out a section at 11. Trip was cold. Country looked beautiful – and I thought a good deal of what I would do after the war. A few biscuits for luncheon. Back at 3.30pm. Short stop in Les Islettes then back. Mail came – letters from Joe, Sally & Mama. Full moon – wrote letters. Bed."

On 14th November, Frank, on the *Wyoming*, the flagship of the Commander of the US Atlantic Fleet, at Scapa Flow, applied for 12 days leave to see his twin brother Captain Maurice Roche in France. His request was granted on the understanding that he might miss the *Wyoming*, in case she were ordered home suddenly. Four days later, his leave was granted.

On 21st November the *Wyoming* and three other American battleships joined the Grand Fleet to escort 74 ships of the German High Seas fleet into the Firth of Forth, on their way to be interned at Scapa Flow, following the cessation of hostilities. Inexplicably to his family and friends, Frank chose to miss this great, historic event. The truth was that Frank was suffering from depression and had a pressing need to get away from Scapa Flow.

On 29th November he was detached from USS *Wyoming* and ordered to report for duty in the Communication Section, US Naval HQ, London where he remained until he was repatriated in July 1919.

When his mother heard of this action, she was very sad and distressed at what she saw as his shameful dereliction of duty. She felt he had brought disgrace on the family and chided him in an emotional letter:

"…Oh I am sad to think that now you have done something to live down & that no one will ever forget – and I have cried again from grief and disappointment for 2 nights! How could any one around you let you do such a suicidal thing? How could you contemplate it? I am so distressed and sorry for you. What did all the previous good conduct and luck on getting on that splendid ship count for since you threw the whole thing to the winds for a few days of social <u>amusement</u>!! Oh, it is too, too sad! Did the war teach you nothing? It is a sad Xmas in spite of peace. *Your Mother.*"

"Nov 15th

Salkin[175] is paying my life insurance policy today. Gorgeous day – without a cloud. After some sport went down to the com and bought some cigars from the company fund. All kinds of rumours about our train being split up. Wrote letters, after luncheon and then took a ride down to the railhead – back at 4 after going out to the dumps. Had some guests for supper. Have

---

[175] Family lawyer.

been chosen to take some trucks to the other division. Bed at 10.

Nov 16th

Spent the am arranging train of AECs which had to be taken to the first division. Finally got started at 11 – bitterly cold day. Arrived at Ramarque at 2, only to find that the division had moved on to Verdun, arriving there at 7. Kept waiting until 9, before we go to the first division park. Turned over the trucks, then returned. Reached home at 2am. Glad to be back.

Nov 17th

Ordered to entrain – got off by noon – very cold – stood around the station at Ste. Menehould & caught cold. Had a pleasant afternoon with the French people I met the other night, talked all the pm with them. Good dinner with Marcus, then took the train at 8.45pm. The Kitchens, Quinn, Marcus and I weren't much prepared for such a trip – but I bought some paté and sardines. I slept on the bench.

Nov 18th

A poor night's sleep on account of my cold. Up at 6am. Most uncomfortable time without water etc. Many hours' wait, then we got under way. Passed thro' pretty country all day, going always towards the south; then towards night it got even prettier. Conversation mostly about what could happen after the war. Took the floor this time for my bed.

Nov 19th

Better night sleep. Off (the train) at 10am. at Marigny (le Cahouet); spent the am looking for a place for the company. Nice luncheon. Not much to do in the pm. Early supper and bed at 8pm.

Nov 20th

Much better today. Went to Semur. Very pretty place, nice people. Lunch with the officers. Came back with Mayor. Supper with the company – sat around & talked with the officers. Beautiful moonlight night – Bed.

Nov 21st

Went over to Semur to get company stuff – met Marcus & went to Dijon. Most beautiful trip. Cloudless day & very cold – arrived in time for lunch. After lunch with Cris, Marcus, did some shopping & saw an interesting French review and presentation of medals. Bought a fine pair of gloves. Back by six pm. Sat around and talked. Hear we are leaving tomorrow for Semur. Rather glad as there will be more to do and see.

Nov 22nd

Up at 7am. Beautiful morning. Reached here in time to billet the men. Semur is one of the most picturesque towns in France – such quaint streets and old corners. Am billeted with the priest – couldn't be nicer – beautiful view on the square. Good luncheon – then we arranged to have a dispatching system; looked around the Company which is quite well arranged – then introduced to a charming gentleman who asked me back at 8. I thought it was for dinner so I didn't eat; arrived and found it was just for a musical evening – very pleasant altho' the piano was not in tune – sat around and talked until midnight.

Nov 23rd

Up at seven. Breakfast with the Company. Bought some things at the Commissary – some handkerchiefs – met Dave Milburn who asked me to luncheon. Lunch very nice – Dave, French officers and his wife, excellent luncheon and very gay. Back to the company to arrange for the passes. Home to write a few letters – much to my surprise I got a telegram saying "Ensign Frank Roche will arrive at hotel on square, Nancy, on Wednesday morning." Don't know what to do. Anxiously awaiting to hear from him. Sat around after supper – Bed."

Letter to Frank:

"Nov 23rd

Dear Boy,

Now that the censorship ban is lifted, I can send you some news of where we are billeted in the rest area. Our journey from the fort occupied two long days & nights in the train in which time I caught a bad cold, but I am quite ok by now. You have read so much about the closing hours of the war, that I can add very little. It was extraordinary to hear the firing become less and less often, finally ending completely by 11am. Immediately our division turned about and came here.

Boy, all France began to make merry and the towns are now flying all the allies' flags. The Great War is over! Beginning tomorrow, our men go on seven days leave. The officers not as yet. I shall put my name last on the list so that I may join you & Lucy somewhere and we can have a party together. I wish you could come here. This is a charming place. I am billeted with the priest & simply could not be more comfortable. The view from my room is marvellous. Those towers in the view were built in 1041. The church opposite me was started in the fifteenth century.

Semur-en-Auxois, headquarters of the 78th Division from the Armistice until May 1919

Left: House of the Abbé Didier, Semur, where Maurice was billeted for six months, November 1918-May 1919. Right: Stained glass window in the church of Notre Dame, Semur-en-Auxois, dedicated to the memory of the 78th Division, American Army

I've been wondering if you had the good fortune of seeing the German fleet being turned over to the British. It must have been a glorious sight & I am glad you saw the last of it on sea while I the last on land.

Boy aren't we lucky? To think that we have survived this great historic epoch, and go back to civilian life again! We hear all kinds of rumours of what is going to happen to us – but I think that for the present, we shall surely remain in France. Perhaps you may return soon. At any rate let me know your plans.

I am arranging to have some turkey for Thanksgiving Day. I found a butcher who knows where he can get some. I shall buy them out of the Company fund.

As I have had no letters lately, I cannot give you any news. I presume that everybody is delighted at home over the whole thing. When I think of it, today would have been the Yale-Harvard football game. Just think! How many we have seen!

I am waiting to hear from you . If you get to Paris and they don't know where the 78th is, we shall very likely be here at <u>Semur</u>. You can easily find me & as I have said before. I am at the priest's house opposite Notre Dame Eglise. I do hope to see you . If you come by motor, I shall give you all the gas you want when you get here.

I can't make up my mind what I shall do after this war. Have you decided?
Much love Affec. MR."

"*Nov 24th*
Sunday morning. Looked at some antiques. Church at 10am. Very good music. Enjoyed it very much. Luncheon. Back to the antiques – always expecting my brother – again at 2pm to Vespers. Supper. Talked to Sgt Kreoh for two hours. Found Marcus at 8pm and went to the Roblots where I had a very enjoyable evening, listening to their music. Back at 11pm."

"*Nov 25th*
Raining slightly. The time is passing rapidly. Passed some time writing. Sent Mama a wire saying: "Am well"– After luncheon received many letters – Salkin, Zenabru, Barclay, O'Brien. Wrote several letters in the pm. Up at headquarters – supper – hear we may be leaving shortly for home. A poor day. Sat around in the evening. Wrote letters. Bed. Saw about getting listings."

One of the letters he wrote that day was to Dr Drury, asking him to investigate the practicalities of installing electricity in the Chapel at St Paul's School:

"Nov 25th '18

My dear Dr Drury,
As I look at the calendar, I see that Thursday is Thanksgiving Day. It certainly will be a real Thanksgiving Day this year. All France at this moment is rejoicing. The towns are flying the colors of the Allies.

We are in the rest area. For the moment nobody knows just what will become of us, so much depending on the behavior of the Germans. However I do not think there is the slightest possibility of our going home before the early months of next year. Everything takes time.

I have heard several times from Frank – he is trying to join me here in France for his leave. I shall be so glad to see him.

Dr Drury, you have often spoken of the problem of putting electricity in the Chapel instead of the ancient gas system. Will you be kind enough to look into the question of doing that & at what cost? I might suggest that you have a man come from Caldwell's, New York, and if he thinks the present fixtures not proper for the placing of the wires, let him make proper drawings with estimates and I should be very glad to have the work done at my expense.

I am at present stopping with the priest (Abbé Didier) of this fifteenth century church. He is a charming man and I have had some very pleasant talks with him.

I do hope that you have had a very good term and that you all will have a very happy Christmas. With kind regards to you both,

Yours ever. Maurice Roche."

"Nov 26th
Still wet day. Went to an officers' meeting. Then looked around town. Had some difficulty getting a money order cashed. Met the Roblots who asked me in tonight. Looked around to try to get some turkey for Thanksgiving. None to be had. Received a nice letter from Cynthia, clippings from Helen. Also "Life". Good supper. Sat around and talked to Sgt. Kreoh. To the Roblots at 8pm, talked life & ate chestnuts and white wine. Bed at 11.30. Chimney fire which caused some excitement.

Nov 27th
Six months ago today we left America. It seems much longer. Passed this am arranging for tomorrow (Thanksgiving), taking my wash, sewing torn clothing. Luncheon, afterwards to the Roblots where we had some music and a chat – later with Capt. Hoyt to his place. More letters from Helen. Alice W Rubuens – Sat around and talked to Sgt Kreoh. Back to room,

then walked about town. Bed at 10pm.

Nov 28th

Letters from Brinley, Drury, & Elizabeth B – Thanksgiving Day. Prepared for the morning service. Took about 25 men to the church which was full. After church I lunched with the priest and four of his friends. Had a very pleasant time. We talked of the war, religion, NY. After luncheon I bought some things for the men's mess. No turkey! to be had so I have some excellent mutton, cauliflower, salad. Sat around in Marcus' room – back to write letters, had an invitation to go to Capt. Hoyt's mess. Excellent food, drank a lot of champagne – sang, had a really fine evening. Home at midnight.

Nov 29th

Officer of the day. Meeting at 9am, I inspected the Kitchens, went for a walk about town; it is a beautiful place. Spent the pm with Mrs R – very pleasant time. Bed early.

Nov 30th

Again officer of the day. Censored letters and bought some fish for the Company. Very pleasant luncheon with Mess 30; sat around & talked until 2pm. Heard some more music. Bad news that Hakes had died of pneumonia. First man in my company to die overseas. Talked with some very pleasant people until 9pm. Bed.

Dec 1st

Up at 5.30. Great trouble in getting things started at the Park. A beautiful day. Saw my man Hakes who had died. Arranged for the funeral. Luncheon. Received some mail – Brinley, Helen, Elizabeth Z. A walk in the park, to the 3pm vesper. Arranged the funeral – supper Mme R at 8pm, to hear some music and have some eats. Bed at 12.

Dec 2nd

Fine day – had a rendezvous with Monsieur R at 9am and we arranged for the making of the coffin, took a walk around town which was very beautiful. 1pm back to his house again. Saw to the final arrangements of the funeral. At 8 went to the Roblots and had a very pleasant evening. Bed at 11.

Dec 3rd

Up at 7.30. Arranged for funeral. Everything went off well. Company assembled – firing squad. Funeral at 10. Major Howard only other officer present. March to the funeral and service quite appropriate – firing squad and taps. See the death notices of three of my friends in the Harvard Bulletin. Nat Simpkins, Charles de Rham and Logan Scott. Spent a delightful day with the Roblots. They are charming people and I sat in the bedroom of a girl who was ill. We had a very pleasant pm. After supper I went to the Roblots, where I brought two bottles of Chablis and some excellent chestnuts, and we passed a very delightful evening. Bed at 11.

Dec 4th
Officer of the day. Gray day. Censored letters and passed the day thus. Had a very pleasant talk with a cabinet maker. In the evening went to the Roblots where we had a very pleasant time eating chestnuts and drinking white wine. Back late.

Dec 5th
Major Howard gave me some rather annoying news that I might be transferred to make room for Milbrandt. Took a Ford ambulance – with the La Prostes to Dijon. It was an amusing ride and it had its funny side. Arrived at Dijon at 12.30. I had a charming time at the La Prostes, and a good luncheon which I enjoyed. Met Schroeder and Turner and I told them the news and I came back with them in the motor. Supper – around to see Kris. – to the Roblots where I told them of the trip. They are such "snob" & rank people. Bed at 12.

Dec 6th
Beautiful day. Breakfast – had a hair cut. Saw Major Howard – things seem to have been fixed up. After luncheon at Mess 30, I went to the Roblots where we went for a walk. Beautiful view, back for tea. Found a letter from Grace R; had a cup of tea, wrote several letters and after supper I went back. We had some chestnuts and tea. It was all very good. Bed at 11.

Dec 7th
Nothing much in the am. Went to the commissary & wrote letters after luncheon, and then I passed the pm chasing around, and at 7pm went to the Roblots, where we had an excellent dinner of woodcock and wine. A very enjoyable evening. Bed at 11.

Dec 8th
Very nervous. Breakfast & to headquarters. Everything going well. Back to write letters and around to Mess 30. To the Company, then had an excellent luncheon at 2pm, turkey and pie. Roblots took some photos. Had supper with McDonald around to visit, very boring time. Bed at 10.30.

Dec 9th

Up at 6.30 to see that the priest got off. Raining – inspection – up to the Park – everything going well. Attended funeral of an old lady. Wrote letters & censored. Luncheon – after to the Park – letters, 2 from Helen, Salkin, Edith. Glad to get Salkin report – said Aunt Lucy was on the way over. To the Roblots, to the com. – cup of tea – supper – wrote several letters. Roblots at 8.30- music – nuts and wine – Maj. Roller there. Bed at 11.

Dec 10th

Up at 8.30 – park – Censored letters and looked around- everything going well. After luncheon saw to Trimmer's return to the hospital. To the Park. In the evening had a marvellous dinner – wild boar! Dave Milburn, Ray Belmont – tried to get in but door was locked so went to the Roblots where I spent the night.

Dec 11th

Up at 7. At the Park – spent the morning censoring letters and seeing to the business. Luncheon – afterwards went to the commissary and bought some things for the Roblots etc. back to headquarters. Nice letter from Frank, Maman and Helen. Wrote Frank my plans. He is now en route meeting President Wilson. He expects to get transferred to some Staff job. At 8.30 I met the Huquenets, very pleasant people who were extremely nice to me. We sat & talked life over. Bed at 11.

Dec 12th

Today we earned our first service stripe. I feel very proud to have it. It has been a fearful day of incessant rain – went to the commissary – and to see about the Harvard dinner; excellent luncheon – up to the Park, then to take a bath. Bad news at 7 to hear that I probably have to go to the Motor Transport School – hope I don't have to go. Will make the best of it just the same. Dined at the Roblots but was too upset thinking about the transfer to enjoy it. Back at 11.

Dec 13th

Poor night's sleep. Over to see about the transfer. Nothing doing as yet. Got my pass to Paris. Am going at all costs – why worry. At 2pm took French priest and went to Les Laumes. Long wait until almost five before train came. Just before train came, talked to such a nice lady – had a bite to eat before entraining. Trip up was very crowded and I had Mrs Colombes to talk to. She was very nice & we had a very nice time on the trip. Arrived at the club at 9.30, fixed up and went to Place de la Concorde to see the changes and how it looked since I had last seen it. To a hotel where there were a good many poor women. Bed 3."

On this day, following Maurice's instructions, $10,000 of Bonds were shipped by registered mail to St Paul's School in memory of Richard Elliot.

"Dec 14th '18. (Woodrow) Wilson Day!

Up at 8. Breakfast, saw to the extension of the passes. Had a shower, watched the crowd collect for Wilson parade. Had great sight – thousands of people – stood in the Place de la Concorde. At 10.30 Wilson passed. Went to Maxims. After we had a champagne cocktail, then to the Ritz. The same old place. Mrs French lunched with me. Met a countess who asked me to tea. I had a nice walk with Mrs French and at 5 went to the Countess of Briandiere. Had a very nice time at tea, danced. A beautiful house. Decided to give up going to the Harvard dinner – dined alone with the Countess – went on to the show with Lord Wimborne. Back and spent the night – up at 3 to go home."

The *New York Times* described the parade:

"The carriage bearing the Presidents of America and France passed through the blue-clad ranks lining the wide passage across the Place de la Concorde. This little scene struck the deepest feelings in France's heart toward her guest. More than Wilson the statesman, Wilson the champion of liberty, more than even Wilson the President and the standard bearer of mighty America, the people of France are welcoming Wilson the peacemaker,[176] who brings back home their loved ones in safety from out of death's shadow..."

Dec 15th
Did not sleep very long, off to station, caught train at 7.45. Pleasant trip to Les Laumes – found a truck & went to Semur. Found order to go to the MTC. Much upset. Read mail and got ready to make trip. After supper back at 7 to read letters. Bed at 9.

Dec 16th
Prepared for trip. Took the 12.20 train to Chagny. Pleasant time. No room at Chagny so went up to Caborse. Talked with an aviator who owed his life

---

[176] President Woodrow Wilson was awarded the 1919 Nobel Peace Prize for his peacemaking efforts.

to a detachable tank. Finally got a seat inside, arriving at Decize at 11.45 Room at a hotel. Had a glass of beer and bed.

Dec 17th

Up at 7. Out to the trucks. Find I am with three other Captains. Attended a lecture on physics, then another on company administration. Very busy pm spent in viewing motors and driving, all most instructive. Think I shall get a good deal from the course. Supper. Am with some nice officers at table. Rules very strict, in by 8pm. Stood retreat and then got my things. Supper, bought some necessities – arranged my bed. Bed at 10pm.

Dec 18th

Stood reveille at 6.30 am. Lectures as usual until 12. Raining hard all day. Felt much better today, I like the other men I sit at table with. At 1pm we were marched to the Park and I took out a Ryder with several other officers. I drove part of the way – backed. It was a pleasant pm, tho' it rained. Back at 4.30pm, shave, supper. Went to the hotel and arranged for my mail – wrote letters – Bed.

Dec 19th

Another bad day. Sent off a few letters – interesting lectures in am. After luncheon, a practical demonstration in motors, then a drawing class. I like that work very much. Again a pleasant supper and a walk thro' the town back to write letters.

Dec 20th

Lectures in the morning as usual. Quite interesting. After luncheon we took some Packard one and a half-ton trucks. It was a fierce pm. I drove part of the way and stood up on the inside of the truck and thought of them all back in the US. It is now that they are having the Christmas shopping, from what the papers say. Frank must be getting there soon. I hope he does. After supper went to see the baker's family, then back at 8pm. Wrote letters. Bed.

Dec 21st

Nice day for a change. The sun is out. Have signed off for the weekend. Nice day for a trip. In the pm had some practical demonstration and a short quiz. Then the theory of ignition system was explained to us. In the evening, I went to see some friends at the hotel where I spent the first night, discussing labour questions. Bed at 10.

Dec 22nd

No reveille. Went to town, shaved – church at 10 – a nice old place, then back to lunch. Afterwards I wrote letters, it was raining. At 3pm went to the baker's family, where I spent a very delightful afternoon and had a cup of tea. Supper, went to the hotel and found a letter from the Countess, which I answered. Bed at 10pm

Dec 23rd

Lectures as usual in the am. It rained hard all day. Pm practical demonstration. In the eve, went to the Hotel and had a nice talk. Bed at 8.

Dec 24th

Lectures in the am. At 1pm we went on a convoy. How it poured! Drove home a Liberty truck. It was a fierce day before Xmas. Went to the Hotel and danced and had a fine old time until 3am. Had my letter returned from Grace. Letter from Roblot, Keogh. Bed at 3am

Dec 25th Christmas Day

Horrid cold morning – went around and bought a wristwatch for Line. Very pleasant luncheon. Afterwards had a shave and wrote letters there. At 3.30pm went to see Line – thought of Xmas at home – had some white wine and a good supper. Snow falling. Danced and drank until 10.30pm. Had a very happy time."

Maurice wrote to Dr Drury, Christmas Day 1918, telling him that St Paul's was as usual in his thoughts:

"Dear Dr Drury,
I am thinking of dear old St Paul's today, for it is always first in my thoughts. Here we are having a pleasant day – under the circumstances. We are promised a good luncheon and the YMCA is arranging entertainments. Hope you all had a fine vacation.   *Kindest regards. Maurice Roche.*"

"*Dec 26th*
Still raining. Lectures in the am. At 12 noon, work stopped for the day. After luncheon walked to town, had a shave – went to see Line – wrote seventeen Xmas cards to everybody. Stayed there for dinner and talked until 10pm. Bed."

In New York, Fanny waited with Cynthia, from early in the morning in the cold and snow, for the arrival of the Atlantic Fleet. Fanny was overcome with emotion and disappointment as the *Wyoming* came into sight – without Frank on board!

"Dec 27th
Lectures in the am. Wrote letters had a shave, met Line and had a nice talk under the trees. Talked life, then back to see a tannery – interesting . Back to the hotel where I had a talk with a French captain. Good dinner – talked with Line – bed at 10.

Dec 28th
Lectures until 12. Pm went to see Line – read *Oliver Twist*. Returning bought paper which gave me the bad news that Hobey Baker[177] had been killed flying, another St Paul's boy. A fine athlete gone. A nice letter from the Countess. She writes very nicely. Learn by the papers that the *Wyoming* is home. Frank must be there. After supper wrote the Countess a letter. Went around and talked to Line. Back to bed.

Dec 29th Sunday
Dull gray day, drizzle. After a shave, I went to church and then back to the barracks – then to see Line.

Dec 30th
Lectures in the am. After luncheon had a shave and found Line. She took me for a walk along the canal, which is beautiful, and talked of life and certainly she has a brute of a husband. He treats her dreadfully. Had a few letters – Brinley, Josephine, Sgt Kreoh who told me how they passed Christmas. To the Hotel, supper, then back after a marvellous night, at 1pm.

Dec 31st 1918
The last of this year! Glorious day. The sky is cleared for once. It has rained every day since I've been here. Lectures in the am. Had to wait some time until I could get a shave. To see Line and back to the barracks, to Line's for dinner, danced which was good fun – wish I had stayed later but came home rather dejected. Bed at 11.30pm

Jan 1st 1919
After breakfast this am sat around and got fixed up. Think, another a year has gone by! I shall be 34 this year. Went to town & bought two nice

---

[177] A student at St Paul's School from 1903-1911. He was the finest amateur American athlete ever – an outstanding ice hockey player and footballer. He was killed when the plane he was testing crashed near Toul in France, the day before he was due to come home.

umbrellas, some small pins for the women of the hotel. Had a very nice lunch with Tartral family and stayed around & danced until five. When I came back I gave the waitress a small present. Poor thing, she is wearing it tonight! Back to the hotel where we danced until 11pm. What a charming girl.

Jan 2nd

Lectures as usual. A medico Sgt made an ass of himself. Goes to show that concentration is necessary for all things. In the pm there was a convoy. Drove a Liberty. After retreat, went to Line's where I got some dozen odd letters. To my horror, Reggie Lanier writes me of Charles' (his brother's) death. I simply couldn't believe it. Poor Charlie is dead. We have known each other for twenty years. Letters from Brinley. Helen, Alice W Madame Colombes. Stayed at the hotel for supper. Back to Line with Schroeder and Campbell. They came around to the room where we talked until midnight. Damn tired.

Jan 3rd

Felt tired today. Lecture in the am, a lecture on renewal decisions. Wrote Reggie Lanier and others letters of condolence. Pm spent time on motors. At 5pm got a telegram to go to Nevers. After supper went to the hotel & found Line, so trip to Nevers is off. Wrote Howard a letter, also Kreoh. Glad not to be going away. Had a nice talk – bed at 9.30pm. In good spirits.

Jan 4th

Lectures as usual. In the pm there were two quizzes. In the evening I went until 9pm to the baker's, then to Line's where I joined the wedding party, drank a good deal of brandy and went to bed at 1.30am at the hotel.

Jan 5th

Felt pretty foul until luncheon. Back to the barracks where I got fixed up and cleaned. Good luncheon. Nice day when I got out in to the air. Much amused to see a German prisoner rescue a pig that was drowning. Went to the baker's, then back and had supper at Line's and sat around and talked, back at 10pm.

Jan 6th

Things reached such a stage last night, that this morning I decided to move. That unspeakable medical officer got drunk last night and behaved so that there was nothing else for me to do but go. Thank God, I have been looking for the chance. I am now in a large room where I think I shall be happy.

Moved up after breakfast. Am 'all in' from a fierce night. Lectures as usual. P D in pm. At 5.30 went to see Line. Good supper. Letters from Cynthia, O'Brien, Frank, Kimball and also Frank sent me the Rector's report, which I read with great interest. 31 St Paul boys have made the supreme sacrifice. Fifteen of them I knew personally. Wrote Lucy a letter then, as I had a pass, I stayed out till midnight.

Jan 7th
Had breakfast at Line's, which was fine. Steak and coffee. Lectures in the am. In the pm we went on a convoy and I had the job of being a file closer. Nice day but I was tired. Back to have a review of the work. To Line's for supper, then here at 8pm. & wrote letters.

Jan 8th
Lectures in the am. Practical demonstration and an exam. Given a ticket to go to the theatre. Letters from Mama. Dined at Line's then to the play. Not much. Back to Line's. Bed at 12.

Jan 9th
Lectures am. More rain. Started out on convoy. Such numbers I have never seen. Pulled out a quad, then on to road. Nothing interesting to report, back at five. After luncheon I had a talk with St. Means and will send his name into Drury. He would be a great asset to the school. To Line's where I had supper. Back at 8 to have a bath. Bed at 8.30pm.

Jan 10th
Lectures in the am. Beautiful day. At 1pm practical demonstration. Word from Line to meet her in the park. Cut the drawing class & found her in the park. Had a nice talk about life in general. Back for retreat. Then to dine with her and at 8 went to the Martins, where I had a very pleasant talk. Back at 10. Bed.

Jan 11th
Lectures in the am. Exams in the pm. To Line, where I found a letter from Madame Colombes. Went to bed at the hotel.

Jan 12th
Slept fine. Awakened to find three letters from Frank with photos. Very fine day. Lunched at Line's and then to the movies at 3pm. Back to Line's where we had quite a jolly evening. At 10 to bed. Wrote Frank."

Letter to Frank:

"Jan 12th '19,
Decize, Nievre.

Dear Boy,

It is only today that your letters of the 10th of Dec, 23 & 30th came. Until now I have been without your address and as I had no news from you. Of course I believed that you had returned to the States.

Many thanks for the photos, also the details of your letters were interesting & I envy you being in London. I am pleased that you say I was 'right' when I used to rave about dear old London. Of course there is no place like it, and I only wish I were there now instead of this place. I do hope you won't get in wrong in any way & for Heaven's sake remember that our family is famous for making 'bulls' and getting into 'messes'. For God's sake, think of that. I shall remember that fateful April 1913 which still hangs over my head.

Boy, don't forget that I am a member of Prince's Club, Knightsbridge & there is the best court tennis possible, so you can play. Also don't miss going to Westminster Abbey for the 7pm service, if you want a sensation.

Boy, will you do something for me? You know that England makes the finest stained glass windows in the world. Will you please find out the name of the firm that put in the rose window in St Thomas? Get their prices, for sometime I would like to put a rose window on the north side of the Chapel with the Chapel tower, where there is at present just the wall. They may have a catalogue of prices and I would like to put one up in memory of the 31 SPS boys who fell in the Great War. Please do that for me.

I have already completed four weeks of this school. I have two to go. As I said in a previous letter I shall be in Paris the 26th perhaps, anyway the 27th, 28th – also to return on Feb 1st or thereabouts. Would love to see you of course, for it is nine months since I left you. I'm damn sorry Mama jumped on you as she did. She certainly hasn't any right to do so. I have had scarcely a dozen letters from her since being here, half of which were typewritten. Nothing very warm about them either. Not a damn thing for Xmas. All the officers got packages of candy etc., or something to mark the day. I had nothing.

I think we may be able to get discharges here. If so I go to London surely & would like to go home by way of Australia, New Zealand. I have a horror of returning to the States for there will be some scenes surely.

Boy, I am not fat at all. I look just the same as I did when I left you in May. I still have plenty of money. Just think, I brought over $2,000 – and haven't spent it all as yet. I sent home five months pay besides & have just got three months pay I shall cash in Paris. Will write more fully tomorrow. Let me hear from you, if there is any chance of seeing you.

Much love. Watch your step. Affec. Maurice.

Jan 13th
This begins the fifth week. Lectures not good. Practical course in pm. To the bakers, where I had a long talk with Madame Quenant about American doctors. To Line's where I found a letter from the Countess. She was nicer to me than ever. Back at 8.

Jan 14th
Two poor lectures in am. In the pm there was a convoy but I went walking with Line. It was a beautiful day and there was a smell of spring. We sat by the river and had a divine time. Also dined there, back at 8 to write letters.

Jan. 15th
Attended the first lecture. At 10am started for a walk over the canal. It was like a spring day. Passed a big country place; down to the canal café where they were unloading wine. At 4pm went to town then back for retreat. To Line's where I found 8 letters. Had news of Mr Dole's death. Back at 10pm."

Letters to Frank:

"*Jan 15th '19.*

Dear Boy,
Here are the photos. You may care to send them elsewhere.

I have but ten more days here, then on to Paris. Boy, it has been pretty gloomy at times. As you know there are no distractions at all; also it seems to rain every other day.

I shall try to profit by any holiday I get, and after I get discharged I certainly am going to make the best of things.

I have no news. Mama hasn't written for ages. Grace Rogers has been so rude to me over here that I have ceased writing to her; she has no feelings at all, and I never intend doing anything for her again.

Do send clippings & any letters you get from home that you can forward to me. That Miss Sykes I spoke of is at Claridges Hotel. So long.

Love affec. Maurice."

"Jan 16th

Dear Boy,
I got eight letters last night. I am sending these on. Poor Dole is dead. He was a faithful old man. I had heard that he was desperately ill in a previous letter from Brinley.

I am so damn sick of our officers that I can hardly speak. Of course the greatest majority are not gentlemen. I have the greatest contempt for all officers from the southern States and Middle West. They couldn't be worse. Thank Heaven we don't live out there. The eastern officers are alright – they are fine. Boy, those western thugs are always drunk & insulting all the nice French women they see. How the French hate them. They have no manners & are ruffians.

We are having some fine weather for a change.

Love affec. Maurice Roche"

"Jan 16th
Lectures in the am. A letter from Frank and Aunt Lucy. At 1pm started out on a convoy. Drove the first party of the journey. It was a glorious day. Just like spring. Stopped half way and talked to the children. Back and had a shave, to Line's for supper, which wasn't very nice. Back at 8pm.

Jan 17th
Lecture at the first period. No instruction the second, so we left. Attended the first lecture and met Line at 2.30. Went to the edge of the river where we took photos and had a nice time together until 4. Went to get some money cashed. Shaved – supper out, back at 8pm. Soon to bed."

In a letter to Dr Drury, Maurice suggested that with a professional coach, St Paul's boys would greatly improve their rowing skills. He offered to pay the salary & expenses of the best English coach to be found.

"Jan 18th
Lecture in the am, got my checks cashed. Put my name down for Moulins. Letters from home, Maman, Helen, Brinley. Have decided to go to Moulins. Hate to leave Line – her husband coming. In charge of crowd. Started at 6pm. Pleasant drive and got there at 7.30pm. Played around until 11pm. Went around to the various cafes.

Jan 19th
Had a good night's sleep in a good hotel. After breakfast, looked around

the town, which is quaint, looked into two churches. Back for lunch with three officers, then to the movies. At 5 to the officers' club where I met some nice girls and had a jolly time. Dinner and back at 8pm. Chauffeurs made a mistake so it wasn't until 10.30pm till we got back. To Line's where I found 2 letters from Mama, 1 from Cynthia, Zenabru.

Jan 20th
Our last week. Morning lectures. Wrote Kreoh, Mama, Cynthia. Practical demonstration, then drawing class. To Line's where I found a letter from Frank with photos. Back for supper, bed at 10.30 after an hour's bridge.

Jan 21st
Lectures in the am. At 1pm we motored to Verneuil where we visited the huge repair plant. It was a marvellous place. Every kind of machine and all kinds of repair work. Back at 5pm, to Line's then to the Martins where I passed an amusing evening.

Jan 22nd
Lectures as usual. Practical demonstration & exam. At 4pm went to see a girl who had a story to tell me about an American who had been with her. To the barber's and Line's. Went to the Brunochets where I had a nice evening. Up at 8.30.

Jan 23rd
Had a cup of coffee at 8.30. Got in OK, telling the guard that I was in a convoy. Lectures in the a.m. In the pm, I drove a Packard truck and it was very cold. Back to Line's where I had a cup of tea. No reveille. Back to supper. Nice eggs and steak. Forgot to say I had lunch there. Home at 8pm. Cold. Some snow to-day.

Jan. 24th
Lectures in the am. Practical demonstration in the pm. At 3pm Col. Robinson called me in and asked me to come to the next camp as an instructor. In view of the fact of the trouble Frank caused by leaving the *Wyoming*, I decided "no" after seeing St Means. Would like to be staying on for I hate to leave Line, she has been so kind. I shall always be grateful to her. There for supper. Back at 8pm. A good bath. Bed.

Jan 25th
Last lectures of course. In the pm kicked a football and then met Line and had a drink. Back at retreat. Had a wire from Major Howard telling me to

report back before going on leave. Hope it doesn't mean that I shall have to be transferred. Am leaving tomorrow night for Paris just the same. Passed the evening at Line's and then back at 1am.

Jan 26th
Given our travelling orders. Will leave tonight for Paris. Had luncheon with Line and at 3pm went back and packed up. Back to Line's where I dined, deciding to put off the trip on account of the snow. Bed at 11pm.

Jan 27th
Three inches of snow on the ground. Went to get a shave and say goodbye to the Martins and the Brunochets. Came back & caught the 10.20 to Nevers. So sorry to be leaving. Arrived at 11.30, had lunch and caught the 1pm train to Paris. Had a seat for which I consider myself lucky. The whole trip alone; thought over the past six weeks. Arrived Paris 6pm. To the St James, stung 65 francs for the room which is regal. After a hair cut and shampoo to Aunt Lucy's. Very glad to see her. She looks well and of course I can see that she does not intend to go into her work seriously. Polly Hare had gone to the canteen. I went back & got a hot bath and danced and we dined at the Ritz. I saw Charlie Avory and Amos Lawrence who were with two women. Had a very pleasant evening talking with Aunt Lucy until 12.30."

Aunt Lucy was divorced from Peter Cooper Hewitt at the end of 1918. He remarried Mrs Bruguiere. She sailed for England on the *Adriatic* in mid-December and moved to Paris to do war work.

"*Jan 28th*
To the Ritz for breakfast at 8.30. Shave, to the Guaranty Trust Co. to cash check. Several purchases. Back to the Ritz where I got Aunt Lucy's car and went to the Countess. Lunched at Ritz, nice time, then to the Pharos with Aunt Lucy which was interesting. To La Rue's to order dinner and we went to a play which was very poor. To the Murats where I stayed until 4.30. Lots of people – much dancing – Nini – and others.

Jan 29th
After some hours sleep, up at 6. Got to the station and boarded the train as per schedule. Had breakfast and felt very tired. Arrived on time, then found transportation which brought me here at 2pm. Found that I was only needed for Council book etc. Everything else fine. Was delighted to find mail with the good news of the Memorial endowment having got thru'. Mrs Elliot is

overjoyed and I feel sure that I will very shortly find a letter from her. Had a letter from Line and went to the Roblots who were pleased to see me. I go on leave the first. So tired I went to bed at 8pm.

Jan 30th

Slept 12 hours. My, it was fine! Busied myself around all morning. It was fine. Had a good breakfast at 9am. Lunched and afterwards had various things to do. At four went to the Roblots; again at 8 to have some chestnuts and tea. Bed at 11. Wrote two letters.

Jan 31st

Meeting at 7am to arrange my Council book. Passed the morning thus. After luncheon tried to write letters. Had a meeting at 2pm. Wrote to Cynthia, Frank and Mama. Go on pass tomorrow. This is such a depressing place! To the Roblots for a while, then to bed.

Feb 1st

Up at 8. Breakfast then to an inspection. Decided to go to Paris. Packed & saw Kurtzman & at 1.45 drove to Les Laumes and just caught the train. Had to stand in aisle all the way. Arrived at 7.30 & passed the RTO. Came to Ritz, found Aunt Lucy just going out so I went to Choiseul. No room. Found Miss Sedgewick and had dinner with them. Very pleasant. To the Theatre Francais where I saw an excellent play.

Feb 2nd

Up at 9.30. Breakfast downstairs. To the Ritz, shave, met Aunt Lucy, to the American church. Poor sermon by Bishop Perry. Lunch with Lucy and Polly. Met Julia Meyer & Brambilla. Talked over old times. Met Linda Thomas & Mrs Mathews with Miss Sedgewick to call. Back to Ritz where I dined with Lucy. Play. Bed at midnight.

Feb 3rd

Up at 8.30. Cafe for breakfast, where I wrote to Frank & while waiting for a shave, I dashed off a letter to Line. Then to Dolly Watts where I had a nice talk. Back to Aunt Lucy's. Paid calls & took a drive thru' the Bois. Lunched with Mrs Maxwell. Went to see pictures with Lucy & then to the station to check in. It worked beautifully. Met Julia Meyer and went to see Mrs Barclay's sister who is charming. Saw her children. Then to La Rue's where Nannie Tiffany and Lucy dined & to the opera Manon Lescaut, which brought back many NY memories. Back to pack & off tomorrow at 7.45.

Feb 4th

Up at 6am. Got the train in good time. Bought ticket to Nice. Uneventful day. Had a seat which I gave from time to time to ladies that were without them. Arrived at Marseilles at 2am. Went to the Red Cross where I bought some sandwiches. Back to the train where I had a seat.

Feb 5th

Slept very little. Started at 5.40. Beautiful trip to Cannes where I got off but the MPs refused to let me check in, so I fortunately was able to re-catch the train to Nice. Found a room at the Astoria Hotel. Slept a bit and went out. Ran into a Capt. Nixon and we had a fine dinner together but very expensive, which I paid for. Went to dance until midnight.

Feb 6th

Beautiful am. Breakfast at 9. Watched some poor tennis, then to the Promenade des Anglais. It was gorgeous! Such sunshine and warmth. Played with some girls. Lunch at the Ruhl. To the band concert where I met a nice girl who took me for a walk. Had some friends for dinner, then to the dance which was good fun. Bed at midnight.

Feb 7th

Up at 9. Tennis in the am. Good fun. I found I had lost very little of my form. To the Negresco where Cris & I had a fine luncheon. Met a demi-monde lady afterwards. Went for a long walk with the Pace sisters, a gorgeous day. Back to the Ruhl for tea. Dinner at 7.30 with Cris and two women. Sat around & listened to the music until late. Bed at 12.

Feb 8th

Shortly after 9 am it rained & did so all am. Had a very pleasant talk with a regular army Colonel. He was in the Philippines & also an instructor for four years. Such a nice man. Lunch at the Negresco. It was raining so went to the Officers' Club where I met Mrs French, Lady Chelsmore & the Curtis girls. Took tea there. At 8pm went to the Negresco where I dined alone and then danced afterwards. What a life this is! When I think of all this money spent, as it is, for no purpose at all. Bed at 12.

Feb 9th

Am leaving today. Beautiful cold day. Spent morning on the promenade enjoying the sights and taking a last look at the Mediterranean. Lunched at 12 & caught the 1pm. Sat in a compartment with a Miss Studd and another girl from Chicago. They got off at Cannes. While standing in the aisle, I saw an English lady wearing the French transport uniform. I liked her expression and without any reason I asked her if I could find her a seat. Found her very attractive. We had tea together and had many ideas in common. I was fortunate enough to get a seat next to her in her compartment. We dined at 8.30 and returned and prepared for the night. There was no steam, and I got my sweater and put it around her feet. The night passed pleasantly. She gave me her address (Miss Wethered, 157 Sloane St SW, London) and thanked me for my attention. I said goodbye at 4am & found Cris at the Red Cross, where we had a cup of coffee & sandwiches which were most welcome. Very lucky in getting bed at the RC & retired at 5am.

Feb 10th
Much refreshed. Up at 11. Had luncheon with Cris & caught the 2.10 to Chagny. Had to stand but had a very pleasant talk with a Lt. Arrived at C. and then on to Decize at 4.30. Trip uneventful. Arrived at 10.30. Line pleased to see me. I had something to eat then to bed at midnight.

Feb 11th
Up at 9. Had breakfast. To the barracks where I saw Lt. Pratt. Things have changed a good deal. The two French officers have left & everything is poor. After lunch I went to the Martins where I had a pleasant talk. Back & I had a few words with Line as I find they have been talking about us. Things have changed. How I wish I had not returned. Felt sad. Before and after supper we danced. Bed at 11. Gave the servants their tips.

Feb 12th
 Called at 6. Line and Mrs T. came to the train. Train late. Had a nice talk with a girl. Arrived at Chagny and had luncheon with Suzanne Wropez. Finally got the train & it seemed never to leave. Arrived Dijon at 9.30. Spent the night there. Supper, bed at 10.30.

Feb 13th
A glorious day! Up at 6.30. Breakfast & caught the 7.40 train to Semur. Arrived to find some 20 letters from Alice Wainwright, Grace Rogers, Cynthia, Maman, Mrs Lanier, Salkin, Drury, etc. etc. Spent the am reading them. To lunch. Paid the men, bought things to eat. To the Co. then back at 5. Messed with officers. To the Co. then back here to write to Frank, Lucy. Bed at 11.

Feb 14th
Up at 8 much refreshed. To the Post Office where I sent a cable to Drury.
Wrote letters. To the headquarters. Luncheon. To the Disciplinary Det.
Back to the Co. where I got 3 letters from Mama. Wrote letters in the pm
until 5pm. Buy a room fire. To supper. At 8 went to the Roblots where I
passed a pleasant evening."

Maurice in a letter to Dr Drury:

"I spent my leave on the Riviera. It was wonderful to get away from the
snow & the cold to the sunshine & summer heat…
    We are rather anxious at present for the Germans are preparing to give
us trouble. Will this never end!"

"Feb 15th
Up at 7.30. To the Co. & prepared for inspection which took place at 9. To
the park & a meeting at 11am of officers, train talk. After luncheon to my
room where I wrote some letters. To the barber's, to tea with Quinn's friends.
Very pleasant. Supper Schroeder. Talked over a business proposition. Nix.
To the Roblots at 8 pm where we ate chestnuts and white wine. Major
McDowell & Bowles. Bed at 11.

Feb 16th^v
A rainy am. To the company. To church. After luncheon I saw them bury
three more of our men. It seems disgraceful that not a single officer is
present. To the Roblots where I met some fearful "7" people. To the mess.
Back at 7.30. Built a fire and wrote letters.

Feb 17th
Up at 8. To the Park, then to the repair shop where I saw several cars in
process of reconstruction. After luncheon wrote letters until 3.30 Letter
from Brinley and Mama. No news. Raining most of the pm. At 8. I went to
the Roblots where they had a host of "7" workers and we had tea and sat
around and were amused by them.

Feb 18th
Up at 8. To the company & to the Park where I made out my pay voucher
for two months. Attended a funeral for a man in E. company. After luncheon
wrote letters & at 4 pm to the Roblots for tea. Letter from Lucy, wrote to
her and Dorothea W. To the Roblots until 10. Good deal of rain.

Feb 19th

Not raining. To the company. Back here to write – Frank, Mrs Lanier, Marjorie Oelrichs. Called to Major Howard and given a roasting for not getting into the barracks. Back at 4. To the Auberts where I heard some good music. Back at 7. Bed at 10.45pm.

Feb 20th

Stopped raining. Up at 8. After breakfast to the Park where I saw to the arrangement of the barracks. Passed the hospital as they were taking four more dead soldiers to their graves. Bought this book. Long letter from Frank announcing Howard Henry's suicide due to a nervous breakdown. It is fierce to hear of such things. Luncheon. Back to write to Frank. At 2pm went to Madame Claret's which was a real museum. It was wonderful and I studied the house very carefully. Have some photos of it. Stayed until 5pm. Received a long letter from Maman, Elizabeth Z and the Heury girl. Back to my room to read. To the Roblots at 8pm & to a friend across the river where we talked and had a cup of tea. Bed at 11.

Feb 21st

Up at 8. To the park, saw to the barracks – inspected the cars. Back to lunch – seven letters from Helen, Mama & Alice Wainwright. Glad to hear. Hair cut and shave. Officers meeting at 2. Had some mail for the men. Played with the headquarters' dog. Back and read letters. Received such a nice one from Mrs Wethered, which I answered at once. Sgt de Liege met me at 8 and took me to the Cruzats where I passed a very pleasant evening. Bed at midnight.

Feb 22nd

Washington's birthday. To the company and then did some shopping for tonight's supper. Some oranges and biscuits and chocolates. Back to write to Elizabeth Zenabru. After luncheon a long letter to Helen. Then to headquarters and on my return met St Quinn and we went for a long walk, which was very pleasant. Back for supper. At 8 went to the Roblots where I saw lots of "7" workers, heard music and stayed until 11.30.

Feb 23rd

Sunday. Jeffrey going to London so am writing Frank to get me a fishing rod and an overseas cap. Shaved, church at 10am. Back to write. Drizzle. At 1pm went to the Roblots where I had a cup of coffee. Back to the room for a nap. Bought the daily papers, then to supper. Have news that our division is sailing the end of May. What I am going to do with myself when

I get home! Sgt Kreoh came to get me and I passed a very pleasant evening at the Cruzats, hearing some good music. Bed at 11.30

Feb 24th
Up at 8. To the Park and barracks. To the officers' club. Back and found a telegram from Aunt Lucy and also a letter from Dolly Watts and Aunt Lucy. Plenty of mail at lunch time. Salkin, Edith Travis, Zenabru, Mama, Eileen, Mrs Rivers, Mrs Archer. Great to get that news. After luncheon back to write. Gabrielle and Mr Salkin. To the Auberts for tea. At 8pm went to the Roblots where I stayed until 1. A fine day because I had so much mail."

Dr Drury wrote thanking Maurice for his latest generous donation, which will provide accommodation for three masters' suites in the Lower School. He goes on to offer Maurice a position at the school as assistant business manager with special care of grounds and buildings. He would receive a salary. Maurice might like to build himself a small habitation in the school grounds where he would be independent yet connected with the life of the place.

Feb 25th
A stormy morning. To the company headquarters. To the commissary where I bought some milk, pens, jam. After luncheon to the Park where I read a Town Topics that Mama sent me from home, with the usual amount of trash. Back & wrote several letters. After supper went to the Roblots where there was singing and plenty of people. Bed at 11.30.

Feb 26th
A nice day until 10am, when we had some more rain. To Headquarters then back to the room. In the pm I was in my room until 4pm when I went to the Auberts; nice time. After supper I had two long letters from Frank which gave me much pleasure. Charlie Dickey, a St Paul's Alumnus is dead. To Madame Claret's where I spent a very delightful evening; bed at midnight.

Feb 27th
Up at 8. To the Park and inspected trucks. Back to write Frank a letter in answer to his. Lunch. After it wrote Aunt Lucy and a letter to the Roblots. At five to the Auberts and after supper to the Cruzats where I stayed until 10.30. Very pleasant time. Bed at 11."

Letter to Frank:

"3, Place Notre Dame, Semur
Feb 27th 1919

Dear Boy,

Your long letter and the one containing the other letters came last night and was most appreciated. You have no idea how nice it is to get them. Picture a town in France, dismal, where we eat supper at 5.30pm, & a long evening ahead.

Before I go further I want to tell you that I never wrote Mama that you were not writing, only saying that I hadn't "heard from you lately." She is certainly getting "loony" – each letter she repeats herself & is always harping on the same things. It is I think chiefly because she hasn't her mind on what she's doing & her letters are for the most part insincere & she doesn't mean a word she says.

Just a word about the money proposition. Don't forget for an instant that you & I are entitled to $60,000 (sixty thousand) per year & if ever you are thinking of marriage, you can count on that. Salkin told me that last spring. Maman is really spending our money at present. But as we really are very well off at present, it is best to leave things as they are.

What you say about scheming English girls doesn't surprise me. Bridget Colebrook was quite the same. I have always known that you and I would be far happier married to girls who are not in the first rank. Besides being far nicer & simpler and grateful, they are much the nicest people. Take for instance how much better it would be to be married to a girl like Mildred Rives that was, than that fierce, vain, conceited Julia Robbins! who just would raise several kinds of hell and then get your goat about them.

Boy, to hell with these people. You say Lady L wouldn't permit her daughter to marry you. Just tell them to "fuck themselves" as they say in the army. They ought to be honoured that you even asked her!

It was quite right of you to send the French girl a present. I'm glad you didn't kiss her, for you don't know her well enough. My God what a damn fool her mother is. She has no head at all. She's in Aunt Lucy's class. You may think that I'm an awful "crabber". All I can say is that I think Aunt Lucy is the limit. Here I am only five hours from Paris when there is an excellent hotel & she never has even volunteered to come to see me, but prefers dashing about Paris aimlessly and trying to do God knows what! Now she passes within a half hour's ride from Semur to the Riviera & can't even stop off. I don't blame Cooper for getting rid of her. She and Mama are the most selfish people I know – everything for themselves!

248

Boy, the French women of France haven't "come across" in the relief work at all. They treat the "poilus" disgracefully here. Mrs Lanier, Mrs Whitney Warren and Mrs Henry Clews have my respect. They are fine women.

If you can, do try to come over. There are several nice families that we can visit in the pms and evenings, all anxious to see you. We have continual rain, but as those higher up say we shall be heading homeward in four weeks we are all pleased, of course.

I know I speak better French than any officer in our division. They all say that it was the biggest crime I ever was allowed to stay in the supply train. I should be in G.2's office [a G.2 officer is responsible for military intelligence] – but that's our army. Glad you are well and enjoying yourself. Those letters were fine, send more.

Affec. MR"

"*Feb 28th*
Stopped raining. Censored letters then to the Park. Met Mr Roblot and I went about with him. Received my pay. Was broke until then. After luncheon had a cup of coffee with the Roblots. To an officers' meeting. Then to take some photos at the Gontards. After supper to the Lizets' where we danced and had a good time generally. Bed at 11.30 pm.

March 1st
A clear cold day. To the company, Judge Advocate's office. To the Park. Back for luncheon. Shave. Roblots. Took a fine walk to the dam which is a peach. Then back for tea. A beautiful day. After supper I found a nice letter from Frank who has bought me a fishing rod and "overseas" cap and is waiting for Jeffrey to put in his appearance. Tomorrow the time is advanced an hour. To the Roblots at 9pm for an hour."

Letter to Frank. Undated:

"Dear Boy
I want to thank you very much for the trouble you took getting the fishing tackle.

I would have given anything to have seen that wedding.[178] You should consider yourself awfully lucky to be in London and I can't see why you wish to resign because you are from time to time uncomfortable. What an opportunity! With Princes' Club, all those attractive people and with spring

---

[178] On February 27th 1919, Princess Patricia of Connaught, granddaughter of Queen Victoria, married the Hon. Alexander Ramsay in Westminster Abbey.

etc. Boy, so few people realize, know a good thing when they have it. Do you want to go home?

Do you want to join me on a trip to Canterbury, New Zealand this fall? They say it is the finest place and it will be summer there then?

I have no news. We know definitely that our return is in May – and some say much sooner. I can't make up my mind if I am pleased or not. It has been such a wonderful ten months over here, with nobody to nag or anything uncomfortable to worry me. Boy, thank you so much for getting me that fishing tackle and it will help me pass many pleasant hours. *Love Maurice.*"

"March 2nd
Breakfast and then to church. To luncheon, then to the room & for a walk. Rain fell again. To the Auberts for a while, read papers. To the Cruzats where I had a very delightful evening, music etc, Bed at 11.

March 3rd
Up early. To the Co. & Park. After luncheon I wrote letters and at 4 to the Auberts. Back to supper. To the Lizets where I played bridge rather indifferently. Bed at midnight.

March 4th
To the Park. Meeting at 9 am. Back to the Company. Letters from Elizabeth, Mama, Cynthia. Arranged for a bath. On the way up got an invitation to lunch tomorrow. To a meeting which never amounted to anything. Wrote Elizabeth Zenabru and Cynthia. After supper went to the theater where I heard Miss Margaret Wilson, the President's daughter, sing. Not good. Returning I went to the Roblots where they invited me to the Clarets. Lots of people, the General & Miss Wilson, whom I met. Very pleasant evening until midnight.

March 5th
Up promptly. To the Co. and to the Park where I found a Ford and went to Vitteau. Things went smoothly. Picked up Monsieur Benoit and his wife. Bed at 12. Letters from Reggie Lanier, Elizabeth Z. Mama. To Madame Q. for luncheon. Shown around the place, the cattle and chickens. A beautiful walk back, like a May day. Glad to be alive. The country never looked more beautiful. Back to supper, to the movies and then to the Roblots.

March 6th
Up at 8. To the orderly room. Back to write letters to Edith and Elizabeth. Luncheon. To the Park. Everything getting set for the barracks. A letter

from Kitty Kimball. To headquarters. Back to the Kitchens. At 5 I went to call on Madame Claret, where I had a very pleasant talk with her. To the Lizets at 8.30 for bridge. Quite pleasant. Bed at 11.

March 7th

A clear cold day. To the company. Wrote Mama a letter. To the Park. After luncheon a letter from Aunt Lucy. Rather ridiculous. Officers' meeting. To the orderly room where I picked up Sgt Kreoh for a walk to the Auberts for tea. See that Frederic Schenck has died. Was a classmate. To the Roblots at 8pm. Bed at 11.

March 8th

Up at 8. Inspection of Co. To the market place to get potatoes and at 10.45, I took Mr and Mrs Roblot to visit a cousin, 14 kils. away. A pretty drive, along a canal, arriving at 12 noon. The cousin, an old lady of 70. Excellent luncheon & wine. Brought back some eggs. Walked thro' the Place which had some beautiful trees. Back at 3, with the rain. To the Duflos for tea. Nice girls. To the Roblots at 8. Letter from Frank telling me that he was coming here the 18th. Bed at 11.30.

March 9th

A beautiful day. To the company. Back to write. Bought some oranges and nuts for the Duflos girl. Had an excellent lunch at the Roblots and at 2pm, I went to the Duflos and heard music for two hours. To the company and back to write. To the Cruzats at 9-11. Bed at 11.30. A very pleasant day. Wrote Mrs Wethered, Lucy and Frank.

March 10th

Up at 7 & had a cup of coffee. Walked halfway to Chevigny and got a lift the rest of the way. Arrived in time to see the execution of the big pig. Difficult getting her tied by the leg, then thrown on her side – then bled. Finally it took place. Watched with interest the whole process. Had a cup of coffee and returned in a Ford. Turned out fine day. A letter from Dolly Watts. She will not come here, I fear. To the Park after having written several letters. To the Auberts for tea and croquet. To mess and then to the Company, where I had a long talk with Sgt Kreoh about the need of good schools in America. Bed at 10.30.

March 11th

A gorgeous day. Not a cloud. To the Park and barracks. After a shave I went and found a bicycle and went to Chevigny, where I had a perfectly wonderful luncheon, the best food I have had for sometime. Back at 3.30.to the Company. Then to Madame Claret's and she took me to see Madame Bruiand's house which was quite pretty. Back to mess. Took a walk and then to bed at 10pm.

March 12th
A letter from Moppie Trimble on arising. To the Park and then back to the room to write to Moppie. After luncheon, to headquarters. A letter from Elizabeth S. At four went to the Gontards where I had a very pleasant talk with the mother and daughter. Bought some pickerel. Gave the priest two. To the Roblots. Bed.

March 13th
Not a nice day. To the Park, back to write to Frank – a letter from him. General unrest with him. He does not know what he wants to do. To the basketball game & then to the Duflos for tea. Back to buy the papers. Supper – a letter from Line who wants me to write. To the Lizets for bridge. Bed at 11.30.

March 14th
Company moved to the barracks. Everything moved very smoothly and we had excellent weather. Tried to get some potatoes etc. At 1.15 attended a meeting at Col. Strutt's office regarding mess prizes for the best Kitchens. At 3.30 went to the Auberts where I had a very enjoyable pm, playing croquet etc. To the Roblots for dinner to eat a carp which I furnished. It was excellent. To the Park at 9. to see how everything was. Bed at 12. Beautiful moonlight.

March 15th
Cold and clear – not a cloud in the sky. Bought potatoes and cauliflowers. To the Company where I paid the men. After luncheon had a hair-cut and shave. To the Cruzats where I saw their garden. Then to the company and arranged to pay the men on the work-detail and at 4pm I went and had a delightful evening with Madame Claret. She is fine.

March 16th
Eight years ago today Grandpa died. To the Park when I paid some men and at 11, I got a letter from Elizabeth Z. and seven letters from Helen. Luncheon. Afterwards to my room. At 2pm I went to the Roblots and then to an excellent concert which I enjoyed. To the Duflos and to supper. At 8.30 I went to the Gontards where we played bridge until late. Rather pleasant evening. Bed at 12.

March 13th Not a nice day. To the Park, back to write to Frank. a letter from him. Several arrived with him he doesn't know what he wants to do. To the basket ball game & then to the Dufflepee tea. Back to buy the papers. Supper - a letter from Line who wants me to write. To the Legion for booze - bed at 11.30

March 14 Company move to the barracks. everything moved very smoothly - and we had excellent weather. Tried to get some potatoes etc. At 1.15 attended a meeting at Col. Statt's office arranging new prizes for the best kitchens. At 3.30 went to the Roberts where I had a very enjoyable time. playing croquet etc. To the Roberts for dinner to eat a cup which I furnished. It was excellent. To the Park at 9, to see how everything was. Bed at 12. Beautiful moonlight.

March 15 Cold & Clear - not a cloud in the sky. Bought potatoes & Cauliflowers. To the Company where I paid the men. After luncheon had a hair-cut & shave. To the Cruzats where I saw their garden, then to the Company - & arranged to pay the men on the north detail.

A page from Maurice's war diary.

March 17th

Up at 8. To the barracks, censored mail and paid men. Bought $30 worth of groceries. Back to the room. After luncheon to the Commissary where I got some candy for the men. Brought some to the Duflos girl. Much pleased. Sat & talked. At 4.30pm went to the Auberts where I had an excellent time. Gave them some candy. Had a nice letter from Cynthia and Helen O'B. Frank comes tomorrow. Am giving him a time.

March 18th

Bought things for luncheon and dinner. Had a shave and returned to the room. With Quinn, I set out for Les Laumes and the train was on time and I saw Frank getting out with the fishing rod. He looked fine. Had a nice drive home. He shaved and we went to the Roblots for luncheon, then to the Duflos and to the Barracks, to the Auberts and to our mess at 6. Had some champagne which was excellent. To the theatre, to the Roblots where there was singing and it was very pleasant all around.

March 19th

Up at 8. Frank stayed in bed. Back to room at 10 and then we went to the Clarets and took pictures about town. To the Cruzats and to the Roblots for luncheon and then after took some photos. Frank left at 1.35 and I went to our officers' meeting. Major Howard is leaving. A most beautiful day. So glad Frank came and I think he liked it. In the evening I went to the Roblots where I had a nice time. Bed at 11, very tired. Letter from Miss La Proste.

March 20th

Much refreshed. To the Park where I occupied myself with company duties. Rain falling. Back to my room and had a long wait in the barber shop. Then to the barracks where I took a motor to the country & bought seven dozen eggs with Sgt Wiler. Major Howard left the train today and Capt Milbrandt is to take command. Wrote Mrs Wethered a letter. To the Roblots for a while. Bed at 12.

March 21th

Officer of the day. To the Park. Inspected quarters and Kitchens. Back to the room. Wrote to Miss La Proste. After luncheon back to the room, while it snowed hard outside. To the company where I signed many papers. Back to tea at the Auberts. Bought some letter paper. To the Roblots. Bed at 11.

March 22nd

Up at 7.45.Bought some flowers on the market place. To the Company. Censored 65 letters. To the headquarters. Mail – Mama, Joe Sally & Helen Henderson. Bad day for the trucks. Wrote Helen Henderson and Joe Sally. At 5 went to the Auberts. 8pm to the Roblots and then to the Auberts. Bed at midnight.

March 23rd

Beautiful day. To the company and headquarters. Back to the room where I wrote Mama. After luncheon I went off fishing, trying a few cuts here and there. A poor day and no luck. Extremely clumsy. Back at 4 to the Duflos. To the Park. A letter from Helen O'Brien and one from Frank tonight. He returned quite in good time and in good company, found a friend on board ship that was nice to him. Have a fierce headache. To the Huquenets at 8.30. Had a very pleasant evening until midnight.

March 24th

Awoke much refreshed & in good health. A beautiful day. Wrote Mr Knox a letter – & Frank also. To the Roblots and then to the Park, where I had a long talk with Jake S. about his trip to Paris. Three of them spent 10,000 francs in three days. Its fierce. To the Roblots, then to supper & afterwards to see June Bryant's place & hear the story of her life.

March 25th

Up at 8. To the Park & Co. Nothing of note. To the court martial at 9.00. Five officers tried for reporting late to a divisional school – most interesting – lasted until luncheon. To headquarters where I got a car and took Rasmussen and we gathered 13 doz. eggs. At 3.00pm back, shaved, to the Duflos. After supper to the Park, an early start tomorrow, 4.15am. Pershing reviews the division. At 8pm went to the B. where we had a fine time until 1am."

On March 26th General Pershing reviewed the 78th Division. He decorated the regimental and battalion colours with ribbon streamers to commemorate the battles in which they fought. At the end of the ceremony, he addressed the division, commending the officers and men, for the valour and vigour with which they took part in the last two decisive battles of the war.

"Semur, Cote d'Or. Twenty thousand men of the famous Lightning division from New York City and State, New Jersey, Delaware, Ohio and Illinois, who compose the National Division, stood in solid massed formations,

255

while the commander-in-chief, followed by his personal staff, galloped around them and later made a close personal inspection on foot. The impressive military spectacle was witnessed by a large number of the county folk, who came from miles around. A massed band took up its position at the reviewing stand as the troops marched past. A striking feature of the march past was the heavy artillery, drawn by immense caterpillar tractors."[179]

"March 26th
Never slept at all. Called at 2.45am. Breakfast at 4.30am. Took 12 trucks to Flée. Companies I. & M. 310 Inf. To the debussing area at 8.10. Come into line at 10.30. Passed the am policing cars. Had a cup of coffee & sandwich at 1. To the field where I saw the Division. It was very impressive. Rained most of pm. Got away at 8. & arrived at Flée at 10.30. Good dinner – bed at 12. 30am rather tired. Letter from Mrs Wethered.

March 27th
A holiday. To the Park and shaved. To the room. After luncheon received 2 letters from Mama & at 1pm went to the barrage with John and tried to fish. Not a sign of one. Very cold & windy. Back at 4. Tried to visit a bit – feel tired after these past two days work. A rotten rainy day. Damn this weather anyway. To the Gontards at 9pm where I had a very pleasant time & we laughed a good deal – bed at 12.30.

March 28th
Up at 8. After that at the court martial until 11.30. In the pm to the Roblots & to the park & at 4.30 I went to the Auberts where I had a cup of tea. Has snowed and rained all day. At 9, I went to Roblots until 11. Bed very tired.

March 29th
Raining as usual. Busied myself as usual & at 2.30 went to Dijon. Rained almost the entire way. Arrived at 5 & went to the La Prostes where they greeted me. I stayed for dinner, and after a pleasant evening early to bed.

March 30th
Up at 8. To the barbers & then officers' club. Bought some cakes. Back to a good luncheon. At 2 said "goodbye" to the La Prostes and to the offficers' club for a while and at 4 met Quinn, Snell & Brebe. A word or two with Miss Scott of the Red X. Much snow had fallen. Back at 7. Letter from Cynthia, Eileen and Helen O'B.

---

[179] An unidentified cutting from a newspaper.

March 31st

Up at 8. Nervous as anything. Censored many letters. Back to the room &
wrote to Frank. He sent me yesterday Town and Country and some letters.
To the Gontards at 2.30 where I had an interesting time, hearing their
story of the girl's life. To the company. Had a letter from Frank & Mrs
Wethered. Was so tired that I wrote Mrs W. a letter and then went to bed at
9.30.

April 1st

A cold clear day. To the Park. Back to write letters – to Frank, Cynthia,
Maman. At 1.30 took the Dodge and went in search of eggs. Saw some
nice people – returned at 4.30 with 16 doz. Received my pay cheque today.
Eleven hundred francs. Back to write to Alice Wainwright & Cricket Barclay.
To the Roblots until 11.30. Bed.

April 2nd

A beautiful day. To the company where I worked all morning. Cashed my
cheque. Back to the room. Nothing much until 4.30 when I called on
Madame Serene. Rather unsatisfactory visit. Very formal. At 9.30 attended
a boxing match between French and Yanks – the balance of power to the
French. To the Roblots, where we ate pop-corn.

April 3rd

Another glorious day of sunshine. To the Company, then inspected our
trucks. Back to the room. At 2.30 went to the Duflos & then to the Camp
Hospital where I had tea with Miss Dunn. At 7 I dined with the Roblots
and they had a musical evening. Bed at 12.

April 4th

A rainy morning. To the Company. Back to the room. After luncheon I
decided to go to Marigny to see about the baggage. Saw Col K and then
walked back. It was poor going, but made the walk in one and half hours.
Am going to Paris tomorrow for a three day leave. To the Roblots at 9 and
to bed at 11.30pm.

April 5th

Up at 8. To the Co. Censored mail. and prepared a report. To the Duflos.
Had to wait for a shave. Lunch & caught the car at 1.30. Train a bit late.
Read the newspaper. To my surprise Miss Vanderbilt has married a young
fellow of 28. How I remember the days of 1907. They were happy. Arrived
Paris & to the hotel at 7. Went to the Theatre Francais where I witnessed an

excellent play. Back, had a short walk. Paris quite the same old place. Bed at midnight.

April 6th
A good night's rest. Out by 8. To the Wagram & to the barber shop, then walked to the Champs Elysees. To the Bois. Couldn't believe it was the same old place! Saw some wonderful people. Met 3 '7' ladies. Took a walk with them. Had a pleasant walk. Invited them to luncheon at La Rue's & it was all very nice. To the Pantheon of the War. It is remarkable. Back to tea. Had a nice time & got to know these ladies, who related their experiences and their troubles. The usual woman troubles. Back & got a seat at the Theatre Francais, saw an excellent play, well acted. Thought over life. Back & bed at 11. Glad I am leading a sensible life. Believe I am getting old.

April 7th
Up at 8. After breakfast to the Louvre then to the Bois de Boulogne. Such a beautiful day. Talked to a nurse. To the hotel to get Miss Clarkson & Miss Buck. In the pm I walked the Tuileries and at 4 came home to dress. To Mrs Phipps where I got a cold reception. To the opera with Miss B – Manon – Sat around in the open until 1.30 am. Told the story of my life. Bed.

April 8th
Up at 9. Shave. To Notre Dame & then to the Bois where I met Mr Ronalds & talked about NY. Got Miss B & had a quiet luncheon. Back to the room. Brushed up. Spent the pm walking around & bought the Duflos each a little bag. Met Hunt who wanted to persuade me to stay over. Had supper & at 7.30 went to the Theatre Francais where there was an extremely dull play. Had a long talk with Sally. Bed at 12.

April 9th
Didn't sleep well. Awake at 5.30. Caught the train, no trouble with the MPs. Breakfast. Went into the compartment with some Sgts. and saw an attractive woman. Ate luncheon at 11. back & while Frenchman had his lunch, had a long talk with this same lady. Bade her goodbye before reaching Les Laumes. Upon arrival she gave me her book in memory & I went back & thanked her with a good kiss. It was a pleasant experience. To the Co. where I paid off my men. Off to get 8 doz eggs at 4. To the Roblots at 8 after having written to Miss Buck. Bed at 11.

April 10th
A fine night's sleep. To the Co. On the way back met Cox who told me of a

trip to Poland. After luncheon to the Roblots & to the Park where I found about 15 letters – Brinley, Drury, Lanier, Salkin, O'Brien, Hope Beale, It was fine getting them. To the Duflos where I gave them each a nice bag which pleased them so. At 4.30 to the Auberts & then to the Co. Sgt. Kreoh, Macphee, Dwyer back. Glad to have them. Had no supper. Back to the room to read letters of today. Drury asked me to return (to St Paul's) as master. To the Auberts at 9.

April 11th

A gloomy morning. To the Co. where I censored & paid the men. Had to look up the baggage question. A meeting at 11.15. Shave and 1.15 received 2 letters from Elizabeth Zenabru & a six page one from Scudder who gave me the details of the coming rowing season. The Duflos took me to Avalon where I enjoyed the town. Very pretty ride back. Supper at the Co. To the Roblots at 9 to pass the eve.

April 12th

Up at 7.30. To the Company. Stayed until 10 & missed the inspection. To the Company. Back to the room. Wrote to Cynthia regarding the Dole Memorial. After luncheon had a fine hot bath. To the Company. Back to the room. Wrote letters and at 7. went to the Company where I found a memo to explain my absence this am. These small minded people. Six years ago today the Alcedo affair! To the Auberts.

April 13th

Up at 8. To the Co. and then to church, Palm Sunday. After luncheon talked to the sergeants in the medical station. Rained very, very hard. Back to the room. Ran into the Gontards & walked back to their house with them. After supper to the Gontards alone. We played bridge. Bed at 12.

April 14th

To the Company at 8. Bought several purchases at the Com. Lye and shoe polish. Back to the room where I found a nice letter from Miss Buck, my '7' friend. After luncheon letter from Mama, Helen, Elizabeth. Off in a Ford to get eggs. Had pretty good luck & got 20 doz, @ 4 francs. Back and got a case of milk. To the Company. Cold and raining. Wrote to Miss Buck. To the Company until 10.30pm.

April 15th

Up at 8. To the Company. Rained very hard. Back to the room. Bought the priest a carp & then to the Roblots where I had a cup of coffee. To the

Auberts at 7. Bought them a chicken. To the Auberts at 9 pm to say goodbye.

April 16th

After inspection, to the officers' club where I saw some officers. Then to say goodbye to the Auberts. After luncheon wrote to Frank. Had received a long letter from him this morning. In the pm to the Duflos for two hours. To the Company & in the evening I went to the Roblots.

April 17th

To the Co. & after a shave had an excellent luncheon here at the Rectory. To the Company & at 4pm to the Cruzats where I had tea. At 7 went to the Roblots where we ate the chicken that I had bought them the other day. Also had music until about 11pm.

April 18th

Up at 7. To the Company and as it was Good Friday I went & bought some carp. Officers' meeting at 11. Discussed plans for leaving. At 1pm as it was a beautiful day, I went walking with Adams, Renner & Turner. Back a 4. To the Duflos, then to the Company where I found there was no supper, so beat it down to get 12 doz eggs which were eagerly eaten. A gorgeous day, loved every moment of it – What a sky! What a view! It was something too splendid. Glad to be alive. Trees just coming out and spring just appearing. France certainly did look too beautiful for words. Talked about life & dealings with other people. After supper just sat in my room & read & wrote to Helen. Bed at 10.

April 19th

A marvellous day, not a cloud in the sky. Had the company out on the drill field for inspection. It was done quite well. Saw to several more matters. 3 letters from Helen & 2 from Mama telling of Elise French's marriage to a man 12 years younger then herself. To the Company after lunch & then to the Commissary to buy cherries & cocoa. At 2pm started to the barrage with Jean & Lt. Adams. A fine day like yesterday. Didn't catch a thing as might be expected. Towards five came home. No letters from Frank nor Miss Buck. Duflos until 10 pm.

April 20th Easter

A beautiful day. To the Company. At 10am went to church at Semur & at 12 lunched with the priest. Gave him 500 francs which seemed to please him a good deal. Walked to the hospital at 3pm. Sat & talked and fooled about. Bought 12doz eggs for the men. Went to the Duflos. Read the papers.

Generally depressed today. There's nobody to see here. To the Roblots at 8 & then to the Cruzats where we had a very interesting evening until 11.

April 21st
A beautiful cloudless day. To the Company, then to the officers' club & then talked to some girls in a shop. Back to the room. Got a lot of letters from home, Cricket, Helen & Mrs Travis. At 1pm met Madame La Proste & Hilarme. It was a beautiful day. Wrote a letter to Cricket and at 7 dined at the Gontards who were so nice to me. It was a delightful evening in every way. Stayed until 11.30pm.

April 22nd
A gorgeous blue sky. Cold. Company work until 10. Shaved & then set out to Verchizy, arrived at 12, met the Rolland family who were great. I had a regal lunch and spent the afternoon walking about the place with the boys & girls. It brought me back so far, to a period that I had never known before. Back at 5. It was a fine day & I enjoyed every moment of it. At 8pm went to the Roblots & then to that wedding breakfast where I had a nice time, drank a little too much and got home very late. It was very amusing all the same & I laughed. Tired.

April 23rd
Felt badly this am. To the Park, back and had a nice letter from Frank, also Town Topics. A nice long letter from Marjorie and Cornelia which I read eagerly. At 2pm started out in sidecar to visit Précy-sous-Thil and the chateau. A gorgeous day, so clear and cool. Enjoyed every moment of it. Could see for miles and miles. Back at 5 and to the Cruzats where we played a little croquet & at 8.30 to Madame de Chambures where I played some bridge. Bed at 12. Dead tired. Wrote Frank at 6.

April 24th
A cloudy day & rain. To the Park & Co. Wrote Marjorie a letter & Cornelia. Back to my room. After luncheon found several papers & a Harvard Bulletin waiting for me at the Co. Pictures of the 27th Div parade. To the room. Should be leaving soon. To the Duflos until 4.30. To the Company where I saw to the evening meal. After supper wrote to Mama. Read "Town Topics". To the Roblots when they had pop corn & music. Bed at 11.

April 25th
A dull day. To the Company – duties. To the Commissary at 9.30am where I bought some flour for Madame Huquenet, jam for the Company. In the

261

pm to the Duflos where I stayed until 5pm, listening to some music. Wrote Frank a letter in answer to his in which he says he is to be home by June. The papers speak of the first detachments of the 77th being landed in the States. Wrote letters etc. until 9.30, then to bed.

April 26th
Up promptly, after a long, restful night. To the Company, then at 9.30 to the Court Martial of an Italian soldier who in a fit of rage stabbed a Corporal. We heard both sides and finally gave him two years. He certainly looked a bad lot. To the Co. Letter from Brinley & Helen. We shall very likely leave here May 6th. Bought some rations, sugar and peaches for tomorrow. After supper went to the Roblots, where I saw General McRae and heard some singing and talked with the Gontard girl. Back at 1am.

April 27th
A nice day. Up at 8. Long talk at breakfast. Have been gone eleven months from home. Expect to have another ten days here in this house. Censored mail and back to the room. After luncheon to the Park while I got some second class mail from Elizabeth Zenabru – pictorials. Went for a walk, a beautiful pm. Talked with people here and there. To the Duflos. To the Park, bought papers. Supper. At 8.45 to the Gontards where I passed a very pleasant evening. Bed at 11. It snowed hard as I went to bed.

April 28th
A beautiful cold day. In the distance, all the hills were covered with snow. Censored letters and saw to my record card. Back to my room where I wrote a letter to Deacon Brinley and sent Mr Sims $250 for the Lab. which should prove useful. After luncheon walked around by the Station, then to the Company where I met Lt Phillips and he returned with me and we went to the barrage. It snowed very hard. Had a cup of coffee at the Lake restaurant. He told me about his life in the Philippines, which was most interesting. Back to the Company. Papers state that New Zealand won the boat race. Back to my room. At 8pm went to the Roblots, then on to the Gontards where we played cards. Snowing hard. Bed at 12.30am.

April 29th
Up to find the ground covered with snow. A fine day. To the Company to censor letters. Back to get a hair cut and shave. Got a nice letter from Frank. Pouring rain. Wrote Frank a letter to the Park, back to the hospital where I saw Lt Kurtzmann. Bought him some cake and candy. To the company to superintend the supper, which was good. To my room after

supper, then to the Roblots where we ate pop corn until 10.30. Walked home.

April 30th

Snowing hard & rain. To the Company where I censored letters and saw to the court martial. Saw to the officers' mess at the hotel. Ten francs per day. Nothing of importance on hand. Gontards have invited me to dinner tomorrow night. Went there at 1pm & stayed until 3. To the hospital to see Kurtzmann until 4pm. It snowed hard all day & rained. To the Company where I rejoiced at the sight of much mail – Salkin, Wainwright, Zenabru, Mama, Moppie, Delafield. It was raining so hard that after reading the papers & writing several letters to Moppie, Mama & Edith Travis I went to bed. Goodbye April.

May 1st

Still a rainy day. To the Company, then after censoring letters, to the Commissary where I bought some milk. Nice letter from Cynthia & Lt Sheridan. Paid the men and had lunch at the hotel. Very good. To the company where I paid off the men. Back to write letters. Wrote one to Col Battle to try to get an M.P. job. It may be a mistake, perhaps not. At 7pm got dressed up and went to the Gontards. Very nice dinner. Sat around afterwards & had game of bridge. Bed at 12. Letters to Cynthia & Frank.

May 2nd

Still overcast & rain. To the Co., read the Tatler & waited around until 11 but there wasn't any officers' meeting. Am anxiously waiting to hear if there is any chance of my being transferred to Paris. I hope I am. There will never be another war like this & it is the most interesting place to be at the moment. On the way to the Company met Col. Roler. To the Huquenets where we met Madame H. To the Officers' club. Very pleasant talk for an hour. At 8 went to the Company & at 9 to the Roblots' where we talked America. Bed at 11.

May 3rd

To the Company. Bought some salad for the Company & ordered cake. Back to the room. To the Co. for inspection, returning to my room. Found a long letter from Aunt Lucy, Miss Buck & Line. After luncheon wrote to Lucy & Frank. To the Company & at 5.30 had supper with Col Roler at the camp Hospital. Went to the nurses' quarters afterwards and had a nice talk with Miss Bell, Miss Cooper, Miss Childs. Bed at 11pm.

May 4th

Up at 8. Lt Pratt has returned to the Company. We had a long talk regarding the Americans in France. They have behaved so badly. To the room. After luncheon went to the Company & it was glorious & hot. Met Cris and we climbed the church steeple & heard them ring the big bell. Had coffee together, bought some oil for the Company, shaved & went up after supper. Had an amusing supper. This is our last Sunday in Semur. Am glad to be leaving. Never very happy here. At 8.30 went to the Huquenets where we had an amusing evening. Bed at 11.

May 5th

Up at 7.30. Breakfast & to the station expecting to see the Morissy children leave. They put it off. To the Roblots & then to the Park. Most gorgeous day. Here we are these last days in France. The day after tomorrow we leave. At 2pm I found the Gontards and we proceeded to their country place which led us thru' the country & woods. It was a lovely day & I did enjoy the walk. Arriving found an ugly house but nice view. Had some wine & returned. Got back at 7. To the Company & at 9 went to the Roblots until 11 when I came to bed.

May 6th

A calm, cloudless day. To the station, busied myself with a claim, started packing & gave the young boy my fishing rod. Lunched with the priest & afterwards saw to my luggage & the claim. Court martial at 3.30. Officers' meeting. Went for a walk with the Duflos girl. Most gorgeous evening. After supper to the Cruzats, Gontards & Roblots. Home at 12.30. Bed at 1 am. Off to-morrow.

May 7th

Up at 5.30 am. To the Company. Had breakfast & at 8.30 walked the Company down. Back to say goodbye to the Gontards. Bayets, Duflos. Cruzats at the station to say goodbye. Train finally pulled out at 11. Beautiful day. To Les Laumes & north. Off at La Roche. To Bourges. Spent the pm looking out of the window. Bed at 10.30 on a bed sack.

May 8th

Poor night's sleep. Long wait at Limoges. Beautiful hot day! Rest of the day spent on & off the train. Had enough food. At 10 arrive at Bordeaux. Not enough trucks. Had to stay around until 3.30am before we got away. Don't mind it though! Bought the men some doughnuts. Slept on the floor.

May 9th

Up at 9. To the Knights of Columbus[180]. Had a cup of chocolate. Men there. Had 2 letters from Mama, Zenabru, Harvard Bulletin, Delia. Busied myself around. Saw to the Companies' Mess. After my men fed, censored in Council Book. Cashed my cheque. Raining hard. At 7.30 Cris & I went to Bordeaux where I saw a "revue" with him. Sat in a box with some women. Back at 12.30.

May 10th

Up at 8. Missed breakfast. Saw to the transportation, then all around to see to the movement. Had a bite at 12. Moved to permanent camp. Reached here at 1 pm. "Deloused", had a physical test. Supper at 5. Back to the billets where I took a bath & then got the men their mess. Had supper with Cris Kurtzmann. Back to the billet to prepare for the night. Raining hard. We shall pull out very soon. Over to the old camp to get sailing baggage lists. Back on foot. Bed at 11.

May 11th

Up at 6. Not much rested. To the company, then fixed up. Made out baggage lists & at 9.30 held an inspection which went thro' all right. Passed the pm by going with Contelessa to the other camp. Got my money changed & found some mail. When I got back had letters from Alice Wainwright, Alice Hopkins, Mama, Helen and enjoyed them all. Went with Cris to Bordeaux where we had an excellent dinner, then to 'Tosca' which was very good. Enjoyed this day very much. Nice ride down the river in a boat. Had some Harvard Bulletins and two books that I shall read on my return to the States. Bed at 12.30.

May 12th

Felt very tired. Had to report a detail at 8 a.m. Spent the am looking at my letters & reading the Harvard Bulletins. Have felt terribly today to read in the Harvard Bulletin that Richard J Hunter, my playmate in college had been killed in action, August 25. We played soccer & cricket together in Harvard. Has been a terrific hot day. Had an excellent lunch. In the pm, about the barracks, wrote letters. To the old camp to hand in baggage lists. Back to write to the Duflos girl, Aunt Lucy & read the papers. Am in good spirits. Will go back to the States to make good.

---

[180] A Catholic relief Agency, founded in the US which set up centres for American soldiers in France, buying property at centres and embarkation ports on which to erect Knights of Columbus huts.

May 13th

Another beautiful day. Not a cloud in the sky & real summer heat. Had a good nights sleep. Up at 7. Breakfast, back to the Company. Wrote Frank a letter. Stayed around the Company & barracks. Have no idea when we shall be leaving. After luncheon, had my hair cut and the heat was fierce so that we all sat around in the barracks and kept as cool as possible. Wrote letters and looked around. Don't think we will get away for some time yet. Am looking forward to our return eagerly. After supper went to the '7' where I heard music & read the English pictorials.

May 14th

Somewhat cooler today. Watched a baseball game & went to the '7' where I wrote to Madame Roblot & Gontard. Luncheon. Afterwards bought a victory ribbon & had two letters from Helen & one from Alice Wainwright. Talked to Miss Colby about the American officers. Tomorrow is my birthday– 34! Expect to go to town tonight. No news as to when we are sailing. After supper took a boat to town and wandered about the city. It is a pretty place. At 8 bought a seat & saw 'Manon. (Lescaut)'. Enjoyed it a good deal. A lovely lady in the next box. Back at 12.30.

May 15th

My birthday – 34. It had rained last night so it is cool today. A good breakfast. Talked afterwards to Glen Bowers. Watched some baseball & read. A beautiful day. Read most of the pm. & at 6.30 played two sets of tennis. Lost both. Came back and caught 8.15 auto to Bordeaux & with a piece of good luck got a seat with some French soldiers for 'Aida.' It was pleasant and I'm glad I went. Bed at 1 pm.

May 16th

Hear we are off today. Had baggage ready at 8. A cloudy day. Sat about & read the New York Times & packed up. Nothing much doing. After luncheon sat around. Watched baseball game & talked to some French people. Tomorrow we go. Baggage has left. It is to take 12 days, I believe. Goodbye France. Went to the C & then back, to bed at 9.30. So much noise I couldn't go to sleep.

May 17th

Up early. Leave at 10. Breakfast, shave. All is ready. Had Company ready at 9. Marched out to the parade ground at 10. Very warm. I had my suit case & raincoat. A long hike to the docks. Band played as we left the camp.

The heat and dust was terrific. Had numerous stops. Arrived at 12. The

Red Cross gave us an excellent cup of coffee & sandwiches. How like a year ago! Nothing prevents our getting aboard at 2. Am in a stateroom with Major Daly & a Capt Dyett. Arranged my things. At 5.30 the boat drew away. Down the river and our last views of France. My, what a wonderful year it has been! Thank God I was saved from this ghastly war! Had a good supper at 6. Went on deck & had our last view of France. I shall come back! Sat around & read until 9 and then turned.

May 18th

Out of sight of land! Slight ground swell. Feel fine. Had breakfast with Lee Marcus. Spent the am listening to the music and reading Burke which Mama sent me. It was a glorious day & the sun was hot, a gentle swell that made some of the men seasick. In the pm had a meeting where we discuss ship discipline. Am to go to boat 6. Lay down for a while – read & slept. Good supper. Sat around as usual. Bed at 9.30.

May 19th

Up at 8. Had quarters ready for inspection. It was overcast & we had fog for about an hour. The wind has freshened up a bit. Read Burke until luncheon. Am getting used to this life again. It isn't much fun. Read & at 4 pm we had the boat drill. Wireless report that the English Sopwith plane had started on its voyage. Good luck to him! In the evening sat around & talked to Turner in our cabin. Bed at 11.

May 20th

A gorgeous blue sea! Ship is tossing a bit. Was officer of the day. Almost ten before they got around to our station. Had a shave & sat in the sun. At luncheon heard that the English plane[181] had come within 40 miles of the coast of Ireland & had fallen. What luck! Expect to be another ten days on this boat, arriving about the 13th. Hope I can get to school for Anniversary! Am still reading Burke. Played bridge until 10.30.

May 21st

Beautiful day. Listened to the music & read up on deck. At 11 we came into a school of tuna. They jumped out of the water and were about 40 lbs in weight. After luncheon had some bridge – Daly, Marcus, MacKenna & I. Usual drills at 4. Nothing important today. After supper played some

---

[181] The English plane was a Sopwith machine flown by Australian-born Harry Hawker with Lt Commander Mackenzie Grieve as navigator. They ditched after 13 hours aloft and were rescued. The first non-stop flight was by British aviators Alcock and Brown of the RAF the following month

bridge with Lt Johnson. Talked France & the work the engineers had done in Europe. Bed at 10.30.

May 22nd

Felt better today. Read in the am & played bridge. Some fog in the pm. More bridge. Nothing new. Passed the Azores today at 3pm. Had a walk for an hour and was on the bridge. Talked to a naval officer at the bridge. After supper played some more bridge until 11pm.

May 23rd

Weather still overcast. Heard stories of some people who had the shame of paying $25,000 to escape the draft & went into the Navy yard. They ought to be killed outright and branded! Played bridge all pm. Fog at times. Up on bridge after supper. There was a tremendous wind storm. Bridge until 10.

May 24th

A clear day with much wind. Was down in the hold until 11.30 waiting for inspection. Felt ill because the ship rocked a good deal. We reached the half way mark at 3pm. Hear that the English plane has been found. The men have been lost. Sat in my cabin the entire pm reading. Should be home a week from today! It will be fun to see New York again. Got very rough in the pm and the boat rocked terribly. Talked about England in the evening. Kept awake until 11. Very nervous – there was so much movement.

May 25th

Very much calmer. Beautiful clear sky. Sat on deck in the sun. Sea getting calmer & calmer. About 12.30 the *Lancaster* sighted. At 1.30 watched some very poor boxing. Back to my cabin when I wrote some in this book and read an excellent article by Briggs of Harvard. Passed the *Lancaster* at 8.30. Bridge until 10pm.

May 26th

A very warm night. Sea as calm as a mill pond. On deck this am in the sun. Sighted several vessels. At noon we had news that the English aviators had been picked up in good health. Three cheers! Boat is doing splendidly – nearly 300. Four more days! At 1.30 there was boxing – one knock out. I sat around on deck. Engine slowed down for repairs to boiler. In the evening there was a glorious sunset. Played bridge, one rubber lasting two hours, 8-10. It was good fun. Bed at 10.

May 27th

Rained hard at 8. By 9 the boat was going full speed again. Unable to go on deck. Spent practically the entire day reading a camping book, which was most interesting. Loafed around in the pm & read. Made out a Court Martial charge and signed some slips entitling the men to wear the second gold chevron. One year ago today, we left Camp Dix. Boat made a poor run. Played bridge in the evening until 10. Read.

May 28th

A good night's sleep. A nice day. Boat making good headway. Am full of plans for future. It was a glorious day. Found a most interesting book giving the lives of famous American Belles of the 19th Cent. It made very interesting reading. At 2pm I saw some good boxing, one bout in particular being very bloody. Nothing important. Read much of the pm & played bridge & hearts until 12.

May 29th

Another nice day. Listened to the music & felt much better than yesterday. Finished the interesting book that I had begun yesterday. A lazy pm & at 4pm the boat stopped completely for some trouble. Resumed its run at 6pm, thank heaven. Should be in by Sat. Have had a pretty good time on the whole. Have been much benefited by the books I have read on this trip. Played cards all evening. Bed at 12 after some jam & crackers.

May 30th

A clear windy day. Listened to the music and translated a letter into French. Should reach quarantine at midnight tomorrow night. It is a great relief to know that this trip is over soon. It has been too long. Watched some boxing and made a very interesting visit to the ship's engine room. Today is Decoration Day. Have felt very nervous all day. In the evening I saw a beautiful sunset & played bridge & talked until 11.

May 31st

A gorgeous day. Sea as calm as the Hudson. Am officer of the day. On the job at 10am. Passed a vessel & saw some porpoises. Listened to the band. Thought of getting home tomorrow. It hardly seems true. Hope I can keep my resolutions.

  i.   Am determined to be more manly.
  ii   To cease all dancing.
  iii Not to forget how few people were nice to me while away.
  iv   To never forgive SR & DK & Marks.

v   Not to drink & have perfect control.

vi To be able to say "no".

At 2.30 unfortunately, our port engine broke down. We are proceeding with one engine. Delighted to receive three (3) radiograms from Mama, Cynthia, & Salkin, all eager to see me. We dock at 9.30am. Sent Mama a radio to that effect. Sea is dead calm. Should be thankful that the breakdown occurred only today. Just think New York tomorrow! Home! Took a bath at 5. Feel fine. Sat around & talked & at 8pm we had our first view of land. Lighthouses! Played a little bridge until 3.45. Had a good cup of coffee at 12. Up the channel & anchored.

June 1st

A three hours sleep. Great reception as we came up the Harbor. Rockets and other boats whistled. Reached dock at 10.30 After inspection, to see Mama who was there with Joe Sally. Glad to see her. At 1 pm we took the ferry to the Penn & reached here at 4.30. Camp Dix. How strange it all seemed to be back. Went to the Hostess house for supper and then after that I walked over to our old barracks to see the change. The place has deteriorated & it is all badly taken care of & worn out. Bath & bed at 10.30 in building 404.

June 2nd

Up at 7.30. Breakfast at 8.30. To the Company then back to an officers' meeting, where we began to arrange lists for demobilizing. Heat terrific. Read in the Times that Mr Bacon[182] had died, his funeral today. Sat around after lunch. Had a shave & at 4pm had the company picture which ought to be good. Supper at 6 . Wrote some letters. Bed.

June 3rd

Passed the am. in the most terrific heat. Lunched early & at 2 took the company down to be "deloused". That lasted all the pm in a fierce heat. Back to our new area. Company settled. Had a little supper & then got fixed up for the night. Went down to the old barracks. Bed at 11.

June 4th

Another hot day. Turned in some records & after luncheon went to the "mad house" & made out final statements. Had supper then to the Hostess house & back to bed.

---

[182] Col. Robert Bacon. Harvard Club of New York.

June 5th Anniversary

From June 5th to the 12th the life at the camp was tedious and under very trying conditions. On June 8th the entire company went AWOL & returned Monday.

The day before they got their discharge I gave a farewell "spree". We had strawberries & ice cream with the other company – B.

Before leaving the camp the men gave me a silver cup that I appreciated very much. Finally on June 12th, I received my discharge from the US Army."

Frank too was relieved from active duty from the Navy in mid-August, 1919. He received a discharge gratuity of $60 along with thanks for the patriotic services he had rendered to his country in the war against Germany.

After the war, the title of General of the Armies of the United States was conferred upon Pershing, the only officer in American military history so designated. The Great War, "the war to end all wars" as it became known was over. The scale of its destruction is unparalleled. The total of those mobilised on both sides was 65 million, of whom 10 million died and 20 million were wounded.[183]

[183] BBC News Special report. 1998. World War I.

Part III

Life in England

23

Maurice Roche becomes Lord Fermoy

Maurice was thankful to have returned from the war unscathed. He had had a marvellous experience, in spite of the harrowing sights, the tragedy of death and his own moments of intense fear. One thing was certain. Life would never be the same for him again. Already dissatisfied with the pleasures of the social round, he was now determined to make something of his life.

His bank balance had been building up while he was away, and he soon began donating to St Paul's School. In June, he had been elected a Trustee. On July 4th Dr Drury wrote asking him to guarantee the shortfall ($10,000) required to build a new road at St Paul's, diverting the main road from the centre of the School to one side. Maurice sent a telegram immediately agreeing to do this. He also contributed $9,000 towards a rustic stone bridge with three arches, where the new road crossed the Turkey river. He donated a "pasteurising machine" for the farm and paid for the repainting of the squash courts.

At the end of August, Maurice went to St Paul's, which he found looking beautiful. He was delighted with the new Lower School improvements and the new bridge under construction. Preparations were under way for the boys' arrival. He journeyed from there to Danbury to the school camp where he spent a few days. He was impressed by the new building, which he described as a very complete structure and much appreciated by the staff and the boys. He described himself as a crank on "better living conditions". He had done everything in his power to make it attractive.

In the autumn, Maurice set about actively building an endowment fund for St Paul's. He founded a scholarship of $10,000[184] in memory of Richard McCall Elliot, a St Paul's boy who was killed at sea in March 1918, in a heroic attempt to save his ship and the lives of his fellow-officers and crew. Maurice was deeply affected by the death of his friend, as he was by all the deaths of St Paul's boys during the War.

Aunt Lucy now had a fine home on the River Hudson – Woodburn Hall. At the end of 1918, she was divorced from Peter Cooper Hewitt. She wrote to Maurice in the spring before his demobilisation, expressing her loneliness and need of him: "I want you to like Woodburn Hall and me. I want to mean something to you

---

[184] Market value of the scholarship in 2007: $182,879.

– also I need you myself very much. I have cut off the past. I have no roots. You have no idea how pining and pointless I feel." In the same letter, she urges him to plunge into his new purpose, without going to Newport where his good intentions and impulses will be sapped.

In early January, he returned to work in the Superintendent's office of the Lackawanna, as he found his time was hanging heavily on his hands. He took a holiday in Castine, Maine, staying with Mr Brinley, the St Paul's master who was his good friend. In August, he went to Europe, first to Sandricourt-par-Meru, (Oise) in France to visit friends from the war. While he was spending a few weeks in London, his father inherited the title of Baron Fermoy.

On 1st September 1920, the second Lord Fermoy died at Barmouth in Wales where he was living. He had one daughter Sybil[185] and through lack of a male heir, the title passed that day to his brother James, who became the third Baron Fermoy. Jim was living in Artillery Mansions, Westminster. At the end of his eventful life of financial peaks and troughs, bankruptcy was pending. Yet as the photograph opposite shows, taken soon after he became Fermoy, he was still a fine-looking man, holding himself proudly and erectly, fashionably dressed. Every morning his commanding figure was seen walking across St James's Park to Brooks', his club in St James's Street.

Maurice saw him in London and returned to New York at the end of October. A few days later he was shocked to hear of the death of his father. Forty days after he inherited the title, the 3rd Baron Fermoy died at his home. This personal tribute sums up his most unusual character:

"A vital and expansive personality has been extinguished by Lord Fermoy's death. He never looked, though he had fully lived, his sixty-nine years. One of the handsomest men of his day, well over six feet and powerfully built, he retained to the last a fresh and imposing presence, just as he kept his buoyant disposition and the capacity for spurts of youthful interest which was part of his Irish birthright.

He seemed to have been everywhere, and to have tried his hand – one gathered fitfully and not over-successfully – at most ways of making a fortune; and having a retentive memory, a shrewd eye for a situation, and a wealth of humour, his stock of reminiscences was inexhaustibly beguiling. A quick sense of the drama of life never left him, and under the manipulating artistry of his imagination, no facts remained arid or featureless. His mind like himself had rather roved than assimilated, but his information which was variegated, but hardly profound, had always in it so great a quality of entertainment that one accepted it much more on that basis and as a revelation of the man, than as a contribution to knowledge.

---

[185] Sybil Roche married Godfrey Nigel Baring.

Maurice volunteerd his services to fire the engine of a train to the Lackawanna terminal during a strike of railroad men, 1920

Maurice's father when he became Lord Fermoy, September, 1920

Kindliness was with him an instinct; he delighted in doing people good turns; and the punctiliousness of his courtesy and consideration towards all who served him was an engaging trait in a man as naturally careless of appearances and opinion.

At the practical things of life he was little good but the world never ceased to present itself to him as an affair of radiant possibilities. Not much ever came of his manifold schemes, taken up with unquenchable ardour and fertility; but no sooner had one collapsed than he was busily chasing its successor with the same undaunted ineffectiveness. An adventuring optimism was the very salt of his being. The baulked achievement, the constant anti-climax of non-fulfilment, faded from his mind: there remained to feed his romantic memory, the inspiration, the desire and the quest. In that, as in his love of sport and his passion for horses, he was a thorough Irishman. The passing of such a man means nothing to the world at large; but to his friends and acquaintances it is one of those losses they know can never quite be made good. It will be long before they cease to think and talk, smilingly but with absolute affection, of J B Roche."

Bewildered and anxious at the stunning news of his father's death, Maurice immediately wrote to Frank, who was enjoying a hunting season in Leicestershire.

"Nov 1st 1920
Tuxedo Park

Dear Boy,
I cannot begin to take in the fact that our father has died. I also am unable to know what to do. I am hoping that you will attend to the funeral arrangements and also get a good lawyer & find out everything as to the estate & what taxes etc are due. I think it would be a good thing to have an inventory of the estate made & also I suppose I will have to pay a big sum to the "crown" if I accept the title.

Spent the weekend at Aunt Lucy's. Place looked lovely. Tennis court is fine. Have no news; am anxiously awaiting full details and dope on the whole matter.

Tomorrow is election day. Harding is sure to win. I go to Concord for the next weekend. Saw Ray & Wardour yesterday. Never have I seen such golf. All Tuxedo turned out to see it. Perfect day & not a breath of wind.

Take good care of yourself.

Love MR"

The funeral service took place at St Martin-in-the-Fields. Jim's brother

Edmund,[186] his sister Countess Hochberg and his son Frank were among the principal mourners. (His daughter Cynthia was in America.) The congregation included his lifelong friend, Moreton Frewen. He was buried at St Marylebone Cemetery, Finchley.

On the day his father died, Maurice became the 4th Baron Fermoy. The unexpected death presented him with a potentially difficult choice. When his uncle Fitzy believed that he could transfer the title to a nephew if Maurice refused to assume it, he was ignorant of the law. Until the Peerage Act 1963,[187] it was not possible to disclaim a peerage. Maurice could not get rid of his hereditary title, although the option was open to him to remain in America and simply not use it.

In fact the death of his father coincided with a vacuum in Maurice's life, when he did not know what to do with himself – how to live up to the resolutions he had made when the war ended. Settling in England as Lord Fermoy, offered an escape from a life of ease, pleasure and frivolity which he had outgrown, and that was fundamentally unfulfilling to the serious side of his nature. He decided to give it a try, embracing the hope of a new life and suffering only a few moments of wavering and doubt.

According to the New York press reports, Maurice offered the title to Frank, who already had a house in Leicestershire, England, at the time of his father's death. However Maurice himself made it clear to Frank that these reports were incorrect. It appears that it did not take him long to make up his mind to resume his British nationality. This he was able do, in spite of having spent his life in America and being a naturalised American citizen, because he was born in London of a British father. There was no obstacle to him assuming the title of Baron Fermoy.

"Alumni Association of St Paul's School. November 22 1920
Office of Secretary 23 West 53rd Street, NYC
Nov 22nd 1920

Dear Boy,
I got all your data today. I must tell you here that I never said a word about passing the title. It was all the papers' invention, of our being twins etc.

I don't see how you can be in such a hurry to pay these debts. I have told you several times that I am going to pay half of them, but I think you should engage another lawyer than Holt. He has already the largest claim against the estate. That looks bad. How do you know he earned that? Salkin agrees with me that you should engage a new lawyer and tell Holt to file his

---

[186] Hon. Edmund Burke Roche, 5th son of the 1st Lord Fermoy, who emigrated to Canada and married Elizabeth Clapham of Quebec. They had no children.

[187] This act was introduced by Tony Wedgwood Benn, then second Viscount Stansgate. Irish peers were still not covered by this Act.

claim against our father's estate. Have all his papers gone over; then a man is sent to each firm or shop to get in writing an itemized bill of what is owed.

I am anxious to know something about the estates. Can you get some idea of what there is left? If any. I see that you have paid one bill and I sincerely hope you will get a full list and go over carefully all our father's bills before paying them.

Things have not brightened up here in the least. Mama who seems to have as much "guts" as a chicken is hanging around the house, depressed or friendless. Her debts in France amount to 74,383 francs. She now intimates she wants to live in England with us & now that you have invited Cynthia, she is sailing and plans to keep house for us next spring. Result, the whole family on <u>our</u> hands for good. Cynthia never makes an effort and with Mama to nag, and this group, you can imagine what will happen.

You will see that St Paul's was beaten 1-0 by Groton. There was four inches of snow on the ground & everybody who saw the game said we had better backs & ends & had the game been played on dry ground, we would have certainly won. Here is a clipping. The game was lost on a fumble with just 50 seconds more to play! which is more galling.

I saw Harvard beat Yale 9.0 Saturday. Three field goals. Harvard came down the field six times & couldn't put it over.

Boy, how can you get proof that these money lenders lent our father that money? We have a year to pay these debts. I think we should go into each debt with the greatest of care. You should notify all the people that my father owed money to place their claims on file. Glad you are having a good time and have found a nice car. Keep an accurate list of all expenses you've incurred thro' our father's death.

Much love Maurice"

"Woodburn Hall, New Windsor-on-Hudson
Thanksgiving Day, 1920

Dear Boy,
If you could just look out from here & see the lawn & the trees all covered with beautiful snow. Last night when I took the train from the Grand Central, it was starting to fall & today we have a real old fashioned thanksgiving.

Aunt Lucy has nobody up here so that makes it rather dreary. This am we went to church & then walked about the place. After lunch, I strolled about & saw the pool, the rose bed & thought a great deal about my future. I am now spending my last days in America & next year at this time I shall be settled somewhere with you abroad.

You can say what you like, but there are some very nice things about this country; only business life is not attractive. The people are more real and genuine & when you talk to somebody over here, they do listen & are not just saying "Oh, really"!

Christmas is with us a month from now. If there are any things you care to have done let me know. Cynthia sails the 23rd and I shall give her additional hair tonic for you.

There's no news. Business is very bad over here, no buying & prices are going down something fierce. You will be pleased to hear that they have passed the million & a half mark in the SPS drive.

Let me hear often. Nothing to report.

Very best. MR"

Jim Roche, the late Lord Fermoy, had been on the verge of bankruptcy when he died, and Maurice and Frank had to pay off his substantial debts. Maurice wrote bitterly to Dr Drury:

"I am still aware of the fact that I owe some eighteen hundred dollars on the bridge. The unforeseen always happens. This time, it was my father's death & his pending bankruptcy. Of course Frank & I had to clear his name. The curse of the Englishman's private life seems to be these money-lenders, who lend easily at high rates of interest. To these men alone we have paid some two thousand pounds. Thus the reason for my not paying my bill before."

As the time approached for his departure, it troubled Maurice that his mother would not be able to afford to run the house in New York, once he had gone. He paid a large sum every month into the housekeeping budget. She would have to move and ten staff would lose their jobs. He tried to persuade Frank to return for the following winter.

"Racquet and Tennis Club,[188] 370 Park Avenue.
Wednesday, Jan 27th 1921

Dear Boy,
I am sorry that you haven't written much lately but I know that you have been expecting me "overseas". Of course you understand that when I go some ten people in our house are discharged & the place closed. Mama cannot afford to run it herself. This winter I have been paying five hundred

---

[188] Racquets is an indoor racquet game, called in English, "hard rackets" to distinguish it from "squash rackets".

a month for my board and lodging. That is only fair.

I wish you would think it over, if there is the merest chance of your spending next winter here. Will you give this a week's thought? For if not the house must be sold & our identification with NY ended. Certainly if I find no job in England that is constructive, I shall come back for the winter. You have no idea how nice NY is, the fine houses, etc.

I expect to go to Palm Beach & sail sometime in March, the first week. Let me have your plans.

Love MR

Cathleen Vanderbilt[189] married Sidney Colford yesterday."

"Alumni Association of St. Paul's School
Office of Secretary 23 West 53rd Street, NYC
Jan 31st 1921

Dear Boy

Just what I expected has happened and it pains me very much that Cynthia arrived to make you change your plans. Of course she is the most spoilt person in the world & after my experience in 1913 when she left me after three days in the Maine Woods, when conditions were extremely nice, I think you have been a saint, for I feel sure that I would have acted quite differently under the circumstances. Damn that Miss Sherwin!

I am glad that you have seen the Prince & the Queen and what you said in connection with them was interesting.

Saturday, I played for the Tennis & Racquet club and we had a pretty busy time. I am pleased to report that I played well, hitting the ball crisply. Here is the clipping.

I expect to sail in early March. I don't think I want to go to Cannes. Take care of yourself. Write often.

Love MR

I'm glad you did well with the debts."

"Racquet and Tennis Club, 370 Park Avenue
Wednesday, March 16th 1921

Dear Boy

Ten years ago today Grandpa joined the great majority. This am Aunt Lucy and I went out to Green-Wood[190] & placed carnations & other flowers

---

[189] First wife of Reginald Vanderbilt.
[190] There is a Frank Work family plot (Section 75. Lot 3585/86) at the Green-Wood Cemetery, Brooklyn, NY, at the intersection of Grove Avenue with Juniper Path. It has an elegant marble obelisk.

on the graves. I believe it was the first time she had been since we buried him. I think it is a shame that neither she nor Mama have ever even thought of any kind of memorial, even a bed in a hospital. But that's their business. She sails Saturday and I presume you are going to all meet in Paris.

I have seen quite a lot of the Wernhers & they are having an excellent time staying with the Neely Vanderbilts. I took them to a dance last night. She told me of the excellent joke played on you & how you danced with a man dressed as a woman! He is sort of an ass and the conceit of them both quite galls me.

I leave three weeks from tomorrow. I don't think you will be in London when I arrive. I expect to go to some small hotel upon landing. I think the Cavendish. It depends on the price.

The Hoffmans sail very soon after that. Marian has been trying to get me to come up this weekend but I don't want to. There is absolutely nothing to do and I refuse to be bored.

I presume that you are planning our trip to the Riviera. It seems a bit late, but perhaps you may enjoy it. I hope you get a few good matches, as that will please Cynthia.

Rumour has it that Uncle Cooper and that woman are to be divorced.

There is no news. I hope to hear soon. Trusting that you are having a good time.

With love MR"

"23 West 53rd Street,
March 6th 1921

Dear Boy,
You have no idea what a perfect day this is. Fifth Avenue thronged with people & real spring air. It must be seventy at least – really warm.

The Junior League show took place last week & it was excellent, on the same scale as in previous years. I went Friday night. There seemed to be so many pretty girls.

I have but a month left. I wish that you might come to spend next winter here. That would enable us to keep the house. I saw in the paper that the cost of living came down 43% in the past year. The clothing people are suffering something fierce, failures everywhere. Damn it, they deserve it.

I see the English court tennis championship is to take place the 25th of April. I hope that I may be able to win a match in it. I'm playing a more aggressive game than before, forcing & it seems to count.

Hope everything is ok. Old man Senator Butt died the other day.

H A C Taylor is also very ill at present.

My operation on my teeth cost $450. Do you think it much? I don't.

love MR "

A week before Maurice sailed for Europe, his mother wrote to Frankie to explain a letter Maurice had written to his brother, in which he expressed his affection for America and his doubts about leaving. This letter had upset Frank very much. Fanny reproached Frank for finding it difficult to understand Maurice's position.

"But it is very natural. You are there enjoying all & everything. He is here having not tasted any of the pleasures that may arrive from his situation, only feeling that this portion of his life is over forever. He feels sorry in a way that it is finished & sorry to leave so much that is pleasant.

You know how you have felt upon sailing for Europe. Last time you were in a fever of uncertainty. You felt very badly, I remember. You both have had a wonderful time & there is naturally a wrench to break off old ties & associations. I am sure that once M goes over & settles himself (I do hope he will find something to do, for it is deplorable not to have it) he will be happy..."

She adds that she is not shipping her saddle horse Sportsman when she travels to Europe the following month. She will wait and see. Ben, her groom, can send him over if he is wanted.

24

Settling in England

On April 7th 1921, Maurice Burke Roche, now Lord Fermoy, set sail for England on the Cunard liner, RMS *Mauretania*. As an Irish baron, his destination should have been to Ireland, where a long line of Roches had lived since the twelfth century.

They were originally Norman warriors, who had come over with William the Conqueror in the eleventh century. The Abbey of Battle, seven miles from Hastings, was erected as a memorial to those who shared in the victory in 1066. Their names are listed in the Roll of Battle Abbey,[191] which purports to contain the family names of the knights who fought with William. Roche is not listed in the Roll but Rochefort is. The name Roche in early Latin documents is *de rupe*, "of the rock". Rochefort is *de rupe forti*, meaning "of the mighty rock".

A century later, King Henry II sent some of the land-hungry Norman warlords to subdue the Welsh in South Wales. There they built stone castles to defend their newly acquired territory, of which Roch[192] castle survives. In 1167 an Irish chieftain who had been exiled by his enemies, sought help to retrieve his lost land. With the approval of the Pope, a Cambro-Norman force sailed from South Wales to the south of Ireland. They quickly conquered most of the country. According to the legend Adam and David de la Roche were among the Norman knights who took part in that invasion.

They are the forbears of the Roches in Ireland. Through advantageous marriages they became one of the most powerful families in the south and south-west of the country, completely integrated into an Irish way of life. In the thirteenth century "the barony of Fermoy consisted of 23 parishes and therein were 190 plowlands and 69175 plantation acres".[193] It was known as Roches Country.

In the fourteenth century at least five distinct branches of Roches were in existence. They were large landowners in Wexford, Cork, Tipperary, Kildare and Louth. The Roches' chief castles were at Glanworth and Castletownroche. They

---

[191] There are several lists and their authenticity is disputed, as some names have clearly been added centuries later.

[192] The type of rock the castle is built on is one of the oldest in the area. It is pre-Cambrian, probably about 1,000 million years old. It is called Roch rhyolite, a most resistant rock, which weathers almost white. From *The Geology of Pembrokeshire*.

[193] *The Roches of Fermoy* by W J Roche.

owned many others as well. The town of Castletownroche derives its name from the Roche castle.

"Maurice Roche was mayor of Cork in 1488 and several of the name were mayors through the next centuries. To one of those Queen Elizabeth presented the silver chain now in the museum at Fitzgerald's park."[194]

In 1585 Lord Maurice Roche claimed the title of Viscount Roche of Fermoy. and sat in the Irish House of Lords. There is no patent extant for this title and the Crown appears to have issued a peerage by writ. In 1733 Ulick the last viscount died without male issue.[195]

Maurice's ancestor, Edward Roche was living at Trabolgan in County Cork, in 1678, but that ancestral home had been sold in 1889. Kilshannig,[196] another family home, had also been sold and there was no longer any property in Ireland in Roche ownership. His uncle Fitzy, the second Lord Fermoy, ended his days living in Wales and his father had no stake in Ireland.

Even if Maurice had inherited an estate in Ireland, the situation there had reached a peak of violence. An Act of Parliament giving Home Rule to Ireland had been passed in 1914, but was repudiated by the Liberals in 1916. This hardened the attitude of Irish nationalists, who became republicans, wanting independence from Britain. Starting in 1917, for the next five years, a bitter war of terror ensued, between the British army and police on the one hand, and extreme Irish republicans on the other. This was the cause of many deaths and serious injuries on both sides. These in turn were followed by brutal reprisals.

The British government recruited English, Scottish and Welsh army veterans to bolster the numbers of the Royal Irish constabulary. There were not enough black uniforms and some wore army surplus. They became known as the Black and Tans and were ruthless in their methods.

With any thought of going back to his Irish roots being impractical and unadvisable, Maurice came to England, with the intention of finding 'constructive' work in London. Two months before he sailed, he was quoted as saying that he had not made up his mind as to whether to go into British politics. The railroad business was another possibility. He intended to spend three months of every year in America. If he ever had a son, he would go to Harvard.

One of his fellow passengers on board the *Mauretania* was to prove very influential on his future life. Maurice wrote to Dr Drury from the ship: "I have had the good fortune of sitting at table with Lord Queenborough who has given me much information & promises great help when I am in England."

---

[194] John T Collins. Cork Historian. 1961
[195] From the report of J P Brooke-Little, College of Arms, London, 30th June 1980
[196] Trabolgan was at the entrance to Cork harbour. Kilshannig was 25 miles inland, due north.

Maurice's conversations with Almeric Paget,[197] Lord Queenborough, at meal times at the Captain's table, had an important influence on the course of his life in England. Almeric was born in 1861, one of 14 children. He was shipped off to America in 1879, penniless, to Iowa where he was a cattle rancher. He was a contemporary and friend of Maurice's father, Jim Roche, and later of Fanny as well. Unlike Jim, Almeric made a fortune in real estate. Like Jim, he married a wealthy heiress, Pauline Whitney, daughter of a nickel king, who was heiress to a fortune of £8 million.

Because of his wife's delicate health, the Pagets came to live in England, renting a house in Norfolk in the first place. From 1910-1917 Almeric was MP for the constituency of Cambridge. He was given a peerage in 1919 as a reward for services to his party, and took the name of Lord Queenborough of Kent. Politically to the right, he was an opened-hearted man and a friend to aspiring young men.

Maurice had encountered "a man with business acumen, a genial knowledge of the world, a wit and specialist on things American; ...a friend to young men as they rose."[198] It is easy to imagine how the warm-hearted, older man, would have responded to the very charming Maurice. Speaking from his own experience, Lord Queenborough recommended going into politics as a good way of integrating oneself into the life of the country. No doubt he encouraged Maurice to believe that with his personality and considerable financial resources, he could be elected to Parliament.

For Maurice, who had no idea what he was going to do, this advice was welcome and timely. The help which Lord Queenborough offered him was exactly what he needed at that moment. The meeting on the *Mauretania* was a crucial one and pointed him to his political career. He now had a powerful referee in Lord Queenborough, who was president of the Eastern Provincial Division of the National Unionist (Conservative) Association, and carried weight at the Conservative Central Office.

Apart from the first evening in London when he did not know what to do with himself, Maurice plunged into his new life. His mind was concentrated on the Amateur Real Tennis Championships at Queen's Club, Baron's Court, in which he was a competitor. These were, in effect, world championships. Maurice had the care of the American champion Suydam Cutting,[199] a fellow member of the Racquet and Tennis Club in New York, meeting him on his arrival and rushing him to Baron's Court to practice.

---

[197] Robert Sencourt. *Heirs of Tradition: tributes of a New Zealander.* Carroll & Nicholson, 1949.
[198] *Heirs of tradition.*
[199] American court tennis champion who later became famous as an explorer of Tibet and was the first westerner to enter the forbidden city of Lhasa.

"Claridge's Hotel, Brook Street, W1
April 19th 1921

Dear Boy,

I was so glad to get your telegram when I got in last night and answered you early this am. I had hoped to hear before. It was very dismal arriving and not knowing what to do.

Anyway I know where you are. I saw that Rocksavage beat you but I suppose he has much practice.

I met the boat train off the *Acquitania*, the Hoffmans with Suydam Cutting. Suydam C was delighted I had booked courts & after a hasty luncheon, I took him from Dover Street to (*Queens Club*) Baron's Court. Quite a large gallery to see him play. He said after that he was discouraged with the balls & never thought there could be such a vast difference. Everybody in the Gallery thought him very good & that he would easily win the All Comers.

Boy, there are 28 entries which seems a lot. They were not willing to make any prediction about his chance with Baerlein,[200] but I think it depends on how Suydam progresses. Am now waiting to see Marian. They forgot to have their passports visa-ed & came very near having to go back to US. I must say it was fierce but the papers at home said no passports were needed.

If you see Cooper or his wife you must not speak to them. Before I left Mr Sturgis told me that Cooper's obstinacy about selling Chicago & Mo. stock has resulted in a paper reduction of four millions in Grandpa's estate. Both Salkin[201] & Trundall wanted to sell and buy US Steel Pref. Now Chicago & Mo is at 5% stock & US Steel at 7%!

The tournament begins the 25th. I am playing fairly well. I hope to win a match as there are lots in my class. There are two Frenchmen.

I may come over the first part of May, if you wish. Please look out for Mama & meet (Aunt) Lucy off the boat train, *La France* sailing New York 20th. Be nice to her – she's depressed. Had a nice weekend. Met the Erskines, distant relatives of ours. The daughter gets married Thursday; am going to the wedding. Am most comfortable at the Cavendish, valet et al.

Much love M"

"April 26th 1921

Dear Boy

I had a terrific match yesterday (*at Queen's Club*) & it was a great disappointment as I lost it by 1 point!

---

[200] British real (American=court) tennis champion
[201] Loeb Salkin, family lawyer

There was a large, large gallery for everybody was there to see Cutting play & I came after. In fact there wasn't a seat in the dedans![202] I played. Mr Latham[203] who is as good a player as Charlie Sands is today. For I play Charlie even now, tho' I don't beat him. Boy, I started fine, hardly made a poor shot & cut balls down & played so well that I won 6-3. The second set, lots went against me & the crucial moment was when it was 5-5 & I was 40-30! Damn if I didn't cut the easiest of balls into the tape of the net! Latham won that set 6-5. Then started to play even better & won the next 6-1 and had me 3-0 the next set! Here I just said I will do or die! Mrs Rose, the entire Eyres family & Cutting were vigorously applauding me. I won the next three games so got to be 5-5. Latham had me 40-30 and I got a nick making it deuce & by serving uncommonly well won the set 6-5! You should have heard the applause!

It was now 2 sets all! Well – the effort just killed me. The first three games in each I had advantage & 40-30 but I dropped them all by sheer bad luck. Latham even bounced a ball into the grill on me! The match now had been going 2 hours and a half & it was a quarter to seven! The light was poor & I was dead beat. Latham won the deciding set 6-3! I have no excuse. We are not good stayers & have fierce nerves for a five set match. I should have won the 2nd set & that would have given me the match!

I forgot to say that Latham is an ex-racquet champion! I lost 26-21 games which isn't a bad beating from such a man. Please return the clipping. Am taking it easy today. Stiff as a post.

I see Percy Pyne & Taylor P's father has died. No other news.

Let me hear about the motor trip in France. Look out for Maman.

Love M."

"Cavendish Hotel, London
May 1921

Dear Boy,

I found that Clifford had packed your overcoat in my trunk. It needed repairing so that it has only just returned from Burkinshaw. It surprises me that you make such a fuss over such a thing. It dates back from 1913. Have you no overcoat at all?

You have misunderstood my letter. I only said that I had Capt. Ryan to consult on the possibilities of job. I am going to get one too!

Cutting won the All Comers today. So far he hasn't lost a set. I would give anything to have him beat Baerlein. Baerlein hasn't got the stuff on the

---

[202] A division, at one end of a tennis court, for spectators.

[203] Peter Latham was British rackets world champion from 1887-1902 & real tennis world champion four times. Charlie Sands was a former American court tennis champion.

ball that Suydam has & his service is poor. Suydam has a fair chance.

I wish Cynthia would come over for a day or two. Lady Derry's house, has five master rooms, 3 baths & all her servants, is to be had June 1st- August 1st.

Glad you're having such a nice time.

Affec M"

Maurice's hopes were to be disappointed. Baerlein the British real tennis champion beat Suydam Cutting in straight sets.

"Wiston Old Rectory, Steyning Sussex
May 16th 1921

Dear Boy,

Your friend Gladys Newbury of Biarritz very kindly asked me down here. It is a charming little spot in Sussex, not far from Brighton. There are just four of us, Mrs Marshall & the Sheldons. The only thing I have hated is the bridge. They all play so well & of course all the time I am very handicapped.

England never looked more beautiful than today. At this moment of writing there isn't a cloud in the sky and with the freshness of spring, nothing could be more ideal.

I think you will like Lady Derry's house, 19 Gloucester Place. I shall be on hand to get it ready when you come over. June 1st is the day of the Derby. When do you think you will come over? Give me an idea of your plans when you get them. Are you having good tennis? Also are you going to Newport for the summer?

I sent the overcoat over by Edgar Leonard. I hope you got it. I had it relined because it looked so shabby.

No other news. Let us make this 36th year a good one. I saw Mrs St George the other day who worked for you. Am wonderfully rested. I suppose you're on the go the entire time in Paris.

My best. Maurice"

Frank was in Paris, working at the Guaranty Trust Company of New York, staying at the Hotel Crillon where his mother was also residing. Not for the first time in his life, he was suffering from a bad attack of "nerves". Fanny sent a letter to his room:

"Hotel Crillon
May 1921

My dearest Boy,

I have been terribly saddened by finding that you are in such a deplorable mental condition. I am terribly worried and upset over it. I had a long drive today; and your miserable face as you handed my letter back to me haunted me.

I sympathize with you very much; it is hell. There is no other word for it;

& the sad and awful part is that nothing that anyone can say, and nothing that anyone can advise, is going to help you one particle.

You must do it all yourself. And where to begin? And how? Some woman who heard from you when you were in the North Sea, promptly retailed it all to me, as people very naturally will if you talk about your affairs and feelings. I wish you had written it to me. I would have possibly said things to you that might have prevented you leaving the ship.

If I were you, or if I were ill myself, I would go tomorrow to see Dr Aumont. He has made wonderful cures. Many men have been really, really ill physically, all in pieces. Sign up for a month's treatment & put yourself absolutely in his hands. Money ought not to stop you. You have plenty; & if he were twice as costly, it does not matter. You can't go on feeling, looking like that. You may be either consoled or the reverse when I tell you that I have lived, suffered and agonized & nearly died over the same complaint.

Dear boy, let us help. We are all anxious & eager. You can lift yourself out of it surely.

Love FR"

Aunt Lucy was also at the Hotel Crillon and wrote a letter to Frank, which implies that he was suicidal. She was sympathetic and encouraging.

"Hotel de Crillon

My dear Frank

After all, I am the only one that understands how you feel – I am sure you have not got better since I saw you, because doubtless you have been worrying about all sorts of things. I want to say to you I quite understand your wanting to go to London & not wanting to stay here so long but I do hope that you will arrange to come here in the autumn & try & get well.

I can't use any further argument if you don't want to listen but I can't see you throw yourself from the top of a high house without begging you not to do so. Remember that you are young & have a long life before you. Your grandfather was ninety-two, your father almost seventy. Do get well again & be happy. I assure you it is worth the bother. When you are well again, you will not be sad & blue, only too glad to be happy & at peace. Please think this over & believe me I am <u>right.</u>

Very affectionately, Lucy"

Maurice was naturally very distressed when he learned that his brother was in such a bad way. He revealed that he too had suffered from "nerves" and offered to help Frank, inviting him to come to London and get involved in studying English constitution. He urged him to adopt a positive attitude and look on the bright side.

"Queen's Club, West Kensington, London W.
May 1921

Dear Boy,
I hear from Mama that you have had "nerves". Take my advice & come over here. I have lots for you to do & I think I can soon cure you.

I had them "fierce" last year & I couldn't concentrate on anything. I just hated things.

The world looks glorious to me now. I have entirely conquered myself. When you get here, I'll begin & study with you. I have the man. We'll study English constitution, public speaking.

Another thing is <u>rest</u>. Why! I don't know what it is to be tired. I've cut out dancing.

Boy, we ought to be so happy. Just think what a good beginning you made. Best Boy medal – Harvard in 3 years. Boy, the school expects so much of you, too. I wish you & I were sailing tomorrow (on the) *Adriatic*, to be present at the (St Paul's School) boat races. Its to be the 50th anniversary of the Club. Every captain is going back. They are rowing in brand new shells I gave them. They row for your cups too.

Just say yourself, I'm alright. Marian Hoffman wants to see you.

Boy, it makes me unhappy to have you feel this way.

Love M"

In May, Fanny's sympathetic attitude towards Frank has changed to one of exasperation and anger.

"Hotel Crillon
May 25th 1921

Dear Frank,
This I opened immediately among a great sheaf of mail. I send it at once. I have nothing further to add about your condition. I told you always: "The child is father to the man."

You are reaping what you have sown; & in bitterness, as all bad harvest must be gathered! You should have everything taken away from you! Give Charles a holiday. Get up in the morning and go out & break stones if necessary! But you won't!! ...

The strong help themselves & only by effort, by pain, by discipline. No one can do it for you! I love you. I pity you. I know all about it, but you can get up, as I hope.

FR "

Two months later, in a long letter his mother confessed her own faults and urged Frank to make an effort to make his mark in the world.

"15th July 1921
No address

My dearest Frankie,

I am writing this to possibly go by your steamer. I don't dare address it definitely to the ship, to you on board because in that way it might just miss you!

Yours has just come and I want at once to say that I am only too interested and anxious for your happiness & welfare and that I have never got the slightest inclination to crow over you or say I told you so.

First, my one desire in every way is to help. I have, we all have, each one differently manifested, faults & it is for each to help the other and dwell as much as possible upon the good qualities.

Lucy for instance & I are poles apart! I am hot; she is cold. I am large; she is small. She is entirely self-centred. I am an ass in the opposite direction, giving away my money, letting myself in for extravagances I can't afford, entertaining a lot of perfectly indifferent people, for whom I really do not care, and making myself very uncomfortable and cramped in consequence. Will either entirely change? No! But can a character become modified and improved by experience? Yes, I think so. I shall never again run into debt in the old way! Never. 20 years ago, having seen a beautiful Sir Joshua (Reynolds) or a lovely ruby bracelet or a tapestry, I would have immediately taken it, with no funds to pay: scraped up a first deposit – and trusted to luck for the rest. It was a stupid, extravagant way to live. I have been brought to see it! Of course, I always ought to have: but for years I lived on this very false and bad principle.

Now one mania still exists, therefore is to be fought in consequence and eradicated. It is the mania for being sociable, entertaining. I feel that I know art people, make it pleasant for them, "give them a good time" as you say. I feel that if I see a poor artist I want to help: to patronize; to provide him with work! This is perhaps a laudable feeling. It couldn't be called very selfish. But it is a <u>vice</u>! I have not the means to do this!! And all uncontrolled feelings, whether it is a bad thing or possibly a fine, generous impulse, carried to excess is <u>vice</u>.

I am now in one of my moments of having gone ahead too fast. It was that silly party. A beautiful well-ordered, well carried-out party with every detail carefully thought out and very successful as regards flowers, seating. Harry Lehr came and helped me place the cards & he is very good at such things and the dinner was very well chosen & the music and recitations delightful. And I would have lived in peace & security and not known any anxiety for three months in good hotels for what *in toto* it cost me! Now do you not see how annoyed I am with myself? And what a jackass I feel I was to do all this! The tips for the entertainment practically represented one month & the dinner, of course, the heaviest item!

Well! I go in detail about myself & show you that we all, if we are honest with ourselves, can regret & deplore things that we know are errors. But if there is any stuff in one – and I feel that we all have that quality of breeding – we can shut our teeth & say: "Hang it I can do better & I will" Now you, to come home to you again, have half expiated your fault by recognizing that you were wrong. Do not stop there: Say: 'I am not such a fool that just because I thought a life of ease & pleasure would keep me going, & I found it can't, & Mama instanced Mr Canfield and all the other men who did nothing & lived life with tears in their eyes, and that it was the curse & bane of their lives.'

My father said many wise things!! This was his axiom. "You show me a man or woman that doesn't get up in the mornings & I will show you a man or woman who will never amount to anything." Naturally if you are interested in life, you get up because it is interesting! But if you like ease & pleasure & comfort & loafing in your room, you are (I don't mean you – I mean one) not going to make your mark. 'NOT WITH THE CROWD TO BE SPENT.' The line is Mathew Arnold's. Learn it by heart. And when you have learned that, it is enough for one lesson.

Turn to Henry V and say to yourself 'If it be a sin to covet honour I am the most offending soul alive.' Read that whole speech before Agincourt. Try & get some spirit into your blood. Doing even your little task goes well, as soon as you put that infusion into it. Be a man & try to find a man's work & let all the little trivialities go...

By the way thank you for your very full interesting & well-written talk about M(aurice) & Marian & all!! Yours was an excellent letter!! Oh if you were only poor! You could do so well! So well!

The plan I thought of for you: you like horses, open air & breeding etc I truly think if you can think of nothing better, there is a good business in finishing polo ponies, hacks. They bring big prices in Paris. I can see a little place near: plenty of riding & congenial surroundings, picking up subjects & finishing them for market. Mr G is a very good man. He knows nothing of my thought. He is reliable & knows his business. He was 14 years with Count Potemkin as groom. We could pass up subjects & he could train them. Love & trying to help.

FR."

Maurice wrote to Frank from Blickling Hall, Norfolk, which his friends the Hoffmans, have taken on a long lease. He has paid his brother's bills and is all prepared for a return to Semur, and a tour of the battle area in France. He also confides that he is thinking of getting married.

"August 6th 1921

Dear Boy

I was delighted just before coming up here to the Hoffmans to get your letter from the steamer. I'm so glad that you had a pleasant voyage and more so, that you didn't get the "blues". I feel that your next letter from Newport will also give me the news that your depression has gone. I think it was change you needed & you were right to go when you did.

The time flew and before we knew it, August came. It was with a sigh of relief that I signed the last cheque. I was delighted when I gave Irvine his last cheque for £100 – and paid the house bills. Your £300 was a great help, for Cynthia, as you might expect, never even volunteered to pay a cut for Irvine, or repay me for the £25 that got Helen and Miss S. to Scotland. I was astonished when at dinner the other night she said that with the favourable rate of exchange, her monthly allowance came to over £700! As you well know, C has no idea of what it is to play the game. If she can stick either of us at any time, she'll do it!

Fortunately we are not like that. However after everything has been paid, and I am prepared to go to France, I have £257 for the journey, which is ample.

My plans are a follows. I go to Paris – deposit trunk & with golf suit & necessities, I go to Semur for several days then to Vitrey. On the 18th Chappy Scudder,[204] Alice Hopkins and a Mrs Dewey go as my guests on a three day motor trip – Rheims, Amien and [Chemin des] Dames, Verdun etc. I then go to Deauville for tennis & back here.

Marian has been unusually kind & nice of late. We have passed so many happy days here & you would have loved our picnic the other day. We speak openly of marriage and I think that in this way, I have come to accept it as a very likely thing in the future. I realize that it has every advantage & that with her eighty thousand, much can be eliminated that might be troublesome.

I'm so glad you're going to Castine & Maine. Hope you have a good time. Look into the court question at SPS & write often.

Love M."

---

[204] Willard Scudder, classics master at St Paul's School and rowing coach who became a good friend of Maurice and Frank.

Maurice could not attend the Trustees meeting in October 29th. He offered to resign, but his resignation was not accepted. All appreciate his wonderful all-round interest in the school.

"Hotel de Crillon, Paris
August 10th 1921

Dear Boy

I'm so sorry you're not here. Tomorrow I go to Semur and Vitrey and on the 18th, Scudder, Alice Hopkins & Mrs Dewey go as my guests on a four day trip – Rheims, Verdun, Argonne etc. Scudder is so keen about it. He is the official photographer. I got a good car today & it will be well worthwhile. Boy, Paris is just great. I go tomorrow to Semur – if only you were going too.

We should have such wonderful lives & we must make the best of them.

I took Mrs Rose to the country today. It was just marvellous. I got my English passport OK. It is good until 1923!

I suppose you are in Newport now. Boy, please try to get a job for the winter. You will be so much happier. I'll come over for Xmas & we'll have a nice year. After the motor trip, I go to St Moritz perhaps. Am so grateful for the money you sent me.

Had a wonderful weekend at Marian's before coming over. Am anxiously waiting news from you. For heaven's sake don't get discouraged whatever you do. Will drop you a line all the time. Am in wonderful frame of mind.

Much love M"

The next letter is from Semur, where he is staying with the priest, sleeping in the room he had for six months after the Armistice.

"August 13th 1921

Dear Boy,

Here I am back again in Semur! Everything looks just the same; there hasn't been a change of any kind. All the old people like Roblots, Auberts, Gontards have welcomed me. I walk around from place to place, every street has some sort of association.

I went to the American Cemetery. They have taken away over a hundred and sent them home. In October, they take the remaining ones & place them all together, those whose parents refused to have them returned. My man Hake is still here.

As you have been here, you know how pretty it all is. The fields in the country look lovely and the peaceful scenes of France certainly hard to beat. I leave tomorrow for Vitrey. It's always a mistake to stay too long. I hope to come every year – this is my second annual visit.

Yesterday at the Auberts for tea, I was the only man and eight girls. The Bruizard girl is a peach. I could hardly keep my eyes off her. She's so attractive.

Nothing else to say. Am here in my old room, everything just as I left it – now two years past.

Hope everything is going well.

Love Maurice"

"Vitrey
August 16th 1921

Dear Boy,

I passed by here on my way to Paris and if you remember correctly, it is the first place our division visited when we landed here from the States. Madame Riche was delighted to see me and fortunately I sent the children some nice toys from Paris last year, so I was in OK with the family. I have already been around the town and seen the people who are always pleased to welcome us.

I return to Paris tonight and on Thursday, Scudder, Mrs Dewey, Alice Hopkins & I start on our motor trip. If I can persuade them, I want to do the Château district a bit too. I think four days of 'front' will be a little too much. I expect to see Aunt Lucy before her return to America. I do hope you will go and stay with her at Woodburn Hall for I think it will do you good & be nice for her.

As I haven't seen the papers for a long time, I cannot comment on anything that has taken place. When I get back to Paris, I hope to hear from you.

You will hear soon again. I hope this finds you well. I feel that you are having a nice time this summer. Take care of yourself.

Much love. Maurice"

"Aug. 21st
Paris

Dear Boy,

The auto trip was the <u>greatest</u> possible success. It gave me real pleasure to see Chappy Scudder, Alice Hopkins and Mrs Dewey, so happy. I got an excellent car and we left last Thursday getting back Sunday night. We took in everything between these points – Loisins, Rheims, Verdun, Metz, Toul,

Chateau Thierry. I paid for everything, rooms, food, and auto. It was the "big thing" today & I am very glad. We had lovely weather and I only wish that you could have been with us. The car cost me $167 in American money. 870 kil. covered – 2,125 francs. 500 francs a day all expenses paid by chauffeur. I tell you I loved every moment of it.

I have just met Aunt Lucy & am returning at 1pm to take her out to lunch. My next letter will give you more news. Hope you are well.

Much love. Maurice

From all accounts the tennis in America must be wonderful just now."

"Hotel Royal, Dinard.
August 1921

Dear Boy

When I got back from my motor trip, I found a telegram from Mama telling me not to join her in Switzerland & that she would be back in Paris the 3rd, so I decided not to go to Deauville and came here. I took the night train from Paris in order to save a day. You know it is ten hours. I found a nice room here & think I will like it. I went to the tennis place, joined & am now entered for the big tennis week, which begins Monday. I wish you were here to play in the doubles with me. There is Miss Dallett from Philadelphia whom I met in North East, Mrs Richard Stevens, Dorothy and several familiar faces.

I am particularly equipped for tennis, have a Dion & the Maas racquet I liked so in London this year (a new one $14\frac{1}{2}$). I played very well this am, which was encouraging. I want to take this tournament as a sort of a getting in shape one. I now know that I have always played with too light a bat. You need weight behind services & ground strokes. As you well know, the courts here at Dinard are vastly superior to Deauville. Besides, they are sheltered. The ball today was excellent & had height.

I have written to the Guaranty to expect a large envelope of mail & I feel sure it will contain one from you. I saw Gordon Douglas the other day & he said he had seen you in Newport. I do hope you have not been over doing & are well.

Uncle Cooper has been desperately ill. Yesterday's paper said he had pneumonia, a temperature of 104 & breathing 36 – all most alarming you know. He was operated on for intestinal trouble two weeks ago.

Tonight I am dining with the Stevens. I'm not going to dance at all – just get into good shape. The place is just crowded with young people: kids. I shall have a good time for a week & then go.

After seeing Mama, I shall return to London. Boy, last night I went to the casino and met all your friends – of course that beautiful M Sirian who said so many nice things about you. I remember your telling me about her last year & her refusal to meet a Boche. I expect to see her today. Beatrice Pratt is here and many others. The Casino was amusing, some pretty women I thought.

On the whole, I am most comfortable. My room has a fine bed & running water. I have every reason to believe that my two weeks here will be good fun. I'm glad I didn't return to Deauville. By the way, I saw that Sarbes won the tournament again this year, also the mixed.

This must go. Write me first how far you got with S. She certainly is pretty at night. Hope everything is well.

M"

"Paris,
Sept 6th 1921

Dear Boy,
My ten days at Dinard closed last night. My only regret being that you weren't there too. Much to my surprise I won the handicap-mixed doubles with Peggy Dallett. We played some very close matches, in one being within a point of losing. I played really well the entire week. I 'starred' about four times on the championship court, and as you know there is always a fair gallery. I owed my success to that 'Mapwap' racket which I think is easily the best I have ever seen.

I saw quite a good deal of 'Winnie' Surian who was most kind to me. I think she is unusually nice & pretty. Of course I feel very sorry for her in her position.

I found Mama here in good form & she has a perfect summer & has not quite decided when to go home. I shall play around with her for at least a week, then go on to England.

I feel sure these days you must be en route to Maine and making certain visits. I hope that you can make Brinley see that his sixteen years as 'head' of the Lower is a fine thing & that his place should be taken by a younger man.

I saw in the paper that Uncle Cooper's body had been taken home last Saturday on the *Aquitania*. I am most anxious to know if he left all his money to that Bruguiere woman. I certainly hope not. I suppose you know by now that he died of cancer of the stomach.

I never saw Paris as attractive this glorious day – just cool enough for pleasant walking. Boy, I have had such a fine summer. If you had only been well – for Dinard was tenfold nicer than Deauville. You didn't tell me how nice it was and never expensive. I feel wonderfully well. I expect to go away for the weekend with Mama.

I'll write soon again. I have absolutely no news at all. Beatrice (Pratt) Gibson told me she is divorcing Preston. Do take good care of yourself.

Much love, Maurice"

"Paris,
Sept 8th 1921

Dear Boy

Marian Hoffman writes that the talk of Newport is your devotion to Helen Moran. Helen wrote Marian that 'she likes you in spite of certain things'. I want you to realize that she has a *mauvaise langue*[205] and that she is a girl frightfully on the make. I hope you don't get in too thick with her all the same. I never cared for her.

The enclosed clippings gives you the final round of Dinard. [Maurice and Peggy Dallet won the mixed doubles of the lawn tennis tournament.]

Maman is giving me a good deal of preaching. She is on the crest of the wave again. Dangerous! I see new things arriving at the house tho' she assures me no spending. I think she will return about the 20th. She goes to Lucy's & makes visits. This weekend we go away, then I return to London next week.

I hardly ever enjoyed a month more, what with the motor trip, Dinard & Paris, it has been perfect. The truth of it too, has been that I never have been too tired.

I hear the Schuyler Parsons are to be divorced and Fanny Kissell writes that the Fowlers look bored already! Let us appreciate our freedom!

Am anxiously awaiting news from you. This time of the year must be ideal at home. Remember all the wonderful things you and I have.

Much love. M"

---

[205] A malicious tongue

25

Maurice's Irish grandfather

The *New York Times* had reported in July that Lord Fermoy was on the list of candidates likely to stand for parliament as a candidate for the Anti-Waste league. This was a short-lived political party formed by Lord Rothermere to attack the excessive government spending. The report went on to say that Fermoy might have stood in August in the Abbey Division of Westminster, if he had not thought it presumptuous for one who had so recently come to England to try for Parliament. The newspaper further speculated that he was most likely to stand at the next general election for Marylebone, which had been his grandfather's constituency.

My father never spoke of his mighty Irish grandfather Edmund Roche, 1st Baron Fermoy (1815-1874). He died 11 years before Maurice was born, and as Maurice was separated from his father from the time he was two years old until he was 27, he grew up knowing nothing about his family history on the Irish side.

Edmund Roche was born on 9th August 1815, at Kildinan, the home of his father Edward Roche. Edmund's grandfather, Edmund ("Mon") Roche of Kildinan,[206] had transformed a tract of waste land into cultivated land. He invented a strong mountain plough hauled by two bullocks; he treated the soil with ash and lime from his own kilns; he divided the land into parcels of 40 acres with a dwelling on each; he rotated the crops; he gave long leases, with the whole of the rent allowed to the tenant for ditching for the first seven years. In all he created "a very fine place richly furnished with plantation and in all respects a suitable residence for a gentleman of fortune. Mr Roche's success in the improvement of the northern part of the county deserves to be recorded as the greatest attempt of this nature in this county and perhaps one of the most remarkable in the kingdom." [207]

Edward, Edmund's father, was married to Margaret Honoria Curtin, a cousin of the illustrious Edmund Burke.[208] The battle of Waterloo had been fought in June two months before the birth of his son and heir, after ten years of marriage. His only daughter, Frances Maria, had arrived four years earlier.[209]

---

[206] In 1798, he was charged with promoting the rebellion of the United Irishmen and was tried at a Court Martial in Cork. He ably conducted his own defence and was acquitted of the charges.

[207] *A General and Statistical Survey of the County of Cork.*

[208] See Appendix B.

[209] She married James Kelly MP In 1856 she published a book of poems written by her governess and herself entitled *Poems by Rose and De Rupe.*

Edward Roche inherited the Kildinan estate, near Rathcormack, from his father and the Trabolgan estate and 20,000 acres from his uncle Col. Edward Roche. The latter died in 1828, his only son having predeceased him, dying in 1803 as a prisoner of war at Lyons.

Young Edmund Roche took over the management of Trabolgan when he was nineteen years of age, although his father did not die until 1855.

Trabolgan

In 1814, Trinity House embarked on plans to build a lighthouse at the entrance to Cork harbour. The land they required was on the Trabolgan estate, which then belonged to Col Edward Roche (the great-uncle of E Roche MP) who strenuously objected to the sale, claiming that the tower on the land had been built as a banqueting house, and was the only place where he could get a good view of shipping and Cork harbour. His arguments forced up the price to £1,500 and the purchase was eventually completed in January 1816. The lighthouse, on Roche's Point, was in operation the following year. In 1995, the keeper was withdrawn and it now functions on automatic operation.

We get an idea of the liberal and humanitarian traditions Edmund inherited. When his father Edward Roche left Kildinan to take over Trabolgan, he gave a large sum of money to the Roman Catholic priest so that he could complete the plastering and ceiling of his Chapel. He wrote that it was given in recognition of his respect and regard, and in gratitude for many acts of kindness heaped on him over fifty years. He told the Rev. P Sheehan in a letter that the bigots in his church regarded him as a stray sheep, but in fact he was an unswerving Protestant, who believed in religious liberty and in loving one's neighbour of whatever persuasion.[210]

Edmund's great-grandfather, Edmund ("Mon") Roche, was a Roman Catholic, a wealthy and popular man married to a Catholic, Barbara Hennessy. He held the office of High Sheriff and was presumed to be Protestant. The story goes that one day he confessed to a priest that he was a Catholic and his true religion became public knowledge. When he discovered that the question of the validity of his marriage would affect the transmission of his property, he re-married in a Protestant church. Therafter the Roches were Protestant. There was no need for the women of the family to convert. Young Edmund Roche's sister Frances Maria was a Catholic.

Edmund Roche's granddaughter Moira Somerville, informed by her father and aunts, speaks of him somewhat waspishly as:

"A large man of florid good looks and rather pompous manner, exceedingly conscious of his position (as were most of his contemporaries) and an only son, married to an exceptionally, handsome woman. He seized upon every opportunity for showing off these advantages. He kept his own hounds at Trabolgan and hunted them himself, riding beautiful heavyweight horses. His barge, picked out with gold and manned by six rowers, took him into Queenstown by sea in fine weather." [211]

He was highly intelligent, very well educated and a keen sportsman. He did the grand tour in Europe accompanied by his Catholic tutor. From an early age he was interested in politics. Edmund Burke, his illustrious first cousin twice removed, was a great inspiration to the young Edmund. When he became a peer, he introduced 'Burke' into the family name.

Edmund Roche was elected Member of Parliament for County Cork in the year 1837, the year of the death of King George IV and of the accession of Queen Victoria, who was one year younger than him. It was the usual practice at that time to hold a general election after the death of the monarch. This was the last time the custom was followed. It was in this general election that Edmund Roche, then aged 22, was elected MP for County Cork, the largest agricultural constituency in Ireland.

Roche ran a successful farm, Trabolgan being well placed for Cork markets, and for transatlantic and UK exports. His farming concerns were reflected in his speeches at Westminster. In 1842, he protested against Sir Robert Peel's amendments of the tariffs of the Empire, which were injurious to Irish interests.

---

[210] *The Times*. September 13th 1828.
[211] Family stories told me by my father and the Aunts. Moira Somerville. Papers of the late Edmund James Burke Roche, 5th Lord Fermoy.

He objected to the high duty on corn, one of Ireland's main imports, whereas the low duty on meat was manifest injustice to the meat interest. As one who reared beef cattle, he was personally affected. However being a reasonable and practical man, he proposed a deal. The Irish would make a sacrifice to help the English. In return, he wanted the Government to consider the important question of the building of railways in Ireland.[212]

Edmund stood for Daniel O'Connell's party as a Liberal (Repeal). O'Connell was an Irish Catholic landowner and barrister from Kerry. He had a commanding personality and a great voice. He was one of very few who dared to speak out against the Act of Union, 1801,[213] which had been forced on Ireland, achieved by bribery and corruption and the presence of 100,000 soldiers.

O'Connell was a champion of the powerless majority in Ireland and was enormously popular. In a general election in 1828 he had a historic victory against a Cabinet Minister in Co. Clare but the law did not allow a Catholic to take his seat in Parliament. The Duke of Wellington (Prime Minister) warned the House of Lords that there was a risk of civil war if the law was not changed, and persuaded Robert Peel (Home Secretary) to introduce the Bill for Catholic Emancipation in the Commons. The Bill was passed in 1829. Catholics could now sit in both houses of Parliament, though they were excluded from becoming monarch, prime minister and other high offices.

Daniel O'Connell took his place in Parliament. Having achieved Catholic emancipation, he worked towards getting the Union dissolved, so that the Irish parliament could run internal affairs. He had no wish to completely sever the connection with the Imperial Parliament and was loyal to Queen Victoria. He was against the use of violence.

We know from his correspondence that Daniel O'Connell stayed at Trabolgan for a weekend when he attended a public dinner in his honour in Cork. In a letter dated 17th July 1841, he wrote from Cork: "I go tomorrow to Trabolgan, the seat of my colleague's father and will remain there until Monday when I am to be entertained at a public dinner in this city." [214]

O'Connell inspired young Roche to fight for the same causes. Roche belonged to his party and adopted his policies. From 1841-47 they were joint Members of Parliament for Co. Cork in 1842. Their opponents had threatened to present a petition to the Commons, complaining of the late election of O'Connell and Roche for Co. Cork. In January Roche wrote to O'Connell:

---

[212] Hansard 1842 vol. 63, p. 395.

[213] The Irish Parliament was dissolved, the Parliament at Westminster legislated for both countries. The Union had a disastrous effect on Ireland. Industry collapsed, unemployment increased, England dumped surplus goods on Ireland.

[214] Correspondence of Daniel O'Connell. Vol II, pp. 278-9 Ed. W J Fitzpatrick. John Murray: London 1888

"Kilshannig
22nd January 1842

"My Dear Sir,
It is now fast approaching the time when we should be making preparations
for defending our seats. You know how ruinously expensive a thing of this
kind is to a private individual. As far as I am concerned it is a thing that I
never could undertake out of my own resources and I am sure you neither
would nor could you be expected to do so. Under these circumstances we
must rouse the county." [215]

Daniel O'Connell wrote back three months later in a state of agitation,
expressing the urgent need to find resources to fight the charge of a late election,
pledging £300 himself and instructing Roche to do likewise. It was vital that "the
County must not be sacrificed to the demons of the ascendancy." [216] A select
Committee a few days later declared O'Connell and Roche duly elected.

Throughout his parliamentary career, Roche fought injustices against the Irish.
Speaking on the causes of the discontent in Ireland, Roche defined himself as a
decided and pledged Repealer. To Members who spoke of a willingness to conciliate
the Irish people he said: "Soft words butter no parsnips!" If he were not to have
their votes, he despised their speeches. The people of Ireland would never be
quiet until their grievances were addressed. All he implored was that they should
set out on the journey at once "for the golden opportunity of conciliating was fast
passing away".[217]

He spoke eloquently and vigorously and made his point with force and clarity.
Addressing a motion on the redress of grievances, Roche summed up the most
grave of these in a passionate speech. He said it had been asserted that Ireland
was in a state of treasonable rebellion. If this was the case, how he asked had the
Government met it? Had they reasoned with the people or treated them as
reasonable beings? No; they had tried to put down the agitation by the strong
arm of the law. But could they suppose that Ireland with her *bona fide* grievances
would submit to be bullied out of it?

He asked how the Franchise was to be dealt with. The people of Ireland required
not only a fair and reasonable franchise, but a fair representation in Parliament.
They could not have confidence in the legislation of that House while they knew
that their representatives were in a miserable minority, as compared with the
representatives of England.

He complained that Government was not alive to the dangers of their Irish

---

[215] O'Connell papers, NLI 13649.
[216] Unpublished letter from O'Connell to Roche. In the papers of the late 5th Baron Fermoy.
[217] Hansard.1843 Vol 70, p. 1047.

policy. Parliament did not hold Ireland by a strong military possession.

"You hold it by the strong affections and deep love and unchanging loyalty of the Irish people for their present sovereign. Her Majesty held possession of the hearts of the Irish people. This meant that Ireland was far more securely held than if all the armies in Europe were in that country." [218]

Roche supported a motion that a committee should investigate the way the Irish Parliament had been dissolved. He stated that the House:

"had always hitherto misgoverned that country (Ireland), because they being Englishmen and foreigners did not know how to legislate for it... Their legislation had rendered life and property insecure and had reduced the country to such a condition as was presented by no other in Europe. It therefore devolved on the people of England as much as it did upon the people of Ireland to unite in repealing the Act of Union between the two countries. A time might come when they would want the people of Ireland; and he would tell them that if the people of Ireland were neglected and their grievances were left undressed, when that time arrived they would not have the people of Ireland. The people would say: 'We asked you for redress but you refused it'."

At every opportunity he attacked the Church of Ireland, a Protestant church which was imposed on a country where 90% of the population were Catholic:

"Was there on the face of the whole earth anything so anomalous as that they should have this moment in Ireland the poorest, most miserable, and most degraded population existing, in contrast with the richest, most luxurious and rampant religious institution in the world? The people were actually dying of starvation by hundreds and thousands while the bishops of the Protestant establishment were dining in the greatest opulence. That gross and intolerable monopoly stood at the head and front of Ireland's grievances. [219]

He claimed that in Ireland they had a country possessing the richest soil in the world and yet that country was inhabited by the poorest and most helpless population. Their duty as practical men was to bring that rich soil and the poor people together, which they never had done, and never would do until they were bold enough to give up their squeamishness

[218] Hansard. 1844 vol. 73, pp. 298-302.
[219] ibid. 1849 vol.102, p. 881 and ff.

about what was called the rights of property and passed a sound, practical, comprehensive and sweeping measure, regulating the tenure of land in Ireland." [220]

Much of the blame for the deaths from famine, which was caused by the potato crop failing from 1845 to 1851,[221] was laid at the door of the Irish landlords. Roche was a good landlord. In 1846, supporting the Protection of Life (Ireland) Bill, he informed the Government:

"that it was time to take action to prevent the horrors of a national starvation. Hundreds of people were having to eat seed potatoes...the government had changed its mind with regard to the distribution of Indian meal and the people of Ireland were to be thrown upon their own resources.

Hundreds and thousands of people would get up tomorrow morning in Ireland without knowing where to get a supply of their daily food...the government ought to order supplies from America."

Roche told the House that he personally employed four hundred people and would go next week to Liverpool to obtain supplies of Indian meal for them. In 1847 speaking after Members reported a repeated outbreak of potatoes affected with disease, he was happy to state that there was no potato disease in Co. Cork. He recommended that farmers who discovered disease should take them up and plant late turnips. He had planted a hundred acres of turnips last year after potatoes and they had turned out exceedingly well.

He was a very practical man, invariably offering a remedy for the problem he was addressing in the House of Commons. His remedy for pauperism in Ireland was for the Government to invest in the cultivation of flax. Given the demand for flax in England, remunerative employment might be given for every man in Ireland. His suggestion was pooh-poohed by the Chancellor of the Exchequer and his proposal was ignored.

He himself grew flax on his estate. In April 1853, he had two thousand acres growing flax. His inventive mind developed a 25-horsepower engine to operate a scutching[222] mill, as well as a range of farm machinery. All the waste products of the flax scutching were profitably used. When the flax was harvested, it was transported in bales on horsecars to be shipped on board a small vessel belonging to him, and then taken to the quay at Cork and placed in the hold of the next steamer bound for England.

---

[220]   Hansard 1849 Feb. Vol 102 p881 and ff.

[221]   The famine was a great disaster. Over one million people died of starvation and disease. Another million emigrated.

[222]   The scutching process extracts the linen fibres from the flax plant.

He himself travelled frequently to London from Cork for the parliamentary sessions in London. His granddaughter Moira describes the journey which she heard about from her aunt Eleanor:

"They went from Queenstown to Bristol by packet boat, taking with them horses, carriages and cows! Edmund Roche did not consider that London milk was fit for humans to drink. Naturally all the servants, the governesses and tutors came too, which with eight children and two parents made quite a Noah's ark of it.

When the boat arrived the party boarded a train, the carriages being strapped on to open trucks. The ladies and children travelled inside them, the gentlemen alone daring the 'Common carriages.' The smuts and dirt were dreadful so that windows could not be opened, and the heat and confinement of the carriages must have been appalling. Once in London, the girls rode with their father in the Park. Caroline's beauty even at that age causing a sensation so much so that my father refused to go out with her! They also used to feed the cows on Sundays with carrots bought off the costers' stalls, carrying them down to the mews in little baskets. But the children hated London and longed to get back to the delightful freedom of the Irish countryside."

Roche had been a Member of Parliament at Westminster for 11 years when he married Eliza Caroline Boothby, daughter of James Brownwell Boothby and his wife Charlotte Cunningham,[223] who was half French; Eliza was the great-aunt of Robert Boothby MP.[224] Her granddaughter describes her as a splendid looking woman although her portrait reveals a very plain and rather depressed-looking one. The Boothby family owned Twyford Abbey, a large gothic mansion which still exists, though in a neglected state, in what is now the borough of Acton.[225]

Edmund's wife, Eliza, had some firm ideas, which no doubt reflected the values of her milieu at that time. "Religion is only for females." "It is effeminate for men to be musical." "Girls are bound to be married and the sooner the better, otherwise what are they for?" "Happy? I should like to know who is happy." Everything she did not agree with was "odious nonsense". She wrote in a letter: "I hear Alexis (her third son) is to have another child – most unnecessary." She herself had eight children, five sons and three daughters.

Moira her granddaughter learned from her father and aunts:

---

[223] Her mother Suzanne Guinand came from a family of Parisian bankers. She married General Alexander Cunningham.

[224] 1900-1986. Created Lord Boothby in 1967.

[225] In 2006 it was due to be demolished to make way for a residential housing development.

"that the Roches were not a loving or united family. Fierce individualists all of them and at least two of them endowed with lightning wit and tongues dipped in acid. The fact that they had to share tutors and governesses who were utterly unable to control the wild tempers and vagaries of their charges must have made life extremely difficult for everyone, more particularly for the younger children."

Eliza Boothby (centre) with her parents and siblings.
Twyford Abbey, 1837

Her Aunt Ethel told Moira that:

"No hell could have been worse than what I suffered as a child. I was very fat; my mother had not wanted me and hated me as I hated her. If it had not been for my governess, I really think I should have killed myself. The boys teased me unmercifully. I was afraid of the sea and they used to throw me into it saying that I was too fat to drown. I was given a pony that ran away with me. I never remember being anything but miserable."

In August 1849, Queen Victoria, accompanied by Albert, paid her first visit to Ireland. She wrote in her notebook, on board the Royal Yacht *Victoria and Albert,* of the approach to Cork Harbour, after she had rounded Roche's Point. "When we went on deck after eight in the evening, we were close to the Cove of Cork and could see many bonfires on the hill, and the rockets and lights that were sent off from the different steamers."[226] The bonfires on the Trabolgan estate were spectacular. Servants of Edmund Roche accidentally set fire to fourteen acres of fir plantation so that the royal yacht was bathed in a blaze of light! Messrs. Power and Roche, the joint MPs of County Cork made a welcoming speech when she stepped on shore.

In September 1855, Lord Palmerston, Liberal Prime Minister, elevated Edmund Roche to the peerage of Ireland as Baron Fermoy.[227] Although Palmerston was born and lived in England, he was himself an Irish peer. Much of his income was derived from his estates in Co. Sligo and Co. Dublin. He was sympathetic to the plight of the Irish people. He defected from the Tories in 1830 because of his support for Catholic Emancipation.

Palmerston believed that the problems of Irish Catholic nationalism could be improved by greater political integration of Ireland with Britain. In the light of their shared policies and ambitions, the elevation of the moderate, liberal Edmund Roche was a means to that end. Roche was very popular, a good landlord, and although he was a Protestant, he was an active supporter of Catholics.

In February 1856, the Earl of Derby[228] informed the House of Lords that the creation of the Fermoy peerage was unconstitutional. He explained that a patent which been granted to a gentleman called Roche, constituting him Baron Fermoy in the peerage of Ireland was invalid. The Crown had the power to create one Irish peer upon the extinction of three Irish peerages. As there were only two vacancies when Fermoy was elevated, the creation was unconstitutional, even though a third vacancy had since occurred.

The case was investigated by a committee of the House of Lords, who voted to refuse the petition of Edmund Roche to vote as a representative Irish peer. They then issued a new patent, putting back the date of the creation to 1856. A great deal of parliamentary time was devoted to debating this point of constitutional law!

In November 1856, Fermoy was appointed Lord Lieutenant of the County and city of Cork, on the death of Lord Bandon, a position which he held until his death. Fermoy, having been made a peer could no longer stand as a Member of Parliament in Ireland. However as an Irish peer he did not have a seat in the Lords and could stand for Parliament in England. In June 1859, a vacancy occurred when Lord Palmerston, the Prime Minister, promoted the Member of Parliament for the Borough of Marylebone to the peerage. Lord Fermoy presented himself as a potential candidate for the ensuing by-election.

---

[226] *Leaves from the Journal of our Life, 1848-1861.* p. 247.
[227] Edmund changed the family name to Burke Roche when he became Fermoy.
[228] Conservative leader of the House of Lords.
[229] *The Times.* Wednesday June 24th 1859.
[230] Before the introduction of the secret ballot in 1872, people had to mount a platform and publicly announce their choice of candidate to the officer who then recorded it in the poll book. This exposed voters to punishment from employers and landlords.

He appeared before the electors to explained his policies.[229] He told them he belonged to the Liberal party and listed his reforming policies. He was in favour of the introduction of a secret ballot. It was cruel to give a man the vote without protecting him in the exercise of it.[230] He had supported the repeal of the Corn Laws although they were not in his interest as a landowner. He did so because they cut a slice off the loaf of the poor.

He was duly adopted as Liberal candidate, and once a Member of Parliament again, resumed his battle for justice for Ireland with his indomitable passion and energy. He constantly advocated reforms that would benefit those who suffered under the prevailing legislation. He asked for help for the poor and the starving, for the rights of fishermen and farmers, for fair taxation. He appealed for united education, that is, for education for Catholics and Protestants alike.

As a representative of a London Borough, he also turned his attention to metropolitan concerns. He supported the refusal of an individual's request to build on Hampstead Heath, "one of the most beautiful spots near London." He rejected a number of proposals on practical grounds. He asked who was going to pay for the Thames Embankment – a new street from Blackfriars to the Mansion House. He objected to the coal tax being used for this purpose.

Although a staunch supporter of Palmerston,[231] Fermoy did not hesitate to criticize him for his plan to spend eleven million pounds fortifying Portsmouth.

"The idea of a French invasion was a mere myth, and it was perfect madness to buy £11 million in works, while they had in Lancashire and Ireland, an amount of poverty and unemployed labour which was a disgrace to them. The Prime Minister had adopted an erroneous course, a course not only injurious but suicidal to the Liberal party."[232]

Always keen to help Ireland, Fermoy inquired if the postal communication between Galway and America, which had been cancelled because of lack of means, could be renewed. If so, he asked if the claim of the harbour of Cork would be considered, describing it as the most commodious in the world. Palmerston, first Lord of the Treasury, replied that when the proper time arrived, Galway, Cork and Foynes would be considered on their merit.[233]

On a motion to regulate street music[234] Fermoy said he was glad to hear there was so much musical taste in Belgravia and thought that street music was a legitimate occupation and afforded a greet deal of innocent pleasure. In England,

---

[231] For example, Fermoy warmly commended the Prime Minister for his position of neutrality in regard to the civil war in America. Hansard. 1863. Vol. 170 p. 94.

[232] Hansard. 1863 Vol. 172. p. 974.

[233] Hansard. 1861 Vol. 164. p. 1890.

[234] Hansard. 1863 Vol. 172. Three bands in Eaton Square and one in Eaton Place had been heard playing at the same time.

no provision was made for music, and street music was the consequence.

His last speech in Parliament rang with a positive note. Fermoy rejoiced to hear of the increase of the number of children attending schools in Ireland. The effect of people being better educated led to an increase in emigration in the hope of bettering their condition. However education materially increased the tranquillity of the country and put an end to agrarian outrages.[235]

A few months before he died, he wrote to the Prime Minister, Mr Gladstone, leader of the Liberal party, wishing him success in the coming general election campaign, and expressing hopes for his support for Home Rule. He received this letter from Mr Gladstone, in which the PM left open the possibility of being converted to Home Rule, on certain conditions. Roy Jenkins, in his biography of Gladstone, saw this non-committal letter to Fermoy as "a remarkable paving exercise for his (Gladstone's) 1886 conversion." [236]

10, Downing Street, Whitehall
Jan 23rd 1874

Dear Lord Fermoy,
I thank you for your letter and good wishes. In my address I have endeavoured to state clearly the principles on which I should endeavour to deal with all questions relating to the local and sectional powers in the United Kingdom. With respect to Home Rule, I have not yet heard an authoritative and binding definition of the phrase, which appears to be used by different persons in different senses. Until this phrase comes to have a definite and certain meaning, I have not thought myself justified in referring to it: but I indicated plainly in another form the test which I should apply to its interpretation.
Believe me, faithfully yours Wm. Gladstone.[237]

Edmund Burke Roche, 1st Baron Fermoy died unexpectedly at 2.00pm on September 16th 1874. He was in his sixtieth year. He was taken ill while taking his morning bathe in the sea. At 10.30 am, the doctor was called and came as quickly as possible, travelling by special steamer from Cork to Aghada. Fermoy "received a stroke of paralysis shortly before his death". On hearing the sad news, the county went into mourning. The Cork Corporation adjourned the Council out of respect. No band was played at the Cork races. The stewards did not wear scarlet and wore black mourning badges. The Queenstown Magistrates adjourned the court "in consequence of the demise of the lamented nobleman".

[235] Hansard. Vol.179. 1865. p. 1252.
[236] *Gladstone*. p. 378.
[237] *The Times*. Monday February 2nd. 1874; col d.

Edmund Burke Roche MP
1st Lord Fermoy

Fermoy was famous as a hunter. He was Master of the Foxhounds and considered to be the best rider, of his weight, in the south of Ireland. He popularised the ancient sport of hawking. His genial manner made him a great favourite. Old friends of the hunting field and friends in Cork presented him with a portrait of himself.[238]

The Chairman of the Magistrates, who had known him for thirty years, spoke of his great kindness, his genial disposition and his loyal friendship. "As a resident landlord, those good qualities made him a great favourite with all classes and creeds. To the humble man his lordship was always accessible and his kind, graceful manner made all who approached him feel quite at home." [239]

"The funeral of the late lamented Lord Fermoy was solemnized five days later at 8am. It was strictly private. A strong desire was expressed by many persons in the county and by a large number of residents in the city of Cork, to have a funeral of a public character, but it could not be complied with, and the coffin of the deceased was borne quietly on the shoulders of his tenantry from Trabolgan to the family vault outside the demesne, amid a sorrowing crowd of friends and neighbours, without any ostentation." [240]

---

[238] From his obituary in the *Freeman's Journal,* September 18th 1974.
[239] The *Cork Daily Herald.* September 19th 1874. p. 3.
[240] *The Times.* Thursday September 24th, 1874 (from the Dublin correspondent).

His funeral was a quiet, simple affair but his flamboyant, expensive and extravagant life style left his heir Edward FitzEdmund Burke Roche, 2nd Baron Fermoy[241] (Fitzy) an estate weighed down with debts. The Norwich Union Assurance Company held two mortgages on the estate, totalling £70,000. A life insurance paid off half of the sum owing.

A month after his father died, Fitzy held an important auction of a valuable herd of 200 dairy cows, several thoroughbred bulls, one hundred head of young cattle, 80 horses, 200 pigs, a collection of farm implements and quantities of fodder. In 1881, he put the 19,000 acre estate on the market, pressed by the principal mortgagee, the Norwich Assurance Co., but only about eight years purchase was bid and the sale had to be abandoned.

Between 1871-78 Cork property realised 20 years purchase. In 1879, the Irish Nation Land League was formed, which combined all nationalists in a campaign against landlords. This "Land War" and the agrarian agitation severely depressed the value of land. It was not until 1889 that a court ruled that the Norwich Union's offer of £32,000 for the estate was a fair price, and they became the purchasers.[242]

[241] He married Cecilia O'Grady, only child of the 3rd Viscount Guillamore, from whom she inherited the Rockbarton estate and Caherguillamore House, where Fitzy lived when he had to give up the Trabolgan estate.
[242] *The Times* March 28th, 1889.

26

Preparation for politics

M aurice was not ready to follow in his grandfather's footsteps, presenting himself as a candidate for the Borough of Marylebone. He was continuing his political studies and at the same time taking care of his brother's affairs – his house, staff and horses.

Frank had been suffering from nerves and insomnia for the past year. Following the advice of his friends, he put himself in the hands of Dr Austen Riggs, (a psychiatrist) who diagnosed a case of "mismanagement". Not enough work and too much play had started a conflict which had caused a breakdown.

Frank put this down to his selfish life of ease and comfort and took steps to remedy the situation. Instead of going to England as planned, where he had taken a house with his sister Cynthia in Melton Mowbray, he denied himself a season's hunting and took a job in New York. This gave Maurice the responsibility of finding homes for his horses and a position for his groom.

"London
November 9th 1921

Dear Boy,
Perhaps I've gone contrary to your wishes but I have practically closed a deal whereby Mrs Hoffman takes your horse & Harris for the winter – feeding them & caring for them for nothing. Both Mrs Hoffman & Miss Preston have taken up riding. They will never jump of course. I presume that Kitchener & the other horse will be carrying them around the fields of Norfolk. It was impossible to let Harris go at once because the positions for winter are all filled. When you cabled me, I had to find out all these details for I was entirely ignorant.

Well Cynthia now has got the reputation here of having "run off" with (Ikey) Bell. They go everywhere together and God know what the final will be! Our family certainly takes the cake!

Tomorrow I go to the House of Commons. It is my first visit. Excuse me for opening this note. I thought it might be important & about the house.

Try and write more often. There is a fierce fog today. I just got into the Bachelors' Club. It cost me fifty pounds, worse luck.

Much love M"

"Bachelors' Club, Piccadilly. W.
November 11th 1921

Dear Boy,
As you can see I am a member here. For the moment, the only advantage is that I can stand and look out on Piccadilly, much as I would do at the Knickerbocker in New York. However it is a Club & will prove useful. As you and I are very conservative and don't drop hundreds of pounds here & there in betting & hell raising, it is worth it. It gives me a certain status here.

A cable came giving me the good news that you were cured. I hope you won't get discouraged in finding a job – that is what I am afraid of. It is easy at our age. And then again we like roaming about the world. I'm looking forward to St Moritz and the hockey and life there. I go there Tuesday the 27th. I shall pass Xmas with Cynthia. I saw her the other day and she is quite OK for the winter. The only thing I'm rather sore at is the way she got me involved about giving (Aunt) Caroline[243] an allowance. On Dec. 1st I have to hand over £125 – I believe you are supposed to do so too. Have you been advised? The money should be turned in to Cynthia, who is giving her the full sum.

Today I stood at the Cenotaph at 11am. It was a great moment & thousands of people. Nothing could have been better done. I went with Gorst.

Am waiting for a letter from you. I've only had four since July!

Have nothing to report. Hope this finds you in good health. I'm gradually meeting more & more people and have liked my autumn over here a good deal.

Don't forget to send my skates when you have a chance.

Much love. M"

"London
Nov 14th 1921

Dear Boy,
I was glad to get your letter of the 4th. I'm not as lonely as you think & my days are so full I haven't a moment to myself. Beginning next Monday, I go

---

[243] Countess Fritz Hochberg.

into Sir George Younger's office where I shall learn politics. It means no expense & will give me no end of experience.

I certainly hope you won't be angry because I didn't sell your horses. First, it wasn't fair to discharge Harris, for at this time of year he could get no position. Mrs Hoffman and Miss Preston couldn't possibly hunt the animals and then in the end they could always be sold another year. I sent you a cable today to let you know that fact.

Thank you for sending over the skates, and in your next letter tell me what you really want to do with your car. Under no circumstances can I use it. Also what price.

By the way, I certainly don't think you should pay that four thousand you speak of to the Orphans' Home (St Paul's School). Just think every single month I send a cheque for $125. That means fifteen hundred per annum! If you continue, you will find they will be after you each year. If you care to send a thousand that would be ample.

I see that Princeton beat Harvard, also that Yale beat Princeton. Harvard has no team this year, they can't develop a line, the Bulletin says. It can't hurt to lose sometimes.

By the way, you must go to Tiffanys' and get Reggie (Lanier) a present. Think it would be better to have a nice big one from us both. We'll divide the cost. You should be very complemented to have the job.

Boy, the Halycons have placed an order for a shell[244] at Sims'. They cost £125, so I ordered another for Shattocks.[245] I love working over these things. Boy, do try and get interested in something like that. It makes life so worthwhile. Wait till you get the germ some day.

I see that Mrs Gould dropped dead on the golf course. I must say, I admire Julie Noyes for his years of devotion – he's been on the job for about twelve years. I'll bet he had a happy time for say what you want, the Goulds certainly did things to the King's taste.

Don't forget about the present for Reggie.

Much love. M"

"November 30th 1921

Dear Boy,
I had hoped to hear by now, if you approved of my having given the Hoffmans the use of your horses. I have already described to you at length my having been there, their condition. Harris needed fifteen pounds so I gave it to him. Let us have some sort of agreement about him.

---

[244] A long, narrow racing boat propelled by oarsmen..
[245] Halcyons & Shattocks were the rival rowing teams at St Paul's School

Will you let me know if I am to be responsible for him & to what extent?

I had another excellent pheasant shoot last week. I am going to the Hoffmans to one this Sat. & also to one on the 9th. I had to buy a gun at Purdey's but instead of getting a new one at 125 guineas, I bought an ex-officer's for 60. It is just as good as new – so says Purdeys. Each week also I go to the London Shooting School and fire over 200 rounds at flying targets. Watson says I have the making of a fine shot. Seems I'm quick. I just love the sport. On Sat. I got two high pheasants as I stood in an avenue between two covers. Several people saw it.

My work goes on the same. I am busy each day until 5.30. No nerves for me! I look well & feel fine! Have a drink when I want it & refuse to worry. I'm going to address some young fellows soon, and am not afraid either.

Hope you got Reggie a nice present. Do give me a line. What are you doing?

Love. M."

"Date Dec. 18th 1921

Dear Boy

I was more than delighted to get a letter from you on my return from Lady Markham's. Today the skates arrived for which I thank you. I was beginning to despair of ever getting them & as I leave a week from Tuesday for St. Moritz, I wanted them badly.

I was distressed to see in the papers that Charlie Appleton had died. I wonder what of? I now see that Jack McCullough has gone too. What a wasted life his was! Its just dreadful when one thinks of the wasted opportunities of these drunkards. Just think what poor Uncle George missed by "boozing".

I don't suppose that I have ever been as happy as this year. My work with Gorst is just splendid. I write speeches, compose things, talk for one and a half hours everyday except Sat., and have been doing so since October 8 and haven't finished yet. I give him £30 a month and as I think happiness is paramount, I'd pay anything to get it.

Yesterday I went to the Brandbury Ball at Brandbury & saw lots of your old hunting friends who mistook me for you.

That chauffeur was Chauncy Beaver and was a good man in my Supply Train. I sent them all a Christmas card again this year, addressing them all myself. Last year I got 82 cards from the "boys".

Boy, I hope your difficulties will be solved. I can't impress upon you what we both have & how criminal it is to waste. I'm going to stand for election some day, and if I get beaten, well I won't care, there's no disgrace. I have every qualification. I am (1) not trying to grind an axe, am (2)not looking for a peerage. I have one & (3) cannot be tempted as (4) have money. The whole thing is to have the proper backing & people to speak for you. The people want somebody to represent them who will be fair, straight & a gentleman! You must not discourage me, but say "go for it" & that you're damn glad. That's my goal. I'm not afraid to face the music.

I am sorry to hear Aunt Lucy is ill. What a wasted life too! Money swilled away. No return! What has she ever done for France!

I wish you were coming to St. Moritz with me. How on earth you got in this nervous way I can't imagine. I never was freer of nerves in my life. People have been splendid about asking me and I've made friends galore.

Hope you have a Happy Xmas & prepare for a good New Year. Write often. Just look forward to a new beginning & try & make us happy, as it is your duty to try to do so.

Much love. M"

At the end of January 1922 Maurice was adopted prospective Conservative candidate for the Horncastle Division, a rural constituency in Lincolnshire. He was given a warm welcome by the selection committee when he rose to address them. He told them that he had a great interest in agriculture, particularly in dairy farming. He was convinced that the farming industry was of superlative importance in any country, and the farmer should be encouraged in every way. With regard to agricultural policy, he felt that the industry should be free from government control, operating independently to ensure a profitable return to the farmer and a fair wage to the farm worker.

His service in the American army in the war had given him great sympathy with ex-servicemen and he would always be ready to help them. He had always held the opinion that those who were better off should live useful lives and endeavour to improve conditions generally. He intended to study all the local problems and local conditions and no class would find him wanting in sympathy.

He felt strongly about the friendship of English-speaking nations. He assured them that he had a deep interest in the sick and hospital work. He had a great desire to do what he could towards the better living conditions of people of his constituency. He assured his audience that his motives were serious and he was prepared to put all his energies into the work of being elected. Finally, he hoped to be able to live amongst them and to be able to help them with all that lay in his power.

The local paper commented on his transparent sincerity which created a most favourable impression upon those present. Although he was not an accomplished orator he had a very happy way of expressing his views, and there was no doubt

Lord Fermoy at St Moritz with Captain Adamson of Cambridge University in an ice hockey match, 1921

Hagnaby Priory, Spilsby, Lincolnshire

of his ardent enthusiasm.[246]

Maurice lost no time in renting a property, Hagnaby Priory, Spilsby. He set about touring the constituency, addressing meetings. He increased his knowledge of agriculture, studying the system of rotating crops. He impressed on his constituents that ten tousand women in the constituency would be able to vote at the next election, and eight million throughout the kingdom.

Despite the desperate efforts of the suffragette movement, who fought for votes for women in the decade preceding the First World War, by 1914 they had failed to achieve their objective. Women made such a vital contribution to the war effort that in 1918 Lloyd George, the Prime Minister, gave the vote to women over the age of 30, who were householders, wives of householders, owners of property with an annual rent of £5 or graduates of British Universities.

In February, Maurice wrote to Frank from his new abode:

"Hagnaby Priory, Spilsby Lincs.
Feb 7th 1922

Dear Boy,
Mrs Barnwell has just sent me a line saying that she expects to give "Kitch" a good home and also to get about £200 for Stockholm.[247] I wired my approval. When the money comes, I shall place it in your bank and cable you.

Boy, I have taken a great liberty. When I got here the first thing I had to do was to get a car. So I telegraphed Irvine to bring your Morris. Words cannot describe what a real comfort and pleasure it is. I immediately engaged a chauffeur (local) as good as Aunt Lucy's Ball, & he drives me out & everywhere. You know what it means to me. It is so comfortable and I go out in the cold and wet all closed in. I promise you I haven't driven it a mile. Warender, the chauffeur, is in fact the best driver & man you ever saw & I promise you that no harm will come of it. Boy, it just is the best machine for this work in the world. I pray you don't disapprove for you know if it were my car I would let you take it willingly too.

Here are my meetings for the week. I go to London for the week-end to get my clothes etc. The work is going forward. I'm fine & not in the least worrying over this thing. I find there are the best grass courts at the Spilsby Tennis Ground.

Let me hear, affec. M"

---

[246] From the *Lincolnshire Standard*, 28th January, 1922
[247] Frank's horses.

"Hagnaby Priory
Feb14th 1922

Dear Boy,
The most encouraging letter came from you today. I was so glad to hear that you were at work again and I hope you will realize that it is the only solution to a happy life. When you either get a holiday, or move to London as you expect, you will just love the change.

Now to answer some of your questions. You know that I take the NY Times so I get all that is taking place in New York. I see about the cuttings and all such events. As for the Cable, I don't see why you couldn't see it. "Hoffman property" etc of course meant that I was clear of Marian. There was no tie. I realize that she very likely isn't the person for me.

I am writing to Salkin to change my membership to non-resident. Also last week I was duly elected a member of Brooks' Club & have paid the dues & everything. I also belong to the Bachelors', a Piccadilly club. Marvellously run!

I'm so glad you are going to SPS and hope to hear all about it. I know you will write fully on it. All I can say is that I think this year should be a very good year for us. I'm so comfortable here that I can't believe it. This house runs like a charm. With the lengthening of the days, it is getting nicer and nicer. I told you that the Spilsby tennis club is one of the best in England. I have two meetings each night this week and am subscribing etc and giving prizes. Boy, there is the nicest little chapel on my place and I intend going there.

The house runs smoothly. I have taken it for six month – £150 or about 17s 6d [248] per day. Living up here is not expensive. Salkin has just sent me a thousand pounds so I have the money on hand for an election, which I judge won't come anyway before May. I'm giving large prizes at the Skegness cattle show & tonight I'm giving out the prizes at a whist drive. I'm giving a ton of coal as a prize!

I have already written you about the Harvard Endowment Fund and from what you say in your letter, I feel that you will help me in this matter. Then we shall have each given $5,000. You know it is in 5 year instalments.

Try and keep interested in things. I feel sure that you have conquered yourself & just console yourself with the fact that if you quit tomorrow, in a month's time you would be in a sorry plight again.

I've never been happier than now.

My best."

---

[248] 87 pence in today's money.

Maurice was deeply affected by the deaths of St Paul's boys during the Great War. He commissioned Dent clockmakers in London, who designed the Big Ben clock, to make a clock in memory of the fallen alumni of St Paul's. He wrote to his brother Frank asking him to meet the clock and send it on its way to Concord:

"April 23rd 1922 Sunday

Dear Boy
I'm thinking of you as being in Tuxedo today. I miss fishing very much. I remember so well when we used to spend our vacations there, when we were at school – now so many years ago. Boy, before I forget it, I wish you would arrange to be at school when the clock is dedicated. I think you will like it.

The Rector thinks it will be best placed on the Lower Grounds between the tennis courts & the football fields. It has two faces and stands some thirteen feet from the ground. The inscription is: "And time itself shall not efface the glory of their sacrifice", followed by the scroll & the fifty names. As a timepiece, Dent says it won't vary more than seven seconds a month and many hundreds of years after we're gone, it should be performing.

When it starts for the States, I will cable you & please rush it to Concord to be there for Anniversary. If the time is very short, I wish you would hire a motor lorry and send it direct. For the ceremony, they are going to place it on a wooden stand so as to alter the position if it is not suitable. You might send Charles along on the lorry with it to see that it gets there. I'm rather worried that it may not get there in time.

England is beginning to be nice and spring like now. Of course Lincolnshire is the windiest and coldest place you've ever seen. If I fail in the election, I won't stop there after the expiration of my lease. I think I may take a trip to Australia to look around, but I'll go to America first to see you. I think there is every indication that the election will be in October. It is too late to have it in the spring.

I hope that Mama will find something to do this summer. I'm so afraid she will come over and camp on my place and that I shall have her on my mind.

Well, I get plenty of news on reading the NY times. I see Lady Astor is turning around the US. They hate her in the house. She made a pussyfoot speech the other day and you know how Englishmen feel about that. They practically hushed her up. Women shouldn't have the "brass" to go into the house.

So glad you are better, and do have the satisfaction of knowing that you are missing nothing over here this year. Write often.

Love M "

The Memorial Clock in its original position at St Paul's School, 1922

The Lord Fermoy Memorial Clock at St Paul's School today, with Dave McCusker and Bob Rettew

"*May 14th 1922 9.30am*

Dear Boy

It is such a wonderful day here. Altho' it is just 4.30 am with you I shall think of you all at the picnic you have planned and tomorrow is another milestone in our lives, 37, almost the half-way mark! Think of it! Also how many of our friends never even reached it. Charlie Lanier, Hooker Bruce, Nat Simpkins etc.etc.

I hope we both make this a brilliant year, and that unlike most people, that we shall improve with vintage. We <u>must</u> make good, and do something.

324

I wish I were never going to hear of your engagement to the Trombly girl.

Everything looks so big beforehand. Boy, just think of this job of mine & the audiences I face & have to talk my way into Parliament - that's what it comes to. When you think it over afterwards – there's nothing to it. This Friday I have Mr Noble who is coming for the weekend – he is a coach & prepares skeletons, (of speeches). I never fail to be able to talk if I know what I'm to talk about. He is to give me "dope"

I see the *Mauretania* has arrived and so then the clock too. I hope you have done all I asked and have dispatched the clock to the school. I am certainly awaiting your letters. Nothing new to report. Aunt Lucy has just written me a nice letter. She is thinking of taking a house for a month in London. I hope so for I shall be very glad to see her and if the election doesn't take place in June (as it most certainly won't) I shall have a place to go.

Marian Hoffman sent me a nice present and I must thank her. My best.

Yours ever M

P.S. I hope you will surely go to Anniversary."

In the middle of June, Maurice has a visit from his mother and her friend Miss Grosvenor. Before she leaves Paris, she writes to Frank of her elder son in tones of praise as well as strong criticism! She has heard that he has put on weight!

"Hotel de Crillon, Place de la Concorde, Paris
June 13th 1922

My dear Frankie,

The time is approaching when I go to England. In a week, I cross the Channel & see again that lovely, dear country and those dear people for whom and because of which I made this misery & failure of my life. However I am sure to love it. I did so earnestly when I was young.

Maurice has written very little lately: short letters! But I suppose he is engrossed with his work. I hear much praise of him & all seem to think that he has qualities of head and heart that will carry him far.

But a small comparatively personal thing is a pity. I have not seen him and I will not make any but favourable comments when I do. They all say he has grown very fat & gross-looking. It is apparently a fact that the family has a tendency to coarseness. I never dreamed of it. At over sixty I may be permitted to grow heavier, but people still on the sunny side of forty are certainly displeasing if they expand & have a swollen fed-up look that is so much to be deplored. He always bolted his food in a cannibalish way.

It is so funny to observe that very soon after maturity in one way or another, & generally in several, we must begin to exercise self control..."

Fanny's visit is a success. She is happy with the place and the people. But she confides in Frank that she fears Maurice has not enough knowledge of English politics to go before the electorate. She approves of him making the attempt and would see no disgrace if he were to be defeated. He would have gained experience and presented himself to the public as an ambitious young man wanting to do something for the good of his country. There is no use standing on the brink in life.

Dr Drury writes that the clock will be placed on the lower grounds as Maurice wishes. The base will be prepared and the clock put in position in August.

"Hagnaby Priory, Spilsby, Lincolnshire
July 12th 1922

Dear Boy,
On Friday last, I took Mrs Boys, a lady near here to Wimbledon to see the semi-finals. It has been said on all sides that the standard of tennis this year has never been poorer. When I saw Paterson beat Anderson, Paterson served 18 double faults in the match! I went again on Saturday. I wish you had been there to see Mrs Mallory[249] get the worst "hiding" you ever saw. Well the result tells the story – 6-2, 6-0. B Fisher told me that he thought Lenglen[250] played the most perfect tennis of the week. In the entire match, she never put one ball further than a foot out of court – and if ever, just missed the side ones by inches! I believe that Mallory is clamouring for a return match.

Boy, London was extremely nice. I took in two good plays and had a general look round. The weather was generally rain in the pm and at the tennis, each day we were kept in the seats while it rained. The new Wimbledon is a wonder but sad to relate, too small already. It is under cover and one sees pretty well from the entire place.

I have returned to take up my life here again. Am busy with Fetes & other things – tennis. I shall be here the entire summer, I think. Haven't heard from you of late.

Boy, can you send me some of those pens? They are the only ones I can write with. Send me about 50 please. How the years fly, another has gone since we said "au revoir." Mama has sent me a perfect "Maplap" tennis racquet and I'm delighted. Have no news.

It is entirely "off" between Marian Hoffman & myself. We just fought the entire time and I wasn't going to be "bossed" by a little ass like her.

---

[249] Norwegian-born American champion.
[250] Suzanne Lenglen, world-beating French tennis champion.

326

They sail on August 2nd and I'm delighted to feel free again. There's nothing like it.

Take care of yourself. Much love M"

"Hagnaby Priory
July 19th 1922

Dear Boy

I was very glad to get your letter of July 4th telling me all about your holiday to dear old Newport. I can well imagine all the memories that were recalled – somehow that all seems so far back – the fort, Jim Quinn, the cherry tree, our daily drive to the beach on the old chestnut horse! Racing the Laniers.

I'm glad you sent Eleanor Conover the present and do ask Salkin to pay you my share on it.

Before I forget, Scudder is coming up here Monday to visit me. I'll give him some golf and ask a few friends to meet him. I'm not worrying.

I took in the Lincoln tournament this week. The first day I played perfect tennis and beat A M Stokes, one of the finalists of last year. I had a new racquet Mama sent me and I don't think I ever played better in my life. I won again but yesterday a match player, Gaunt, beat me 8-6, 6-4. The courts are perfect and beautifully situated, with the Cathedral as a back ground. At 6pm last night the entire gallery watched us in the mixed doubles – very close. Miss Thomas and I lost 6-4, 6-4. You & I would have done well in the doubles as the pace of the court suits us.

Today the big agricultural show at Skegness. So you see I've been busy

England is lovely this year and I'm full of hopes and in the best of spirits. Your letter was the first I had had since your visit to SPS a month ago! When you see Marian Hoffman don't be too nice to her. Also if she jumps on me stand up for me.

Love M."

"Hagnaby
July 22nd 1922

Dear Boy,

I'm thinking of you as being in Newport today. When I look at Town and Country sometimes, I get rather homesick – for at times it is pretty lonely taking all of one's meals alone. But I have other moments when it is perfect. I have had a most interesting year, so many new experiences.

I never enjoyed anything more than this prize day. Over a hundred and fifty nice boys & girls all in uniform. After the prizes I gave them a short talk on sportsmanship, its value, and wished them all success & luck in winning further honours. It took place at the Cricket ground and there were present the parents and friends.

Boy, ask Salkin to pay this please. I've been looking over the directory of old boys and it is rather sad to see how many of them have died that we know. In your next letter do tell me just what work you were doing at the school, or are you giving it up?

Monday.

I have just returned to Hagnaby and am dumbfounded to hear of Cynthia's marriage. Never did I believe such a thing possible! Her cable came today. I hope she will be happy and "make good". And what an income too! Of course Bertie Goelet gives him vast amounts to do. Well, I'm delighted and I hope Cynthia produces a few children before she's too old.

Your letter of the 14th at hand. I'll try to follow your advice about hitting the ball – my tennis hasn't improved a bit. Have just bought two small black pigs to eat up the left-overs. Do you know where I am on the map of England? Look. Wish you were here to enter the Spilsby 'show' (tennis) with me next week. This must go. Scudder comes this pm to stay with me.

Love M."

On 24th July, Cynthia married Guy Fairfax Cary, a successful lawyer with a lucrative practice. He had wanted to marry her twenty years earlier but he regarded himself at that time as having insufficient wealth. Her first husband Arthur Burden had died. She was married at her mother's home, Elm Court, which was:

"transformed into a forest of flowers, eleven thousand roses being brought by truck in an all night ride from a Connecticut greenhouse. The entrance to the house was lined with blue hydrangeas leading into the main hall where there were standards of American Beauty roses."[251]

Her brother Frank gave her away. There were 75 guests.

Fanny, her mother, was enchanted with the news in Paris. She thoroughly approved of his family background and his fortune and also liked him – in that order! She was also glad that Cynthia's loneliness was at an end, as well as the uncertainties and dangers which a young attractive woman was exposed to if alone. She had been very much afraid that some many-titled fortune hunter or detrimental person would entrap her daughter.

The announcement of his sister's marriage in Newport had unfortunate repercussions for Maurice in Lincolnshire. Maurice was equally enthusiastic and delighted until an article appeared in a local paper, exposing the family's dirty

[251] *New York Herald.*

linen, under the heading "Horncastle's Candidate". It reported that his mother had married her coachman. Indignant and angry he wrote to Frank:

"Hagnaby Priory,
August 7th 1922

Dear Boy
Cynthia's marriage certainly has given the opposition a chance to land one on me! God damn them, they put in this article which of course does me harm. Well, I've decided to see this thing thro'. There is a good deal of jealousy here but I'm taking on this job. Sir Archibald Weigall, who owns this paper, is a bounder & a cad. I saw him yesterday and instead of his saying he would do something about it, he just said nothing.

I went to Oakham the other day to play in a tournament (American). I stayed with the Dixons (Gunthorpe). They said they know you. Also many asked after you. I won the tournament. Had great pleasure in beating Capt. Sherwood. Am going to Deauville August 17th to see Lucy.

Love M."

Perhaps to counterbalance the potentially damaging article on his family history, the very supportive local newspaper[252] reported that:

"His Lordship appears to have become very popular wherever he goes and one realises as one knows him better, that he is the ideal gentleman to represent Horncastle in London. He has made himself fully acquainted in every hole and corner of the division since he came to reside among us. He has the welfare if the people at heart and there's not an institution but that has his wholehearted support."

"Hagnaby Priory, Spilsby, Lincolnshire
August 16th 1922

Dear Boy,
Your letter of August 7th just came with the excellent picture of the wedding party. I read with equal interest your times in Newport and you know I would have loved to have returned this year. But I just couldn't think of it. All over Lincolnshire I am constantly opening fetes, two yesterday & one today. And then I could never know what might happen here. Then, Boy, I know that I'd just raize hell and never get to bed etc and then the expense of keeping the servants going here - wait until another year. And I just had

---

[252] *Horncastle News & South Lindsey Advertiser,* July 29th, 1922

to busy myself about the division

Boy, I'm so very glad to hear that you are doing something to the class rooms, all of which will do so much towards making the boys happier - and then I think it is nice to be associated with SPS like we are, and just think what we can do there for the next twenty-five years with the start we've got already.

I think the picture just excellent of you & Cynthia etc. How well I can make out the background and even here sometimes I make a trip down the (Bellevue) Avenue from my bed. Today I'm expecting Mama and Miss Grosvenor. I hope they will spend the night – I have anyway tomorrow to go to join Aunt Lucy and to motor back to Paris with her.

About the Morris car – she has never gone better. I wouldn't part with her for anything. So very comfortable and just the thing for Lincolnshire. As I told you before I never drive it, and we have done over seven thousand miles since February! I couldn't have found a better fellow than Warrender. He knows every inch of the country here. I give him £2 a week.

I wish I had more news. I get plenty of mail from the States and am kept in touch with things. Boy, I am going to marry an English girl, when I do. Take it from me!

You certainly did look your former self in the photo. Of course, work is the tonic of life. Am well too. Will write again.

Love M."

Letter from Willard Scudder (Classics master at St Paul's School, Concord and rowing coach), expressing concern for Maurice's solitary life.

"August, 1922

Dear Maurice,

The chance to see you was in all ways a delight & the visit very interesting. It was specially so in watching the operation of 'nursing a constituency', & you in the new role of candidate. One could see & with no surprise at all, that you had gone a long way to winning votes by winning hearts, & I hope that when the election comes there will be no doubt of a thumping majority.

Of course, it is hard work to get at a lot of strange folk, not much helped by your solitary life. The only thing which gives me concern is that. One feels as if there were not enough society for you, as if the circle in your side of the country were small. You'll have to get a lot of people down from time to time to counteract the limitation of the Horncastle division. And you ought to do so for your own sake, lest you do get too much tangled up with a lot of meetings of the women & of the local rustics.

You've such a strong sense of duty that I am a bit fearful that you'll overdo your job! Don't.

It was good to see something of you again, to find you well, comfortably looked after, busy & interested! I shall write again soon again.

Love W.S."

A letter from Aunt Lucy:

"Royal Deauville
August 10th

My dear Maurice,
I really meant to wait until the Polo match today was over because the King of Spain[253] is to play and every thing is expected of its being a good match, but unless I write in the morning, I know I won't have time.

I am beginning to settle down into my life here. I had a weekend that seemed to unsettle me for Deauville life. I went Friday of last week to have tea with Lady Patricia Ramsay[254] to see two paintings she had been doing at Versailles & I said, why don't you & Captain Ramsay come & lunch on Sunday with me at Bois Joli[255] (I was going to spend the night) & in the end they decided to go too & spend the night.

He drove his car with the luggage and she came with me. We painted all the afternoon although there were sharp showers & Monday it did not rain, so she found a lovely spot & painted a very excellent painting in two sittings so to speak, all morning & then after lunch until 4, when we had tea & then parted to go our different ways. She said she had met you & they are to dine with us on Tuesday the 22 in the Bois before I sail. I can't begin to tell you about her because it would take too long – she is very interesting, so attractive & above all so <u>simple</u>. They are so happy together – it was such a delightful atmosphere to be in & I am really lucky to have made two such really attractive friends..."

Maurice joined Aunt Lucy in Deauville, expecting to spend a few days with her before she returned to the States. He was not best pleased with her change of plans.

---

253 Alphonso XIII, King of Spain called himself the Duke of Toledo in his life as a sportsman, believing this gave him some privacy. He was passionate about polo. From *Courts and Countries after the War* by his aunt HRH Infanta Eulalie of Spain.
254 Princess Patrica of Connaught was a granddaughter of Queen Victoria. She gave up her royal titles when she married Capt. Ramsay (later admiral), an aide-de-camp of her father Prince Arthur. She was a talented artist.
255 Hotel Bois Joli, Bagnoles-de-L'Orne.

"Dinard
August 25th 1922

Dear Boy,

I don't mean to "crab" but I haven't enjoyed these days in France as I might. The truth is that playing about with Aunt Lucy isn't a treat. You see when I joined her at Deauville, I expected her to sail to the following Wednesday. Well, she put off her sailing and instead of going on my own for a few days, I'm just terribly 'stuck'. We arrived here in Dinard & immediately I was asked etc. but I have had to refuse. There are a lot of Harvard men etc. and I just have to sit up & take her everywhere.

The most ridiculous thing about her is that she thinks she is still young, and I am mortified when at these dance places, I have to take her. It is sad, and I hope that when I'm old & gray-haired I won't be like that. It's pretty hard on me, because I've been working steadily up there in Lincs. and this is my holiday. Instead of leaving me here to enjoy a few days, I have to motor all the way back to Paris with her, then catch the train Sunday to London. There Mama is camped at the Berkeley waiting for me & God knows what she intends doing but she's not going to return to Hagnaby for the winter. I couldn't stand it. She's always moralizing & nagging and repeating her prat which is all too clear in my head already. I forgot to add that I pay for entrance fees, polo & racing. Enough of that!

I'm looking forward to returning to England. For once I'm financially in good standing; the shells & clock are paid for and I've got only a single bill in London – Burkinshaw & Knight. No more promises. Today we watch tennis. Yesterday we went to Mont St Michel and I thought it disappointing. The whole thing is "killed" by hordes of the shopping people yelling from the doorsteps, pleading you to buy a souvenir or some rotten stuff. The Abbey is interesting on account of its age and history.

Hope you're well.

Love Maurice

Aunt Lucy sails 30th *Homeric*. Meet her if possible."

In the following letter, he expresses his thankfulness to have ended his relationship with Marian Hoffman. He thinks he has had a lucky escape!

"Hagnaby Priory
Sept 5th 1922

Dear Boy,

I got your nice letter of August 25, enclosing pictures, telling me of your tennis and tea with Marian. Marian just was too impossible for words & never on time, always tired. Mad at me for not leaving Hagnaby at a moment's notice etc. Just too undisciplined for words. That mother of hers is a terrific person when the "fur flies". I'm well out of it.

Very pleased that you did well in tennis – and your description of the dances & life and Newport was extremely clear.

Am back on the job again. I really never could have returned to Newport this summer as I had to get Ramm[256] & I have done a tremendous lot of work here. Then I know that I would never get to bed and just be dead beat after a few days.

Do you remember the Dixons of Oakham? I was with them the other day & they spoke of you. Barbara, the eldest has since married.

Have a good time; and for heaven's sake realize that it is your job that is making you so happy & is keeping you in this frame of mind.

Love M"

In a letter to Dr Drury, he contrasted the attitude of parents to their children in England and the States and commented on the wealth of average families in America.

"Hagnaby Priory
Sept. 28th '22

Dear Dr Drury,

As usual I was glad to be included among those who received the letter to the "Alumni in College". In fact I wish you would write a good stiff letter to the "Alumni out of College". I agree with all that you say and since living in England, I feel that the root of the trouble lies more with the parents. Here in England the boys have more obligations put to them. Obligations of estate, of soldiering, of inheritance. If a family has been represented in the Life Guards for years, so must this link continue. There is also more of the idea of "noblesse oblige" and not that careless "passing of the buck" that we have in America.

Also, since living here I realize the ease and comfort of the average St Paul's boy. What stacks of money the average family we know do have! And

---

[256] His parliamentary agent.

so is free from money & troubles! As I sit here in this little island, I read each day of the general unrest of the Empire; I am ever ready for the war that is threatening in the East – of all those moral obligations, and aside that, this stupendous job of standing for Parliament. How little did I think when I left America that the obligation of being a Peer of the Realm called on me to take the Chair at a large gathering, and that I am to have the honour of introducing the Bishop of Lincoln! But I'm delighted to be so privileged. Somebody said we have no rights, but duties.

How can I help? I think it would be an excellent idea to have a series of lectures at the school on 'Careers.' Boston is full of magnificent men. Why not have the leading man of his profession come and give a talk? Even if his words impress but 15%, it's worth it. Yes – talk on 'Careers'. I'll contribute largely to such an undertaking. Let me hear.

I regret that I am to miss another Trustees' meeting, but the excellent financial statement received from Salkin today consoles me.

With best wishes to you all.

Maurice"

The general election was held on November 15th 1922. The results for Horncastle division were:

Pattinson Liberal	10,797
Fermoy Conservative	9,158

Maurice had increased the Conservative vote by more than a thousand but had failed to be elected. The disappointment was great among his supporters. The crowd were dumbfounded and refused to believe the news when the results were given. Fanny and Frank were present. Maurice announced his intention to stand at the next election.

Nationwide, the Conservatives, led by Andrew Bonar Law, had a majority over Labour. It was the first election where Labour surpassed the combined strength of two Liberal parties, in votes as well as seats.

27

Lord Fermoy, Member of Parliament

After his annual visit to St Moritz in January 1923 Maurice resumed the task of nursing his constituency. In May, he wrote to Dr Drury telling him that the government was taking five dollars out of every twenty-dollar bill that came to him in England, which he regarded as an enormous bite. He was obliged to reduce the amount of the Roche and Work Scholarships by half.

In June 1923, he visited A E Hillard, the High Master of St Paul's School London, and as a way of cementing the connection with his own school, he donated ten scholarships of £45 each to be known as "The St Paul's School of America Scholarship".

He gave up the lease of Hagnaby Priory in August, and returned to the US, sailing on the Red Star liner *Lapland*. He was interviewed on arrival and spoke optimistically of labour conditions in Great Britain, where fewer than ten per cent were out of work. There was much work in Canada for British labourers, harvesting the year's bumper crops. He proceeded to Newport to stay with his sister Cynthia Cary.

Maurice had already left Lincolnshire when a general election was held in January 1924. Presumably with the prospect of a safer seat elsewhere one day, Fermoy abandoned his intention to stand again for election as MP for the Horncastle division. Meanwhile he was not a candidate for the January election.

The Conservatives had won a clear victory in 1922 but the government did not last long. Bonar Law resigned from ill-health and Baldwin became Prime Minister. He decided to introduce import duties to make the cost of foreign goods more expensive and thus give a boost to British industry. As this policy was contrary to that of Bonar Law, who had stood for free trade and had promised not to introduce tariffs on imported goods, Baldwin felt it was only fair that the electorate should have the opportunity to vote for or against trade protection.

A general election was held on 6th December 1923. The Conservatives, led by Stanley Baldwin, won the most seats, but Labour, led by Ramsay MacDonald, and the Liberal Party, led by Herbert Asquith, gained enough seats to produce a hung parliament. The Conservatives had fought the election on their intentions for tariff reforms which were opposed by the other parties, so they clearly could not govern. Ramsay Macdonald became Prime Minister and the first ever Labour government was formed.

In April 1924, Maurice was adopted as prospective Conservative candidate for the King's Lynn, Norfolk Division in April 1924. The town of King's Lynn is situated on the Great Ouse river, about two miles from the Wash, a deep indentation of the North Sea. It was one of the largest towns and most important seaports of medieval England. During the late Middle Ages it belonged to the Hanseatic League, a powerful mercantile trade union of North German origin, which controlled ports around the Baltic Sea and neighbouring countries.

The name dates from the sixteenth century when Henry VIII took control of the town. Many fine buildings survive today from the medieval period. King's Lynn is the central market town for the large surrounding farming area of West Norfolk and the Fens. Once again Maurice's agricultural experience played an important part in his selection.

The Editor of the *Lynn New & County Press* was clearly very impressed when he met the candidate for the first time. He introduced him to his readers in warm terms:

"Lord Fermoy, the newly-chosen Conservative candidate for the King's Lynn division honoured me with a visit this morning, and we had a long and interesting chat about everything except politics.

You will thoroughly like Lord Fermoy – his strong, alert figure, his keen grey eye; his very slight Irish-American accent; the pleasant suggestion that his manner carries, after five minutes' conversation, of his having been friendly with you for years.

I specially appreciated the way he spoke of Lincolnshire farming men and methods, of Lincolnshire town and village life, of political helpers and opponents, of Boston 'Stump'.

Here we have a man of education, world-wide experience, extensive commercial knowledge, who is ready to devote his life to the public service by assisting to make and administer his country's laws. It behoves us all, then, in the first place to thank him for making this offer. After all, you know, he is in a position to live a life of indolent leisure, cynically ignoring all public claims upon his energies. Are you quite certain, my socialist friend, if your income and social position were as amply secured as Lord Fermoy's, that you would embark on the arduous career to which he has committed himself? After our talk I took Lord Fermoy to see some of the Guildhall's treasures and those of St Margaret's Church. He proved a most intent and appreciative visitor, and revealed by many questions and comments that he has read up the history of the borough very carefully." [257]

---

[257] *Lynn News & County Press.* 20th May 1924.

Maurice took up residence in Heacham, a coastal town close to Hunstanton, 13 miles from King's Lynn. He rented the Shooting Lodge for £80 a year. It was an attractive brick residence, set in an acre of land in the grounds of Heacham Hall and one mile from the coast. It had three reception rooms, seven bedrooms and one bathroom. There he lived alone, with a household of staff. He was too busy to feel lonely, spending the week at Westminster and attending engagements in his constituency throughout the weekend.

Having set up his home, he devoted all his energies to becoming known in the area. During the next six months, Maurice was tireless in his attendance at whist drives and dance evenings, open air meetings, fêtes.

One of his first appearances was at a whist drive at Terrington St. Clement where he distributed the prizes. The first prize for the Ladies was a silver cake-basket which he donated. The headline of the column reporting the event read "Bachelor King of Hearts".[258]

He received a very hearty reception. His speech began:

"I have been in the division a month and my reception everywhere is extraordinary. You good people cannot know what it is for anyone like myself to arrive in Norfolk and find you have so many friends about. You are all men and women with a great deal of intelligence and business ability. The most important thing for me is to see what I can do for you, especially in the field of agriculture which is the most important thing to you all.

There are men and women in this room who get their livelihood from the land. You will all agree with me that the question of the present-day wage is a most important one to us all. I have been in various big enterprises and I know that 25 shillings a week is not a living wage. (Hear, hear). I come forward in this division in the interests of agriculture. I want to do all I can to help the farmer. To-day there is no department of farming that pays. There is no industry in England at the present time which is taxed so much as land."

In the vote of thanks the speaker said there would be nothing like a good old bachelor to win the ladies. In 1924 who better than a handsome, charming bachelor to win their important votes?[259] In the dancing that followed, Maurice joined in enthusiastically, leading off every dance.

The key issues of agricultural wage, housing and unemployment featured in most of his speeches. At Hunstanton in May, he alluded to the British Empire Wembley Exhibition which he said showed the vastness and importance of the British Empire. The exhibition was opened on St George's Day by George V.

---

[258] *Lynn News & County Press* 27th May 1924.
[259] It was not until 1928, under a Conservative government, that women were given the vote at 21, at last giving them equal rights to men.

Fifty-eight countries were represented. Later the Empire Pool became the Wembley Arena. The Wembley Stadium, although intended to be a temporary Stadium, survived as the home of English football until 2002 when it was demolished.

He joined the Royal Antediluvian Order of Buffaloes, a philanthropic organisation whose mission was to help widows and orphans, the aged and the infirm. Their orphanage supported 150 fatherless children each year. The members called him Brother Roche. In October he presided as host at a dinner for members in Heacham. Proposing the toast to their host, Brother Barwood said that during the short time that Brother Roche had been initiated into the Order, he had proved himself to be a right good and loyal brother and worker.

From their observations of the kind and the friendly actions of his Lordship, he was sure Lord Fermoy had his heart and soul in Buffaloism. It was apparent he had a large heart and great sympathy for the fatherless and widows. He had never known anyone to take such a keen interest in the Order as Lord Fermoy who he was sure would always succour and defend all its worthy objects.

The general election of October 1924 came unexpectedly. The Labour government had been in power just ten months. One of Prime Minister Ramsay Macdonald's first actions had been to give full recognition to the Soviet Union, the sovereign state formed by the Communist party of

Maurice

338

Bolsheviks who had seized power from the tsars in the Russian Revolution (1917-1920). Macdonald wanted to restore normal trade relations. He negotiated an Anglo-Soviet trade treaty, to be followed by a guarantee of a loan to the Bolsheviks. The Conservatives and Liberals were strongly opposed to the ratification of the treaty. MacDonald took this as a matter of confidence and when his party lost the vote, he resigned in October, ten months after he came to power.

Maurice was formally adopted Conservative candidate three weeks before the election, called for on October 29th. His published manifesto naturally followed the Party line. He stood for the immediate development of trade especially with the Empire; the reduction of taxation and encouragement of all business enterprise; a safe British foreign policy, as the surest way to peace; the firm handling of German reparations; legislation for the revival of the agricultural industry. He stood against loans to Germany or Russia and unnecessary bureaucracy and nationalisation.

Fermoy's speeches during his election campaign picked up many of his manifesto issues. He reported that Ramsay Macdonald had lifted the import duties on luxury goods and this had resulted in a loss of jobs in the motor, watch, clock, piano and film industries. Collieries and steel works were closing. The very first thing Mr Baldwin would do, would be to re-impose the McKenna duties on certain industries which today were facing unfair competition.

Fermoy deplored the abolition of Colonial preferences and spoke of the debt to the Colonies who had made great sacrifices during the war. The government was tumbling over itself to trade with Russia and would do nothing for their own flesh and blood, who came over in thousands to give their lives for the old country in the Great War.

"You cannot ask the Colonies to come here and fight for you and shoulder the rifle for you if you are not going to do them a good turn. The taking away of Colonial preference has been a very serious thing. The Colonies were our best customers. The previous year they had brought us £22 million more than the rest of the world put together. Mr Baldwin intends to restore Colonial preference which will mean a reduction in the cost of living."

He deplored the abolition of the Singapore base whereby Mr Macdonald had deprived Australia and New Zealand of the protection of the British navy from the envious eyes of the Russians, the Chinese and the Japanese.

When he was asked how water mills in the district could be restarted, he replied:

"I have a scheme. Even though some of those mills may be wind-mills, you cannot start them on air. You need capital. Therefore, instead of lending money to Russia, let us let you have it to restart these mills. The Russians owed us six hundred million pounds, but by a stroke of the pen, the Soviet government, when they came into office, renounced that debt. And now Mr Macdonald wants to lend them another forty millions. I am against that and I am sure every man and woman in this room is."

The question of the Russian loan featured in the Conservative election posters in King's Lynn. One showed a British working-man and a Russian, with £'s running from the former to the latter. It read: "The unemployed say if that money were kept at home it would give us work. Keep it here by voting Unionist (Conservative)." Everywhere there were posters in favour of Fermoy, one reading "Fermoy for all, all for Fermoy".

On the subject of agriculture, Fermoy said that if successful he hoped to make a study of the question. Only one fifth of MPs represented agricultural constituencies. There was no question that the industry needed a great deal of help. Twenty-five shillings a week was not a living wage and he sincerely hoped farm workers would get an increase in the weekly wage. In the King's Lynn Division, they wanted the government to invest in sugar beet and bacon factories. Railway rates and taxation were entirely killing the industry and he was in favour of a big reduction in railway rates for agriculture. These were things that would be attended to if Baldwin were returned to power next week.

He spoke of the enormous debt that the nation owed to ex-servicemen, their widows and dependents. As an ex-serviceman himself, he would do his utmost on their behalf. Mr Baldwin would set in motion many schemes for employment for men, including ex-soldiers. He hoped too that Mr Baldwin would give the country a housing scheme, which was badly needed. There was a dire shortage of houses and no houses were being built. With regard to steel houses, they would need to go carefully about the proposed erection of this class of dwelling. Something attractive was required and not houses that would resemble petrol tins.

At a meeting of the Women Unionist Association in Hunstanton a week before the election, he made a direct appeal to the women present. He said that perhaps it was because he was a bachelor that he found it difficult to talk to a number of fair and wise ladies. There were 17,000 women (in the constituency) who had the right to vote in this election. It was a very sacred privilege that had been given to them, and not all women seemed to realise this. Women suffered the most from a bad Government and social evils of every kind. Under the late Government there had been a great increase in unemployment and the cost of living had gone up in consequence; no houses were being built and he wondered if women realised that there must be a change.

Mrs Coxon, the Chair, said the women had it in their hands to redeem the past and win back the lost seat. No doubt she sent shivers through her audience when she told the meeting that she thought the return of Ramsay MacDonald would mean revolution, and she reminded the audience of what revolution had meant in France and Russia!

Four days before the election, a letter from Grigori Zinoviev, a leading Soviet communist politician, was released by the Foreign Office and published in the *Daily Mail*. The letter, marked "Very Secret", exhorted the British Communist Party to strain every nerve in the struggle for the ratification of the Anglo-Soviet Treaty, by stirring up the masses of the British proletariat and infiltrating the armed forces in order to paralyse the military. This lettter is now generally believed to be a forgery but it served to strike 'red' panic in many hearts and added momentum to the defeat of the Labour Government.

At the General Election on October 29th 1924, the Conservatives had a landslide victory, winning 419 seats. The Liberal party lost three quarters of their seats which made Labour again the second largest party. In King's Lynn, Fermoy triumphed! The Conservative candidate for the King's Lynn Division was returned with a big majority, turning a Liberal victory at the previous election into a Conservative majority of 2,526 votes. The declaration was made in the Assembly Room of the Town Hall. The beaming new Member of Parliament appeared at a window at the front of the checkered façade.

"On the open space in front of the Town hall an immense crowd had assembled. When Lord Fermoy, the first man at the opened window triumphantly waved his hat, there was vociferous cheering mingled with hearty groans. Lord Fermoy for some minutes vainly endeavoured to make himself heard. When he did obtain silence enough for a few words, he shouted: 'Are we downhearted?' This was answered by a yell of 'No! 'It has been a great victory,' he shouted. 'I am in by 2,500. It is a glorious victory.' Cheers and counter cheers."

Lord Fermoy smilingly acknowledged the enthusiastic cheers of his supporters. The broad smile on his face showed his elation. After the meeting at the Town Hall, he was carried shoulder-high to the Working Men's Club, where a very enthusiastic and numerous gathering welcomed him with the singing of *For he's a jolly good fellow* and cheers. He addressed them briefly saying, "Thank you all for electing me – it is a magnificent victory – that I, who was practically unknown to you six months ago, should go in with a majority of 2,500. I thank you a thousand times over."

For an American who had spent only three years in the country, his election to Parliament was a remarkable achievement. The question he had asked himself so

King's Lynn Town Hall, 31st May, 1929: Declaration of poll. Candidates at window, from left to right: Mitford, Liberal; Maynard, Labour; Fermoy, Conservative.

often: "What am I going to do?" was answered. His new responsibility centralised his life and give it the serious purpose and meaning which he had been seeking for many years. His total pay, including expenses, was an allowance of £400 a year.

Victory celebrations in the constituency followed his election. At a smoking concert[260] at the Lynn Working Men's Conservative Club, he was given a very warm reception. He assured the meeting that he would do all he could for agriculture. He had been saddened when he visited the poor people in the villages, who were trying to exist on 25 shillings a week. He rejoiced to hear that the wage had been raised that very day to 28 shillings, and hoped it would become still larger. He promised to do all he could to further the cause in the King's Lynn Division, and to do what he could for any man or woman, irrespective of their politics.

In December, over two hundred people sat down to tea in Emneth Central Hall. The toast was the Conservative Cause. The new MP, who was given a rousing reception, responded to the toast. After he had expressed his enormous gratitude to his supporters for their splendid work which had led to his victory, he told them:

---

[260] A performance of live music often held in a hotel, where men smoked and talked politics.

"I wish you had been with me at the Albert Hall the other night. There was one of the most remarkable gatherings ever seen since, perhaps, the days following the war. There were in that Hall ten thousand faithful Conservatives. And as I sat there and listened to Mr Baldwin's speech, I was hoping that the two million people who were listening in by wireless, were experiencing the thrill that I was at that time."

His speech ended with an encouraging note, asserting that a world of prosperity lay ahead. Unfortunately, this view turned out to be wildly optimistic.

28

First term as MP

Now that he was an MP, Maurice set about conscientiously fulfilling all his
election promises. He led a very full life, spending the week at Westminster
and cramming into the weekend as many local functions as he possibly could. He
received many invitations to dances, smoking concerts and whist drives, events
raising funds for sport or charity. On a single day in May, he opened a bowling
green at Gaywood; he attended the annual meeting of the Infant Welfare Centre
as a visitor, in order to ascertain whether he could do anything in the House of
Commons at any time for the Centre; he attended the Mayoress' party for widows
with children an orphans.

In the summer, he opened many fêtes, including one at St Germans in the
cause of repairing the picturesque church of St Peter. He was president of the
King's Lynn and West Norfolk Stallion show, the League of Nations Union and
many other organisations. Whenever there was an opportunity to dance, such as
the Hospital Ball in aid of the West Norfolk and King's Lynn Hospital or at the
Wiggenhall Football Club, he was never off the dance floor. On every occasion he
contributed a prize or a gift of money.

At Westminster, he was a member of several committees. He attended regular
meetings of the Second Chamber Committee of the Conservative Party, which was
considering the reconstitution of the second chamber on a more democratic basis.
As a representative of a large agricultural constituency, his interventions in
Parliament were mainly concerned with the plight of the farmer. His first speech
in February 1926 applauded the help the King's Speech gave to the industry:

> "I think I am right in saying that in no civilised country to-day is the outlook
> for agriculture poorer. That is due entirely to the high cost of production
> and the slump in prices…I am glad to see that we are to have State grants.
> I hope they will be for long terms, and that interest will be very low, so that
> men can pay them off in easy payments."

The only Private Members Bill he introduced benefited agriculture in particular.
The Auctions (Bidding Agreements) Bill was aimed at preventing rings and knock-
outs. Rings, he explained in moving the second Reading of the Bill,[261] are composed

of dealers who enter into agreements not to bid in competition for articles at auctions. Through lack of competition, the bidder obtains them at lower prices than their value, sells them on at a profit and then divides the profits among the members of the ring. The knock-out is the subsequent auction of the article which has been obtained by the ring.

Maurice and Frank outside the House of Commons, 1924

The Bill was a step towards protecting the public against fraud. Agriculturists were particularly badly hit by rings. The farmer brought his stock to market when they were in the prime of their condition, but, unlike other sellers, he was not able to put a reserve upon them, and was unable to bring them back to the farm, because he had used up all available feeding products.

The Bill made it a criminal offence to enter private bidding agreements. The penalty was a fine or six months imprisonment with or without hard labour for six months.

His questions in Parliament were mainly addressed to the Minister of Agriculture. He asked Mr Noel Buxton,[262] if he would take action to have the embargo removed on the importation of potatoes imposed by both Canada in the USA; he asked him if he was aware that the cost per ton wholesale of potatoes in East Anglia was £3 whereas the retail cost in London was about £8; he informed the Minister that the fishermen in the River Ouse near King's Lynn were having their livelihood taken away from them by the effluent from the local beet-sugar factory; he asked for special assistance for the canning of agricultural products.

261 Hansard. February 1927. p. 2061.
262 Minister of Agriculture and Fisheries 1930.

He asked the Minister, Sir John Gilmour,[263] if his Department had investigated experiments aimed at freeing crops of weeds by spraying, and whether, in case it was satisfied, he intended to assist in popularising their use. The Minister replied that he presumed that his Noble Friend was referring to the experiment in the destruction of charlock in spring oats by spraying with dilute sulphuric acid. He had been advised that it was desirable to await further results before commenting on this.

He asked the Home Secretary[264] whether he would consider some means of suggesting to employers of labour that, where possible, salaries and wages should be paid by cheque and not in cash, so as to diminish the temptation to theft on a large scale. Sir Herbert Samuel was not impressed with this practical idea. He replied that he did not think it would be practicable for him to give effect to this suggestion.

His speeches were well prepared, no doubt discussed with his parliamentary agent, Aubrey Ramm.[265] He often included a report on the national and international scene. In early May, at the first meeting of the newly-formed Sandringham and West Newton Men's Conservative Association, he spoke of the dangers rising from von Hindenburg being returned as President of Germany on the previous day. Hindenburg was a friend of the Kaiser and a Nationalist (Nazi). This put the payment of reparations in question. He maintained that it was a serious thing for the country, for the security of France, and for all the things which have to do with securing peace throughout the world.

On the same occasion he spoke of the plight of the shipbuilding industry which employed 500,000 men:

"If we could encourage our own shipbuilding, we should be reviving other industries. I am sure you deplore, as much as I do, that we have been placing orders for ships in Germany and Holland. It is a terrible thing to think of them having our orders when our own men are out of employment. Really it is very easy to understand. Their standard of living is much lower than ours, our wages are about 30 per cent less and they work longer hours. Then again we have to deal with the rates of exchange." [266]

His Liberal opponent at the election, Col. Woodwark, took issue with him for calling himself a colonial, and with the constituency for electing a stranger from America. In a speech in the spring of 1925, the colonel said he was waiting for his Lordship's maiden speech in the House of Commons. He had not yet opened his

---

263 Minister of Agriculture 1932.

264 Sir Herbert Samuel. Home Secretary.

265 Conservative Agent for the Lynn district from 1919-1962. He was a man of great ability and a master of election campaigning.

266 *Lynn News & County Press.* 5th May, 1925.

mouth, and the speaker was betting that he never would! His socialist opponent reported in the local paper that Lord Fermoy had arranged a tennis tournament for fellow MPs between May and July.

In April as a result of his intervention with the Ministry of Agriculture and Fisheries on behalf of Brancaster fishermen, he was successful in obtaining £549 from the War Office as compensation for these men. In October, he successfully negotiated on behalf of dockers with the Ministry of Transport to improve methods of handling timber traffic at the Lynn docks.

He was a vice-President of many organisations, including the King's Lynn and District Motor Cycle and Light Car Club. His friend the Marquis of Cholmondeley was President and races were held at Houghton. Speaking of his own interest in motoring at the annual dinner of the club in October, Fermoy said that he had driven thirty thousand miles in Norfolk in the past fifteen months. On the other side of "the pond", he had driven to the summit of Pike's Peak in Colorado which was 14,000 feet high. (The climb involved 156 switchback bends and was 12 miles long.)

Ever mindful of those in need, of the poor and of the underprivileged, and ever ready to help them, he suggested that those members with cars should take the poor children of Lynn to the seaside on one special day. He also thought it would be a good idea if the Club got together on one day a week to take convalescent patients from the hospital out for trips. He would willingly lend his car for both those purposes. His suggestions were met with applause.

The British coal industry had serious economic problems in 1925. Coal exports were down because of the strength of the pound following the return to the Gold Standard.[267] Germany and Poland were producing cheaper coal. The mine owners were forced to lay off workers and to reduce wages. The miners, backed by the Trade Union Council, would not accept the new terms. The Government intervened to avoid a coal strike, with a subsidy of £10 million to cover the miners' wages, this to last for nine months while the coal industry was reviewed.

At political meetings during August in his constituency, at Dersingham and Middleton, Fermoy expressed his views on the very serious situation in which the country found itself. He believed that faced with the possibility of a coal strike, the £10 million Government subsidy was cheap compared with such a happening. The Prime Minister had done a very wise thing in arranging to tide over the very serious problems of the coal industry by guaranteeing the miners' wages. Although it was called a subsidy, it was really a form of dole, because the money would have been paid in unemployment pay to men thrown out of work had the strike taken place.

He believed that without government intervention, there would have been a

---

[267] Under the Gold Standard the monetary unit was gold. The Bank of England guaranteed to redeem notes on demand for their fixed weight in gold.

general strike on the railways, and most of the industries of the country would have ceased to work. Great hardship would have been inflicted upon the country. The greatest number of unemployed was in the great industries of coal mining, shipbuilding, iron and steel. The most important industry was coal, for the price of coal affected the price of ships, of steel and of nearly every commodity. It was very important that coal should be produced as cheaply as possible. Not only were wages higher than in the continent, but there was the further serious point that ours was a 43-hour week against their 54-hour week.

The Shooting Lodge, Heacham, Maurice's first home in Norfolk, England

He assured his audiences that during the next nine months the entire coal industry would be looked into by gentlemen representing both sides. Everyone knew that the price of coal was almost beyond their pockets. He had never believed that he would have seen the day when he would have to pay what he had to pay for a small supply of coal at Heacham.

One of Fermoy's more unusual engagement took place in December when he attended a smoking concert at the Eagle Hotel in Kings Lynn, organised by the Fellowship of Freedom and Reform. This had been formed to combat the growing menace of prohibition. Total prohibition meant that it was illegal to drink a glass of beer not only in a pub but also in a club or at home.

Once the war was over, many Scottish communities took advantage of the Temperance Act to ban the sale of alcohol. One famous example, Stewarton in Ayrshire, held a poll under the Act in November 1919. The following June, all the town's public houses were forced to close down. They remained closed for 41 years, until a vote in 1961 reversed the decision taken in 1919.

Voting was taking place in Scotland in December 1925 and reformers were hoping to vote 'dry' 70 new areas. Fermoy expressed his desire to be associated with the society. On his last visit to America in 1923, he found that prohibition in that country had made one hundred million people law-breakers. To be forced to have a drink on the sly was an abominable thing. A man who opened a bottle of whisky consumed the whole bottle, with two or three friends, in a few minutes for fear of being caught.

Poor people resorted to drinking hair tonic and methylated spirits which made them very ill, even killed them. After a big football match, as many as twenty men had been found dead after drinking evil concoctions. So long as he was in Parliament he would do everything he could to defeat prohibition.

In early 1926 Fermoy reported the government's achievements:

"They had done their best and tried to fulfil election pledges. They had helped the Colonies; there was the Lucarno Peace Pact[268] for which Sir Austen Chamberlain deserved much credit; the McKenna duties had helped and not hindered trade in our country and new factories had sprung up in consequence of them. Then there was the Widows' Pensions Act, an excellent thing and a very cheap insurance for the widow of the worker and his family.

Agriculture was not to-day in a prosperous condition but it was difficult for Members for rural areas to do what they would wish, owing to the opposition from town representatives."

He invited anyone who wanted his help to send him a post-card and he would be with them. Alas! The coal subsidy did not prevent the General Strike. In March 1926 the mine owners issued new terms to the miners, extending their working hours and reducing wages. The miners would not accept them and responded: "Not a penny off the pay, not a second on the day."

On May 1st the TUC announced a general strike "in defence of miners' working hours and wages." On May 3rd, workers from key industries – railway, transport, iron and steel, printers and dockers – joined the General Strike. On 12th May, the TUC called off the strike, having achieved nothing. The miners refused to return to work and the coal strike carried on for another six months, until eventually hardship for themselves and their families forced the miners back to work, defeated. Many were victimised and remained unemployed for many years.

---

[268] "The Treaties agreed at Locarno were intended to secure peace in western Europe. Germany was treated as an equal, not a defeated power. "The greatest achievement of British diplomacy between the two wars…" *The Drift to War.*

Those that were employed were forced to accept longer hours and lower wages.

In August Fermoy, through his agent Mr Ramm, approached the Secretary of State for Mines to express the plight of domestic coal consumers and small food-producing companies, as a result of the high cost of coal. The Minister wrote to Fermoy informing him that a limited amount of cheap imported coal was available for distribution to the consumers through the Divisional Coal Officers. This was described as an act of political kindness by their MP in the local paper.[269]

1927 saw a repeat round of invitations. In February, he attended a meeting of the Lynn Conservative Working Men's Club. He listened to Alderman J H Catleugh outlining the plans to take over the supply of electricity for the area within a 22-mile radius of the town. The National Grid was established through the Electricity Supply Act of 1926. Prior to its operation, the public supply consisted of a variety of authorities servicing restricted areas.

Catleugh turned to the matter of the serious housing shortage. Private enterprise had failed to build affordable houses. The Council planned to build houses for rent, as people could not afford to buy a house at £400 or £500. Fermoy told the meeting that he was on the Housing Committee of the House of Commons and realised it was no use talking about rural cottages at five shillings a week, because a man could not pay it. He was hopeful that Mr Chamberlain would do a great deal towards rural housing in the next two years.

In August, he opened a fête at Castle Rising. The vicar first listed the needs of the church and the community. The schools were over one hundred years old and the children deserved better accommodation. £100 was needed to improve them by installing central heating and putting in larger windows; a further £100 was needed to overhaul the organ; the church clock no longer chimed and £10 was required to repair it. Fermoy immediately put himself down as a contributor and appealed to the audience to give what they could towards the collection of this sum. In October 1927, he gave a billiards table to the Snettisham Conservative Club.

In November, he was recognised by a reporter playing a prominent role in an energetic game of ice hockey, in the Corn Exchange in King's Lynn, exhibiting his remarkable skill on skates. The observer went on to comment that he noted with pleasure the remarkable progress of Lord Fermoy as a speaker. "He is gaining the knack of assembling his facts in good order and dealing with them according to their merit. The humour he introduces is very amusing and in good taste."[270]

Maurice found every opportunity in his speeches to open windows to the outside world, sometimes to activities at Westminster, sometimes to the international scene. On one occasion he turned to the situation in China and supported the action of the Prime Minister in sending forces to protect British

---

[269] *Lynn News & County Press.* August 8th, 1926.
[270] *Lynn News & County Press.* November 2nd, 1926.

lives.[271] The forces were being sent on the definite understanding that they were there to protect life and not to take any part with either the army of the north or the army of the south.

He pointed out that British in China were living under very unattractive conditions, in order to sell British goods and to carry on trade. What would happen to these people, he asked, if serious trouble arose and the mob got out of control, when it took five weeks to make the journey from England to China? He was satisfied that the trouble was being properly taken care of, and they had the satisfaction of knowing that America and Japan were also sending forces to protect their citizens, who were similarly threatened.[272]

The highlight of the summer was the annual fête, which was held in the first week of July, in Gaywood Park, by kind permission of Major Sir Richard Bagge, the Chairman of the Conservative Association. There was a full array of stalls, competitions and amusements. The sun shone throughout the afternoon, the beautiful gardens and park of the Hall were looking their best, and the supporters came in big numbers. Lord Fermoy gave prizes for whippet racing. There was a lawn tennis tournament and a bowls competition. William Horace Jarvie, won the baby show for the "under one year" category; William Denman for the over one year! Two hundred people took part in an open-air whist drive on the lawn in front of the Hall in the evening.

There was a large audience for the open-air meeting. Captain Douglas Hacking MP [273] opened his address by paying high tribute to the work of Lord Fermoy in Parliament and spoke of the high esteem in which he was held by his fellow members:

"Lord Fermoy" he said, "is seldom in the limelight. He does not desire the limelight. He is a hard worker; he is also a sportsman. He is an enthusiastic and loyal supporter of the government; he has ability, and above all he has no axe to grind. (Applause) His ambition is to do his best for the people he represents. He is undoubtedly one of the most popular Members in the House of Commons and his name will go down in history as being the man who passed through the Commons the Auctions Bidding Agreements Bill, which will do a great deal to help the agricultural community in our midst."

After the fête closed, a carnival dance was held in the Conservative Hall.

In the summer, the King's Lynn Labour Party adopted Sir John Maynard as

---

271 They were at risk of being caught up in the war between the Nationalists and the Communists. Chiang Kai-shek, the leader of the Nationalists, was hostile to foreigners.

272 *Lynn News & County Press*. February 1927.

273 Member of Parliament for Chorley in Lancashire, later 1st Baron Hacking.

prospective candidate. He was a formidable opponent, having spent 40 years in the Indian Civil Service, where he was particularly connected with agriculture in the Punjab. He had been Chancellor of the Punjab University and Finance Minister for the Punjab province. He lived in London but proposed to spend his holiday the following summer in the King's Lynn Division.

In the middle of August, Maurice and 21 British Parliamentary representatives sailed from Southampton in the Royal Mail liner *Arlanza* on a visit to Brazil, at the invitation of the Brazilian government. The objective was to develop trade relations. The British party included Sir Herbert Cayzer MP, Dr Watts MP, Colonel Applin MP and Mr Herbert Wragg MP. Forty more delegates from Europe and Asia joined the *Arlanza* at Cherbourg.[274] *The Times* reported from Santos on September 19th that the delegation had inspected coffee estates and had been entertained at a banquet presided over by Senhor Antonio Desalles, Secretary of Justice, on behalf of the President. The visitors had been astonished at the possibilities of Sao Paulo. They had set sail in the *Alcantara* on September 21st.[275]

The delegation also became aware that the British ambassador had no embassy and conducted business from a hotel! Questions on this regrettable state of affairs were asked in Parliament in the following November by Col Applin MP.[276]

On a cold, windy day in November, under an overcast sky, Fermoy opened two hard tennis courts in Hunstanton. In declaring the courts open he said that as the French had just won the Davis Cup, which would now be contested in France where there were no grass courts, it would be necessary to practise on hard courts in England. Hampered by the wind, he then played and won the first match, a keenly fought singles against Dr F J Willans.[277]

In May 1928 Maurice invited the world-famous marathon swimmer, Mercedes Gleitze, to open the new sea water swimming pool in Hunstanton. The previous month she had become the first person ever to swim the Straits of Gibraltar. In 1927, Mercedes was the first British woman to swim the English Channel. People came from all over East Anglia to see the famous Miss Gleitze demonstrate her swimming strokes in the new seawater pool. Lord Fermoy set in motion the machine which pumped in the sea water. Miss Gleitze was invited to swim the Wash, which she did in the following year. She was making for Hunstanton but landed at Heacham!

At a fête at Heacham on July 1st 1928, Duff Cooper[278] spoke of the government's achievements. Fermoy referred to the reintroduction of the petrol tax, at the rate of four pence a gallon. He pointed out that the cost of that tax was £1 per 1,200 miles.

---

[274] *The Times* August 10th 1927; p. 10.
[275] *The Times* September 20th, 1927; p. 13.
[276] MP for Enfield 1924–29. Hansard. Vol. 210. November 1927.
[277] Surgeon Apothecary to the Royal family at Sandringham from 1924. Knighted 1933.
[278] A prominent politician. Financial Secretary to the War Office. Later became Viscount Norwich.

A gallon of petrol cost 1s 6d.[279] The tax had been introduced specially to provide for the relief of industry. It was thought at that time, that because those who used motor cars or vehicles were generally prosperous, they could afford to pay this tax.

July and August were busy months for Fermoy, as he attended as many fêtes and functions as possible before going to the States for a holiday. On one occasion he invited Bob Boothby[280] as a guest speaker. At a fête on July 4th he reminded his audience that it was Independence Day. He forecast that Britain would soon hear of the cancellation of her debt[281] to the USA, as a result of conferences in that country. He thought the Kellogg[282] peace proposals would have a great deal to do with outlawing war in the world in the future.

A speech he gave in August reflected the Conservatives' change of policy on imposing a general tariff on imports:

"It had been rightly stated that this country did not require a general tariff. There were, however, many like himself who felt that the iron and steel industries might be added to the list of those industries who were being helped for the moment. In the case of those industries which had been safeguarded, it had been shown that the imports had considerably decreased and the exports increased. In view of the large and increasing amount of unemployment in the heavy industries and in the coal industry it might be wise at some time to help those people who were so greatly distressed to-day. Over four million tons of cheap steel were imported every year."[283]

In August 1928, Maurice met up with his wartime friends when he attended a reunion of Company D, 303 Supply Train, 78th Division at Cedar Hotel, Waterwitch, NJ. He visited St Paul's School, his warm-hearted interest in his old school never abating. His visit to the school farm gave him the idea of giving the school a Friesian bull, which he duly found on his return to England! With regret he was obliged to stop paying the scholarships as he was badly hit by double taxation.[284] In addition, the obligations of an MP made heavy demands on his income.

---

279   Seven and a half pence in today's money.
280   Elected MP for East Aberdeenshire in 1924. Parliamentary Private Secretary to Winston Churchill 1926-1929. A cousin of Maurice.
281   Britain borrowed £850 million from the USA in WWI, the equivalent of about £40 billion in today's money.
282   The Kellogg-Briand Pact, signed in Paris on August 27th 1928, was an international multilateral treaty "providing for the renunciation of war as an instrument of national policy."
283   *Lynn New & County Press.* August 7th 1928.
284   He was taxed in the States as well as England. Double taxation relief was not introduced until 1946.

He picked up the theme of tariffs in a speech in Lynn in November:

"This summer I had the privilege of going to America. No country in the world had so high a tariff. The Americans are very clever people. Why did not Germany, France and other countries not give up their tariffs? Simply because it paid them and stimulated their industries. For that reason, many of the European countries are exporting huge quantities to England when really England had the coal mines to supply her own requirements. But, instead the miners have little work, the pits are idle, and the growing unemployed are a burden on the State. The Conservative party are out to help the country..." [285]

Early in 1929, speaking at a social gathering organised by the Lynn Women's Unionist Association, Lord Fermoy MP took the opportunity of placing his "record" before the meeting:

"I may say in passing, that not only under the leadership of Mr Ramm and the various committees has great work been done, but I have single-handed been able to attend over 1,000 gatherings during the past four years. I have made over 260 visits in each of the past four years – (Applause), therefore whatever may be the result of the coming election, I hope that we have not failed to put forward the cause."[286] (Applause)

[285] *Lynn News & County Press.* November 6th 1928.
[286] *Lynn News & County Press.* January 29th 1929.

29

Second term as MP

Just over two weeks before the General Election held on 30th May 1929, Fermoy was again adopted candidate for King's Lynn and District. Captain Lance, the chairman of the Lynn Conservative Association proposing the motion that he should be re-adopted, spoke warmly of their member:

> "You all know Lord Fermoy. He has been our Member for the last nearly five years and during that time, he has endeared himself to the whole of the constituency. (Applause) He has shown himself a man of the utmost generosity. I do not think any hard luck case can have been brought before him without him helping it in some material way, or doing his best to improve it. He is, as you all know, an extremely modest man, very diffident indeed, and I think that has endeared him to us. That diffidence showed itself at first in his not caring to speak very much but he has got over that, and we are very pleased that he is a very much improved speaker now after five years in Parliament."

The resolution was carried unanimously and Fermoy received a great reception when he entered the room. He expressed his pride in having been adopted for the coming fight. He reviewed the government's achievements of the previous four years, highlighting the improved grants for agriculture. There were two provisions which showed encouraging prospects for the future. From October to March, the Home Forces would be fed entirely with British beef. (Cheers) Another provision was that no less than 25 per cent of the flour used in the making of bread would be from English-grown corn.

> "My friends," he concluded, "to-morrow is my birthday. I do not know of a finer birthday present you can give me, believing as I do in the working classes of this country, and of the splendid working men of Norfolk in particular, than to do all you can to ensure the return of Mr Stanley Baldwin at the head of the poll on the 30th May. Nobody can call me a very strong Party man. I have tried to the best of my ability to ease all the troubles and to relieve any sadness that takes place in my division, to look after pension

cases, and everything that comes to me or to my house at Heacham. Everyone knows I am not an orator, but, perhaps, a hard-working person who tries to do his best. (Applause)" [287]

He campaigned energetically but did not always have an easy time. At the end of May, in an article headed Election Liveliness the *Lynn News* reported that:

"Lord Fermoy had rather a rough time at his eve-of poll meeting in the Central Hall, King's Lynn. He was subjected to a torrent of abuse, catcalls and whistling. Eventually several policemen had to be called in, and took up their positions in various parts of the hall, but even their presence did not deter the rabble." Hecklers shouted: "For God's sake give us some politics not charity." They accused him of living in the lap of luxury while thousands starved. When Lord Fermoy stood up to speak, there was booing from the Socialists, but this was quickly drowned by the lusty cheers of the Conservatives. However the incessant tirade from the Socialists made it very difficult for the audience who wished to listen to hear all that was said.

At a mass meeting in the Central Hall, Lynn, he was asked how it was he was able to attend so many engagements in his constituency and do his proper duty in the House of Commons as well. Lord Fermoy replied that he had done his work in the constituency between Friday night and Monday morning."

The chairman Capt. H W Lance speaking in his support said:

"Lord Fermoy is known to all and has made himself the best-known man in the district of Norfolk during the last five years. You all know him in various characters. You know him first of all as a very good sportsman. You all know he is very keen in shooting and he is a first class tennis-player. He is interested in any form of clean sport that you engage in. You also know another side to his character. He is the most hard-working and energetic Member of Parliament. And any of you who have had any cause to go to him for advice or help know that he has a most charming personality and a great big generous heart. A voice: "That is the only thing." The Chairman: "Yes, quite right. That is the only thing that counts and it goes a long way. (Applause). That advice and help has been freely given to every member of his constituency, whether these people have the same political views as he or not. At the last election you all backed a winner when you sent in Lord Fermoy – (Applause) – and all I can say to you is – go ahead and back another winner." (Hear, hear).

---

[287] *Lynn News & County Press.* May 21st 1929

In spite of stiff opposition from his Labour opponent, Sir John Maynard, Lord Fermoy won the seat by a majority of 3,500 votes. The local newspaper reported the sensational result:

"After the Town Clerk of Lynn had made a public declaration of the result from a Town Hall window, each of the candidates thanked his supporters for the help they had given him. When Lord Fermoy emerged from the Town Hall, he was hoisted on the shoulders of two of his supporters, and borne to the St James's Club, where he was overwhelmed with congratulations.

Speaking from an upper window, Fermoy said he was quite overwhelmed with the splendid victory which he had just achieved. Later he spoke at the Working Men's Conservative Club, where he attributed his great victory to the work of his agent, Mr A Ramm, and to the splendid organisation of the army of his supporters in every parish in the constituency. He was very proud to be their member and he wanted to be worthy of their choice. They all knew the disaster which had overtaken the party elsewhere and it was all the more striking that at Lynn they had been able to increase their majority."

Fermoy had triumphed against the trend. In the general election of May 1929, the Conservatives lost 140 seats and their majority in Parliament. The Labour Party had won the largest number of seats, although not as many votes as the Conservatives. A Labour government was formed without an overall majority, with Ramsay Macdonald the Prime Minister for a second time.

Speaking at a Junior Imperial League meeting shortly before the King's Speech at the opening of the new Parliament, Maurice gave his views on the policies of the new government, saying that he understood that there would be two important issues in the speech.

The first was the withdrawal of British troops from the Army of Occupation in Germany. When he had visited Germany the previous year, there was concern that these would be replaced with French troops and this would create a difficult situation.

The Treaty of Versailles, 1919, determined that German territory west of the Rhine should be occupied by the Allies for periods varying from five to fifteen years. The British occupied an area where the withdrawal was due after ten years. The rest of the area was occupied by the French. France had invaded the Ruhr in 1923 for a short period, because Germany had fallen behind with war reparations. Consequently the Germans were hostile to the French and the French remained fearful of aggression from Germany.

Secondly he was concerned at the effect on the coal industry of the eight-hour day, and the consequent drop in production and the possibility of another coal strike.

A few weeks after the general election, an article headed: "All-round acts of generosity," the *Lynn Advertiser*[288] announced that: "Lord Fermoy MP in friendly gratitude to his constituency is making the following noble gifts to deserving local causes." The largest amount – £1,500, was to provide a motor fire-engine for Lynn. This had two engines, a large one as well as a smaller one, which could be towed behind. He donated £1,000 to the West Norfolk and Lynn Hospital.

A gift of £1,000 for the forming of a new British Legion Club was gratefully received. Maurice said he was pleased that they had accepted his offer. He expected that £800 would be spent converting and equipping a suitable building and £200 on billiard tables. He wanted it to be clearly stated in the new rules, that the club would be strictly non-political, and that no Member or Candidate for Parliament should be on the committee.

"I am not doing this for political purposes, and I do not want you to feel under any obligation to me. You ought to have a good club in Lynn. You can make one if you try, and I am staking £1,000 on the result."[289]

His smaller donations ranged across the constituency – to schools, churches, village halls, benevolent funds and youth organisations. He donated a specially bound new *Encyclopaedia Britannica* to the library at a cost of £25. The gifts totalled £5,000[290] and made significant differences to the recipients, enabling improvements and changes, and sometimes wiping out burdensome overdrafts and debts. Later in the year, he gave the ingredients to make a Christmas pudding to 24 poor widows in Terrington.

The newspaper was effusive in appreciation of his generosity and praise of the allocation of the gifts:

"Every gift aids a cause which will be universally regarded as a deserving and needy one; and every gift is bestowed entirely without consideration of political bias. The allocation of the gifts is admirable. It would be difficult for Lord Fermoy to spread his benefactions over a wider field, both urban and rural. Practically every person in Lord Fermoy's constituency derives benefit from his splendid act of generosity.

It behoves us all therefore to offer to him an expression of our personal gratitude. Moreover we do not think that acknowledgement should cease with mute appreciation. Lord Fermoy already holds the highest public

[288] July 7th, 1929.
[289] *Lynn News & County Press.* June 25th, 1929.
[290] About £1 million in today's money.

honour which the area can confer; but at any rate Lynn, as its urban centre, can add thereto its own most exalted mark of distinction – the conferring of the Freedom of this historic borough."[291]

I have no doubt that his philanthropy came from the heart. Just as his generosity to his old school came from love of his surrogate family which the school had become, so his warm heart embraced all his constituents and he was happy to share his large fortune with the town. I wonder if Maurice would have been as generous had he known of the disaster that was to hit the financial world four months later!

In August there were reports in New York[292] that Lord Fermoy was engaged to wed Mary Carter, the daughter of a clerk in holy orders. This report was denied the following day by his brother and sister who were in Newport. They knew nothing about the reported betrothal. Fermoy was not expected to visit the US that summer.

On Black Thursday, 24th October and Black Tuesday, 29th October, the New York stock market crashed. Share prices had soared to a great high in September with many transactions financed by unsecured loans. Signs that these loans were about to be called in led to nervous sell-off and share prices plummeted. This triggered a worldwide economic crisis known as the Great Depression. The repercussions hit nearly every country in Europe, where unemployment had been a major problem since the war. The next two years brought great hardship and misery to many people in England.

Fermoy's main theme in his speeches towards the end of 1929 was how to deal with unemployment. He deplored the fact that the Minister of Labour had seen fit to extend the dole to the younger people. He had grave fears that this would be very detrimental to the country and very demoralising to the young men and women. He thought that money should go in the form of providing work. Referring to the raising of school age to 15 years, he said that in an agricultural district like his, he was anxious to know what benefit it would be to boys of the age of 15. He thought it would mean great hardship to many families where boys who went to work at 14 made life just possible. Boys showing promise could go on to higher education.

What was needed was the improving of trade. No country was taxed as we were. What the socialists had brought forward during the last two or three weeks, would mean a heavy burden on industry. There was no wonder at the captains of industry being anxious about their factories.[293]

---

[291] In fact Maurice never received the freedom of the Borough. 35 years later, ten years after his death, it was his wife who received this great honour.

[292] *New York Times*. 23rd August 1929

[293] *Lynn News & County Press*. Nov. 26 1929

The Conservative Party at this time had a clearly defined policy supporting Free Trade. Following the party line, Maurice was against the imposition of a general tariff. He reported that the McKenna duties on luxury goods were an exception and had proved successful. Unemployment in the industries concerned decreased, the cost of articles went down and export trade went up.

The Empire could not supply all the commodities the country needed. Lancashire depended on America for seven-eighths of its cotton and Americans bought British goods. The imposition of tariffs would build a high wall and prevent that trade. Ninety per cent of steamers coming into the port of Lynn came from the Continent. A general tariff had not cured the problems of Germany, who had two million unemployed.[294]

In March 1930 Maurice left his Heacham home and moved to the nearby village of Sedgeford. He was presented with a silver salver signed by some 150 Heacham residents, as a token of their appreciation of his work for the village during his five years of residency. Mr Bartle, presiding, described Fermoy's role in the community.

> "We meet him tonight on more or less common ground – not only as a gentleman of social standing but as one whom we are all acquainted with as a friend and fellow resident. By his courtesy, kindly interest and advice he has been the friend of us all (applause) – not only in this parish but throughout North-West Norfolk…"

Lord Fermoy responding said he had had five of the happiest years of his life in the parish of Heacham. They were meeting that evening as a family gathering. He was extremely grateful for the beautiful silver salver. After speaking of the value of the Heacham fire brigade, he uncovered a table upon which was his gift to them of a set of firemen's helmets.[295] His Lordship added that he had no desire to leave the Shooting Lodge, but he hoped that his friends would not fail to brave the steep hill at Sedgeford if they desired his help. "May I say," he concluded, "that whatever my fate may be at any election, I have no intention of leaving Norfolk."

Fermoy rented Sedgeford Hall, an elegant property with a fine Queen Anne façade, which belonged to his friend Holcombe Ingelby, who had died two years earlier. Many large houses were available to let, their owners being badly hit by the depression.

Maurice's busy life continued unabated. 1930 was packed with functions in his constituency. In March, he opened the refurbished Lynn YMCA premises.

---

[294] *Lynn News & County Press.* January 29th 1930.
[295] When the fire brigade was first formed each man was issued with a cap, a belt and an axe. The brigade could not afford the cost of helmets which had been recently recommended.

His gift of a full-sized billiards table had been installed and the lighting improved. He applauded the main aim of the movement which was to provide recreation to get young men away from the streets. It had splendid principles, for it tolerated neither gambling nor the drinking of alcoholic liquors. He announced that he was going to make them a present of a five-valve wireless set.

On many occasions he presented a Fermoy cup – a silver trophy which he had donated personally. On a Saturday in April he opened a bowls club in Dersingham, presented a darts trophy in Snettisham, a bowling cup in Heacham, presented the Fermoy Billiards cup and medals at the Working Men's Club in Lynn followed by the presentation of the trophy to the Lynn and District Billiards League. He regularly attended whist drives and entered dance competitions which he sometimes won.

The late Basil Rix, then a small boy, remembers Lord Fermoy giving every pupil in the village school a green sweater as a Christmas present. On a cold day in May when the bathing pool was opened at Hunstanton he was heartily cheered when he took the plunge. He was best man at the wedding of two of his employees. He played in tennis tournaments at Hunstanton that summer.

At the Annual Conservative fête in July, the chairman of the Association, Captain Lance, described Lord Fermoy as the hardest worked MP in the district. He had been absolutely impartial in his attention to duty, and had become the best known, most respected and most loved man in the constituency. Fermoy in his reply pointed out that the Labour government had failed to keep their election manifesto promises. There was no mention in the King's speech of an attempt to reduce the working day of coal miners from eight to seven-and-a-half, or seven. They were not concerned with stabilisation of meat and cereal prices. There was anxiety in the colonies over the threat to abolish colonial preferences.

In October Maurice attended the annual horse-shoeing contest of the Lynn Branch of the Master Farriers and Blacksmiths. The following weekend, he led the members of the Lynn Cycling club in their run from the Lynn Post Office to Sedgeford Hall, where they were his guests at luncheon.

In the spring of 1931, he took the two Lynn football teams, the "Linnets", to Wembley to the cup final. He got seats for them and gave them tea afterwards at a Lyons Corner House and then visited the Palladium. In June, he took members of six different polling districts in his constituency to the Houses of Parliament, where he personally showed them round. In the afternoon he took them to the Zoo and provided them with tea. The day was considered to be enjoyable and instructive!

By June 1931, the government was in grave financial crisis. The unemployment figures in Britain had reached 2,725,000. They had almost doubled since the beginning of 1930. The Bank of England suffered huge losses trying to support sterling. Foreign investors lost confidence and withdrew gold. An American loan

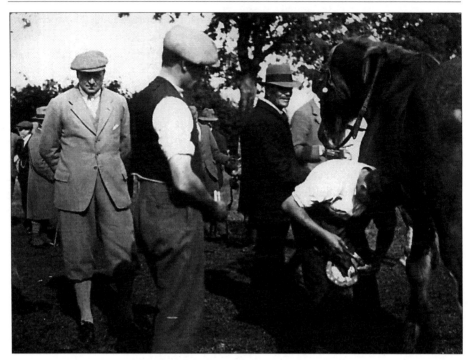

Horse-shoeing competition, October, 1930

of $76 million depended on the budget being balanced. Sweeping cuts in unemployment pay and public salaries were essential to make the necessary economies. The Labour Cabinet could not agree on these emergency measures to save the pound.

In August Ramsay MacDonald went to Buckingham Palace to hand in the government's resignation.[296] Party leaders had convinced the King of the need for a National government and consequently the King refused to accept Macdonald's resignation. After repeated attempts, he managed to persuade Macdonald that he was the only person who could lead the country through the crisis. Macdonald reluctantly agreed to withdraw his resignation and to remain as Prime Minister. The King had played a vital role in the formation of a National Government.

Baldwin, leader of the Conservatives, and Samuel, leader of the Liberals, agreed to serve under Macdonald, and were equally insistent that he should lead the National Government. Philip Snowden, Chancellor of the Exchequer, immediately implemented the emergency measures – a cut in public sector wages and a ten per cent cut in the dole. The Labour party expelled Macdonald and Snowden from the Labour party, for their betrayal of the party and of its principles.

[296] *Ramsay Macdonald.* p. 636.

30

Husband, Mayor and father

On August 25th, two days after the government resigned, Lord Fermoy's engagement was announced to Ruth Sylvia Gill, daughter of Colonel William Smith Gill and Mrs Gill of Bieldside, near Aberdeen in Scotland. She was a lovely young woman, 22 years-old, with golden hair, blue eyes and a delicate, fair complexion. She inherited her colouring from her father, unlike her two sisters who had brown eyes and dark hair and took after their mother, who was one eighth Armenian. Her father idolised her. Being fair-haired was an important part of my mother's identity and she never got over the shock of me, her first child being born with a head of dark hair! She reminded me of this every time my birthday came round!

At the age of 11, Ruth decided she wanted to be a concert pianist and after going to Crofton Grange, a boarding school in Hertfordshire, she continued her music studies in Paris. Maurice met his future wife there when visiting his mother and brother. Ruth had just completed a three-year music diploma course at the Ecole Normale where she studied the piano with Alfred Cortot, a great pianist and interpreter of Chopin. She was his favourite and one of his best pupils, and was destined for a career as a concert pianist.

Ruth was charismatic, she had great charm and was seductive. She once told me that she assumed that men would find her attractive. She had a soft, melodic voice and outwardly personified everything that was good and gentle and beautiful in life. She never raised her voice in anger. She could express her annoyance very effectively in an icy, tacit way! She spoke perfect French and had a lively mind. Everyone loved her.

She was ever ready to laugh and sometimes was overtaken by helpless giggles! Her own brand of humour was rather cruel and she was inclined to make fun of people's weaknesses or unfortunate features. She was affected by how a person looked, and once discarded a friend because she was too big! In spite of all her gifts, her self-esteem was not consistently high and when people were nice to her, she suspected they wanted something from her.

Before the arrival of his elder brother, Ruth was going out with Frank, who worked at the Guaranty Trust Company of New York in Paris and lived at 18 Place des Etats-Unis. Frank introduced her to Maurice who promptly asked her out. After their first meeting, Ruth wrote to her mother: "The dinner with Fermoy went very well but I shall always prefer Frank. He is so kind." However her affections soon transferred to the elder brother, leaving Frank heartbroken. He generously wrote to her on the eve of the wedding, saying how much he wished he was going to be in his brother's place, walking down the aisle with her, but he gave their marriage his blessing and wished her every happiness.

In the same letter he warned her that Maurice would panic as the day drew nigh. "We are both bags of nerves." Sure enough, shortly before the wedding Ruth had to write a robust letter to Maurice who was showing signs of having cold feet. She told him that it was normal to be nervous before taking such a big step, and her strong-mindedness succeeded in getting him up the aisle, where others had failed! He was 46, she was half his age.

Maurice's mother, too, had encouraged Maurice to marry. She wrote to Mr Salkin, the family lawyer, the following year:

"I urged and helped my son to bring off his marriage, for 'his age' weighed upon him, and the fact that Ruth was 22, and loved music and pretty dresses and Paris with a capital letter, disconcerted him. I pushed him unhesitatingly, over the brink. It is the greatest success."

Maurice's friend Dr Drury was delighted to hear the news of the engagement. He wrote from St Paul's School a week before the wedding, with a message for Miss Gill:

"September 11th 1931

My dear Maurice,
From time to time the newspapers have provided hints of your matrimonial tendencies, but this time the indications seem credible and cause your American friends to rejoice. This is just a note to carry our blessings and greetings from St Paul's to your bride and you with the hope that the message will arrive about the time of your wedding.

Won't you say to Miss Gill that you are one of the best beloved old boys at St. Paul's and that some of our most useful, permanent and pleasing things at the School have been inspired by your generous thoughtfulness. Surely you will bring her to America before long. Mind you lead her to Concord and stay with us at the Rectory.

In all these good wishes Mrs Drury most heartily joins.
Believe me, Always faithfully yours,

Sam"

The couple were married at the bride's home in Scotland, in the church of St Devenick, Bieldside, on September 17th 1931. Fanny, Maurice's formidable mother was there and so was his brother Frank. To her sister's disgust, Maurice's aunt Lucy did not come to the wedding. She wrote from St Moritz that she had a dislocated and broken toe, and was also mourning the death of a friend. She had just enough energy to stop off in Paris and grab a few hats before making for Cherbourg and home! Fanny was angry, too, that Lucy did not give the bride a wedding present. Lucy had intended to give Ruth an emerald ring. Ruth had given her the size of her finger, but the ring never appeared.

A boy friend of Ruth threatened to come to the wedding and shoot Maurice, and it was feared that one of his ex-girl friends would cause problems. Luckily everything went smoothly on the day. After a week's honeymoon at Gleneagles Hotel, the couple returned to Sedgeford Hall. The election was not far off and the bride was immediately caught up in campaigning.

Maurice and Ruth on their honeymoon at Gleneagles Hotel, Perthshire, Scotland

Less than a week after her marriage, the new Lady Fermoy made her first speech to the British Legion in Hunstanton, when she accompanied her husband on a visit. She then delighted the company by sitting at the piano and accompanying a number of war-time songs in which the members joined. The next engagement was an "at home" at Sedgeford Hall, to some sixty villagers. The following month Ruth demonstrated her accomplished skills as a pianist to a large audience, when she played some Schumann and a Brahms waltz, at a concert in the Theatre Royal, raising funds for a new wireless installation at the King's Lynn hospital. This was the first of many fund-raising concerts she was to give in West Norfolk.

Parliament was dissolved on October 7th. Fermoy campaigned as a National candidate for North West Norfolk. When he was adopted, he commented on the strange situation of the leaders of the three main parties being united in trying to rescue the country from the current very grave crisis. He paid tribute to Ramsay Macdonald who in forming the National Party, had put his country before his own Party. He also showed his specal concern for schoolteachers.

"This is not a party election. There is to be a National Government and its programme is to be the result of the points of view of the people of all parties and all classes. I appear here under Ramsay Macdonald, in the hope that he will form a government which will end the troubles with which we are faced. He asks the country for a free hand. I greatly deplore the wage cuts but there was no alternative. It was either that or insolvency. May I say to the schoolteachers and others that it will be one of my great aims to see that these reductions are removed when we are in a better position."

The Conservatives no longer believed in Free Trade and saw the imposition of a general tariff on imported goods as the way to save British industry. Fermoy now argued strongly in favour of Protectionism. Foreign countries using cheap labour produced more iron and steel than they required, and exported their surplus to Britain. This practice of "dumping" accounted for one million of the unemployed.

"Now let us take agriculture – the industry upon which we, in this part of the country, thrive. You have in your own parish, week by week, more and more men unemployed who should be at work on the land. Mr Baldwin has said that the cereal grower must have assistance in the form of a 'quota' system and a guaranteed price for wheat. The farm must be secured against dumping. If countries like America, France and Germany use the tariff system, I do not see why we should not do something for our own people... I hope we will be able to discourage the import of the things we ourselves can produce. It is the only solution to our difficulties."[297]

[297] *Lynn Advertiser*, Oct 16th 1931.

In conclusion he said he felt sure that the people of King's Lynn wanted the National Government to take things in hand, putting aside the prejudices of party politics.

Lady Fermoy also spoke at the adoption meeting, saying she felt it a great honour that her husband had been chosen as their candidate that day. "It is a great pleasure to find that the man I have chosen for a husband is so keenly loved in the division." (Applause).

In the General Election held on October 27th 1931, the National Government won 550 seats, and the non-MacDonald Labour Party held only 46. Maurice was re-elected MP with an increased majority.

The following month, Maurice was unanimously elected Mayor of King's Lynn and was installed in a colourful ceremony. Alderman Robert Taylor moved the resolution proposing Lord Fermoy to the mayoralty. He spoke of the grateful appreciation of the town that Lord Fermoy should be willing to take on the Mayoralty. Everyone knew about his work, his public and private benevolence, his support of everything of interest to that part of the country. The Mayoress with her graciousness and charm would be a great help to Lord Fermoy in carrying out his duties of office, and would undoubtedly add lustre to his year of Mayoralty.

Lord Fermoy in reply said he was very conscious of the honour which was his, to follow in the long line of Mayors of Lynn extending back seven hundred years. He thought that one who was both Member of Parliament and Mayor could do a great deal in helping the town's affairs by keeping contact with the House of Commons. "Lady Fermoy and I will do all we can to further your interests. We realise there are no party politics and we shall keep closely to that." Thereupon he drove to Sedgeford Hall and shocked his bride with the news that she was now the Mayoress of King's Lynn!

The opening of the new St James's School in Lynn was an important event in the educational life of the borough. The prevailing serious economic problems resonate in the words of the speakers. Dr Percival Sharp who performed the opening ceremony, said that education would have to bring home to the minds of boys and girls that there was lying before them necessarily a greater simplicity of life – a greater austerity of life.

"Education can and must preach the virtues of the simple life in view of the conditions under which we are now living."

Lord Fermoy moving a vote of thanks to Dr Sharp remarked that schoolteachers gained the admiration of all parties by the way in which they received and accepted the cuts in their salaries in the previous August. When the position of the country improved, all at Westminster would see that these cuts were rescinded.

In January the Lynn Town football club presented Lord and Lady Fermoy with a wedding gift:

As Mayor of King's Lynn, escorting HRH The Duke of Gloucester,
December 1931

"Mr O L Davison, the club's chairman, caused laughter, in which Lord and Lady Fermoy heartily joined, by saying they had been puzzled as to what form the gift should take, until a good friend of the club said the Mayor was using such a dilapidated bag on the golf links, that he was ashamed of it! Lord Fermoy expressed great pleasure at receiving the gift. He said his old bag matched his dilapidated play, and he hoped the use of such a handsome new one would improve his game." [298]

In February the Mayor presented the prizes at the Lynn and District Kennel Society at the Corn Exchange. The King's black labrador Sandringham Stop won Lady Fermoy's special prize for the best bitch in the show. The Lynn Mart, the annual fair, was opened on St Valentine's day with traditional pomp and pageantry.

"Lord Fermoy stepped forward as Mayors of Lynn have done for hundreds of years to read the charter by which King HenryVIII granted to the borough the right to hold a mart in perpetuity. Freak shows and performing lions are still there jostling with daring motor-cyclists on the Wall of Death. An

---

[298] *Lynn News & County Press.* January 26th 1932.

unusual visitor to the Mart this year is Princess Lena who is about twenty five inches in height, is fifty years old and is the King's smallest subject."[299]

Much thought was given in Lynn to helping the town's 1575 workless. Lord Fermoy, MP, Mayor of Lynn presided over a town meeting[300] held at the request of the unemployed's spokesmen, to discuss the problem. Speeches outlining the extent of the problem were followed by suggestions as to how it could be lessened. The distress fund opened by the Mayor for necessitous cases had not so far received any considerable support from the public.

His attitude at that meeting was subsequently praised in the local press.

"[The Mayor] displayed a much better spirit than that of sympathetic aloofness which has characterised religious and public organisations hitherto. The new and enlightened methods which Lord Fermoy favours to stimulate social work among unemployed men in the town are being widely adopted."[301]

Three months later and as a result of this meeting, the Mayor opened the Lynn Workers Club, the headquarters of the Lynn unemployed. They had formed themselves into the Craftsmens' Guild whose members had renovated and decorated the premises without pay. It was a non-political organisation with a thousand members who were prepared to do any sort of work, such as gardening, bricklaying, carpentry. It was work they wanted not charity.

Fermoy was called upon to open the first club of its kind in the United Kingdom. He said that even with all the skilled men they had among the unemployed, it was almost a miracle that they had been able to transform the old pickle factory into such a first rate club. Lady Fermoy expressed her pleasure that the unemployed had so fine a club to spend their leisure and hold their meetings. Their ladies would be pleased that their husbands had somewhere to go and be comfortable instead of wandering about the streets in all sorts of weather.[302]

After only nine months in her new home, Lady Fermoy was on the move again. In May 1932, Maurice gave up the lease on Sedgeford Hall and rented the Mill House, Dersingham. This house dated from the seventeenth century and once had a windmill, which was destroyed in the early twentieth century. The house had connections with Sandringham. In 1907 the then Prince of Wales bought it for one of his equerries who lived there until his death. The gardens were laid out by Mr Cook, the head gardener at Sandringham.

---

[299] *Lynn News & County Press* February 15th 1932.
[300] ibid. February 8th 1932.
[301] ibid. January 1932.
[302] ibid. May 10th 1932.

At the Lynn Mayor-making ceremony in November 1932, Fermoy, the outgoing Mayor, announced his intention not to stand for parliament at the next General Election. Replying to a vote of thanks for his services as past Mayor he said:

"In order that I may not give the impression that I was anxious to use this as a stepping stone, I may say that I do not propose to offer myself as a candidate at the next general election. I hope there will be better times and that the unemployed will drop below two millions. I see better prospects than I did twelve months ago."

The reasons for standing down as an MP were twofold. In the first place, he was now a happily married man with the hope of a family. He wanted to travel and spend time with his wife. Another factor was crippling taxation which meant he could not afford to run a second fully-staffed home in London. His total allowance as an MP was £400.

At the banquet two months later, the new Mayor, J W Raby, Labour, spoke of Fermoy's extraordinary generosity, and described him as "the greatest-hearted man he had ever met." Lord Fermoy was given an ovation on rising to reply. He considered himself ill-equipped for the post but had always been conscious of its great traditions. Lady Fermoy who was also well received spoke of her happy year of office, which coincided with the happy first year of her marriage.[303]

Some years later Alderman J W Raby wrote in an essay entitled: *A Giver of Great Beauty*:

"Lord Fermoy has done much for us as a generous and great-hearted man, but the greatest gift was when he brought home a beautiful Scottish girl as his bride. She is still the unaffected personality that we welcomed some years ago, and has retained that somewhat delicious shyness that adds to her charm."[304]

In September 1933 they rented Hillington Hall. Maurice never owned a house. He had a very large income but did not have access to his capital which was tied up in a trust.

The couple had a long wait before the arrival of their first child. Three years after their marriage I arrived! My parents went to the home of my maternal grandparents in Aberdeenshire, one month before I was due. The newspapers reported that "a blessed event was expected to Lord and Lady Fermoy in August."

---

[303] *Lynn News & County Press.* January 1933.
[304] *The Allotted Span in King's Lynn. 1979-1949.*

"Dalhebity, Bieldside, Aberdeenshire, Telephone; Cults 4
September 10th 1934

Dear Sam

I was very glad to get your nice letter. I'm glad to report that Ruth had a lovely daughter on August 19th. We are delighted with her. We have also been very much honoured by the Queen offering to be Godmother, a very great honour for the child. She is being christened in the crypt of the House of Commons on Monday, October first.

How I wish I could pay you a visit this autumn but it is almost a certainty that we shall be over before the New Year, and a visit to the school will be on the programme.

It has been a wonderful month in Scotland and we return to Norfolk the end of this month. Our address is Hillington Hall, King's Lynn, Norfolk. With kindest regards to you both, yours ever

Maurice."

When I was six weeks old, my parents returned to Norfolk, to Hillington Hall, bringing with them a Scottish nanny, Nanny Chisholm, to look after me and a young girl called Harriet Stewart as a housemaid. (Four years later, Maurice was best man at her wedding to Leonard Bush, a baker's roundsman.) When fifty members of the Lynn Cycling Club arrived at the Hall for tea and refreshments, having cycled one hundred miles on a Sunday in November, Maurice proudly showed off his baby daughter.

He had issued this invitation at a dinner a few days earlier, which he had attended in his capacity as president of the Cycling Club. There he paid tribute to the local sportsmen he had encountered in his ten years as MP. He was involved with twelve branches of sport in the area and had never seen an incident of bad sportsmanship. He had found that people engaged in sport of some kind were the nicest people to meet, because they learned to take defeat in the same spirit as victory. His interest in all kinds of sport had grown from his active participation in sport from boyhood. He had recently won the Parliamentary tennis "singles" competition, beating members twenty years his junior.

He was asked about the world tour he intended to make with Lady Fermoy, which was the reason he gave for standing down at the next election. He replied that he had indeed the intention of going to Australia and New Zealand one day, but had taken a house on the Royal Estate at Sandringham where he intended to live the rest of his life.[305]

---

[305] *Lynn News & County Press*. November 20th 1934.

31

Park House, Sandringham

Once more we were on the move! Sandringham House was bought by the Prince of Wales, the future Edward VII, in 1862, and has remained a royal residence ever since. Over the years, it has been visited by the Monarch for the shooting season, for partridges in the autumn and pheasants from Christmas until the third week in January. Queen Alexandra, who was the Queen Mother after the death of Edward VII, lived there until she died, on 20th November 1925. Only then did King George V move into Sandringham House. From the time of his marriage in 1892, he lived in York Cottage, a house on the Sandringham estate, which was only just large enough for his five children. The King loved Sandringham "more than any other place on earth." [306]

Park House, half a mile away, was built in 1863 as accommodation for the royal household. General Sir Dighton Probyn VC lived there from 1872. [307] Maurice rented Park House from George V and from subsequent monarchs for the next twenty years. He put in a hard tennis court where King George VI played with him on occasions. The house is surrounded by lawns and has some fine trees. It has a wood on the west side and the south-facing façade overlooks Sandringham Park and the village cricket pitch. My father offered a prize to any batsman who could break a window of Park House. Fortunately this was never won!

Park House is a long building built in carrstone, a local stone. It has seven bedrooms and extensive staff quarters. It divides into three sections. The first floor of the middle section was the nursery wing in our day, separated from the principal part of the house by a swing door. The main bedroom, where my mother slept, was south facing, overlooking the park. My father had a dressing room on the other side of the house. The third section comprised the staff quarters.

Maurice's family had connections with the royal family through his remarkable aunt, the Hon. Caroline Burke Roche, who was born in 1857 and died in London in 1940. Known as Nancy, she was the eldest daughter of the 1st Lord Fermoy. She was tall and good-looking and a fine horsewoman.

---

[306] *King George V.*
[307] He was Keeper of the Purse to the Prince and Princess of Wales as well as Secretary to the Prince of Wales. In 1910 he became Comptroller of the Household of the widowed Queen Alexandra.

Maurice and the Bentley outside Park House

Park House in winter

Above: Christening of Mary Burke Roche in the crypt of the House of Commons.
Left to right: Maurice, his mother, Jean Marcus (sister of Ruth), Ruth, Nanny Chisholm,
October 1934

Left: Ruth, Maurice and Mary,
September 1935

It is clear from her correspondence[308] that she played a full part in the social life centred on Dublin Castle during the time Prince Arthur, Duke of Connaught was in residence as Commander-in-Chief in Ireland from 1900-1904. He was the third and favourite son of Queen Victoria. Nancy became friends with Prince Arthur and the Duchess.

In 1904, in a letter to Nancy, Princess Luise, Duchess of Connaught wrote:

"Dear Miss Roche, I wonder if you will give us the pleasure of accepting the smallest of all the presents you will receive from us? It is such a trifle but if you do care to have it as a tiny souvenir of past days in Ireland where we often met it will give us great pleasure. Pray accept our very best and heartfelt good wishes for your future happiness.

Believe me, Yrs very sincerely, Luise Margaret."

The gift was a wedding present. At the age of 48, Caroline chose a husband who belonged to one of the grandest families in Europe. Count Fritz Hochberg was the brother of Hans Heinrich, XV Count Hochberg and Third Prince of Pless. The Counts of Hochberg ruled over vast estates of forest and mineral-rich land in Lower Silesia, and in the nineteenth century inherited the principality of Pless.

Fritz grew up in the magnificent Castle Furstenstein, one of the most splendid palaces in Europe. It had more than six hundred rooms and its doors were always open to the royal families of Europe – to Kings, Grand Dukes, Princes and Princesses. The approach to the castle was wide enough for four kings to drive up at the same time, without any one of them having precedence. There was stabling for two hundred thoroughbred horses and powdered footmen on duty day and night. The Prince of Wales was godfather to Fritz's nephew.

Fritz had grown up in a world of horses, shooting and stalking. He loved England and spent most of his time there. He and Nancy shared a passion for the hunting field and Irish wolfhounds. The two also had a love of gardens in common and shared a particular love of roses and wild grasses. He owned a house called Minstead Manor in the New Forest in Hampshire. An artist and landscape gardener he designed a famous garden in Japan.[309]

His sister-in-law Daisy, Princess of Pless was happy when the two married. She wrote:

---

[308] In the papers of Mrs Corbally Stourton, widow of the 5th Lord Fermoy.

[309] He wrote an account of his travels called *An Eastern voyage; a Journal of the travels of Count Fritz Hochberg through the British Empire in the East and Japan.* He illustrated it with his own watercolours.

"At the end of January 1905, my brother-in-law Fritz Hochberg married in London, Nancy Burke-Roche, daughter of Lord Fermoy. This event pleased us all because Nancy is a charming person. Fritz adored England and hunting and wanted to spend most of his time there; Nancy as befits one who comes of a famous hunting family, was a keen horseman and everything seemed propitious." [310]

The marriage was short lived. According to the family legend, Fritz was a homosexual.

Caroline had met the Duke of York before her marriage. He wrote thanking her for sending him 350 woodcock feathers, in a letter addressed to:

"The Honble. Caroline Roche, Emo House, Portarlington, Ireland

York House, St James's Palace, London S.W. Jan 24th 1900

Dear Miss Roche,
I thank you so much for sending me all those woodcock feathers, it is really most kind of you & I am afraid you must have a had a lot of trouble in collecting them. I have already got over 1,600 & your 350 makes it nearly 2,000.
    Thanking you again for all the trouble you have taken.
Believe me

Sincerely yours, George"

When Queen Victoria died in 1901, the Duke of York became the Prince of Wales. Caroline continued to meet the Prince and Princess of Wales at dinner parties and other social occasions after the end of her marriage to Fritz. Countess Hochberg was in a shooting party at Elveden, home of the Earl of Iveagh, when they were King and Queen.

Caroline was also a close friend of Princess Helena Victoria, a granddaughter of Queen Victoria. She and her sister lived at Schomberg House, a royal residence, until it was bombed in 1940.

Letter from Princess Helena Victoria, Schomberg House, Pall Mall SW1; April 4th 1917 to Countess Fritz Hochberg, Brown's Hotel, Dover Street.

Dearest Nancy, I am enclosing those beautiful words by Ruskin which I mentioned to you yesterday. Tho' written 60 years ago they are as if they had been written for the present moment. It was such a pleasure seeing you yesterday.   *Affectionately, Yours always Helena*

---

[310] The Private Diaries of Daisy, Princess of Pless

It is likely that Nancy introduced her nephew to her royal friends at Sandringham, when Maurice went to live in Norfolk. In any event, Maurice would have met King George V (as the Prince of Wales became in 1910) at shooting parties. The two men had a lot in common. The King was an exceptionally kind-hearted man, without prejudice of class, colour or race. He was unassuming and admired simplicity. He was honest and good; he liked to laugh and was a practical joker. Shooting was his great passion. I imagine the King felt an affinity with the newcomer to the county, who was such a fine shot, and was warm, and had a natural way of being. Ruth's charming and unaffected ways would also appeal to him. In granting Maurice the lease of Park House, he was clearly happy to have them as his near neighbours.

In late November 1928, the King, after a week's shooting at Sandringham, fell dangerously ill. He and the Queen returned to London. A feverish chill developed into septicaemia. He had two operations to drain abscesses in his lung. Maurice's first recorded invitation from King George V to shoot at Sandringham was for January 1930.[311] There were five guns that day – HM the King, Lord Fermoy, Sir Clive Wigram.[312] Col. Oliver Birkbeck, and Lord Claud Hamilton.[313]

On December 29th of the same year, the party consisted of eight guns: HM the King, HRH The Duke of York, HRH The Duke of Gloucester, Lord Fermoy, Major the Hon. Richard Molyneux, Sir Clive Wigram, Sir Harry Verney. They shot 1,529 pheasants, 67 partridges, 72 hares, 14 rabbits and 5 woodcock.

For the next six years until his death, George V invited Maurice to shoot every year, for one or two days in the autumn and two days or more after Christmas. On December 27th 1934, there were seven guns in the party: HM the King, HRH The Prince of Wales,[314] HRH The Duke of York,[315] HRH the Duke of Kent, the Earl of Athlone,[316] Lord Fermoy and Lord Alistair Innes-Kerr.[317] They shot 1,361 pheasants. Maurice was also invited to dine at Sandringham House, before his marriage and with his wife after his marriage. These occasions meant a great deal to him.

Maurice and Ruth spent Christmas 1934 in the States, leaving me behind, confident that I would be well looked after by Nanny Chisholm. Dr Drury was delighted at the prospect of seeing his friend Maurice and meeting his bride:

---

[311] From the private papers of the 6th Baron Fermoy.
[312] Private secretary to King George V. 1931-1936.
[313] Equerry to King.George V 1924-36.
[314] Edward VIII, who reigned for eleven months, from the death of his father King George V until his abdication.
[315] King George VI. 1936-1952.
[316] The King's brother-in-law, the younger brother of Queen Mary, born Prince Alexander of Teck.
[317] 2nd son of 7th Duke of Roxburghe, who married an American, Anne Breese.

Shooting with the King at Sandringham, 1934. Left to right: Sir Derek Kepple, Lord Fermoy, HM King George V, Duke of York, Lord Claud Hamilton.

"*The Rectory, St Paul's School, Concord, New Hampshire
December 28th, 1934*

My dear Maurice,
It is good news which your note of December 16th brings to the Rectory.

You must of course come to this house, feeling all the while quite free to visit about as you like. We can dine at the Upper, where you will see some of your friends, and others can come to the Rectory to meet Lady Fermoy.
I shall book a stateroom on the Sunday night train to New York, January 13th.
Believe me, with greetings to your wife, faithfully yours, Sam."

The King was seriously ill in 1935, the last year of his life, but went out shooting on October 11th with the Duke of Beaufort, the Earl of Sefton, the Earl of Harewood, Lord Fermoy, and members of the Royal Household. In the last two months of the King's life, Maurice was invited to shoot eight times at Sandringham, with the estate manager, Capt. William Fellowes, local farmers and landowners. In

December and in January 1936 the Dukes of Kent and Gloucester were in the party.

The King died on January 20th 1936. My sister Frances was born on the same day. The local papers reported that life and death brushed wings at Sandringham that day. George V had become a well-loved king and was enthusiastically cheered by the crowd at his Silver Jubilee celebrations. "I cannot understand it, after all I am only a very ordinary sort of fellow." Perhaps he enjoyed Maurice's company because they were both modest and assuming.

In March 1935, the Hon. Somerset Maxwell, at the age of 28, was adopted as National Conservative candidate for the King's Lynn division. Maurice's successor had some things in common with him. The heir to Lord Farnham, an Irish Baron, whose estates he managed, Somerset was strikingly good-looking, he had been head of his school at Harrow, a fine lawn tennis player and he was a keen sportsman. He owned a steeplechaser, Egremont. Maurice campaigned energetically on his behalf, accompanying him and Mrs Maxwell at the many meetings throughout the constituency, during the election campaign. Maxwell was elected with a majority of more than 5,000 votes, at the general election of November 1935.

Maurice was now free from his demanding life as an MP. In the early summer of 1936, he made plans to attend the tercentenary of Harvard University. He wrote to Dr Drury:

"14 Hyde Park Street, London W2
June 2nd 1936

Dear Sam,
I have taken my passage on the *Queen Mary* for September 2nd to attend the tercentary of Harvard University. I shall be on my own, Ruth remaining with the children. Of course I shall run up to SPS to see the old school. I know the boys will not be back, but it will be so handy from Boston. Very likely you will be at the big show in Cambridge, so we can return together. Anyway, I'm looking forward to it anxiously.

We are all well. A lovely new daughter[318] arrived the day the King died.

Kindest regards, Yours ever Maurice."

A few days after he wrote this letter his very good friend, Willard Scudder died. Maurice suggested a new building should be named "Scudder House" to commemorate his useful and devoted life to the school. I had a most comfortable

318   Frances Ruth Burke Roche.
319   From *Harvard Observed: An Illustrated history of the University in the twentieth century*. By John T Bethell. Harvard University Press, 1998.

stay there when I visited the school in 2005.

Harvard celebrated its Tercentenary[319] on a grand scale over the period of nearly a year, with concerts and conferences, plays and symposia. It culminated with three days of festivity in mid-September, which drew 10,000 alumni from all parts of the world, including Lord Fermoy. On the final day, an audience of 15,000 assembled in an outdoor, temporary theatre in pouring rain. John Masefield, the British Poet Laureate, read lines he had composed in celebration of John Harvard, a Puritan minister who left his library of books to a small college founded in 1636. Then outstanding scientists and scholars were awarded honorary degrees including the psychoanalyst Carl Jung, the French psychologist Jean Piaget, the Polish anthropologist Bronislaw Malinowski and the British astrophysicist, Sir Arthur Eddington.

President Franklin D Roosevelt, the most important speaker of the day, referred to his dual capacity as President of the United States and as "a son of Harvard who gladly returns to this spot where men have sought the truth for three hundred years".

Back in England, Maurice wrote to Dr Drury that he was delighted with his Harvard visit, where he had seen many of his classmates. He also spent five days in Newport, Rhode Island. He continued to keep in close touch with Dr Drury who regularly gave him news of the school. In June 1937, he wrote:

"The squash committee has now rendered its reckoning for 1936-37. You will be interested to know that from October through April, counting no evenings or Sunday afternoons, there was a total of 10,756 players. This will give you an idea of the immense and important usefulness of your squash courts in the daily life of your school.

Believe me, with much affection, ever yours, Sam"

In January 1937, Maurice was invited to an evening shoot on Wolferton Marshes with HM King George VI and two other guns. A fortnight later the shooting party consisted of the King, the Duke of Beaufort, Lord Fermoy, Sir Basil Brooke and two locals. He shot partridges with him at the end of October and pheasants with the King and the Dukes of Gloucester and Kent at the end of December, on a day when they shot 800 pheasants. The total for that week was 2,033.

This invitation from Sir Piers Legh, equerry to King George VI was typical:

*"Sandringham
Oct 28th 1938*

My dear Fermoy,
The King would be very pleased if you would shoot partridges with him on

Tuesday November 1st, provided you are disengaged. If you are able to come will you be here by 9.15am.

Yours ever, Piers Legh."

As well as the game bags from Sandringham, Maurice also kept the records of shoots from two other two large estates in West Norfolk – Houghton, the home of the Marquis of Cholmondeley and Holkham the home of the Earl of Leicester. He also shot regularly at Six Mile Bottom, the estate of Captain Cunningham Reid, and on many other estates of his friends in the neighbourhood.

I recently spoke with Doreen Fox, who was a Land Girl during the war. She and a friend were beating up the birds at a shoot at Houghton, when they heard a man calling for help. They found a gentleman trapped by barbed wire, his clothes caught between the top and the bottom row of the fence, unable to move in any direction. They unhooked the barbs from his tweed plus fours and set him free. He was very grateful for their assistance! Later they found out that they had rescued Lord Fermoy!

Every year since his marriage, Maurice rented a house in London from February/ March for three months. The address was different each year. In 1937, he wrote from 21 Montagu Square, W1, enthusiastically describing the Coronation of King George VI which he and Ruth attended:

June 25th 1937

Dear Sam,

I was very glad indeed to hear from you. I always read the Horae[320] with great care and see what is taking place in the School life. I was particularly interested in the Squash figures for the year. This must be the 21st year of their existence – if I reckon rightly.

Well it has been a truly wonderful year in London. I shall never forget the scene in the Abbey, where the King and Queen played their part too beautifully. I wish you could have seen my robes; the crowds from the Dominions, America, have packed the hotels, restaurants etc.

I'm afraid I won't get over to America this summer. What troubles you are having with Labour. I must say that I blame Roosevelt[321] for allowing this revolution, in the form of sit-down strikes, wholly illegal. He must be a radical of the worst order.

Do let us know if you are coming abroad.

All well, kindest regards, your ever, Maurice

---

320 The school magazine.
321 In 1937 President Franklin D. Roosevelt, acting on bad advice, slashed public spending which caused the "Roosevelt Depression" with two million unemployed.

On March 20th 1939, Ruth gave birth to a son and heir for Maurice. Edmund James Burke Roche was born at home, at 10 Charles Street, London W1. He weighed nearly 10lb. My sister and I spent the day with our aunt Jean. A month later, we all went back to Park House.

32

Maurice and World War Two

Five days before Edmund's birth, German troops had occupied Czechoslovakia. Six months later, on September 1st, Germany invaded Poland and on September 3rd, 1939, Britain declared war on Germany. The country prepared for a German invasion. On the day war was declared, Parliament passed the National Services (Armed Forces) Act whereby all men aged between 18 and 40 became legally liable for conscription.

The war changed life at Park House. Mawby the butler and Cyril the footman were called up. In order to prevent targets for bombers, no chink of light could show after dark. Blackout blinds and curtains were closely drawn at the windows. Every member of the household had a gas mask, as protection against gas bombs dropped from the air. Maurice and Ruth were engaged in civil defence work, Ruth with the WVS and Maurice with the Home Guard.

The expected invasions did not happen and outwardly there was very little military activity on land in the period between September 1939 and the spring of 1940. This came to be known as the Phoney War. The same was not true at sea, where there were some serious losses. Seven hours after war was declared, SS *Athenia*, a British passenger liner bound for Canada, carrying 1,100 passengers, many of them women and children fleeing from the war, was torpedoed by a German U-boat. Hitler had expressly forbidden the sinking of passenger vessels, but the German commander mistook the *Athenia* for an armed merchant cruiser. On 14th October 1939, the Royal Navy battleship HMS *Royal Oak* was torpedoed in Scapa Flow by a German submarine, with the loss of 833 lives.

Maurice tried to join up but his efforts were in vain, as at 54 he was considered too old for military service. His compensation was an exceptional shooting season that winter. In November, he shot with the King and bagged 600 partridges over two days. On 27th December, the party was: the King, Michael and David Bowes-Lyon,[322] Lord Fermoy, Sir Richard Molyneux, Commander Harold Campbell[323] and Capt. Fellowes. The seven guns shot 931 pheasants, with a total bag of 1,133. With the younger men having joined up, Maurice was invited to shoot at Sandringham eight times in January 1940, four times with the King and members

---

[322] Brothers of Queen Elizabeth, brothers-in-law of the King.
[323] Equerry to George VI from 1936-1952.

of the Royal Household and four times with local friends and farmers.

In February 1940 he at last succeeded in getting a job with the YMCA in France. A week before he left, the Lynn British Legion arranged a "farewell" social to wish him God speed. The chairman proposed his health and spoke of the debt of gratitude to their president, without whom there would have been no British Legion Club in King's Lynn. "When he goes to France he will take with him the good wishes of us all." Fermoy responded: "It is very sad that at 55 a man is considered too old for the Army. But I have got this job and I feel honoured that out of so many applicants I obtained the post."

Maurice in YMCA uniform on the eve of his departure for France, 1940. Mary on Starlight.

The job involved organising mobile canteens to supply the British Expeditionary Force (BEF) with refreshments, cigarettes etc. from mobile canteens. The centres were within thirty miles of the Belgian border, about three hundred miles north of the area where Maurice had operated in World War I. He served three days a week at a centre and three days in charge of a mobile van. His ability to speak French increased the value of his services to the YMCA.

The BEF, commanded by General the Lord Gort, was sent to France in 1939. By May 1940 it consisted of ten infantry divisions, one tank brigade, and an RAF element of about five hundred fighters and light bombers. It was stationed alongside the French army, on the Franco-Belgian border, north of the Maginot Line. This was a four hundred-mile line of concrete fortifications, stretching from Switzerland to the Belgian border, along the borders of Germany and Luxembourg. It did not cover the Ardennes Forest which the French believed was impregnable to a German attack.

The Maginot Line was constructed to avoid a surprise assault by Germany in the event of a future war, so as to avoid the horrific French losses in World War I. It was conceived in the light of experience of that war, mistakenly as it turned out. "(The French) fell into the age-old trap of planning to fight the next war on the basis of the last one."[324]

In the early dawn of 10th May 1940, some eight months after the declaration of war, German forces (disregarding the neutrality of Holland and Belgium), swept across the frontiers of Holland, Belgium and Luxembourg. The speed and ease with which the Germans overran the Low Countries astonished the world. Even though millions of French troops were manning the defensive Maginot Line, Hitler's brilliant *blitzkrieg*[325] strategy caught the Allies by surprise.

Two days later, Hitler ordered the German army to invade France. Twelve hundred tanks broke through the Ardennes Forest, which the French had considered to be impassable. Once in France they wheeled north towards the Channel, trapping the Allies in a pocket with their backs to the sea. Fortunately Hitler called a temporary halt, which allowed the British to start evacuating troops from Dunkirk. After sustaining heavy losses, 340,000 men, one third of which were French and Belgian troops, were evacuated during one week. All their tanks, guns, ammunition and stores were left in France.

On the very day of Hitler's *blitzkrieg*, Maurice was in Calais on his way home. The news that the Germans had advanced into the districts in which he had been operating astonished and appalled him:

"It does not seem possible that such a thing could have happened. It all seemed so peaceful. It was like being in the Norfolk countryside. When I left the district, everyone was saying there would be no war on the western front. We had centres at places like Lille, Arras and Douai and I am wondering how many of those YMCA people were able to get away from there in time.

I was in Calais on May 10th on my way home when the town was bombed. About 4.15am I was startled to hear three tremendous thuds. I knew from my experience of the last war that they were bombs. Later I heard anti-aircraft fire and two bombers flew very low over the town. Bombs

---

[324] *Dunkirk: Retreat to Victory.* p. 10.
[325] *Blitzkrieg*, 'lightning war', involved bombardment by air followed up by a land attack.

fell in the poorer districts of Calais. The bombs were not large and made craters about three feet deep. We were told that the Germans had invaded Holland and Belgium. Boats were stopped. I returned to my area and there I heard there was a boat from Le Havre. I reached here on May 15th."

Maurice gave this interview to the *Lynn Advertiser* when he came home on leave after two months in France. He had been recalled on the recommendation of a British General for a commission in the Auxiliary Military Pioneer Corps.[326] He hoped to return to France in that capacity very soon.

He went on to speak about his life with the YMCA. When he first arrived, there was a great deal of organising to be done and his days were spent interviewing French public officials and owners of premises which were taken over to become canteens. One of the buildings which they took over was a bank, where the staff had been evacuated because of its proximity to the fighting zone. "We took it over just as it was," said Lord Fermoy:

"We served tea over the same counters. Even the steel grills were still in place. We had sixteen cars operating in my area, and I found the work very interesting. Young men in the Army and the Air Force who knew me, kept dropping in to see me. I was struck by the splendid physique and fine spirit of our young men. All of them I talked to seemed determined that the job of ending the Hitler menace would be done."

He described a typical day with a mobile canteen:

"They are beautiful modern vehicles very suitable for the purpose. It was almost a travelling, general shop. Everything was neatly arranged in racks, and a flap at the side lifted up to open the shop. We sold combs, hair lotions, soap, shoe laces, chocolate, biscuits, cigarettes, and a host of other useful oddments. We started from the centre with a full urn of tea. As soon as we drew up in the first village, the troops would come rushing out of their billets to buy cigarettes, tea, and other things they needed. After about a quarter of an hour's brisk business, we would be on our way to the next village.

There were two men in charge of each mobile unit, and the duty of one of them was to pump up the Primus stove and get water boiling for the next village. The washing-up had to be rushed in, whenever we had a moment. It was hard work and very tiring but we enjoyed it. I was delighted at the good manners of our troops. They were very polite. Their discipline and their cleanliness were wonderful."

[326] The AMPC constituted a military labour force, performing light engineering tasks, the handling of stores, laying prefabricated track on the beaches, stretcher bearing.

Other newspapers reported that he personally served tea and cakes to the troops, wearing an apron with his shirt sleeves rolled up. Every morning he got to work with a broom sweeping the floor of the canteen. He also peeled potatoes and washed up.

As the Germans advanced northward through France heading for the coast, the area around the town of Arras was reinforced with BEF troops. By 20th May, Arras was partially encircled by the enemy. General Gort decided on a counter-attack, codenamed Frankforce. Frankforce took around four hundred German prisoners and inflicted a similar number of casualties, as well as destroying a number of tanks. The British were heavily outnumbered but their fierce attack against Rommel's 7th Panzer may account for Hitler's order to halt for two days. This temporary halt provided the breathing space for the evacuation of Dunkirk. The counter attack was eventually repulsed. Lille fell to the Germans on 29th May.

The night after Maurice left his billet in the Arras area, it was bombed and twenty people were killed. Maurice had been lucky to get out alive and without being captured by the Germans.

By 14th June, the mighty German armies were already at the doorsteps of Paris. And on 22nd June, just six weeks after the invasion, Marshal Pétain, on behalf of France, signed the armistice with the jubilant Germans. When war broke out, Maurice's brother Frank remained in Paris and in October 1939, opened a Paris branch of the Lafayette Fund. The object of the fund was the same as in 1917 – to provide comfort kits for French soldiers. As a major benefactor for many years, Frank was deeply hurt when St Paul's School refused to give their support to his cause. He accepted the apology of Dr Nash, the Rector (Dr Drury's successor) but informed him:

"Having spent seventeen of by far the happiest years of my life in France, during the continuation of this terrible war, all my spare funds will go to helping alleviate the suffering and misery of the French nation."

A few days prior to the German army invasion of Paris on June 14th, the officers and members of the staff of the Lafayette Fund moved to Vichy in unoccupied France. Vichy became the centre of the French government after the surrender of France to Germany on June 22nd, when two-thirds of the country was occupied.

When war broke out in Europe, the neutrality laws passed in the 1930s and the spirit of isolationism in America, prevented Roosevelt from giving aid to Britain. Gradually the mood changed. "Hitler's brutality and recklessness were bringing about a great change in American opinion."[327] When the countries of Western Europe fell, and England was threatened in 1940, Roosevelt sent guns and ships to Great Britain without actual military involvement. Finally the attack on Pearl

---

[327] *The Penguin History of the USA.*

Harbour in December 1941 enabled Roosevelt to bring a united nation into the Second World War.

When Maurice came back from France, he was engaged in civil defence work. He also continued to work for the YMCA, taking a mobile canteen to airbases in Norfolk, sometimes accompanied by Ruth.

In the summer of 1941, Maurice had two operations for a fistula.[328] I remember him being in a lot of a pain and sitting on an air cushion for some weeks. In the autumn he joined the Royal Air Force Volunteer Reserve, initially with a commission as Pilot Officer. After a year he was promoted to Flying Officer. His duties were entirely earthbound. He worked alternately in administration and as a clay pigeon shooting instructor, based at Felixstowe and near Brighton. Firing at clays greatly improved marksmanship.

In June 1943, Maurice was appointed personal adviser to Air Marshal Sir William Lawrie Welsh, who was on a special mission to Washington. The Western Allies were under the supreme military command of the Combined Chiefs of Staff. Most of their meetings were held in America, so the British Joint Staff Mission was set up. High-ranking officials from each of the British armed forces would stay in Washington for a period of time. Maurice was chosen for the job because of his intimate knowledge of America and his social contacts there. According to a newspaper report, Maurice estimated he had three thousand friends in the States.

Maurice, promoted to the rank of Flight Lieutenant for the duration of this mission, went to the States by ship and stayed for two months. While he was there, he was given leave to see his family. The visit to his mother was a very sad one, as she had suffered a severe stroke in 1942, which deprived her of her powers of speech. He was happily reunited with Frank in New York, and visited his sister Cynthia and her husband in Newport. While he was in Newport, he addressed the Army and Navy YMCA, telling them what British women were doing to help win the war. He also visited a convent in Washington, invited by the Mother Superior, where the Sisters showed remarkable curiosity as to what women in Britain were doing in the war effort.

On the way back, he sailed on the *Queen Elizabeth* and was thrilled to find himself travelling with fifteen thousand American troops. On his return, he reported that he had travelled over a thousand miles, visiting centres of war production and being amazed at what he saw being produced. He had been most warmly received as a Britisher. He thought that nothing would be able to stand up to the overwhelming fire power and man power the country was mustering. While he was in the States, he had the pleasure of eating the first bananas he had tasted for more than three years!

From 1942 onwards, the United States Army Air Force had begun to arrive

---

[328] An unnatural, narrow channel in the area of the lower bowel which heals with difficulty.

Maurice serving tea from a YMCA mobile canteen to RAF bomber crews at a remote Coastal Command station in Norfolk, 1940

The twin brothers are reunited in New York in 1943. Food rationing in England shows in Maurice's leaner face!

in England. No less than 14 airfields in Norfolk were made available to them. Norfolk was geographically the closest place in England to Germany. With aircraft range being limited in those days, this proximity was a vital consideration and made the area the obvious choice for launching points for bombers heading for Germany. Flying Fortresses flying in formation bound for bombing raids were a familiar sight. I remember hearing distant bombing or shooting during the night and being frightened. I was told they were just practising but this did not take away my fear!

The American airfield nearest to King's Lynn was RAF Wendling, where 392d Bombardment Group (Heavy) 8th Air Force arrived from New Mexico in July 1943. My father quickly became friends with Colonel Irvine Rendle, their Commander-in-Chief, who used to visit us at Park House.

RAF Wendling, August 1944. The christening of the "Birdie Schmidt". Left to right: Birdie Schmidt, Frances, Mary. Maurice and Lt. Col. Lorin Johnson.

There was a special occasion in August 1944 when my father took my sister Frances and I to Wendling for the christening of a Liberator.[329] She was named Birdie Schmidt ARC, after the programme director of the American Red Cross Aeroclub at Wendling. The Aeroclub served tea, coffee and snacks to personnel,

---

[329] The B-24 Liberators were faster than the B-17 Flying Fortresses and could fly further without refuelling

390

taking refreshments to crews returning from their bombing missions before they were de-briefed. They also arranged recreational activities. Birdie, whose image was painted on the side of the bomber, christened the aircraft it, smashing a bottle of coke over the nose gun as she named the plane.[330] A dinner followed that evening to which Frances and I, aged 10 and 8 , were invited. I can still recall my first taste of Coca Cola that evening!

Many foods were unknown to us children during the war. The government could not import enough food and clothes by ships, because of the presence of enemy submarines at sea. Rationing was introduced in January 1940. Each person was allowed a specific amount of the basic foods such as meat, bacon, tea, eggs, cheese, sweets and sugar. There was a complete ban on the making or selling of iced cakes. There were no bananas. Very occasionally we had homemade ice cream, made in a churn which was full of ice and turned by hand.

Our hot-water boiler was fuelled by coke and because coke was rationed, hot water was in scarce supply. Nanny boiled up a kettle of water and added it to a few inches of cold water when we had our daily baths. There was no central heating and getting out of bed in the morning to get dressed was a painfully chilly experience! Later the fire in the nursery was lit but the room temperature remained low. Downstairs there was a log fire in the drawing room.

Clothes rationing on points began in June 1941. There were points for furniture but only if you were newly married, or had been bombed out, or were having a baby. Petrol was rationed so people stopped buying cars. My parents only drove the beautiful, silver-grey Bentley for the annual visit to my Scottish grandparents in Aberdeenshire. The petrol ration was saved up to buy enough petrol for the return trip, twenty five gallons each way. Instead they drove a small Fiat, which my father used to describe as "a rattling good car!" My father always stopped to give pedestrians a lift in his car, which was often very welcome in a rural area at this time. He travelled by bus whenever possible, invariably talking to passengers.

Both my parents rode an autocycle. This had the proportions of a bicycle and had a 98cc engine powerful enough to ensure that pedalling was rarely necessary. It was the forerunner of the moped. It did 120 miles to the gallon. We three children had our ponies and very often rode around the estate at Sandringham, with our governess on her bike. We were too far away to go to pony club meetings or to hunt. Some days (good days as far as I was concerned!) we rode our bikes instead of our ponies.

Living in the country, we were fortunate as far as food supplies were concerned. We had a cow called Nelly who supplied us with milk until the dreadful day when her milk was pink. This caused great alarm and was regarded as a more serious condition than it probably was. Sadly Nelly was put down. We also kept a pig that

---

[330] *The Way It Was: Reminiscences About the American Red Cross Aeroclub at Wendling,* by Birdie Schmidt Larrick

was fed on vegetable peelings and scraps of food. Our hens supplied us with plenty of eggs. We ate a lot of rabbit, pigeons and pheasants in season shot by my father. He derived great satisfaction from combining his favourite sport with feeding his cherished family. There was an exciting moment every month or so when a CARE parcel arrived from the United States from his sister Cynthia. These included tins of butter, ham, cheese, egg and banana powder and bars of Hershey chocolate.

As part of our war effort, the lawn in front of our house was ploughed up and sown with buckwheat. We knitted khaki scarves, balaclavas, socks and dishcloths for soldiers. We had a dugout air raid shelter in the garden, which we never had to use, although a stray bomb was dropped on Sandringham Park, 400 yards away from Park House. My parents put new potatoes in tins filled with sand and put them underground in the shelter. They also preserved eggs by soaking them in a pail full of waterglass.[331]

Before the war, the staff at Park House comprised a butler, a footman, a cook, a scullery maid, a head housemaid, an under housemaid, a personal maid for my mother, a nanny, a nursery maid, two gardeners and a chauffeur. When war broke out and the men joined up, the staff was reduced to a cook (Miss Crisp), a parlour maid (Joan Steer), a housemaid, (Maudie Bullock, Miss Crisp's sister) a gardener and a nanny. We had our meals in the nursery until my brother Edmund was four years old, when Nanny, who had been suffering from cancer for a long time, left and died soon after.

After she left, we had a series of governesses and ate in the dining room. Meals were often tense affairs, with my father bolting his food as if he was half-starved and my sister staring gloomily at her greens which she had to eat up! This could cause a long, silent delay! Attractive women guests caused different problems. My father was much affected by fair complexions and well-manicured hands. He stared unabashed at pretty faces and hands, while my mother at the other end of the table pursed her lips and emitted tacit disapproval! She was more put out by the staring, which was bad manners, than by his interest in the lady in question.

[331] Sodium silicate. Households owning fewer than twenty hens were allowed to keep all the eggs they produced. Any surplus could then be preserved.

33

Back to Parliament

In January 1943 the tragic news was received of the death of Col. The Hon. Somerset Maxwell MP. He died in Libya where he was in some of the thickest fighting, in an armoured division. He was wounded in both knees when he was machine-gunned from the air. After three operations general septicaemia set in.

His wife Susan had been very active in the constituency while her husband was away on combatant duties. She was politically astute and influential friends encouraged her to stand in the by-election that followed Somerset's death. She was not open to this proposal, but publicly pledged her active support to Maurice when he was adopted prospective candidate. She volunteered to accompany him to meetings, just as he had done during her husband's election campaign.

Maurice was elected to Parliament with a majority of 1,669, some four thousand votes fewer than the previous Conservative majority. It was one of few by-elections at the time which had not been won by an Independent. Maurice expressed himself as overcome with joy at the result. After giving the credit for the result to Mr Ramm, his agent, and to the party workers, he described Mrs Maxwell as having been a tower of strength.

When Lord Fermoy MP spoke in the House of Commons in April 1944, he said he had some ideas of his own for new taxes, suggesting they could be raised on daily papers. A penny tax would raise between £10 and £20 million annually. He thought telegram charges were too low. The public were asked to send fewer telegrams and paying more would be a deterrent.

The King's Lynn press viewed the idea of a tax on newspapers in a favourable light, assuming that Lord Fermoy regarded reading newspapers as an essential pleasure and therefore it could be said that taxation was justified!

During the next two years, he asked questions on a variety of subjects related to the health, needs and safety of his constituents. He asked the Minister of Health whether, having regard to the spread of venereal diseases with their consequent menace to the nation, he would now introduce legislation to make the diseases compulsorily notifiable. Mr Ernest Brown replied that he was not at present satisfied that the result of making venereal diseases notifiable would be to help the control of the disease. He would keep the matter under consideration.[332]

---

[332] Hansard. Vol 392 1942-43 Sept-Oct. p. 411.

Parliamentary Bye-Election

FRIDAY, 12th FEBRUARY, 1943

With the Compliments of

Photo:—Bertram Park, Piccadilly, W.1.

FLYING OFFICER

LORD FERMOY

The National Government Candidate

On another occasion, he asked the Parliamentary Secretary to the Ministry of War Transport whether, in view of the large number of fires caused by railway engines that summer, he would see that all railway companies placed tin hoods over the stacks, as was done in America with such good results. Mr Noel-Baker replied that the height of railway-over bridges and tunnels made it impracticable to fit locomotives with the type of tin hood which was fitted in the United States. In addition, because of the British load gauge, devices used abroad were not suitable, as they would reduce the steaming capacity of the engines. However, he assured Fermoy that the railway companies were taking all practicable measures to reduce the risk to crops caused by sparks from locomotives.[333]

Maurice expressed a grievance of Norfolk labourers when he asked the Chancellor of the Exchequer whether he was aware of the discontent evinced among them, owing to the fact that Irish farm labourers did not have income tax deducted under the pay-as-you-earn scheme, until they had worked in a position for a period of six months. By returning home after six months and coming back to this country after a short period, they were able to avoid payment of tax. What steps was he taking to remove this grievance?[334] Sir John Anderson explained that citizens of Eire temporarily resident in this country were left to be taxed by the government of Eire. If a labourer from Eire spent less than six months here, he was not a resident – he was not liable to tax.

On a question of national security, Fermoy asked if the Minister of Information was aware that broadcasts were being made to Ireland from Germany in the Irish language. Brendan Bracken replied that he was well aware that broadcasts in Irish were made from Germany to Ireland but he thought Dr Goebbels did not realise that the majority of people in Ireland understood English.[335]

Maurice was sympathetic to the needs of mothers. He asked the President of the Board of Trade if expectant mothers could have a higher number of clothing coupons in the case of a first baby, in view of the considerably greater strain on resources in the case of a first baby than is experienced with additional children. The Parliamentary Secretary to the Board of Trade answered that he was glad to say that the coupon rate for babies' napkins had recently been reduced. This should be a great help to mothers with their first baby.[336]

Ruth was a wonderful wife. During all the years Maurice was an MP she gave him her total support. From the day she arrived in Norfolk, she met all the demands made on an MP's wife. During the war she worked for the Women's Voluntary Service and served a Voluntary Auxiliary Detachment. She was president of the St John's Ambulance Brigade and wearing her uniform, received Lady Albermarle in 1944 and Lady Louis Mountbatten in August 1945, when they came to

[333]   Hansard Vol. 392 1942-43 Sept- Oct. p. 1244.
[334]   ibid. p. 1244.
[335]   Hansard Vol 396 1944 Jan-Feb p. 1257.
[336]   ibid. p. 1266.

inspect the West Norfolk and King's Lynn Nursing Corps. She wrote to her husband every day he was away from home during the war. She never enjoyed the visits to the States but endured them with good grace, especially when there was a piano available!

In 1943, Maurice tried to get a commission for Ruth's brother Davy. He wrote to Ruth Gill, his mother-in-law, the day after he and Ruth had dined with the King and the Queen.

"Park House

Dear Mummy,
Thank you for your letter received this past week, and I'm so glad the port has given pleasure.

Last night we dined with the King and the Queen. Just ourselves and Tony Crean and the sub-agent. Ruthie looked lovely in black and we laughed a great deal. They are giving a cocktail party this evening and to my great surprise, they are coming to us on Sunday – even the Princess. Elizabeth looked sweet last night. She is so grown up. The King was in excellent form too.

I've been trying to get Davy a commission with Col. Stevenson at Brighton. It may be impossible, but he wants Davy's age and service details. Don't raise his hopes, but it is worth trying. Tell Davy to send them to me at Brighton..."

During 1944-45, London suffered terrible damage from the flying bombs. These were dropped by unmanned small aircraft which came to be known as doodlebugs. The blast did great damage. People were crushed from falling masonry or were buried under their collapsed homes. Speaking in the Fens at Emneth Hospital one Sunday in July 1944, Maurice referred to these weapons of terror and destruction. He said that people in that part of the country were lucky they were not in range of the flying bombs. He spoke in praise of Civil Defence whom he had witnessed rescuing families from the debris of their shattered homes in London.

Towards the end of the war, Maurice often showed parties of American soldiers round the House of Commons. Staff Sgt. William Byrnes wrote home:

"Through the Red Cross we got a pass to go to the House of Commons. Our host was Lord Fermoy. He himself took six of us, all American, on a tour of the place – several hours. He was exceptionally friendly and hospitable. I can't get over him spending so much time with us. He knew the former king and also the present one quite well. Also says he was a guest of Teddy Roosevelt in the White House. He was typically American – everyone around the parliament was calling him 'My Lord' but he said we should call him Maurice.

Bob."

The war was almost over when the President of the United States, Franklin Delano Roosevelt, died of a cerebral haemorrhage on April 12th, 1945. Maurice mourned his death and told his constituents he would attend his memorial service in St Paul's Cathedral.

Less than a month later, on May 8th, 1945, Winston Churchill announced on the radio to the world that the war with Germany was over. He then went to inform Parliament. Maurice reported that MPs got to their feet and cheered the Prime Minister in the House of Commons, when he gave the wonderful news. In King's Lynn, there was great rejoicing – dancing in the streets, parties, bonfires were lit. There was a service of thanksgiving in St Margaret's Church.

A general election was anticipated in the near future. Maurice had earlier announced his intention not to stand again for election. He now actively campaigned for Donald McCullough, the prospective conservative candidate. McCullough was a household name as Chairman of the Brains Trust, a very popular radio programme. His Labour opponent was Major F Wise. I remember the latter's slogan; "Vote for Wise because he's wise!" Voting took place on July 5th but the ballot boxes were sealed to await returns of voting papers from the Service men and women abroad. The full count took place three weeks later.

After 21 years, the Conservative reign in King's Lynn came to an end when Wise defeated McCullough by a large majority. This loss was repeated throughout the country. Churchill had gone to bed confident that he would win the election. He woke just before dawn. "I woke suddenly with a sharp stab of almost physical pain. A hitherto subconscious conviction that we were beaten broke forth and dominated my mind."[337] As the results came in, his premonition proved to be correct. In spite of Churchill's leadership of the nation to victory, he suffered a crushing defeat. The country had turned against the hero of the war. Labour won 400 seats, the Conservatives 210.

A month later, the atomic bomb was dropped on Hiroshima and the war with Japan was over. On August 24th, the country celebrated VJ day with the same spirit of jubilation as on VE day three months earlier.

[337] *Second World War* p. 583.

34

Post-War at Park House

After the war was over, Ruth wanted to give the people of King's Lynn a chance of hearing live the great musicians of the day. In conjunction with the Arts Council of Great Britain, she organised a series of lunchtime concerts in the Town Hall. The series opened with a recital by the pianist Louis Kentner. It was attended by Queen Elizabeth and Princess Elizabeth. The cost of the series of six concerts was 25 shillings (£1.25 in today's money). The musicians gave a second concert for school children, in the afternoon.

The concerts were very popular and continued for the next nine years. The performers stayed one or two nights at Park House and, over the years, I remember meeting the pianists Dinu Lipatti,[338] Moura Lympany, Denis Mathews, Jan Smeterlin, Myra Hess, Benno Moiseiwitsch; the singers Kathleen Ferrier,[339] Heddle Nash, Astra Desmond; the great French violinist Ginette Neveu; the oboe player Leon Goosens; the viola player Lionel Tertis, to mention but a few of the great musicians who performed in King's Lynn at the lunchtime concerts.

Although no longer the Member of Parliament, Maurice continued his public life in the King's Lynn area. He was president of the RSPCA and the Lynn Horticultural Society; he was patron of the British Legion. In May 1946 he was elected Chairman of the Lynn Divisional Conservative Association. Ruth was Chairman of the Women's Conservative Association.

The presentation of trophies to the Lynn Darts and Dominoes League was an annual affair for Maurice. There were 21 clubs and a total of a hundred teams in Lynn and District. Winning trophies and cups was important and they were much coveted. Every year, he opened the bowls at the bowling club at Walpole St Andrew, often winning the competition. In giving prizes for bowling at an annual dinner, he said he was tired of seeing the same old friends winning cups and announced that he would be giving a cup for those who had never been a winner, whom he called "rabbits!"[340]

---

[338] Dinu Lipatti, a Romanian, died in 1950 at the age of 33 of Hodgkin's disease. He was one of the greatest pianists of the twentieth century.

[339] Kathleen Ferrier died of breast and bone cancer aged 41, in 1953.

[340] *Lynn News & Advertiser*. November 9th, 1951.

Rationing continued after the war and became even stricter. In July 1946, acute wheat shortages forced the government to introduce a most unpopular measure. Bread was rationed to avoid bread queues and semi-starvation. The exceptionally severe winter of 1946-7 led to the rationing of potatoes as well. Both these basics were freely available throughout the war. In July 1949 milk was rationed. The introduction of bread rationing in the United Kingdom signalled to the Americans Britain's urgent need for help. Britain was dependent on the United States for essential supplies and the means to pay for them. She was further depleted through her efforts to help Greece in her war against communists.

Food rations in some commodities in Great Britain in 1947 were less than those in defeated Germany. One small improvement was the appearance in March 1947 of chocolate Easter eggs, weighing two ounces, for the first time for many years. They were available with sweet rationing points.

General George Marshall, American Chief of Staff throughout World War II, was appointed Secretary of State by President Harry S Truman in January 1947. Prior to his visit to Moscow to attend a meeting of the Council of Foreign Ministers to discuss the German peace treaty, Marshall requested clarification from the American embassy on Soviet post-war conduct. George Kennan, charge d'affaires at the US Embassy in Moscow, gave him a detailed analysis in a famous Long Telegram. Kennan warned him that "World communism is like a malignant parasite which feeds only on diseased tissue." Many nations in Europe were unhealthy and needed constructive help from America if they were to recover.

His analysis profoundly influenced American foreign policy. On March 12th 1947, in the Truman Doctrine, the President proclaimed that the US would support Greece and Turkey with economic and military aid to prevent them falling under Soviet control.

The Moscow meeting resulted in complete failure. Marshall came away convinced that the Soviets were hoping that the economic situation in Europe would worsen. "General Marshall felt Stalin was obviously waiting for Europe harassed and torn by war and in virtual ruins, to collapse and fall into the Communist orbit."[341]

On his return from Moscow, he instructed the State Department to prepare a European rescue plan, which Truman insisted should be called the Marshall Plan. In June 1947 George Marshall made a historic speech at Harvard in which he explained that the visible destruction caused by the war in Europe was minor compared with the current dislocation of the entire fabric of the European economy. Europe's requirements for foreign food and other essential products – principally from America – were much greater than her ability to pay for them. She must have substantial additional help or face economic, social, and political deterioration.

---

[341] *The Transformation of American Foreign Policy* p. 86.

It was logical that the United States should assist in her return to economic health, in the interests of political stability and peace. He stipulated that there must be agreement among the countries in Europe that they would play their part in using the aid effectively. Marshall stated that the American policy was even-handed "not against any country or doctrine but against hunger, poverty, desperation and chaos." He took care not to appear divisive or anti-communist.

Europe responded quickly to his European Recovery Programme – the Marshall plan. Ernest Bevin, Foreign Secretary in Attlee's Labour government, together with the French Foreign Minister, Georges Bidault, immediately convened an international conference in Paris, at which 16 nations cooperated to produce a plan for the use of American aid. Molotov represented the Soviet Union but denounced the Marshall Plan as a form of imperialism. He rejected the US offer on behalf of Russia and all her satellite states. The Soviets perceived the plan as a threat to their ambitions in Eastern Europe.

Over the next four years the Americans gave 13 billion dollars to Western Europe, which played an important part in the recovery of agriculture and industry, and in the reconstruction of post-war Europe. On the down side, the Marshall Plan brought about a polarisation of the East and West in Europe, and was the first step in the Cold War. When, in 1948, the Soviets seized power in Czechoslovakia, this enabled the American government to more easily sell the Marshall Plan to Americans as an anti-communist measure. Americans were motivated more by the fear of communism than by the starvation of the people of Western Europe.

In King's Lynn and the rest of the country, bread rationing caused some hardship. Normal consumption was cut by one quarter to one half. Bakers were unhappy with the complicated rationing scheme. They wanted to make cakes to supplement the loss of bread. A firm in Lynn was fined for selling tins of corned beef equal to eight hundred weekly rations without taking ration points.

There were also some pleasant events. In July 1946 the King and Queen invited Lord and Lady Fermoy and household to a garden party at Sandringham House to celebrate victory. We three children went and I was photographed with my pony and Princess Margaret. I don't remember why I took my pony!

In 1947, Maurice's mother died in New York aged 90. He had last seen her the previous year. She had been unable to speak since her stroke in 1942.

The winter of 1947 was a very severe one throughout the British Isles. West Norfolk was paralysed by deep snow and ice. Blizzards formed snow drifts more than twelve feet high. Villages were cut off, transport was at a standstill. Ice floes floated in the river Ouse and great blocks of ice were washed up on beaches at low tide. The lake at Sandringham froze hard. The Royal Family skated on the lake and invited a few neighbours to join them. I remember my father teaching Princess Elizabeth to skate, pushing a chair around on the ice.

The Queen confirmed this in a letter to me in which she said that both my

Maurice (centre) during a game of ice hockey on the lake at Sandringham. HM King George VI is on the extreme left. 1947

Edmund Roche sweeping snow off the lake at Sandringham, aged 11. January, 1951.

parents helped her to skate on the frozen lake, and that they used to play dangerous games of ice hockey. She also remembered that Maurice used to make people laugh, which she said was a valuable asset in hard winters. Her Majesty confirmed that my father came across as an American, and that she and Princess Margaret were very intrigued to meet his twin brother as well.

My nephew Robert Fellowes told me that my father was showing off his skating prowess on the same lake and with a great flourish and a pirouette went too near the cave and went through the ice! Splash!

In 1947 Maurice was president of the British Bantam Association. Wearing a bowler hat, he was present at a national bantam show in the Corn Exchange in King's Lynn. He told the audience: "I have a few bantams myself and when I get home at night, they start to crow!"

Maurice made frequent attempts to locate an important treasure. The story goes that King John lost his treasure while he was crossing the quicksands of the Wash in 1216, with his army and his baggage train. One enormous wagon loaded with gold was believed to contain the Crown and the Regalia. There is no evidence that this actually happened, and no-one knows exactly where the treasure was lost. The Wash has receded since those days but Sandringham is a long way from the most likely crossing place. Even so, Maurice, a romantic treasure hunter, believed it might lie in the woods near Park House, and used to take a spade[342] and go off digging!

He was encouraged to pursue this activity by the discovery of a major hoard of Roman silver at Mildenhall, by a farmer ploughing 35 miles from Sandringham. This was declared treasure trove in July 1946. It was acquired by the British Museum. The great dish of the Mildenhall Treasure was the most important find from Rome's administration in Britain ever discovered.

The great event at the end of 1947 was the wedding in November of Princess Elizabeth and Prince Philip, Duke of Edinburgh. Rationing and austerity were set aside for this joyful occasion. Two nights before the wedding, Maurice and Ruth were invited to a reception at Buckingham and Palace. The rooms were decorated with three thousand carnations, given by the French from southern France. On the wedding day, millions were able to watch the proceedings on television, as cameras were allowed into the Abbey for the first time ever at a royal marriage. Maurice and Ruth were among the 2,500 guests in Westminster Abbey. They had good seats and could see the magnificent ceremony very well.

In January 1948, Lord Woolton, the Conservative Party chairman, came to stay at Park House. He was organising the Party's £1 million fighting fund for the next election. In the early years of the war he was Minister of Food. When we left food on our plates, we were told that Lord Woolton would be very angry if we did not finish everything up!

---

[342] Large scale production of metal detectors did not occur until the 1960s.

In the summer of 1948, we all went to the States to stay with my Aunt Cynthia, Maurice's sister, at Elm Court, Newport. We crossed the Atlantic in the Cunard liner *Queen Elizabeth*. Frances, Edmund and I travelled cabin class with our governess, Gertrude Allen. Our parents travelled first class. There was no way that we could visit them! Happily, they visited us every day.

Newport, Rhode Island, 1948. Left to right: Mary, Maurice, Edmund, Ruth, Frances

In Newport we were introduced to banana splits at La Forge Café, the first bananas we had seen since before the war. We had tennis lessons at the Newport Casino and watched the champions during tennis week, an invitational tournament where the Men's Singles that year was won by Bill Talbert and the Men's Doubles by Ted Schroeder and Frank Parker. All three were American champions.[343]

We spent our days at Bailey's beach. How wise those governesses were in my father's childhood days, covering up their charges after a short dip in the ocean! My sister, brother and I were allowed to stay in the water for up to four hours. Our backs and shoulders were soon burned painfully raw by a combination of the salt water and the scorching sun. I suppose my mother from Aberdeen and our English governess from East Anglia had not come across the burning effects of the sun and my father, never having been sunburnt himself owing to the precautions, was apparently unaware of the dangers!

Back home, Maurice was immensely proud of his wife's achievements as an organiser and impresario. Trained as a concert pianist, Ruth retained her skills and from time to time gave concerts at fundraising events. In May 1946, she gave a recital at the Downham Market Grammar School with the Earl of Leicester playing the violin on his Stradivarius. She played works by Chopin and accompanied him in Beethoven's Kreisler sonata for violin and piano. She also played with him at Holkham in 1949.

She gave a number of concerts to raise money for the restoration of the Guildhall of St George including one in Norwich where she played Mozart's Sonata in D for two pianos with Alfred Cortot, the great French pianst, who was her professor in Paris when she studied at the Ecole Normale.

In January 1949, Alfred Cortot, gave a lunchtime concert in King's Lynn. He played Chopin's 24 preludes. The Queen and Queen Mary were present. As usual on these occasions, Maurice was not included in the picture. He willingly kept well in the background when Ruth was running the show.

Maurice's engagements in March included opening the first annual model show of the Lynn Society of Experimental Model Engineers. 220 models were displayed – aeroplanes, sea planes, marine craft and cars. At the end of the month, be was the principal guest at the Wisbech Coursing Club's dinner. He expressed his satisfaction at the recent defeat of the move to abolish blood sports: "The country has been without such interference for many centuries and there is no reason why we should have it now."

In August, after a fête to raise money for local parishes at Sandringham Rectory, a service was held in the grounds of Park House. Queen Mary sat at an open window of the drawing room, facing the area where an altar had been erected. A hundred choirboys sang. They were camping at Heacham and came from all over

---

[343] Talbert won nine grand slam titles. Schroeder won the Wimbledon Mens Singles in 1949. Parker won the Mens doubles at Wimbledon in 1949.

Maurice fishing for pike on the lake at Sandringham

the country. After the service, Maurice escorted the Queen out of the house on to the lawn, where she chatted to some children. A large crowd attended the service. Maurice was the only member of the family at home on that occasion. We were with our mother in Scotland on our annual visit to her parents.

After a full term in power, Attlee, the Prime Minister called a general election in February 1950. Maurice had remained actively involved in local politics, serving as chairman of the King's Lynn Conservative Party since 1946. Three weeks before the election, Commander Scott Miller was adopted Conservative candidate. There was a large audience at the adoption meeting. Maurice reminded the audience of the two main attacks against the Conservatives. The first was against Churchill and the second laid the responsibility for unemployment between 1921 and 1931 on the Conservatives. Both attacks were unjustified, he claimed. The result on

405

polling day disappointed him. Major Wise, Labour, won the seat with a majority of 270.

Ruth now resumed her earlier ambition to be a concert pianist and for the next few years she played the piano professionally. She soon built up an extensive repertoire. In January 1950, she gave a concert in Cheltenham, where she played the Mozart Piano Concerto in D minor, with the London Symphony Orchestra, conducted by Josef Krips. Two months later she played the Mozart again, with the LSO and Krips, at the Mozarteum in Salzburg. The Austrian reviews praised her technical ability, her delicacy of feeling and her expert treatment of tone. Maurice was not there to hear her play but was delighted by her success.

The most important concert of her life took place at the Albert Hall on March 26th 1950, when she played the Schumann Piano Concerto in A minor, with Josef Krips and the LSO. My father and I were almost as nervous as Ruth, for whom the concert was a great ordeal. The Queen was there in the royal box. The reviews were again favourable, praising her technical skills and musicianship. (My brother Edmund was very musical and often used to play the opening bars of the Schumann piano concerto – a flamboyant descending series of chords, following the opening strike by the orchestra!)

The following year, she played the Beethoven Piano Concerto No 1 in C at the Caird Hall, Dundee with the Scottish National Orchestra, conducted by Walter Susskind. One of the reviewers wrote that "she conquered not by might or by power, but by gentleness and grace of spirit." Later that year she played the Schumann at Sophia Gardens Pavilion, Cardiff, again with the LSO and Josef Krips.

Rehearsals and performances took her away from Maurice, who was left alone at home. One of his friends in King's Lynn told me she remembered seeing my father outside the kitchen garden at Sandringham, under the copper beech trees, wearing a threadbare coat with holes in it, looking unkempt and unloved, talking to passers by. He was bereft of his beloved Ruth who was away giving concerts. He missed his children too, who were all away at boarding schools.

In May 1950, he sailed to America for a reunion of the 1905 class at St Paul's School. Before he left he resigned as chairman of the King's Lynn and District Conservative Association, which he had chaired for four years. This caused dismay and disappointment. A vote of confidence was passed in his absence and he was requested to withdraw his resignation and to continue in the role.

In 1950, the whole family travelled in the Bentley to the Salzkammergut, near Salzburg in Austria, for what turned out to be a tense family holiday. We stayed in a hotel at St Gilgen on the Wolfgangsee. Frances and I both fell in love with the same waiter – Gerhard! I was very upset when he showed a distinct preference for Frances! The lake was deep and very cold. My father spent hours in a rowing boat, fishing without any luck and with a lot of cursing and swearing, as his line got caught up in weeds! We went twice to Salzburg Festival to memorable performances of the Magic Flute and Don Giovanni.

In 1945 the Guildhall of St George in King Street, King's Lynn, the oldest surviving medieval guildhall was in danger of being demolished to become a garage. It was built in the fifteenth century and was used as a playhouse from its early days. It is possible that Shakespeare performed there. It was rescued by Alexander Penrose, who bought the derelict site and with the aid of grants from the Arts Council, the Pilgrim Trust and a public appeal, raised money to stabilise it and to reconstruct an earlier eighteenth century theatre.

In 1949, plans commenced for a festival to celebrate the opening of the restored Guildhall. Ruth, the chairman of the Festival committee, was the prime mover in arranging the programme, with help from Dr Patrick Hadley, a composer and Professor of Music at Cambridge University.

Maurice energetically raised money for the restoration of the Guildhall. He undertook the sale of chairs in the theatre, which were inscribed with the name of the purchaser. They had the right to sit in their chair on the occasion of the royal opening of the Guildhall, and on every St George's Day, as well as on special occasions.

He was very well received when in March 1951 he visited Lynn Massachusetts, named after King's Lynn in the seventeenth century. Lynn's leading citizens were expecting a stuffy Englishman and were pleasantly surprised by Maurice's free and easy ways.[344] On being called His Lordship he said:" Never mind that lordship bull! Just call me Maurice! I'm only a miserable baron!"

He was guest of honour at a luncheon in Lynn, Massachusetts, given by the Lynn Daily Evening Item, to raise money for the St George's Hall Restoration Fund. Removing the cover from his dish and catching sight of the roast beef on his plate, the Baron murmured: "My, look at this meat! My goodness, I'll get high blood pressure!" He pointed out in his clipped British accent, that although meat was scarce in England, no one was starving…everyone had plenty to eat." [345]

After lunch, he rose to address the assembled company. He spoke of the duty of the present generation to restore fine old buildings and prevent them from being destroyed:

"The great need for space in England almost succeeded in having the Guildhall destroyed, but it has been saved, and with the aid of Her Majesty the Queen, we have completed nearly 90 per cent of the reconstruction. However the need for money is great and any sum of money would be very welcome from this wonderful city."

He came back from the States having sold 25 chairs to his American relatives,

[344] Daily Evening Item. Lynn Mass. March 20th, 1951
[345] Daily Evening Item. Lynn Mass. March 20th, 1951

his friends and four to Lynn, Massachusetts. His brother Frank subscribed £2,000, the largest donation. In all Maurice raised, on this trip alone, a quarter of the total amount needed.

The opening of the restored Guildhall of St George was a grand occasion. The French ambassador, Monsieur Massigli, was present. General Rene Chaban-Delmas, a de Gaullist MP, Mayor of Bordeaux, ex-leader of the French resistance, was a guest of honour. (He stayed at Park House). He was representing the wine growers of the Bordeaux area whose ancestors ever since the fourteenth century exported wine directly from Bordeaux to King's Lynn. The pageantry signalled the importance of the occasion. The flag of St George fluttered above the Guildhall door. The Queen was greeted by a fanfare of trumpets. Officers and men from HMS *Truelove* formed a guard of honour.

In her speech, the Queen said: "For myself, I can recall no undertaking which more worthily commemorates the Festival [of Britain] year, than St. George's Guildhall, King's Lynn. This lovely place will greatly enrich the life of King's Lynn."[346] After the opening ceremony, the Queen attended a performance of words and music arranged by the Apollo Society, given by Peggy Ashcroft, Leon Quartermaine and Mewton-Wood. Other performers that week were Shura Cherkassky, Benjamin Britten, Peter Pears, Kathleen Ferrier, Joan Cross, Osbert Sitwell, Arnold Richardson, Peter Ustinov, the Boyd Neel Orchestra conducted by Georges Enesco and at a second performance, by Josef Krips.

The Festival had been an outstanding success and the restored Guildhall deserved this celebration. Tributes were showered on Ruth for her remarkable achievement. In a speech on the last night of the Festival, she said that she realised that King's Lynn now had one of the most beautiful halls for music and drama in the whole of England. A week later Maurice showed Queen Mary around the new arts and cultural centre. He was very proud of a photograph of Queen Mary and himself which was taken that day.

The Queen, later the Queen Mother, was patron of the Festival for the next 50 years and attended it annually. The Festival was intended as a one-off but its popularity led to it becoming an annual event. It will celebrate its sixtieth anniversary in 2010.

At the general election on October 25th 1951, Commander Scot Miller was eleted MP with a majority of 937.

Dr Jane de Iongh, the Dutch Cultural Attachee attended the first Festival. She was a historian and highly educated. My mother found her intellectually stimulating and an important friendship developed which continued for the next fifty years. On the home front, my father was increasingly out of the picture. Publicly too, Ruth eclipsed him. During the Festival he took a back seat, only too happy for her to take centre stage.

---

[346] *Lynn News & Advertiser.* July 27th, 1951.

Queen Mary and Maurice outside
St George's Guildhall, King's Lynn.
August 1951

Following the coffin of HM George VI, February 12th, 1951.
First row: The Earl and Countess of Leicester; second row: Capt., and Mrs W Fellowes;
third row: Dr Ansell; fourth row: Lord and Lady Fermoy.

A few months later, on February 6th 1952, the King died at Sandringham. Maurice had been out shooting with him the previous day in a party of six guns who bagged three hundred hares. In an interview with the *Lynn News* after the King's death, Maurice said that at the end of the day:

"The King hurried round and asked us to come again on Thursday. It was a perfectly marvellous day. The Estate looked lovely. The King really enjoyed his day. I had never seen him in better health. He shot awfully well and showed no signs of tiredness. I saw him get nine hares and one pigeon, which he took perfectly cleanly, 80 to 100 feet up."

Maurice added: "I feel that I have lost a personal friend." The following week was a sad and moving one for him and for Ruth.

The Queen arrived at Sandringham on Friday, two days after the death of her father. Shortly after her arrival, the King's coffin was taken on a wheeled bier to the church of St. Mary Magdalene for a lying in state. On Monday February 11th, after a brief service in the church, six Grenadier Guards carried his coffin, which was draped in the Royal Standard, from the church and placed it on a gun carriage drawn by six bay horses. They were ridden by members of the King's Troop of the Royal Horse Artillery wearing full dress uniform and plumed shakoes. The Troop Commander preceded the gun carriage at the head of a procession which followed the coffin to Wolferton station, two and a half miles away.[347]

The Duke of Edinburgh and the Duke of Gloucester walked behind the coffin, followed by a car carrying the Queen, the Queen Mother and Princess Margaret, all heavily veiled. Local families, including Lord and Lady Fermoy, and estate workers walked behind the car. The procession moved in silence except for the sound of the horses' hooves and the rumble of the wheels of the gun carriage. Thousands lined the route along the way, the men wearing bowlers and mourning bands on their arms, the women in dark clothes and hats.

A special train was waiting at the station to take the body of the late King and the Royal Family to London. It was made up of nine coaches, all of them in the varnished teak livery of the former LNER,[348] except the hearse-coach, which was painted black with a white roof. After lying in state at Westminster Hall for three days, the King's funeral was held at St George's Chapel, Windsor, and was attended by nine hundred guests, among them Lord and Lady Fermoy.

In March, Maurice went to America so was not able to accompany Ruth when she received the Order of the British Empire at Buckingham Palace. This was in recognition for her services as chairman of the King's Lynn Festival Committee. I was in Paris. Frances and Edmund went to the Palace with her.

---

[347] From the *Lynn News & Advertiser*. February 12th, 1952.
[348] London & North Eastern Railway.

As its President, Maurice was present at a dinner in April when the Lynn Round Table received a Charter of Affiliation to the National Association of Round Tables of Great Britain and Ireland. Maurice, who proposed the toast of the National Association, said he had just returned from a visit to America where he found that most of the things of prominence had been done by men who had started in a humble way, determined to get to the top in their particular sphere. Round Tables, he said, were groups of men anxious to serve their country and leave it a better place.

Although the Queen acceded to the throne the moment the King died, the Coronation was not held until June the following year. Maurice came up with the idea of Coronation cups, silver trophies which he personally donated, to celebrate the Coronation year. He presented the first of these in January, to the Lynn Cycling Club, of which he was, at the time, the first and only president. He gave a second one to the Lynn and District Angling Club in March.

Disaster struck West Norfolk on the last day of January 1953. North-easterly gales whipped up a surge which added to the high tide and unexpectedly flooded the area. There was no system of flood warnings and 80 lives were lost. Fifteen hundred people were evacuated in South Lynn. Thousands of areas of agricultural land were devastated. Three hundred beach huts were swept away at Hunstanton. Many British and Americans carried out heroic rescue operations and subsequently received awards for gallantry. The Norfolk Flood Relief fund was established. Plans were drawn up for sea defences and advance flood warnings.

On March 24th Queen Mary, widow of George V and the Queen's grandmother, died aged 85. We were all invited to her funeral at St George's Chapel, Windsor, one week later. It was reported that her dying wish was that the Coronation should not be delayed. Maurice used to bring her nylons stockings from the States when he went there during the war and after. She sometimes came to Park House for tea. She was a very kind godmother to me and gave me some lovely presents, always giving me one at Christmas, even during the war years.

35

A dance, a Coronation, two weddings and a christening

O n May 21st 1953, our parents gave a coming-out dance for Frances and myself. The practice of young women having a debutante season was still in full swing until the late 1950s. A debutante was a young lady of an age to be introduced to society and who was eligible for marriage. During a season of coming-out dances, which ran from May to July, she was displayed to eligible husbands. There was a list of suitable young men for hostesses to invite, which included some whom parents would definitely not want as a son-in-law! Frances and I were formally presented at Court, in the form of an invitation to a garden party at Buckingham Palace.

I had been a debutante the year before but my dance was held over so that it could be shared with Frances. These dances were lavish affairs. They were preceded by dinner parties for twelve or so guests, which were hosted by friends of the debutante's parents. There were 450 guests at our dance at Londonderry House, Park Lane, which was elaborately adorned with flowers. It was a white tie affair. Maurice wore his war medals, Uncle Frank a white gardenia. My mother wore her diamond tiara. The Queen Mother was present and her first dance was with Maurice, to the music of "It's a Lovely Day Today". Meanwhile Ruth danced with the American Ambassador, Mr Winthrop Aldrich. There was supper at midnight and breakfast at about 3.30am. Altogether a very expensive occasion for Maurice!

The Coronation of Queen Elizabeth II took place soon after our dance, on June 2nd 1953. Maurice and Ruth were invited. They wore the Coronation robes they had worn at the Coronation of George VI in 1937. These were long crimson velvet cloaks to the ground, trimmed with miniver fur.[349] Maurice had a cape of ermine with two rows of black sealskin spots,[350] which indicated his rank as a baron. A duke has four rows, an earl three. He wore court dress under his robe. Coronets also denoted rank. That of a baron has six silver balls placed on a gold circlet, and is trimmed with ermine.

Ruth's robe had two narrow bands of miniver around the upper arm to denote

---

[349] A white fur in the past from the belly of a grey squirrel.
[350] In previous centuries these would have been black ermine tails.

Family group before the dance at Londonderry House. May, 1953

Dressed for the Coronation of HM Queen Elizabeth II, June, 1953.

her rank as a baroness, and a train one yard long edged with two inches of ermine. The train of a duchess was two yards long and trimmed with five inches of ermine. Underneath her Coronation robe, Ruth wore a white satin dress embroidered with silver. She wore long white kid gloves. Her coronet was smaller than her husband's. We children watched the procession to the Abbey from a stand at the House of Lords. My parents owned four blue, velvet-covered chairs, embroidered with the gold monograms of George VI and Elizabeth II, souvenirs of their Coronations.

In October, Maurice was overjoyed by the engagement of Frances his younger daughter to Viscount Althorp, only son of Earl Spencer. Johnny was acting master of the royal household and an equerry to the Queen. Maurice liked him very much. They had met in January 1951, when Maurice went shooting with the King, and Major the Viscount Althorp was in the party. Maurice invited him to Park House for drinks one evening. Frances was nearly 15 years-old. She immediately fell for Johnny and started knitting socks for him soon after!

Three weeks after their engagement, the couple were separated when Johnny sailed on the SS *Gothic* to Jamaica, where the Queen and the Duke of Edinburgh, who had flown across the Atlantic, embarked for a six-month tour of the Commonwealth. Before he left, Ruth and Frances visited Johnny on board the ship in a London dock to say good-bye to him, Ruth carrying his ceremonial sword!

Maurice received four invitations from the Queen to shoot at Sandringham in 1953. On 28th December, the party consisted of the Duke of Gloucester, Prince William of Gloucester, the Duke of Kent, Brigadier Sir Norman Gwatkin and Capt. Oliver Dawnay. They shot 183 pheasants.

Maurice's public duties in the district continued. In December 1953, he opened a new Memorial Hall at Wiggenhall St Germans which was followed by Ruth giving a recital. He presented a Coronation cup at a Bowls Club dinner. In March, seven former mayors of Lynn met to inaugurate the Mayors' Avenue in the walks in King's Lynn, each planting a tree. Maurice, as the most senior ex-mayor present, planted the first tree – an Indian bean tree. In May, Maurice presented a standard to the new Royal Air Force Association in Hunstanton.

The high standard of performers at the lunchtime concerts continued. In January 1954 the Queen Mother attended the January concert, when Clifford Curzon played. The season ended in April with a performance by Eileen Joyce, the great Australian pianist.

In June 1954 my sister Frances married Viscount Althorp, the only son of the Earl Spencer. It was described in the Press as the Wedding of the Year. The marriage took place in Westminster Abbey where there were fifteen hundred guests. Nine hundred attended a reception in St James's Palace afterwards. Nearly all the royal family were there. The Queen, the Duke of Edinburgh, Princess Margaret, the Princess Royal, the Duchess of Kent and Princess Alexandra were present. The

Frank and Maurice in Newport, 1952

Frances and Maurice arriving at
Westminster Abbey. June 1st, 1954

Duke of Kent was an usher. The royal guests and the venues of Westmenster Abbey and St James' Palace were rare privileges, granted to Johnny who was close to the Royal Family.

Frances and her father set out from 10 Wilton Crescent, the family home in Knightsbridge. A picture of Ruth was taken as she arrived at the Abbey with Frank, her brother-in-law. The twin brothers were still remarkably alike. The caption was Ruth's words: "This is not my husband." It was a proud day for Maurice as he walked up the aisle with his lovely eighteen-year-old daughter on his arm. He wiped a tear from his eye as she came down the aisle with her husband.

At the King's Lynn Festival the following month, Johnny Althorp showed a colour film of the Queen's Commonwealth tour in Australia at the St George's Guildhall. Ruth gave a concert with the great oboe player Leon Goosens which the Queen Mother attended. During the festival week, she unveiled a portrait of my mother painted by Anthony Devas, which hangs in the Guildhall of St George today. It was a tribute to her contribution to the artistic life of West Norfolk. My father was in the audience with myself and my fiancé, Anthony Berry, and Frances and Johnny. On the same day, the Queen Mother was given the freedom of the borough of King's Lynn. Lord and Lady Fermoy attended a luncheon at the Town Hall which followed.

Five months later, I married Anthony Berry, sixth son of Viscount Kemsley, in St Margaret's Church, Westminster. The Queen Mother came to the wedding. I remember my father teasing me until I was on the point of tears as we prepared to set off for the church. He loved to tease but got his timing wrong on that occasion! My wedding was a smaller affair than Frances' but even so there were eight hundred guests at the church. The hymn "Lead us, heavenly father, lead us," was sung as my father took me up the aisle. The Queen Mother was on his arm on the way down. The reception took place at Hutchinson House, off Oxford Street. After the reception was over, Maurice took a bus back home and, a little tipsy, regaled his fellow passengers with a description of the family event!

My parents were relieved to have their daughters off the pay roll! Taxation had greatly reduced my father's large income and I needed to be self-supporting. Although they knew we would have to earn our living, no thought was given to preparing us for a career. At that time and with their life experience, they envisaged marriage as the natural destination for a young woman. And marry we did!

Maurice's last shoot at Sandringham – a half-day for him – was on January 1st 1955, with the Duke of Edinburgh, Lord Elphinstone, the Hon. David Bowes-Lyon, the Hon. Gavin Astor, Flight Lieut C Blount and Sir Michael Adeane. 235 pheasants were shot that day.

In March 1955, Maurice crossed the Atlantic for the fifty-first time, on the liner *Queen Mary*. He was away for six weeks. His brother Frank noticed that he was suffering from high blood pressure. Maurice refused to take his advice to see

Mary and her father leaving home for St Margaret's, Westminster. November 25th, 1954

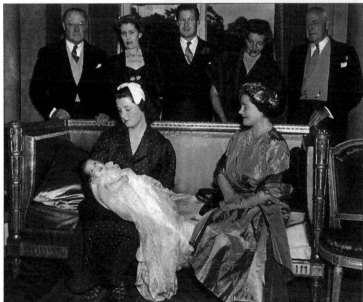

The christening of Sarah Spencer. Left to right: Lord and Lady Spencer, Johnny Althorp, Lady Fermoy, Lord Fermoy; Seated: Frances Althorp and Sarah, HM Queen Elizabeth the Queen Mother.

Edmund with Lady Lemina Gordon at the wedding reception after Mary's wedding.

a doctor and take medication.

He had several functions in King's Lynn on his return in the month of May. As president of the Lynn and District Auxiliary Branch of the Royal Society for the Protection of Animals he addressed their annual meeting. He was photographed speaking in typical attitude – holding the lapels of his jacket with both hands. He went to the open day at Sculthorpe USA air base which was attended by three thousand people. He worked for the local candidate in the May 26th General Election.

On June 9th 1955, two years after the wedding of Frances and Johnny, the family were once again at Westminster Abbey, in St Faith's Chapel, for the christening of their first child, Sarah Spencer. She was Maurice's first grandchild and the only one he survived to see. A reception was held afterwards at the home of the Dowager, Marchioness of Cholmondeley in Kensington Palace Gardens. The Queen Mother was one of Sarah's godparents.

36

The last lap

Three days after Sarah Spencer's christening, Maurice wrote to his son
Edmund, who was away at school as Eton:

"Park House, Sandringham
June 12th 1955

Dearest Edmund,
Mummy and I are spending a quiet week-end here in the rain. She has
been to see the plans for the Festival, which is going well. There will be a
good attendance, the bookings are good, a month to go.
   The Guildhall is being re-painted white which I don't like at all. It looks
cold to me.
   Wonder how things are with you? Mummy thinks we ought to go to
Ireland to Moira's after you have a few days with Frances. Do you like the
idea? What will I do? Sail?
   I think a great deal about you and your future. I want you to be such a
success in life –

Write soon. Much love Daddy."

One week later, Maurice had a stroke while at the hairdresser in King's Lynn.
He was admitted to a nursing home, seriously ill. My mother decided it would be
better if his children did not see him, as his face had become lop-sided. Hospitals,
illness and physical defects were hard for her to bear and she did not want to
upset us. And she did not know that he was going to die.
   Ruth had a professional engagement at the Assembly House in Norwich a
week later, a recital with the viola player Lionel Tertis.
   On Friday July 8th, Maurice was due to leave Gaywood Nursing Home where
he had been for three weeks. The previous day he was considered to have improved
sufficiently to go home. Instead he had a second stroke and died in the early
hours of Friday morning. The news came as a great shock to his family and was
very hard for his children, who had not seen him since he was taken ill. Frank
described his brother's death has the most terrible blow of his life. He would miss

him terribly.

The *Lynn New & Advertiser* devoted an entire page to the report of the death

"of an outstanding local personality. He was truly the friend of kings, statesmen and worldly figures, while still retaining the common touch. Apart from his many services in official positions, it was his friendliness and helpfulness which endeared him to the people of the area – even more than his generosity which was legendary."

There were many tributes, including a quote from a 1929 study of him by Mr T Diggle, editor of the paper at that time. He had written:

"I was curious to hear from his own lips why he was anxious to undertake the hard and wearisome toil of a back-bench Member of Parliament for a huge constituency. When I asked him this question, Maurice replied in a low tone: 'Because I think I might be able to do a little good there.' Why do men usually want to enter the House? A few could do with the salary. Others yearn for the social prestige conferred. To many keen party men, it is the realisation of their life's political ambition. But it is certain that none of these inducements weighed with Lord Fermoy."

Mr Diggle continued that it was rare indeed that any man had acquired such a hold on a constituency. He had kept all his old friends: he had added to their number daily. Why was it? Mr Diggle felt the chief reason was Lord Fermoy's modesty:

"Of all the qualities that wear well, in politics as in other spheres, this wears the best. Watch Lord Fermoy enter such a function as the Railway Concert in Lynn. His seat naturally is the highest one. But into his seat he sidles – seemingly anxious to avoid being seen. When he drops into the hospital, he asks in a half-apologetic way: 'Is there anything you want just now?' This was the usual preface to one of his splendid gifts to the Lynn hospital. The characteristic of his steady and maintained generosity is the fact that his gifts have been carefully calculated to do real good with the money."

Here is an extract from an appreciation by Mr J H Catleugh, a good friend of his:

"How we shall miss his familiar figure with a basket on his arm, doing his shopping in Norfolk Street or High Street. He was president of all sorts of organisations and would turn up at all kinds of meetings – everything where the people were concerned interested him. No-one ever knew when he would arrive or when he would leave, but he loved to be there. He was so much 'part and parcel' of our local life.

All classes will miss him, but particularly the common people whose interests he shared and whose names he remembered. Could any man have a finer memorial than a place in the hearts of the people?"

Sir Patrick Hannon MP wrote:

"It would be difficult to recall any member of the House of Commons in my time who brought greater charm and a more warm atmosphere of friendship to the membership of the House of Commons than Maurice Roche, whose Irish character and qualities of expansive friendship will long be remembered. I addressed meetings in support of his first election and his subsequent in King's Lynn and his popularity was worthily endorsed by the intense interest he took in every local question affecting the welfare of his constituency, and indeed of the whole of the varied interests of East Anglia. His memory will be recalled with affection and the sad reflection that it will be difficult to look upon his like again." [351]

Dr Patrick Hadley, Professor of Music at Cambridge, his friend and neighbour in Norfolk wrote:

"Fermoy was not an orator nor even much of a politician, though he worked very hard to be both. His surpassing popularity was instantly won by his strangely attractive personality. He was indefatigable in his rounds of the constituency. He had an uncanny memory for faces and names and could always recall previous conversations with individuals. During my lifetime in this part of the world there has been no individual so adored by one and all, politics apart."[352]

Maurice's funeral took place in the church at of St Mary Magdalene, Sandringham, where he is buried. The Queen and the Queen Mother were represented. Frank was not there due to illness, but he came over from America a few weeks later. When he walked up the aisle with Ruth to the Sunday morning service, members of the congregation who were unaware that Maurice had an identical twin, suffered from shock! There, before their eyes, was the man they had recently buried!

The *Eastern Daily Press* reported his memorial service at St Margaret's Church

---

[351] *The Times.* July 14th, 1955
[352] *The Times.* July 14th, 1955

in King's Lynn, a few days after he died:

"About 800 people representing all walks of life of West Norfolk, some of them wearing workaday clothes and overalls, gathered in St Margaret's Church to honour the memory of their friend and neighbour, Lord Fermoy. They heard the vicar (the Rev. W A Aitken) describe his death as a gash torn in the heart of the life of the community. 'We all know he is irreplaceable in our midst. No one can be the same, can do what he did, can be what he was in the life of this place,' the Vicar added."

The year after Maurice died, Ruth was invited by Queen Elizabeth, the Queen Mother, to be her lady-in-waiting. Ruth continued in this role for the next 37 years. In 1964, she was given the freedom of King's Lynn. She died in 1993 and was buried in the same grave as Maurice.

His wife and children dedicated the Fermoy Gallery in his memory. It is attached to St George's Guidhall in King's Lynn. Art exhibitions are held there throughout the year.

His brother Frank created the Lord Fermoy Scholarship Fund in October 1955, with a gift of $15,000. It was named in memory of his brother, who had died three months previously. Frank died in 1958. and is buried in the Frank Work plot, in Green-Wood Cemetery, Brooklyn, New York City.

His sister Cynthia died in Newport, Rhode Island and is buried there. On her death, her son Guy Cary (1923-2003), donated to the Redwood Library in Newport, her collection of valuable medieval and eighteenth century books and engravings on architecture, furniture and coach designs.

In 1984, Maurice's son Edmund died by his own hand and is also buried in the family corner at Sandringham Church. His younger daughter Frances died aged 68 in 2004 and is buried in Oban.

Epilogue: My father

His elder daughter Mary is alive in 2008! A great deal of this book has been about the man I did not know. I will now say something about the man I knew.

His humour was a strong characteristic. He could make people howl with laughter at his simple, sometimes rather silly jokes. He liked to play on words. He used to say that his name was More Rice. Mayonnaise was My Knees. He pronounced exactly 'Eggs-actly.' He discovered that the name Parker was Rekrap when spelt backwards. I did not know the word 'crap' as a child so missed the full effect of that one. He called the town of Wareham in Norfolk "I can't". He referred to the opera 'Manon Lescaut' as 'Lets go.'

When I think about the worrying, frightening times of the two wars and the fears for the economy of the 1920s and '30s, what my father provided was in tune with the needs of those difficult times – and perhaps always – for lighthearted, ridiculous relief. His own nervous disposition needed it and so did his audiences, who were ready to laugh at anything remotely funny!

He referred to my twin cousins whose names were Anthea and Jennifer, as Anthracite and Jupiter. Uncle Davy, my mother's younger brother, was Uncle Gravy. Maurice was a dreadful tease. He used to go up to Uncle Davy as if to shake is hand but with his arm outstretched, carried on past him.

He loved listening to music and could make some of his own special brand, which required no instrument. He liked to sound "reveille" – the military wake-up call, played on a bugle at sunrise. He reproduced this sound by trumpeting the tune through closed lips! He was also famous for whistling as he walked through the streets of King's Lynn!

Maurice had a voracious appetite. He loved all game, particularly wild duck or woodcock. He had a passion for eggs and his greatest treat was to eat a whole goose egg. He drank his tea from an outsize cup with a hunting scene painted on the side. A very small amount of alcohol went to his head.

He called Ruth "Boy" or "Beezy-Boo." She occasionally called him "Boy", but mainly nothing. We had a shorthaired dachshund called Badia, named after Badia in North Africa. Maurice also called him Beezy-Boo. He called his son Edmund "Shires", after Art Shires a great baseball player. He called Frances "Funny Face". He had no nickname for me that I can remember.

Once after dining with the King and the Queen at Sandringham he was delighted to tell us a riddle which King George VI had made up. Question: "When is Maurice like Hitler?" Answer: "When he is Ruth-less!"

My father had a strange habit of regularly quoting a line from Macbeth: "There is no art to find the mind's construction in the face." As a child I used to ponder on the meaning of this, without success! Another favourite was to say with an American accent, and all the words rhyming with 'naff': "It makes me laugh to see the calf go down the path to take its bath!" He also came out with, rather outrageously: "Voulez-vous coucher avec moi ce soir?"

Billy Fellowes, his friend and neighbour at Sandringham, a brilliant mimic, did a wonderful take of Maurice's reflection on French soldiers: "Just think, when peace was declared, of all those little Frenchmen in their red trousers scurrying back home, drinking a bottle of vin du pays and then *au lit.*"

From a very young age, we children were dressed in our best clothes to go to church on Sunday mornings. My mother dressed in all her finery for this occasion. We always sat in the same pew, the third on the left-hand side of the church. This was below the pulpit. My father was not always very well behaved. If he thought Hector the Rector's[353] sermon was going on too long, he used to take out his pocket-watch and hold it up, dangling it rather pointedly!

Robert Fellowes told me that he and his sisters Susan and Rachel regarded Lord Fermoy as a hero figure. He had an amazing way with children. Every Sunday after church, he held court outside the church at Sandringham, wearing his grey Homburg hat, making children laugh. Fiona Fraser[354] told me that the first time she met Maurice at Park House as a child, it was the first time she was treated by an adult as if she was a person. He was warm and interested – a remarkable human being.

Some of his jokes were rather rude! I have never forgotten a story Maurice told about two men in the gents' cloakroom, in adjacent cubicles. Both were groaning and straining noisily. Suddenly there was a loud "plop" from one cubicle. His neighbour called out: "Gee! You're lucky." The reply came back: 'No, I'm not. That was my watch." In similar vein, he told the story at a dinner party of how he went to hospital for the removal of a tapeworm. Not everyone was amused!

My father had no interest in possessions for himself. Although as a young man he was always smartly dressed, during and after the war all the available clothing coupons were needed for my mother's finery. She loved beautiful clothes.

He never owned a house, renting Park House from the Monarch for twenty years. After his death in 1955, my sister Frances and her husband Johnny Althorp took over the lease and three of her children were born there, including their daughter Diana, who became the Princess of Wales. When Johnny Althorp became Earl Spencer and moved to live at Althorp, Northamptonshire, the house was empty for twelve years before the Queen gave it to the Leonard Cheshire

---

[353] The Rev. H D Anderson.
[354] Widow of Sir Ian Fraser 1923-2003

Foundation, and it is now a hotel for physically disabled people. When my eldest daughter Alexandra Berry spent a week at Park House Hotel during her convalescence following spinal surgery in 2006, by sheer coincidence she was allocated her grandfather's dressing room!

Park House has been altered in many respects, but my father's den, the first room off the hall on the right, is unchanged. I like going there. There he sat for hours every day, writing to his friends on his typewriter. In the afternoon, he walked up to the Norwich Gates of Sandringham House, where there was a post box. I have his desk and treasure it. After lunch he smoked a cigar, only half a cigar as an economy measure. Then he put it out and relit it in the evening! His main reading material was the *Harvard Alumni Bulletin, St Paul's School Magazine, The New York Herald Tribune* and *The Times*. Almost every year he went by ship to the States, to see his brother and sister and old friends.

My mother told me about some of his acts of generosity. He paid for one of his constituents to go to the States for eye surgery. He once took off his coat and gave it to a man who did not have one. I have been very moved by the discovery of the scale of his generosity to his old school and to his constituency, as I have researched this book.

Maurice loved people. He was the most sociable of beings. He loved public transport. He travelled on buses whenever he could. He always stopped to give pedestrians a lift. He invariably struck up conversations on trains and sometimes invited his fellow travellers to Park House. He was very proud of living on the Royal estate at Sandringham and of his friendship with the Royal Family.

On one occasion when he invited two young women he had met on the train to lunch, my mother shut herself away in her bedroom. It was difficult for her to have such a flirtatious husband. She found my father's uninhibited, warm and personal ways offensive at times. Perhaps his interest in other women alienated her affections, or was it her coldness which drove him to seek affection and more from other women?

No doubt they were happy in the early days of their marriage and Ruth gave him her total support in his public life. They shared a strong sense of duty and a responsibility to give to society. In other respects they were divided by culture and temperament. My brother believed that his own problems with his identity stemmed from the fact that his parents were so completely different.

By the time I can remember my parents, there were tensions in the marriage. The 23 year difference in their ages became a strain. Maurice was always trying to please her. Sadly, the flowers he bought her so joyfully were the wrong colour. One day he came back triumphantly from Lynn with a large piece of middle-cut salmon, which he had bought at Donaldsons the fishmonger. It had been a bargain at 4s.6d. "You know I've done the menus for the week." Ruth told him crossly. I know that pained me, but cannot tell how he received these arrows that punctured his enthusiasm.

My father simply worshipped Ruth and she could do no wrong in his eyes. Meg Rutter, who knew him in Lynn from his pre-marital days, told me "he adored the air she breathed". She also told me that before his marriage, Maurice belonged to the community. He was one of them. Inevitably his new life took him away from Lynn. My mother, with her star personality, eclipsed my father when she took the stage as his wife. He was the first to cede her the limelight, in which he had little interest. He was enormously proud of her beauty and ability to charm. He burst with pride when she gave concerts.

Maurice was always a cautious driver, in my memory, and hooted on every blind corner. He was a nervous passenger and when my mother was at the wheel, he behaved as if he was driving the car. When she put the brakes on, he also pressed down on the floor throwing himself back in his seat! Sometimes he "braked" when she did not, and this, understandably, used to irritate her!

About two years before his death, in spite of his extreme care as a driver, Maurice was involved in a head-on collision. A car in front of him stopped suddenly and he swerved into the path of a car coming the other way. A man in the other car died instantly, of heart failure. Although Maurice was not responsible for his death, the incident deeply affected him and haunted him for the rest of his life.

I have learned much about my father in the course of writing this book. Because of his marriage at a late age, I knew nothing about him as a young man. He was self-effacing and rarely referred to his early life. I have been surprised to discover the thoughtful person who felt things deeply, so well concealed behind the comedian, the jovial façade.

I wish I had known my father better and loved him more when he was alive. I much regret that I did not see him after his first stroke. It was sad that he did not see any of his adored children for the last three weeks of his life. The time I have given to this book has done something to make up for my omissions.

THE END

APPENDIX A

Maurice's Great-grandfather John Wark 1781-1823

John Wark, Maurice's great-grandfather, was born in Plymouth in 1781. He became a civil engineer and emigrated to America when he was 25 years-old. John Wark's father, also called John, was born in 1738 near Glasgow. His marriage certificate describes him as a shipwright. He married Sarah Ham in Plymouth in 1779. The certificate reveals that she could not write and instead put "her mark" instead of a signature.

It may be that he learnt his trade in Glasgow and went to Plymouth where there was a huge demand for shipwrights from 1756 when the Seven Years War broke out. This was followed by the war with America in 1775. Plymouth and other royal dockyards were vital to British forces because they supplied ships of the line,[355] as well as refitting them every year. From 1778 they were fitted with copper bottoms which kept vessels free from weeds and protected their timbers from being eaten by sea-worms, as well as improving their sailing qualities.

There were no formal courses in civil engineering in colleges in the UK when John Wark Junior was a young man. The usual way to train was to serve an apprenticeship in some practical profession. In this way they earned enough to live on and gained experience, eventually reaching the rank of a civil engineer. It is likely that John served his apprenticeship to his father.

The Warks, father and son, probably met John Rennie, the greatest civil engineer of his era, when the latter visited Plymouth in 1806, to draw up a plan for a breakwater to protect the anchorage in Plymouth harbour, which was exposed to storms. As fellow Scots they could have met at the Scottish kirk in Plymouth. Rennie's assistant James Green was employed to survey local rock at Cattewater, seeking to find the most suitable rock for this ambitious plan. James was John's exact contemporary. Both were born in the year 1781. Local surveyors and engineers were required for this enormous project and it is likely that John Wark worked for him.

It is possible that John found his way to America as a result of a recommendation from Rennie when the latter was recruiting a civil engineer for an American company. Or James Green, already well established in his career in his own right, may have passed on an offer he had received himself.

Alternatively John would know of the desperate shortage of engineers and

---

[355] A ship of the line was a warship powerful enough to take its place in the line of battle.

surveyors in the young republic of America. He could have travelled there confident in the knowledge he would find work, as few engineers were willing to undertake the journey from Europe. He may have been inspired by the example of Benjamin Latrobe who had emigrated in 1795. Latrobe designed the Philadelphia waterworks in 1801 and surveyed the Chesapeake and Delaware Canal in 1803. He was an agent for technological transfer. In 1817 he wrote:

> "I am well aware that there is a reluctance very natural and patriotic to the employment of foreigners. But we import blankets, scissors and wine; why should we not import knowledge? A good civil engineer is an acquisition peculiarly desirable." [356]

In 1807 James Green left Devon and John Wark sailed to America with his widowed father then 69. They headed for Baltimore, Maryland where John Wark Jr was first employed. The following year he married Sarah Duncan Boude,[357] whose ancestors emigrated from England in the seventeenth century. They were married in Elkridge Landing, Maryland, her birthplace, when the bride was just seventeen years-old. Their first child was born in Baltimore in 1809. They called him John Clinton after General Clinton, British Commander in Chief of the British troops in the American Revolutionary War. Then came Caroline, born in 1813 in Washington; George[358] was born in 1815 in Baltimore; Elizabeth was born at East Liberty, near Pittsburgh in 1816. Their father's work as a civil engineer was an itinerant profession, taking him from city to city. At some time after Elizabeth's birth, he went to work in Chillicothe where Frank was born on 10th February 1819.

When John Wark and his family came to live in Chillicothe in, say, 1817, it was a time of great expansion of the town. Chillicothe, Ohio lies 150 miles south of Lake Eyrie, 180 miles south-west of Pittsburgh, 300 miles west of Washington, DC. It is situated on the banks of the Scioto River which flows due south into the Ohio about forty miles south of Chillicothe. The Shawnee Native Americans were the predominant tribe to inhabit the area, long before the arrival of white settlers. In 1783, after the revolutionary war, the United States became sovereign of the territory but the British remained in occupation until 1785.

General Nathaniel Massie, a Virginian surveyor, surveyed the land in the Ohio Country in the summer of 1794. He found fine trees growing in the valley between

---

[356] *Biographical Dictionary of Civil Engineers.* vol 1 1500-1830.

[357] Sarah Duncan Boude was born in Elkridge Landing, Maryland, now part of Philadelphia, in 1790. Her seventeenth century Quaker ancestors were immigrants to New Jersey from Lancashire, England.

[358] George Wark son of John Wark was killed endeavouring to prevent a fight between two miners in California. He was Sheriff of Tuolumne, Co. California at the time of his death. From the Wark family bible, in the papers of Mrs Nancy Swan.

the Scioto River and Paint Creek, an indication of the fertility of the area. He measured a walnut tree almost seven feet in diameter An early traveller described the virgin forest with "trees very lofty, straight and clear in their stems, sometimes eighty or ninety feet without a branch".

Massie recognised the potential to support a large population and claimed it for a future town site. The presence of hostile Indian tribes in the area made it too dangerous to start developing the land until after they were defeated by the US army, with the help of the British, in a historic battle – the Battle of the Fallen Timbers in 1794.

Massie and a party of 39 men laid out his town in the summer of 1796. He called it Chillicothe, a name derived from a Shawnee word which means "gathering place". He advertised town lots in Virginia and Kentucky. The area grew rapidly and the new county of Ross was created in 1798. Only five years later in 1803 Chillicothe was the capital of Ohio and held that position, with a three-year gap, until 1816, when the capital moved to Columbus. Today there are about twenty thousand inhabitants.

We know from the journal[359] of Frank's father John Wark that he had a business in Chillicothe. A number of civic buildings were constructed at that time and there was a need for civil engineers. However when Frank was nine months old, in November 1819, his father was employed by the US government to attend to the erection of military buildings in Baton Rouge, a town on the Mississippi a few miles north of New Orleans. He mentions in his journal that he wanted to move his family to Louisiana so perhaps this job seemed to be a way of getting to know the area.

He left Chillicothe on November 19th and describes the route he took. He travelled down the Scioto River to Portsmouth, where it flows into the Ohio River; then along the Ohio to Maysville whence he travelled overland to Louisville on the Mississippi. The rest of the journey was by steamboat down the river. In total the journey took two months and was clearly an ordeal. In his own words: "Arrived at Baton Rouge on Wednesday January 12th after a very unpleasant and tedious journey."

His job was to inspect buildings which were in the process of being erected. He reported:

"that the work was not well done and the mortar was bad in consequence of no good sand or lime therein. I also recommended that precautions be used to prevent the pillars in the basement storey from falling and had new pillars erected before any damage was done."

John Wark was a person of high integrity with puritanical values. He was well

---

[359] In the papers of Mrs Nancy Swan, of Denver, Colorado, his g-g-granddaughter

educated and wrote well, in the very formal high-flown style of an educated man of his times. His diary includes a letter which he wrote to the Mayor of Baton Rouge on behalf of the community. In it he complained that:

> "a band of gamblers or swindlers are waiting for opportunities to plunder the unwary of their all, reducing families to misery and robbing orphans of their expected inheritance. For he who robs the father robs the son, inasmuch as if the root is destroyed the branch must suffer.
>
> It is also much to be regretted that there are houses of perpetual riot both by day and by night where sundry species of gaming are practised, a circumstance very inimical to the tranquillity of the neighbourhood and I may with propriety add, a successive source of inebriation, a practice destructive to the best of constitutions and if permitted to continue, will eventually fill your town with pestilence and your parish with beggars."

John Wark returned to Chillicothe in August 1821, soon after the death of his father. Two years later tragedy struck the family. In 1823 Wark himself died at the age of 42 from an unknown cause, possibly from a disease he had contracted in Louisiana. Frank was only four years-old. No death certificates or obituaries exist from that period. Father and son were buried in Chillicothe. However, their remains were removed and re-buried in the family burial plot in Green Lawn Cemetery, Columbus, Ohio, probably in the early 1870s, when the Presbyterian graveyard became filled to capacity.

The lines on the grave of J Wark Junior read:

> "How loved, how valued once avails thee not,
> To whom related or by whom begot,
> A heap of dust alone remains of thee,
> Tis all thou art and all the proud shall be."

This sober, humbling reminder, which puts glory, wealth and position in a true perspective, speaks of the ethical values of this austere Scottish family.

Sarah, his widow, was left without means to support her large family. She was an enterprising woman and bought a property at the north-west corner of Second and Mulberry Street, which she ran as a boarding house in order to make a living. It was destroyed in the fire of 1852, which ravaged a quarter of the entire town.

Appendix B

"Our foremost friend in Great Britain"[360]

From an address by Whitelaw Reid the American Ambassador to the Court of St James in London, at the unveiling of a tablet in the memory of EDMUND BURKE, 1729-1797, placed on his old residence at Bath by the municipality, October 22nd 1908:

...In Bath he found his devoted wife. Perhaps the most fruitful period of his great public career he spent as the representative in the House of Commons for your nearest neighbours, the people of Bristol. Here he came repeatedly for rest and enjoyment; and here he came too when he knew the shadow of death was upon him. In this very house he spent the last months in which any activity was left him, and he only quitted it for the serene and beautiful death-bed at Beaconsfield.[361]

He shone in every field where his abilities were exerted, and left a great record in many – in economical reform, in defence of the principles underlying the revolution of 1688; in tender care for (Ireland) the land of his birth and the Church of his mother;[362] in resistance alike to the reactionary policy of the Ministry, to injustice in India and to the destructive tendencies of the French revolution. But I may be pardoned for thinking that the highest service of his whole illustrious carer, the most courageous at the time, the wisest and the most far-seeing, was found in his outspoken sympathy with the American colonists, and in his protracted and unflinching resistance to the measure about the American revolution.

No other man in England, hardly one even in America, saw quite so clearly as Edmund Burke that after an unwise Ministry had forced the colonists into a long war in defence of the English principle of no taxation without representation, the only possible outcome of the war by which the real e gland could succeed was an American victory. Yet no other deprecated

---

[360] New York recognised that Edmund Burke was the champion of the right of colonists to tax themselves. He was elected (and employed) as the agent for the New York General Assembly, to represent their interests in Parliament. He held this position from 1770 for five years.

[361] He spent four months there in 1797, taking the waters, to no avail. He returned to his home at Beaconsfield six weeks before his death.

[362] His mother was a Catholic, his father a Protestant.

the struggle so much ; and no other at the outset more sincerely desired to preserve the authority of Parliament and the just rights of the Crown. While there was still a chance to draw back, he pleaded with the Ministry and with Parliament: "It is our business to rule, not to wrangle. It is poor compensation to triumph in a dispute, whilst we lose an empire... Gentlemen say America is an object well worth fighting for. Certainly it is, if fighting a people be the best way of gaining them."

He came to regard the struggle as not a rebellion, but a civil war, in which Englishmen in the colonies fought for old English rights, and in gaining these rights for themselves, made them henceforth forever secure for England, too. In fact, upon this common English heritage he grounded his appeals: "This fierce spirit of liberty" he told Parliament, "is stronger in the English Colonies, probably, than in any other people of the earth. They are not only devoted to liberty, but to liberty according to English ideas and on English principles. English Colonies must be had on these terms, or not had at all."

What Mr Burke constantly sought, in the American business, while it was possible, was reconciliation. His most important utterance during the long debate, from the Stamp Act to the Declaration of Independence, was entitled "Conciliation with America," and English oratory contains no more powerful or persuasive plea for peace. A month after the momentous Declaration, he wrote: "We are deep in blood. God knows how it will be. I do not see how I can wish success to those whose victory is to separate from us a large and noble part of our empire; still less do I wish success to injustice, oppression and absurdity."

This sheer mental inability to support injustice was the key to his whole conduct in American affairs - to his whole conduct indeed in every public affair. He constantly looked to enduring principles for light on current problems. That was the crowning trait in the wonderful equipment which made him the greatest orator of his country, and its most splendid writer on public affairs.

I have only one thing to add. The colonists whom Burke befriended were after all but a feeble folk, less than three millions, scattered along the Eastern fringe of a continent, with the ocean on one hand, and a savage wilderness on the other. They have subdued the wilderness, overspread the continent and stretched out in either hemisphere to the islands of the sea. I am here on Burke's threshold, to utter the voice, feebly and inadequately, it may be, but the authentic voice of that people of now nearly ninety million souls in reverent and affectionate gratitude for the memory, the undying memory of their foremost friend in Great Britain.

(Abridged version)

FIN

Selected Bibliography

Aberdare, Lord *The Story of Tennis* Stanley, Paul & Co. Ltd., 1959

Adams, Charles Francis *A Chapter of Erie* Fields, Osgood & Co., 1869

Akers, Dwight *The story of American harness racing 1938* New York: G P Putnam's Sons

Andrews, Allen. *The Splendid Pauper* Harrap, 1968

Andrews, Wayne *The Vanderbilt Legend* New York, Harcourt Brace, 1941

Ayling, Stanley *Edmund Burke* John Murray, 1988

Baker, Anne Pimlott *The Pilgrims of Great Britain* Profile Books, 2002

Barr, Lockwood 'Dr Joseph Strong, 1770-1812: Philadelphia physician' *Yale Journal of Biology and Medicine*, Vol. 13, No. 4, March 1941

Barrett, Richmond Brooks *Good Old Summer Days* Appleton-Century Co., 1941

Bence-Jones, Mark *A Guide to Irish Country Houses* Constable, 1988

Bohn, Henry *Sir John Rennie: Theoretical account of the Breakwater in Plymouth Sound,* 1848

Bohlen, Charles E. *The Transformation of American Foreign Policy* New York: Norton & Co., 1969

Bourget, Paul *Outre-mer: (Notes sur l'Amerique)* Paris, Lemerre, 1895

Brogan, Hugh *The Penguin History of the USA*. Penguin Books

Brown, Dee *The American West* Simon and Schuster, 1994

Bruchey, Stuart *Cotton and the Growth of the American Economy, 1790-1860* Harcourt, Brace and World, Inc. 1967

Brunicardi, Niall *Fermoy to 1840: A Local History* Fermoy, 1978

Cashman, Sean D *America in the Gilded Age* New York University Press, 1984

Chaffin, Lorah B *Sons of the West* The Caxton Printers Ltd., Caldwell, Idaho, 1941

Chambrun. Col de *The American Army in the European Conflict* Macmillan, 1919

Chevenix Trench, Charles *The Great Dan* Triad Grafton, 1986

Churchill, Winston S *The Second World War* Vol. VI Cassell, 1954

Croffut, W.A. *The Vanderbilts and the Story of their Fortune*. Griffith, Farran, Okeden and Welsh, 1886

Curtis, Edmund *A History of Medieval Ireland* Methuen & Co., 1923

Darwin, H. Stapleton *The Transfer of Early Industrial Technology,* 1987

Davis, Paul *A company of Forts: a guide to the Medieval castles of West Wales* Gomer Press, 1987

Depew, Chauncey M. *100 Years of American Commerce 1795-1895,* Vol. II D O Haynes & Co., 1895

Devlin, Patrick *Too proud to fight* Oxford University Press, 1974

Dickens, Charles *American Notes* Leipzig: Bernhard Tauchnitz, 1842

Dickson, David *Old World Colony: Cork and South Munster 1630-1830* Cork University Press, 2005

Digby, Margaret *Horace Plunkett* Blackwell, 1949

Doctorow, E L *The Waterworks* Macmillan Ltd., London, 1994

Drew, Dennis M & Snow, Donald M *The Eagle's Talons: the American experience at war.* Air University Press, Alabama, 1988

Dwight, Eleanor *Edith Wharton: an extraordinary life* New York: Abrams, 1994

Elliott, Maud Howe *This was my Newport* The Mythology Co.

Ellison, Thomas *Handbook of the Cotton Trade* Longman, 1858

Fenton, Richard *A historical tour through Pembrokeshire* Davies & Co., Brecknock, 1903

Fildes, Valerie *Wet Nursing* Basil Blackwell, 1988

Fitzgerald, Desmond 'A Baroque Palladian in Ireland, the architecture of Davis Ducart' *Country Life, vol.142. No 3682*, 1967, Part I pp 735-739

Fitzgerald, Pat *Down Paths of Gold* Litho Press Co., Midleton

Foster, R F *Modern Ireland,1600-1972* Penguin Books, 1988

Frewen, Moreton *Melton Mowbray, and Other Memories* Herbert Jenkins, 1924

Frewen, Moreton *"Free Grazing": A report to the shareholders of the Powder River Cattle Co. Ltd.* Steel and Jones, London, 1883

Hattersley, Roy *Borrowed Time: The story of Britain Between the Wars* Little, Brown, 2007

Healy, Sarah *Compact History of Ireland* Mercier Press, 1999

Hochberg, Mary T O von *Daisy, Princess of Pless By Herself* John Murray, 1928

Hoffman, Ross J S *Edmund Burke New York agent with his letters to the New York Assembly.* Philadelphia, American Phil. Society, 1956

Homberger, Eric *Mrs Astor's New York; money and social power in a gilded age* Yale University Press, 2002

Hoyt, Philip D *War Story of the 78th Division*

Jakes, John *The Gods of Newport* Penguin Books Ltd., 2006

James, Henry *The Sense of Newport* Harpers CXIII (1960) pp. 343-354

Jenkins, Roy *Gladstone* Macmillan, 1995

John, Brian S *The geology of Pembrokeshire* Abercastle Publications, 1979

Lamb Richard *The Drift to War* E.H. Allen & Co., 1989

Lane, Wheaton J *Commodore Vanderbilt* New York, 1942

Lehr, Elizabeth Drexel *King Lehr and the Gilded Age* Constable and Co. Ltd., 1935

Leslie, Anita *The Fabulous Leonard Jerome* Hutchinson, 1954

Leslie, Anita *Mr Frewen of England: a Victorian Adventurer* London Hutchinson, 1966

Leslie, Shane *Studies in Sublime Failure* Ern est Benn Ltd., 1932

Leslie, Shane *American Wonderland* Michael Joseph Ltd.,1936

Lowe, Norman *Mastering Modern World History* Macmillan Education Ltd., 1982

Lyman, Richard W. *The First Labour Government 1924* Chapman & Hall, 1957

MacMillan, Margaret *Peacemakers: six months that changed the world* John Murray, 2001

McAllister, Ward *Society as I Have Found It.* New York, Cassell. 1890

Marquand, David *Ramsay Macdonald.* Jonathan Cape. 1977.

Martin. Frederick T *Things I Remember.* Eveleigh Nash: London 1913

Mason, Geo. C *Newport and its cottages* Boston: J R Osgood, 1875

Meehan, Thomas F *History of the 78th division in the WW 1917-18* Dodd, Mead & Co. 1921

Montgomery, Maureen E *Displaying women: spectacles of leisure in Edith Wharton's New York* Routledge, 1998

Moody, T W and Martin, F X *The Course of Irish History* Cork: The Mercier Press, 1967

Morris, Lloyd R *Incredible New York* Hamish Hamilton, 1952

Murray, Robert H *Edmund Burke: A biography* Oxford University Press, 1931

Myers, Gustavus *The History of Great American Fortunes* Vol. 2 Charles Kerr & Co., 1909

Nelson, Carolyn Christensen *A New Woman Reader* Broadview Press, 2001

Orpen, Goddard, Henry *Ireland under the Normans 1169-1333* Dublin: Four Courts 2005

Owens, Harry P *Steamboats and the Cotton Economy* University Press of Mississippi, 1990

Owen, H. *Old Pembroke Families in the ancient County Palatine of Pembroke* London, 1902

Pakenham, Thomas *The Year of Liberty: the history of the Great Irish Rebellion of 1798* Orion, 1992

Pershing, John J *My Experiences in the World War* F A Stokes Co., 1931

Queen Victoria *Leaves from the Journal of our Life in the Highlands, 1848-1861* Smith, Elder & Co., 1868

Raby, J W *The Allotted Span in King's Lynn, 1879-1949*

Reid, Whitelaw *Our Foremost Friend in Great Britain* London: Harrison & Sons, 1908

Richards, Paul *King's Lynn* Phillimore, 1990

Roberts, Gary Boyd & Reitwiesner, William Addams *American Ancestors and Cousins of the Princess of Wales* Baltimore: Genealogical Publishing Co.

Roche, W J *The Roches of Fermoy*

Roche, W J *The Roches of Kinsale*

Rose, Kenneth *King George V* Weidenfeld & Nicholson, 1983

Russell, Francis *When Gentlemen Prepared for War* American Heritage Magazine, April 1964, Vol 15, issue 3

Scheer, Admiral Reinhard *Germany's High Sea Fleet in the World War*, 1920

Schlicting, Mary Murphy *A Summer Salon: Literary and cultural circles in Newport, Rhode Island, 1850-1890* New York University, 1992

Sencourt, Robert *Heirs of tradition* Carroll & Nicholson, 1949

Smith, A Howden *Commodore Vanderbilt* Philip Allan & Co. Ltd.

Steele, E D *Palmerston and Liberalism*, 1855-65 Cambridge, 1991

Sutherland, Douglas *The Yellow Earl* Cassell, 1965

Thompson, Julian *Dunkirk: Retreat to Victory* Sidgwick and Jackson, 2008

Townsend, Horatio *A General and Statistical Survey of the County of Cork*, 2 vols. Cork, 1815

Tuchman, Barbara *The Zimmerman Telegram* Constable & Co., 1959

Twain, Mark *Life on the Mississippi* Leipzig, Bernhard Tauchnitz, 1883

Vanderbilt, Consuelo Balsan *The Glitter and the Gold* Heinemann, 1953

Weston, Garth *The Civils: The story of the Institution of Civil Engineers* Thomas Telford Ltd., 1988 edn.

Wharton, Edith *The House of Mirth* London: Virago 1990

Witney, Caspar 'Men and women of the Outdoor World' *Outing*, 1904

Woodham-Smith, Cecil *The Great Hunger of Ireland, 1845-1849* Penguin Books, 1991

Woods, Lawrence M. *British Gentlemen in the Wild West* Robson Books, 1990

About the author

Maurice's elder daughter, Mary, has written this biography of her father. The first thirty years of her life followed the conventional pattern of her family background. She went to a boarding school for young ladies, studied languages abroad, was a debutante, married at twenty and had four children.

At the age of 23, she inherited some money from her uncle, and made two unsuccessful business investments – in a franchise of Hermes, the French luxury goods company, and in an air safari company in East Africa. Although financially a failure, the rewards of the latter were great in important ways. A voyage across Asia in 1963 in a four-seater aircraft changed her life fundamentally.

From belonging to a card-playing, jet set, she developed a thirst for knowledge and a desire for a broader experience of the world. She was a volunteer worker at a settlement in South London. She acquired a BA in Classics from London University and had a short career as a teacher. She managed a youth orchestra and took them to perform in Czechoslovakia in 1988. She qualified as a counsellor and started a counselling service for homeless people at the St Giles Trust in Camberwell, south London.

For the last eight years, she has been developing her interest in history. Now in her seventy-fifth year, this book on family history is her first publication.

Index